Transformation Series
Collection Transformation

14

Setting Course

A History of Marine Navigation in Canada

Sharon A. Babaian

Canada Science and Technology Museum
Musée des sciences et de la technologie du Canada
Ottawa, Canada
2006

Library and Archives Canada Cataloguing in Publication

Babaian, Sharon Anne, 1957–

Setting course : a history of marine navigation in Canada / by Sharon A. Babaian.

(Transformation series, 1188-2964 ; 14)
Includes prefatory text in French.
Includes bibliographical references: p. 145
Includes index.
ISBN 0-660-19626-3
Cat. no.: NM34-1/2006E

1. Navigation—Canada—History. 2. Aids to navigation—Canada. 3. Aids to navigation—History. 4. Navigation—Equipment and supplies. I. Canada Science and Technology Museum II. Title. III. Title: History of marine navigation in Canada. IV. Series: Transformation series (Ottawa, Ont.) ; 14

VK26.B32 2006   623.890971'09   C2006-980080-4

© Canada Science and Technology
  Museum, 2006
All rights reserved.

www.sciencetech.technomuses.ca

© Musée des sciences et de la technologie
  du Canada, 2006
Tous droits réservés.

Printed in Canada

Imprimé au Canada

Table of Contents/Table des matières

Abstract / Résumé v

Foreword / Avant-propos vii

Acknowledgments / Remerciements xiii

Introduction 1

Chapter 1. Navigation in the Age of Exploration 5

    From Cabot to Vancouver: Early Europeans in Northern North America 7

    Out to Sea: Navigational Instruments, 1500–1800 14

    Where Are You When You Get There? Early Charting and Charts 21

    A Safe Place to Land: Early Land-Based Aids to Navigation 28

Chapter 2. Navigation in the Age of Empire 37

    From Sea to Sea to Sea: Building a Maritime Nation 39

    Instruments of the Trade: Navigational Instruments, 1800–1900 48

    Finding the Way to Market: Charting Canada's Primary Shipping Routes 53

    The Longest Coastline: Marking Canada's Coastal and Inland Waters 60

Chapter 3. Navigation in the Age of Electronics 79

    An Economy Afloat: Marine Transportation in Canada since 1900 81

    A New Direction: Shipboard Navigational Advances 93

    From Ship to Shore and Shore to Ship: Two-Way Aids to Navigation ... 96

    Electrification and Automation: Coastal Aids to Navigation 117

Conclusion 141

Bibliography 145

Index 157

List of Maps

1. Champlain's Map of Canada, 1653 12
2. South Coast of Newfoundland, 1774 25
3. Gulf of Georgia, by George Vancouver, 1792 27
4. Lake Huron from Henry Bayfield Survey, 1822 56
5. Gall & Inglis' Map of Canada and Arctic Regions, 1850 58
6. Radio-Telegraph Stations on the East Coast, 1913 97
7. Radio-Telegraph Stations on the Pacific Coast, 1913 98
8. Chart of Lake Winnipeg: Red River to Berens River, 1904 112

Abstract

For centuries Canada, like much of the rest of the world, has depended on marine transportation to facilitate trade and sustain its economic prosperity. Safe, efficient transportation, in turn, demands effective navigational tools and infrastructure. These tools are designed to address two critical needs: the need to establish a vessel's position, course, and speed accurately, especially on the featureless open ocean, and the need to identify, monitor, and avoid hazards, particularly in coastal waters. These requirements have not changed since the turn of the fifteenth century. What has changed, however, is the technology mariners use to meet these needs.

Like all technologies, marine navigation devices and systems are the products of a variety of social, political, and economic influences. In the sixteenth and seventeenth centuries, the search for "new" lands and riches to exploit led mariners to venture far out into the oceans. This search also encouraged mariners and the instrument makers and scientists of the day to find new and better ways to navigate. From the eighteenth century on, the dramatic expansion of trade and commerce and the demands of regular and widespread war prompted further and far-reaching technological change. In more recent years, intense competition and the resulting drive to cut costs have likewise inspired technological innovation in the field of marine navigation.

This study breaks down the history of marine navigation in Canada into three periods, covering three broad categories of technology: shipboard navigation, charting, and shore-based navigational aids. Shipboard navigational instruments establish a ship's position, course, and speed as well as the depth of water beneath the ship. Marine charts serve as both a means to record progress and position and a detailed, graphic source of information about coastal waters. Shore-based aids to navigation, sometimes called seamarks, provide visible and audible indicators of safe routes as well as coastal hazards. In each of these categories, technological change has been driven by a series of specific needs. With regard to shipboard instruments including charts, mariners, scientists, instrument makers and hydrographers sought, among other things, to increase the accuracy of measurements such as latitude, longitude, direction, and speed and to simplify the methods of making, processing, and recording those measurements. In the field of navigational aids, marine authorities looked for ways to enhance the visibility, audibility,

Résumé

Pendant des siècles, le Canada, comme le reste du monde, a dépendu du transport maritime pour faciliter le commerce et maintenir sa prospérité économique. En contrepartie, il fallait de bons outils de navigation et une infrastructure adéquate pour que le transport se fasse avec efficacité et en toute sécurité. De tels outils doivent être conçus de façon à combler deux besoins primordiaux : le besoin d'établir avec précision la position, la trajectoire et la vitesse du navire, particulièrement en pleine mer sans repères, et le besoin de déceler, de maîtriser et d'éviter les dangers, surtout dans les eaux côtières. Ces nécessités sont demeurées les mêmes depuis le début du XVe siècle. Ce qui a changé, c'est la technologie à la disposition des marins.

Comme toutes les technologies, les instruments et systèmes de navigation maritime découlent d'une diversité d'influences sociales, politiques et économiques. Aux XVIe et XVIIe siècles, la recherche de « nouvelles » terres et de richesses à exploiter a poussé les marins à s'aventurer à de grandes distances sur les océans. Cette recherche a aussi encouragé les marins, fabricants d'instruments et scientifiques de l'époque à trouver des façons nouvelles et meilleures de naviguer. À partir du XVIIIe siècle, l'expansion phénoménale du commerce et les exigences des guerres intermittentes et étendues ont suscité un changement technologique plus poussé et de plus grande envergure. Récemment, la forte concurrence et les tentatives de réduction des coûts ont aussi inspiré des innovations technologiques dans le domaine de la navigation maritime.

La présente étude divise l'histoire de la navigation maritime au Canada en trois périodes correspondant à trois grandes catégories de technologies : la navigation à bord des navires, les cartes marines et les aides à la navigation basées à terre. Les instruments de navigation à bord établissent autant la position, la trajectoire et la vitesse d'un navire que la profondeur de l'eau sous celui-ci. Les cartes marines servent à deux choses : enregistrer la progression et la position du navire et fournir une source de renseignements détaillés et graphiques sur les eaux côtières. Les aides à la navigation basées à terre, parfois appelées amers, procurent des guides audibles et visibles pour naviguer avec sûreté et pour repérer les dangers près des côtes. Dans chacune de ces catégories, les changements technologiques ont été suscités par une série de besoins spécifiques. Les marins, les scientifiques, les fabricants d'instruments et les hydrographes visaient avant à tout améliorer la précision du mesurage de la latitude, de la longitude,

and durability of lighthouses, buoys, beacons, and other markers.

With the advent of radio-based navigational systems in the twentieth century and the resulting integration of navigational systems, the divisions between these categories have broken down. Most navigation now relies on the interaction of ship, shore, and satellite-based equipment. This development, however, has not altered the fundamental purpose of all navigational technology: to help mariners choose and maintain a safe and expeditious course to their destination.

de la trajectoire et de la vitesse à l'aide des instruments à bord, notamment les cartes marines, et à simplifier les méthodes pour prendre, évaluer et enregistrer ces mesures. Dans le domaine des aides à la navigation, les autorités maritimes ont cherché des façons d'accroître la visibilité, l'audibilité et la durabilité des phares, des bouées, des signaux lumineux et d'autres balises.

Avec la venue des systèmes radioélectriques de navigation au XXe siècle et l'intégration consécutive des systèmes de navigation, la division entre ces catégories s'est estompée. Aujourd'hui, la navigation dépend surtout de l'interaction entre l'équipement à bord et l'équipement à terre et sur satellite. Toutefois, cette intégration n'a pas changé l'objectif fondamental de toute technologie de navigation, c'est-à-dire aider les marins à choisir et à maintenir une trajectoire sécuritaire et rapide pour atteindre leur destination.

Foreword

Canada has the longest coastline in the world, bordered by three oceans, and remarkable waterways stretching into the heart of the continent. Long ago, indigenous nations were spread out in small groups over this vast land. The Atlantic coast was occasionally visited by Vikings, and recent archaeological discoveries have demonstrated that Norwegians arrived as early as the beginning of the second millennium. This means that well before the arrival of navigators such as the Italian Giovanni Caboto and Jacques Cartier from France, explorers and fishermen had already visited the edges of the continent. You could say that, for the Europeans, the sea gave birth to the New World. And when these newcomers arrived in North America, they used the inland waterways extensively in the development of their colonial possessions.

Because of the huge size of the territory, the development of the continent has naturally captured the attention of historians. However, although naval activities and maritime transport have always taken place and still play an essential economic role throughout the country, their history is not, generally speaking, so well known. Sharon Babaian's detailed analysis of the development of navigational technology in Canada is without parallel. It provides an overview and it puts the development of marine navigation into perspective in both a Canadian and an international context.

Babaian's text highlights the importance of applied innovation in the field of navigation. Such innovation initially assisted navigators to explore farther than they had previously. Later it allowed the state to set up the necessary infrastructure to support the country's economy and to ensure that the shipping lines were safer and more accessible. Depending on the period, the demands of colonization and industrialization persuaded the government to provide an increasingly complex network of aids to navigation.

Belief in the spherical shape of the Earth made it possible to reach the Orient by passing through the Westward Passage. Of course, such a journey was not without obstacles, such as the vastness of the sea and the length of the maritime routes. But these obstacles could more easily be overcome with the magnetic compass and a new type of vessel, the caravel, which made voyages safer. Maps also became slightly more accurate. During the fifteenth century, Western Europe was rapidly expanding and the science of navigation made enormous progress. The king of Portugal, Henry

Avant-propos

Le Canada possède le plus long littoral au monde, bordé de trois océans et de remarquables voies navigables allant au cœur du continent. Jadis, les nations indigènes qui peuplaient le pays étaient disséminées en petits groupes sur le territoire. La côte atlantique était à l'occasion visitée par les Vikings, de récentes découvertes archéologiques attestant de la venue de Norvégiens dès le début du deuxième millénaire. Ainsi donc, bien avant l'arrivée des navigateurs italien Giovanni Caboto et français Jacques Cartier, le continent accueillait déjà sur ses rives des explorateurs et des pêcheurs. Le nouveau monde est en quelque sorte né de la mer. Le corollaire de ceci, à l'époque de la redécouverte de l'Amérique, fut l'utilisation des cours d'eau conduisant au cœur du continent, où les colonies se sont initialement développées.

Bien que l'activité navale et le transport maritime aient toujours été omniprésents au pays et y demeurent un pivot économique essentiel, peu de gens en connaissent les annales. En raison de l'immensité du territoire, c'est vers le développement du continent que s'est naturellement portée l'attention des historiens. L'analyse détaillée de l'évolution de la technologie de la navigation au Canada qu'a réalisée Sharon A. Babaian est un ouvrage sans pareil, qui donne enfin la possibilité de mettre en perspective l'évolution de la technologie dans un contexte maritime historique proprement canadien, tout en présentant en parallèle les avancées de la technologie et le contexte international.

L'ouvrage fait ressortir l'importance de l'innovation appliquée au domaine maritime. L'innovation a d'abord aidé le navigateur à pousser plus loin ses explorations, puis l'État à mettre en place des infrastructures qui soutenaient l'économie du pays et à assurer des voies maritimes plus sécuritaires et accessibles. Les impératifs de la colonisation et de l'industrialisation, selon les époques, sont autant de facteurs qui ont poussé le secteur public fédéral à doter le pays d'un réseau de plus en plus complexe d'aides à la navigation.

En acceptant de croire à la sphéricité de la Terre, on se donnait la possibilité d'atteindre l'Orient par l'Occident. Les obstacles que représentaient l'immensité de la mer et la longueur des routes maritimes sont devenus plus faciles à franchir avec le compas magnétique et un nouveau genre de vaisseau, la caravelle, qui rendaient les périples plus sûrs. Les cartes aussi sont devenues un peu plus précises. Au XVe siècle, l'Europe occidentale était en pleine évolution et la science de la

the Navigator, founded a school of navigation so sailors could explore uncharted waters, an effort driven by economic necessity. Babaian provides an excellent portrayal of this period and shows the fundamental difficulties of what we call navigation, namely the set of skills that allows a mariner to determine his position and guide his ship safely from one point to another.

An important distinction exists between coastal navigation and offshore navigation. On the open sea a navigator must know the route and the speed of his ship in order to determine his location. The compass and log were used in the dead reckoning method of navigation. The navigator deduced his location from the departure point, direction of the route followed, and distance travelled. On the high seas the navigator could also observe features of the heavens, the only thing that differs from one place to another at any given time. Analysing the location of the stars on the celestial concave (cosmography), celestial mechanics, and the notion of time made it possible to determine the position of a ship at a particular moment using astro-navigation. On board, using a sextant, a chronometer, and a nautical almanac, the navigator was able to determine the ship's position with accuracy. In practice, the ship's position was determined by observing the stars only two or three times a day and usually just once a day. If the sky was cloudy, sometimes the navigator was not able to determine his location for several days. Between observations, dead reckoning was used. The method of calculating position by lunar distances and the development of the chronometer opened the way to true scientific navigation.

Through the application of scientific advances navigation on the high seas became easier, which in turn allowed navigators to play a role as explorers in the colonization of Canada. In the early sixteenth century, many voyages were made to Newfoundland and along the St Lawrence. Through trial and error, such exploratory voyages helped to colonize the New World. The initial surge toward the west was also made by way of the Cape Horn bypass route. Subsequent new technologies brought improvements to coastal navigation aids and services, making harbours and interior waterways accessible and safer. All of this contributed to the vitality of maritime commerce, as the author shows.

In 1665, Jean Talon, the intendant of New France, allocated funds for the construction of ships and the training of personnel. The first lighthouse in Canada was built by the French at Louisbourg in 1733. The Nova Scotia government established the first rescue facilities in 1793 by creating a station on Sable Island equipped with a lifeboat. Under French rule, the king's vessels entering the St Lawrence estuary could rely on the port captains to guide them up to Québec.

navigation faisait d'énormes progrès. Le roi du Portugal, Henri le Navigateur, a fondé une école de navigation afin que les marins puissent se lancer sur des mers méconnues, sinon inconnues, les nécessités économiques les y contraignant. L'ouvrage de Babaian campe bien cette période et démontre les difficultés fondamentales de ce qu'on appelle la navigation, c'est-à-dire l'ensemble des connaissances permettant au navigateur de déterminer sa position et conduire son navire en sécurité d'un point à l'autre.

La navigation côtière se distinguait de la navigation hauturière. Au large, le navigateur devait connaître la route et la vitesse du navire afin de déterminer le point où il se trouvait. Pour cette navigation par l'estime, il utilisait le compas et le loch. Il déduisait du point de départ, de la direction de la route suivie et de la distance parcourue où il se situait. En pleine mer, le navigateur pouvait aussi observer l'aspect du ciel, la seule chose qui diffère d'un lieu à un autre à un moment donné. L'analyse du repérage des astres sur la voûte céleste (cosmographie), de la mécanique céleste et de la notion du temps permet de déterminer la position du navire à un instant particulier en navigation astronomique. À bord, à l'aide du sextant, du chronomètre et des éphémérides nautiques, le navigateur arrivait à déterminer le point avec précision. Dans la pratique, la position n'était déterminée par observations astronomiques que deux ou trois fois par jour et même une seule fois le plus souvent. Si le ciel était couvert, il arrivait que le navigateur ne puisse faire le point durant des jours. Entre les observations, on naviguait par l'estime. La méthode de calcul par les distances lunaires et la mise au point des chronomètres ont ouvert la voie à une véritable navigation scientifique.

L'application des avancées scientifiques a rendu la navigation en haute mer plus facile, ce qui a permis aux navigateurs hauturiers de jouer un rôle d'explorateurs aux premiers temps des colonies au Canada. Les débuts du XVIe siècle ont été marqués par de nombreux périples à Terre-Neuve et sur le Saint-Laurent. Ainsi a commencé, par tâtonnements, l'exploitation du territoire et la colonisation des terres occupées. La poussée initiale vers l'Ouest s'est aussi effectuée en empruntant la voie de contournement du Cap Horn. On a par la suite assisté à l'implantation de nouvelles technologies qui permettaient de fournir services et aides à la navigation côtière, rendant accessibles et plus sécuritaires les havres et les voies navigables intérieures. Tout ceci allait contribuer à la prospérité du commerce maritime, comme le démontre l'auteure.

Dès 1665, Jean Talon, alors intendant de la Nouvelle-France, allouait des fonds à la construction de navires et la formation du personnel. Le premier phare au Canada a été bâti par les Français à Louisbourg en 1733 et le gouvernement de la Nouvelle-Écosse a

In the early 1800s, the United Kingdom and its colonies started to implement an administrative infrastructure to improve the aids to navigation in British North America. In Upper Canada, government maritime services first allocated funds to build and maintain lighthouses. In Lower Canada, they established Trinity House in Québec in 1805 to build and maintain lighthouses and other seamarks. New Brunswick and Nova Scotia both established responsible commissions and departments of public works. Canada was no different from other countries in its formative stage. Administrative effectiveness lagged behind social and economic needs, and although maritime services continued to operate well during this period, this was as much due to the loyal and conscientious effort of the vast majority of employees — who carried out their duties without encouragement, as a general rule — as it was attributable to any administrative practice.

Many of the essential services provided today by the Coast Guard and the Hydrographic Service were in demand well before Confederation. After the birth of the new dominion of Canada, the federal government created the Department of Marine and Fisheries of Canada and the Ministry of Public Works, which consolidated most activities relating to maritime navigation. Although initially the role of these ministries was to improve navigation and to establish the necessary legal framework, during the years of expansion they established infrastructure to ensure the safety, profitability, and effectiveness of shipping. On many occasions since their formation, the various ministries and sectors of the public administration have been restructured, and financial resources have fluctuated depending on government policies and economic constraints.

As Babaian explains, the development of maritime infrastructure was important to the economic development of Canada. In particular, she emphasizes two factors that guided the evolution of marine navigation. The gradual technical innovations made before the Second World War led to an increasing number of government branches dedicated to ensuring the safety of navigation and to facilitating maritime commerce. Post-war innovations were both the cause and the result of profound change in the marine sector and the public administration of maritime services. Radio aids to navigation and electronic navigation and communication instruments were developed and underwent continuous improvement. Finally, Babaian provides a glimpse of a new era in maritime navigation, one in which increasingly effective and reliable new technologies and the dynamic integration of systems are revolutionizing marine navigation practices.

In 1986, the International Maritime Organization (IMO) and the International Hydrographic Organization (IHO) set up a working group on the harmonization of

établi les premières installations de sauvetage en 1793, en créant à Sable Island une station pourvue d'un canot de sauvetage. Sous le régime français, les vaisseaux du roi qui entraient dans l'estuaire du Saint-Laurent pouvaient compter sur des capitaines de port pour les guider jusqu'à Québec. Au début des années 1800, la Grande-Bretagne et ses colonies ont commencé à mettre en place une infrastructure administrative afin d'améliorer le service d'aides à la navigation en Amérique du Nord britannique. Au Haut-Canada, les services maritimes gouvernementaux ont débuté par l'allocation de fonds pour construire et maintenir des phares et, au Bas-Canada, par l'établissement de la Trinity House à Québec, en 1805. Le Nouveau-Brunswick avait son bureau des commissaires aux institutions publiques et la Nouvelle-Écosse, son bureau des travaux publics. Le Canada ne différait en rien des autres pays au stade de formation. L'efficacité administrative restait à la traîne et, si les services maritimes ont continué à bien fonctionner durant cette période, c'était au moins autant grâce aux efforts loyaux et consciencieux de la grande majorité des employés, qui poursuivaient leurs tâches sans y être généralement encouragés, qu'au régime administratif.

Nombre des services indispensables qu'offrent aujourd'hui la Garde côtière et le Service hydrographique étaient sollicités bien avant la Confédération. À la naissance du Dominion du Canada, le gouvernement fédéral a créé le ministère de la Marine et des Pêcheries du Canada et le ministère des Travaux publics, regroupant l'essentiel des activités liées à la navigation maritime. Si ces ministères avaient au départ pour rôle d'améliorer la navigation et d'instaurer les cadres juridiques nécessaires, durant les années de croissance, ils ont mis en place des infrastructures sous-tendant les services destinés à assurer la sécurité, la rentabilité et l'efficacité du déplacement des navires. Depuis, les ministères et secteurs de l'administration publique ont fait l'objet de nombreuses restructurations et les ressources financières ont fluctué avec les politiques gouvernementales et les contraintes économiques.

S'inscrivant dans une perspective bien canadienne, Babaian nous fait redécouvrir l'importance dans l'histoire du Canada de la mise en place des infrastructures maritimes pour le développement économique d'un pays en pleine transformation. L'ouvrage fait valoir deux courants d'influence de la technologie qui ont orienté l'évolution de la navigation maritime. Les innovations techniques graduelles d'avant la Seconde Guerre mondiale ont permis aux services de l'État de fournir une infrastructure de plus en plus ramifiée afin d'assurer la sécurité de la navigation et de faciliter le commerce maritime. Les innovations de l'après-guerre ont été à la fois sujet et objet de transformations profondes dans le milieu maritime et l'administration

the use of ECDIS-type electronic map display systems, whose efforts led to the adoption of performance standards in 1995. Used in conjunction with an adequate auxiliary system, these standards made it possible to conduct a satisfactory update of the SOLAS Convention on nautical charts (International Convention for the Safety of Life at Sea) of 1974. Agreeing to replace nautical charts on paper with the ECDIS system facilitated fundamental changes in ocean navigation, which in turn led to numerous computer system applications.

The development of computer technologies improved the performance of electronic navigation systems in terms of both processing speed and the display of information. Navigation systems are now based on the use of ECDIS- or ECS-type electronic card display systems together with an accurate positioning system such as a GPS or DGPS receiver. Current electronic navigation systems take advantage of the interface between positioning, navigation and communication systems, and electronic navigation charts (ENCs). A ship's navigator can superimpose on nautical charts data provided by radar/ARPA, functions relating to trip planning and control, search and rescue (SAR) procedures as well as many other functions vital to the safe navigation of ships.

The progressive establishment of the automatic identification system (AIS) aboard ships and on land brings a new dimension to electronic navigation, by allowing the automatic exchange of information either between vessels or between ship and shore. In particular it has made it possible to provide the GPS or DGPS location, the gyrocompass bearing, and the MMSI (Mobile Maritime Service Identity) of the ship, and to transmit and receive digital messages via the system's VHF channel. The AIS communication protocol also enables the exchange of additional information about navigation conditions (traffic, water level, current, stage of the tide, etc.), information about the state of the channel (buoying, shoal alert, etc.), and, of course, messages relating to safety.

Innovations in computer science and telecommunications are providing extraordinary opportunities for coastal states. Specifically, technology is enabling governments to initiate measures aimed at improving safety and navigation, to review and modify the way in which their services are provided, and at the same time to reduce costs. New technology in the maritime sector requires the state to juggle many competing and often incompatible goals. For example, the modernization of navigational aids has not only encouraged the electrification of buoys and the automation of lighthouses, but also (paradoxically) the establishment and adoption of radioelectric navigation aids networks (Decca, Omega, Loran C, GPS, etc.), which eliminate the need for the same landing buoys or lighthouses. Rigorous modernization results in the abandonment

publique des services maritimes. Des aides radio-électriques à la navigation et des instruments de navigation électroniques et de communication ont fait leur apparition et sont allés de perfectionnement en perfectionnement. L'ouvrage de Babaian laisse finalement entrevoir une nouvelle ère dans la navigation maritime, alors que l'efficacité et la fiabilité accrues de la nouvelle technologie et l'intégration dynamique des systèmes sont en voie de révolutionner la pratique de la navigation maritime.

En 1986, l'Organisation internationale maritime (IMO) et l'Organisation hydrographique internationale (IHO) ont formé un groupe de travail sur l'harmonisation de l'emploi de systèmes d'affichage de cartes électroniques de type ECDIS, dont les efforts ont mené à l'adoption de normes de performances en 1995. Associées à un système d'appoint adéquat, ces normes ont permis de réaliser une mise à jour satisfaisante des cartes nautiques de la convention SOLAS (Convention internationale pour la sauvegarde de la vie humaine en mer) de 1974. En acceptant de remplacer les cartes nautiques sur support papier par le système ECDIS, on a pu apporter des changements fondamentaux pour le progrès de la navigation en mer, ce qui a ouvert la porte à toutes les applications des systèmes informatiques.

L'évolution des technologies informatiques a permis d'améliorer de beaucoup la performance des systèmes de navigation électronique sur le plan de la vitesse de traitement et de l'affichage de l'information. Les systèmes de navigation s'appuient sur l'utilisation de systèmes d'affichage de cartes électroniques de type ECDIS ou ECS jumelés à un système de positionnement précis, tel un récepteur GPS ou DGPS. Les systèmes de navigation électronique actuels tirent parti de l'interface entre les systèmes de positionnement, de navigation et de communication et les cartes électroniques de navigation (CEN). Il est ainsi possible de surimposer les données fournies par le radar ARPA, des fonctions de planification de voyage, de contrôle et de procédure de recherche et sauvetage (SAR) de même que d'autres fonctions vitales pour la navigation sécuritaire du navire.

L'implantation progressive du système d'identification automatique des navires (SIA) à bord des bâtiments et à terre apporte une nouvelle dimension à la navigation électronique, en permettant l'échange d'information automatique ou, spécifiquement, entre les navires et entre la terre et les navires. Elle permet notamment de fournir la position GPS ou DGPS, l'azimut du gyrocompas et l'identité du navire du service mobile maritime, et de transmettre et recevoir des messages numériques via le canal VHF du système. Le protocole de communication SIA permet aussi l'échange d'information supplémentaire sur les conditions de la navigation (trafic, niveau d'eau, courant, évolution de la marée, etc.) et

of a large number of floating and fixed navigation aids. This, in turn, would be an obstacle to the practice of traditional navigation and could jeopardize historically significant properties. However, in the current context of government spending, the maritime industry would not agree to allow the government services to relinquish any productivity gains made possible by technological progress.

Today, not only VLCC or ULCC (very large or ultra large crude carrier) oil tankers and container-carrier ships, but most modern merchant ships on the high seas are equipped with navigation bridges in which the instruments are integrated in such a way to allow the maximum use of the available depth in the navigation channels. Fishing vessels are increasingly advanced from a technical point of view, and pleasure boats can hold their own in terms of high-tech navigation equipment. Qualified personnel — an increasingly rare commodity — become a strategic resource in the maritime field, which is ever more complex and characterized by high technology. Another factor that is sometimes forgotten by Canadians in measures of the competitiveness and relative prosperity of, as compared to, neighbouring maritime economies, is the effective and efficient maintenance by the public sector of safe and accessible waterways. Managers must, however, determine the balance that best suits the various users, while continuing to innovate and to facilitate access to new technologies in order to achieve the sought-after savings and efficiency. By addressing these challenges, Babaian carries her account of the history of marine navigation in Canada right into the present.

Captain René Grenier, MPA
Director, Canadian Coast Guard College
Sydney, Nova Scotia, 2005

l'état du chenal (balisage, avis de haut-fond, etc.) et l'envoi de messages reliés à la sécurité.

Les innovations dans le domaine de l'information et des télécommunications offrent des perspectives extraordinaires aux États riverains, la technologie permettant à l'administration publique de proposer des mesures visant l'amélioration de la sécurité de la navigation et la qualité du service, de revoir et modifier les modes de prestation et en même temps de réduire les coûts à cet égard. Avec l'implantation de la nouvelle technologie dans le secteur maritime, l'État devra jongler avec des objectifs multiples et contradictoires, souvent incompatibles. À titre d'exemple, paradoxalement, la modernisation des aides à la navigation a non seulement favorisé l'électrification des bouées et l'automatisation des phares, mais aussi l'implantation de réseaux d'aides radioélectriques à la navigation (decca, Omega, loran C, GPS, etc.) qui suppriment le besoin de bouées d'atterrissage ou de phares. La mise en œuvre d'une modernisation rigoureuse impliquerait l'abandon de bon nombre d'aides flottantes et fixes à la navigation, ce qui serait une entrave à la pratique de la navigation traditionnelle de certains usagers ou remettrait en cause la sauvegarde de biens ayant valeur de patrimoine culturel. Pourtant, dans le contexte actuel des dépenses publiques, l'industrie maritime n'accepterait pas que les services gouvernementaux se privent des gains de productivité que les progrès technologiques rendent possibles.

Aujourd'hui, ce ne sont plus seulement les pétroliers UGPB ou TGTB (ultragros porteurs ou très gros transporteurs de brut) et les porte-conteneurs, mais la plupart des navires de commerce modernes qui sillonnent les mers équipés de passerelles de navigation où les instruments sont dynamiquement intégrés, utilisant au maximum la colonne d'eau disponible des chenaux de navigation. Les navires de pêche continuent d'évoluer sur le plan technique et les bateaux de plaisance rivalisent en équipement de navigation de pointe. La main-d'œuvre qualifiée, denrée se raréfiant, devient une ressource stratégique dans un milieu maritime de plus en plus complexe et de haute technicité. Un autre facteur parfois oublié de la compétitivité du commerce maritime et de la prospérité du pays par rapport aux économies maritimes voisines est le maintien efficace et efficient par le secteur public de voies navigables sécuritaires et accessibles. Les gestionnaires du secteur public devront cependant rechercher le point d'équilibre convenant aux différents usagers, tout en continuant d'innover et de faciliter l'accès à la nouvelle technologie pour réaliser les économies et l'efficience recherchées.

Le directeur du Collège de la Garde côtière canadienne,
le capitaine René Grenier, M.A.P.
Sydney (Nouvelle-Écosse), 2005

Acknowledgments

When I began this research report I knew that it would be an especially demanding one not only because of the long time period it covers, but also because of the number and variety of technologies involved in marine navigation. Fortunately, I was able to rely on the expert advice, support, and guidance of many thoughtful people during the course of the project. Garth Wilson, the curator of transportation, helped me to develop a workable approach to what seemed like an unmanageably large subject. He also provided conscientious supervision throughout the research, writing, and editing processes and did his best to keep me from getting bogged down in detail and overwhelmed by the scale of the project.

I am also grateful to the three external readers who took the time to read each of my chapters and provide thoughtful and constructive comments on how to improve them. Similarly, the internal reader, Dr. Randall Brooks, gave the whole manuscript a careful read and offered much useful advice and information. The report and its author benefited greatly from their labours.

In undertaking this research project I relied heavily on the assistance of various archivists at Library and Archives Canada and library reference staff at the Canada Science and Technology Museum. I consulted a number of experts at several government departments and agencies and public institutions about the recent history of marine navigation. Ed Dahl, formerly of the National Archives of Canada, helped me to understand the intricacies of the early history of charting in Canada. At the Canadian Coast Guard I sought and received ample assistance from Charles Maginley, Val Smith, Ben Hutchin, and Mike Clements regarding modern aids to navigation. I also spoke at some length to Peter Dunford and Mike Kruger at the Nautical Institute of the Nova Scotia Community College about navigational training and education in Canada. All of these men were unfailingly patient and polite in explaining the complexities of their fields of navigation to a generalist historian with little specialized knowledge and no shipboard experience.

To the many other unnamed people who helped me along the way — by supplying research material, answering questions, and simply expressing interest in the subject — I am also grateful. But for them, this work would not be as complete as it is. Whatever

Remerciements

Lorsque j'ai commencé les recherches qui ont mené à ce rapport, je savais que le travail serait exigeant, non seulement parce qu'il s'étendait sur une longue période, mais aussi en raison de la multitude et la diversité des technologies utilisées en navigation maritime. Heureusement, j'ai pu compter sur les compétences particulières, le soutien et l'encadrement de plusieurs personnes avisées tout au long de ce projet. Garth Wilson, conservateur dans le domaine des transports maritimes, m'a aidée à trouver une façon pratique d'aborder ce vaste sujet qui me semblait impossible à traiter. Il a aussi supervisé mon travail avec attention au cours des processus de recherche, de rédaction et de révision. Il a fait de son mieux pour éviter que je me perde dans les détails et que je me sente dépassée par l'ampleur de l'entreprise.

Je suis aussi reconnaissante envers les trois lecteurs de l'extérieur qui ont pris le temps de lire chacun de mes chapitres et m'ont apporté des commentaires éclairés et constructifs sur la façon de les améliorer. Je remercie le lecteur du Musée, Randall Brooks, qui a fait une lecture attentive du manuscrit et m'a fourni bien des conseils et renseignements judicieux. Les efforts consentis par ces premiers lecteurs ont été précieux pour le rapport et son auteure.

En m'engageant dans ce travail de recherche, j'ai pu grandement compter sur l'aide de plusieurs archivistes de Bibliothèque et Archives Canada, de même que sur le personnel affecté à la référence à la bibliothèque du Musée des sciences et de la technologie du Canada. J'ai aussi consulté un certain nombre de spécialistes œuvrant au sein d'institutions publiques et de divers ministères et organismes gouvernementaux sur l'histoire récente de la navigation maritime. Ed Dahl, autrefois des Archives nationales du Canada, m'a aidée à comprendre la complexité du début de l'histoire des prélèvements hydrographiques au Canada. À la Garde côtière canadienne, j'ai cherché et obtenu un immense soutien de la part de Charles Maginley, Val Smith, Ben Hutchin et Mike Clements, qui m'ont éclairée sur les aides modernes à la navigation. J'ai également eu d'assez longs entretiens avec Peter Dunford et Mike Kruger, du Nova Scotia Nautical Institute, rattaché au Nova Scotia Community College, sur la formation et les études en navigation au Canada. Tous ces hommes ont fait preuve d'une patience et d'une politesse sans faille pour expliquer la complexité de leurs sphères respectives d'activités

weaknesses and flaws that remain are, of course, solely my responsibility.

Sharon A. Babaian
Historian
Canada Science and Technology Museum

dans le domaine de la navigation à une historienne généraliste n'ayant qu'un très petit bagage de connaissances spécialisées et aucune expérience à bord d'un navire.

Je suis aussi redevable envers plusieurs autres personnes que je n'ai pas nommées mais qui m'ont aidée tout au long de ce projet en fournissant du matériel pour la recherche, en répondant à des questions ou tout simplement en manifestant de l'intérêt pour le sujet. Sans le concours de ces personnes, le travail n'aurait pas été aussi complet. Bien sûr, quelles que soient les faiblesses et les failles qui subsistent dans ce rapport, j'en assume l'entière responsabilité.

Sharon A. Babaian
Historienne
Musée des sciences et de la technologie du Canada

Introduction

According to *The Oxford Companion to Ships and the Sea*, navigation is "the art of conducting a vessel from one place on the Earth's surface to another by sea safely, expeditiously, and efficiently."[1] Broadly speaking, there are two types of navigation: coastal and oceanic. Coastal navigation is as old as ships themselves, probably dating back to about 3500 B.C. Its rules were largely drawn from the accumulated experience and knowledge of generations of mariners who carried trade goods across coastal waters to neighbouring states and more distant lands. With only rudimentary tools to help them, early navigators relied on coastal features and built structures to help them establish their position. They also depended on their familiarity with winds, currents, tides, and the seabed to help tell them where they were and whether they needed to alter their course.

These basic skills, often called "dead reckoning," though highly developed over the centuries, were of limited use to mariners setting out across the oceans. Not only were there no familiar features or structures to use as guides, but the winds, currents, and tides were also unfamiliar and often unpredictable. Oceanic navigation demanded a different approach. Mariners turned to the heavens and used the location of astronomical bodies to help them determine their position, keep track of their movements, and set their courses.

Both coastal and oceanic navigation required the development and use of a variety of navigational tools. For the purposes of this discussion, navigational instruments are defined as those devices used by mariners on board ships to measure direction, speed, and position and to establish the depth of the water and the location of hidden hazards. These include the oldest and most rudimentary tools of coastal navigation — the lead and line, for example — as well as more elaborate astronomical devices used to determine latitude and longitude. Twentieth-century navigational instruments such as the gyrocompass, radar, and sonar have made the art of shipboard navigation even more precise.

Other navigational tools are used by mariners on board ships but their effective application relies on interaction between ship and shore. Marine charts, for instance, are two-dimensional abstractions of the oceans and coastlines of the world that allow navigators to locate their ships relative to certain critical land-based reference points. In the open ocean, mariners refer to charts constructed using the Greenwich meridian as a baseline. By measuring their distance from the meridian they can track and record their course on the chart. As they enter coastal waters, mariners compare the graphic information on their charts to the physical features they are seeing from their vessel to confirm their location and tell them how to proceed safely.

Most radio-based navigational systems are also dependent on interaction between a ship and shore-based installations. In the early days of radio the technology demanded active engagement; the ship's radio officer had to communicate directly with a shore operator, who provided position information as requested. Gradually, engineers developed systems that broadcast information automatically so that any suitably equipped ship could gain access to the information whenever it was within range of the signals. A similar trend toward automation of shipboard systems has also eliminated the need for navigators to do elaborate calculations on the received position information to convert it to an actual point on the chart.

When mariners move closer to shore, they rely on aids to navigation to help them set their course. Aids to navigation are coastal devices that provide mariners with additional information about their surroundings when they move closer to shore. They include visual aids — conspicuous natural features and purpose-built structures such as lighthouses, buoys, and beacons — audible aids such as fog alarms, and radio aids such as automatic radio direction finding installations and radar beacons. The term "seamark" is sometimes used to describe all visual aids to navigation, including those that are positioned on land.[2]

Canada has the longest coastline in the world and countless inland waterways and, since European colonization, has been very dependent on international trade for its prosperity. These facts, combined with the imperial relationship with Britain, the pre-eminent maritime power of the eighteenth and nineteenth centuries, made the development and maintenance of safe and efficient marine navigation in Canadian waters a great priority. Governments and the shipping industry have invested an enormous amount of time, money, and energy in building a reliable navigational infrastructure. In conjunction with the development of transportation technologies and systems, this infrastructure has helped to transform Canada from a sparsely inhabited wilderness to a developed and prosperous nation.

To date, the pivotal importance of navigation and navigational infrastructure in Canada has not been reflected in work by historians in this country. Although a number of scholarly books and articles deal with exploration and shipping, they seldom offer any sustained discussion of the navigational techniques, tools, and systems that made these endeavours practical. Non-academic historians, for their part, have produced a few works that explore specific navigational topics and technologies, most notably lighthouses. There exists, however, no comprehensive history of marine navigation in Canada.

This historical assessment is an attempt to fill this gap in scholarship by tracing the evolution of navigational technologies and their application to marine transportation over five hundred years, with particular emphasis on Canada. It is also intended to provide a framework for the development of the Museum's collection of marine navigation artifacts. In keeping with this goal, it identifies and analyses the important themes, events, and issues in the subject area and situates them in the thematic framework established by the Collection Development Strategy. That framework is based on the broad theme "The Transformation of Canada" and the subthemes "the Canadian context," "finding new ways," and "people, science, and technology."[3]

To fulfill these objectives, this study is organized chronologically into three chapters covering navigation in the age of exploration (1497 to 1800), navigation in the nineteenth century, and navigation in the twentieth century, respectively. Each of these chapters is divided into several subsections. The first section in every chapter provides an overview of the major political, social, and economic events and trends that influenced developments in marine navigation. Many scholarly books and articles have been written about the technology of marine navigation and its evolution and application around the world. Few of these books, though, have anything to say about the specific Canadian context of these developments or about how the Canadian story fits into the larger international trends. The significance of marine navigational technology in Canada cannot be fully appreciated in the absence of this historical background. Within this general framework and where applicable, the study also touches on the subjects of education, training, and certification of mariners, with specific reference to navigational skills.

The second section of each chapter focuses specifically on shipboard navigational instruments, identifying the important instruments developed and used in each era and outlining the basic principles of their operation and their period of use. Rather than providing detailed description of these technologies, whose technical and stylistic development has been amply documented elsewhere, this study merely refers readers to the most important sources on the specific technology under discussion.

The third section of each chapter covers developments in charting and hydrography. Many scholars of marine navigational technology have excluded charts from their discussions of navigational instruments and aids to navigation. Charts, however, are essential to the art of navigation. They serve as records of navigational knowledge and infrastructure and, as such, complement and enhance the capabilities of all the other tools of the trade — both shipboard and shore-based. In recent years, with the introduction of electronic charts and satellite-based positioning systems, the chart has increasingly become part of a fully integrated navigational infrastructure that makes its central role in the process of navigation abundantly clear.

The fourth and final section of each chapter concentrates on aids to navigation — the various devices, structures, and systems used to mark coastal waters and direct and control traffic within them. In each chapter, this section identifies and briefly describes the major technological advances in navigational aids. It also traces the evolution of the Canadian system of aids, including the application and adaptation of new technologies to meet our particular needs.

These four major subjects provide the core of each chapter and give the report its basic structure. In each period, though, the basic structure changes somewhat to account for the varying pace of technological change and the unique political, social, and economic circumstances that provided the context for that change. Thus the chapter dealing with the nineteenth century, a period in which there were few major advances in navigational instruments, focuses on the instrument trade in Canada. In writing about the technology of navigation in the twentieth century, it became clear that the adoption of radio-based devices that rely on interaction between ship and shore-based installations had gradually broken down the boundary between shipboard navigational instruments and coastal aids to navigation. In order to reflect this trend, the final chapter has a slightly more complex structure that attempts to convey the increasing level of integration of all navigational systems. This chapter also reflects the problems inherent in tracing the development of recent technology. Not only is the pace of change very rapid, but the technology itself is increasingly complex, invisible, and integrated with other sophisticated systems such as computer and communications networks. This makes it difficult to keep track of all the latest developments, let alone understand fully how they work or judge which will be of enduring importance. To minimize the problems posed by almost constant technological change in this field, the discussion of recent advances generally ends in 1990.

This report is a descriptive overview of the technology of marine navigation based mainly on a synthesis of secondary sources. The nature and scope of the subject and the length of the time period covered demanded a general approach to the technology. At the same time, it was essential to document the Canadian experience due to the critical importance of marine transportation to our economy, both historically and in the present day, and because no one had yet told the story of marine navigational technology in this country. While this Canadian emphasis, hopefully, makes this work unique and valuable, the approach also posed a number of problems and imposed certain important constraints. Because so little has been written on the subject and because primary documents, where they exist at all, are scattered and incomplete, a great deal of time and effort was required just to establish the basic outlines of the history of marine navigation in this country — what happened when and where. A sustained analysis of why navigational technology and infrastructure evolved as it did was therefore outside the scope of the report. Despite these limitations, it is hoped that this formative synthesis will lay the groundwork for further study of this critical field of technological history.

Notes

1. Peter Kemp, ed., *The Oxford Companion to Ships and the Sea* (London: Oxford University Press, 1979), 576.
2. John Naish, *Seamarks: Their History and Development* (London: Stanford Maritime, 1985), 14. Naish quotes the *International Dictionary of Aids to Marine Navigation*, which defines a seamark as "an artificial or natural object of easily recognizable shape or colour or both, situated in such a position that it may be identified on a chart or related to a known navigational instruction."
3. Canada Science and Technology Museum, "Collection Development Strategy," November 2000.

CHAPTER 1

Navigation in the Age of Exploration

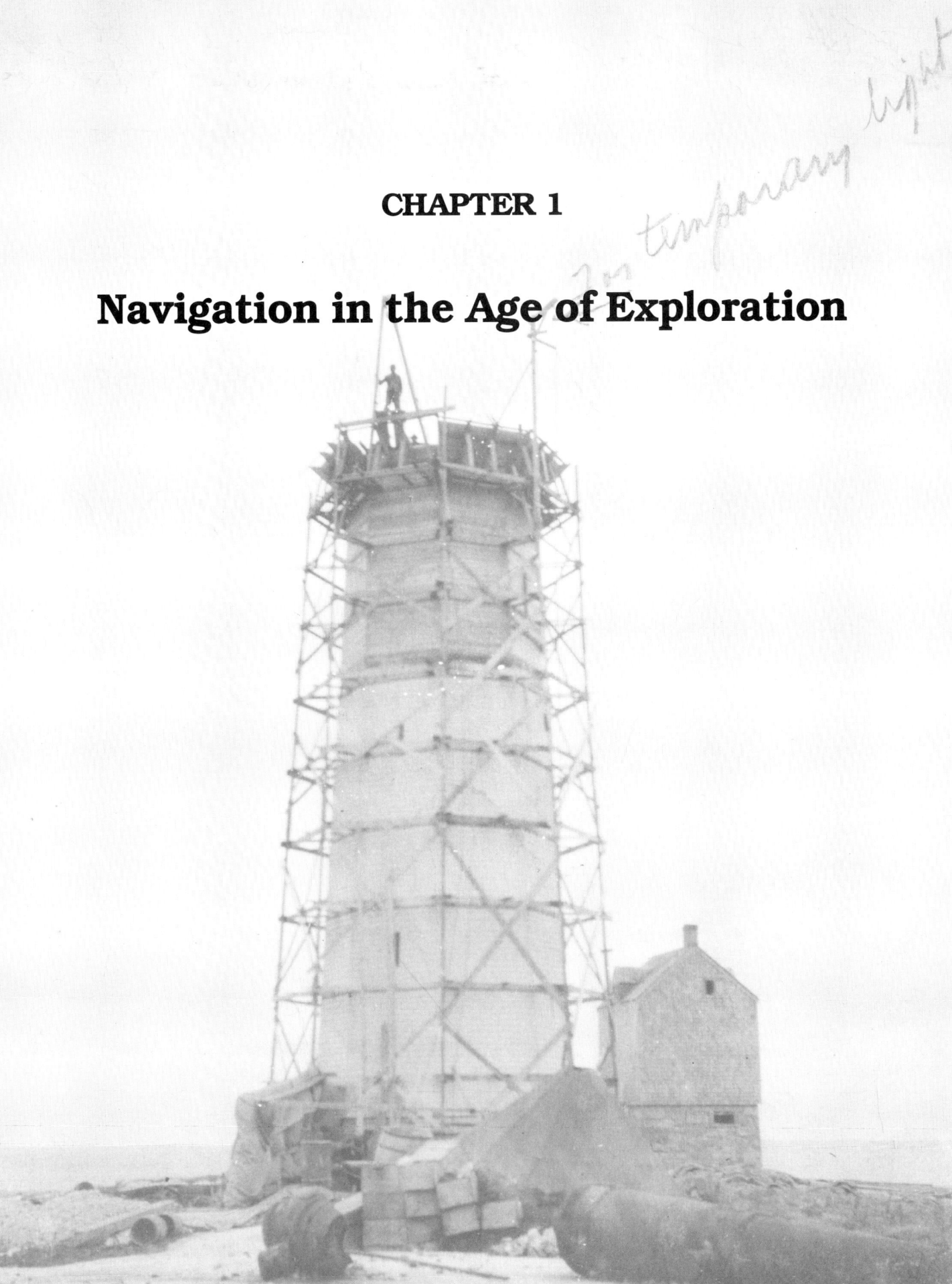

Navigation in the Age of Exploration

The story of water-borne transportation and navigation in what is now Canada did not begin with John Cabot. Many of the indigenous peoples of North America had extensive experience with and knowledge of the coastal and inland waterways of the continent, which they eventually shared with European explorers.[1] Nor was Cabot even the first European to visit this land. The Norsemen had made their way to Labrador and Newfoundland some five hundred years earlier and established a settlement at L'Anse aux Meadows.[2] Yet in the history of marine navigation, Cabot represents an important milestone. With him began the deliberate and determined exploration of northern North America. This type of travel, where mariners journeyed far from familiar shores and waters, inspired the development of more precise and systematic methods of navigation. These, in turn, made it practical for Europeans to explore and map the country, to prepare it for settlement, and to set up the trade and transportation routes essential to its economic development.

This chapter outlines the evolution of navigational instruments and aids to navigation from 1497 to 1800, focusing on the role they played in the transformation of Canada from an isolated and, to Europeans at least, largely unknown wilderness into a viable colonial society and economy. The first section of the chapter surveys the exploration of Canadian coastal and inland waters, highlighting major social, economic, and political factors that led Europeans to North America and eventually encouraged them to settle here. The second section focuses on shipboard navigational instruments. It briefly identifies the tools and techniques available to explorers such as John Cabot, then describes the operating principles of each significant new device developed and introduced after 1500.

A third section examines the early charting of northern North America, identifying some of the major contributors to the process before 1800 and describing some of the challenges they faced in mapping our waters and coastlines. This discussion provides a transition to the final section of the chapter, which deals with land-based aids to navigation. Following the pattern of the previous sections, it begins by mentioning the types of aids that existed around 1500 and those that appear to have been used in what is now Canada. These last three sections focus mainly on tools that were introduced or significantly improved after 1500. They do not include lengthy accounts of the technical and stylistic evolution of these devices and objects but refer readers to the many reliable sources that already provide this kind of detailed analysis.

From Cabot to Vancouver: Early Europeans in Northern North America

Between 1500 and 1800, countless European mariners travelled to the New World. They came to seek personal fame and fortune as well as to enhance, sometimes unwillingly, the power and prestige of their patrons and employers. The key to achieving these goals was trade — finding new routes to known trading regions, especially the Far East, "discovering" new lands with potentially profitable resources to exploit, and protecting both from competitors. These were the primary reasons for persistent European interest and activity in what was, for them, an isolated and inhospitable land.

European exploration in northern North America began with the search for a western route to the Orient.[3] Trade with the Far East had become a very lucrative business in the Middle Ages, but by the mid-fourteenth century the rise of Islamic powers in eastern Europe, the Mediterranean, and Asia had made the overland route very complicated and risky. In response to these developments, the Portuguese pioneered an alternative route by sea around Africa and across the Indian Ocean. With the Portuguese route temporarily closed to them and convinced that a shorter route did exist, other European countries were anxious to explore new options. Thus when mariners like Columbus and Cabot suggested the possibility of sailing west across the Atlantic to reach the shores of Cathay and the Spice Islands, ambitious patrons were willing to listen, and at least a few were persuaded to sponsor, if not finance, these admittedly radical schemes.[4]

When European explorers set out to cross the Atlantic, then, they were not looking for a new continent at all but were hoping to find a more or less open and direct sea route to the other side of the world. Columbus's initial discoveries were inconclusive and therefore interpreted in the best possible light, that is, that the tropical islands he visited were indeed part of the Indies and not evidence of a new continent. Though there were no spices or silks, there were other riches, including precious metals and gems, to exploit. Moreover, Columbus had managed to return safely and to make subsequent voyages to the same general area, demonstrating that the passage was practical.[5]

Encouraged by the promising reports of these exploits, Zuan Caboto — or John Cabot, as he became known in England — approached Henry VII about sponsoring a similar voyage of discovery. Despite his reputedly cautious and miserly nature, Henry did not want to lose ground to the Spaniards in the race to find a route east and thus agreed to sponsor a North Atlantic voyage of discovery.[6] In 1497, Cabot landed in what is now Newfoundland, which, with its rocky shores and cool climate, was clearly not an East Indian island. Nevertheless, it was plausible to believe that further exploration would show this land to be part of northern Asia. There were immediate benefits as well, since the expedition had revealed enormous fish stocks in the area. Though pedestrian in comparison to precious metals and gems, fish was very much in demand all over Europe at the time, and Cabot's discovery led to the development of a large European fishery in North America.[7]

The Newfoundland cod fishery was perhaps the most important result of Cabot's voyage. Fish provided a meat substitute for the many holy days on the Catholic calendar and so was favoured by the many religious institutions of the day, including hospitals, convents, monasteries, and universities. For "people of moderate means," such as artisans and shopkeepers, it was an "affordable alternative to meat." Salted, dried cod was also a portable source of protein for armies and navies. Because of its popularity, demand for cod rose dramatically along with the population of Europe after 1500, leading to price increases that made cod a very valuable resource.[8] Because of this, the fishery was "perhaps the main reason why North America continued to retain the interest of the western European powers, even when they were unable to contemplate devoting any large share of their resources toward exploration of other parts, or undertaking a major commitment to establish colonies there."[9]

Systematic exploitation of the inshore cod fishery brought a growing number of ships to Newfoundland and the surrounding area. Just twenty years after Cabot's first voyage there were already some 50 vessels reported to be fishing in the region. By 1578, the number had risen to 350 from at least four countries. In 1664, the French alone had over 400 ships in Newfoundland.[10] The masters and crews of these vessels, especially in the earliest period, explored the coastlines of the region in search of untapped fishing grounds or places where they could land and dry their catch. Their activities contributed to the development and dissemination of transoceanic navigational skills as well as to the general knowledge of these rich waters.[11]

While the fishery attracted the attention of many merchants and mariners, others chose to follow the more exciting examples set by Columbus and Cabot of exploring the oceans for a passage to the East. Beginning in 1499, a series of Spanish and Portuguese expeditions landed in South and Central America and began to establish the outline of that area. As early as 1498, while exploring the coast of what is now Venezuela, Columbus had suspected that, in his words, this was a "very great continent, until today unknown."[12] Subsequent explorations of the Spanish Main and Brazil seemed to confirm this view, as did Balboa's overland trek to the Pacific Ocean in 1513. Magellan's remarkable journey (1519 to 1522) around the southern tip of South America finally confirmed its enormous size, in addition to showing there was a route around it, albeit a long and treacherous one.[13]

In the north, initial interest in exploration faded quickly after the second Cabot expedition was lost without a trace in 1498. Portuguese mariners sailing either from the Azores or England made a few minor voyages to Greenland, Newfoundland, and Labrador in the opening years of the sixteenth century, but these turned out to be costly ventures, with several ships lost and few gains.[14] Sebastian Cabot's voyage of 1508 to 1509, though perhaps sailing as far north as Hudson Strait and Hudson Bay, also failed to reveal much in the way of promising resources.[15] These setbacks, combined with the obvious appeal of southern exploration — gold, silver, and the glory of conquest — meant that northern waters and coasts were left to the growing number of European fishing vessels exploiting the riches of the Newfoundland cod fishery. Not until the 1520s, when mariners had proved that there was no quick route through or around South and Central America to the Pacific, was European interest in a possible northern passage revived.

For the next seventy-five years, mariners from several European nations sailed across the North Atlantic to explore the coastline of what was still an almost completely unknown land. Although cartographers had begun to give shape to small segments of the east coast of Newfoundland by 1525, its west coast was entirely uncharted, and no one yet knew whether this was an island, several islands, part of a known continent such as Asia, or part of a new one — except perhaps the fishermen who frequented the area but kept their extensive knowledge of it to themselves. Moreover, Europeans apparently knew nothing about the area between the Bay of Fundy and Florida except that it was vast and unexplored. It was natural then that these regions should become the focus of the search for a passage to the Orient.[16]

The French were the first to renew the quest. Francis I, crowned in 1515, alone among the monarchs of Western Europe, had no great discoveries or riches to claim in the New World. His main rival, Charles V, ruled the Hapsburg Empire, which included Spain, the Netherlands, and the Holy Roman Empire. All were benefiting from international trade, but Spain, in particular, was reaping huge profits from the gold, silver, and gems flowing out of Mexico and South and Central America. The Portuguese, meanwhile, still dominated the eastern oceanic routes and, as a result, had a large list of luxury goods that they could sell in Europe and the New World. They were also active in South America. Even England, at this time little more than a second-rate sea power, laid claim to a new land and a new source of wealth — codfish — though they did little to exploit or protect their discovery at the time.[17]

The new French king tried to remedy his situation by becoming an active patron of maritime exploration. Between 1524 and 1542 he gave his support to a series of voyages whose primary goal was to find a northern route to the Orient. In 1524 the Italian mariner Giovanni de Verrazano was commissioned by Francis and financed by a group of merchants and bankers to sail west across the Atlantic "to reach Cataia [Cathay] and the extreme eastern coast of Asia." Verrazano had anticipated, with unfounded optimism, that there would be "no barrier of new land" and that, even if he encountered such a barrier, "it would not lack a strait to penetrate to the Eastern Ocean."[18] What he found, however, as he travelled north from what are now the Carolinas to what is now Maine, was a continuous and large land mass with no obvious passage through to the Pacific. Verrazano hoped to continue his search farther north on subsequent voyages but was killed by Natives in the Caribbean on a voyage there in 1528.[19]

It fell to Jacques Cartier to carry on France's pursuit of the northern strait. In 1534, ten years after Verrazano's expedition had sailed for America, Cartier left his home port of St Malo charged with finding a passage to China and, secondarily, new sources of precious metals. He found neither, but he did circumnavigate Newfoundland, proving that it was in fact an island, sailing through the Strait of Belle Isle and into the Gulf of St Lawrence as far as Anticosti Island and the Gaspé. His explorations, while inconclusive, documented the existence of a very wide and apparently very long inlet or river that could lead through the continent to the Pacific. They also demonstrated the extent and reinforced the importance of fishing activities in the region, as Cartier encountered a number of vessels in areas that he had believed to be unknown and unexplored by Europeans.[20]

Within a year, Cartier sailed again, this time with only one objective — to explore the area and inlet beyond Newfoundland with a view to finding "certain far-away countries."[21] On this voyage, his most famous, Cartier ventured as far up the St Lawrence as he could, making it to Hochelaga, the site of present-day Montréal. From the mountain, he could easily see a stretch of rapids (later named Lachine in mocking remembrance of René-Robert Cavelier de La Salle, who in 1669 sold his nearby seigneury and everything he owned to search for a route to China)[22] that would prevent any vessel from proceeding farther upstream, although the mighty river itself seemed to go on forever to the west. Yet the Natives Cartier met spoke of another river flowing to the west and confirmed earlier tales he had heard of a rich kingdom to the north called the Saguenay. Thus, despite his disappointment at coming to the end of navigable water on the St Lawrence, Cartier was encouraged enough by what he had found to decide to overwinter and see whether Europeans could live in this harsh new world. The toll for this decision was high — twenty-five crewmen died and most others suffered terribly from scurvy — but with the help of the Natives, the majority survived the Canadian winter. Cartier returned home convinced that it would be possible to set up and sustain a colony from which further explorations into the continent, particularly into the Saguenay, could be mounted.[23]

Cartier's last voyage was by far the most ambitious[24] and, in the final analysis, the most disappointing. Under the overall command of Jean-François de La Rocque de Roberval, this expedition, or at least Cartier's ships, left France in May 1541 and three months later began building a settlement near Cap Rouge, near present-day Québec. By June of the following year, though, Cartier and the remaining colonists and crew were on their way home, worn down by hostile Natives and disease and with no apparent hope of relief, since Roberval's ships were now believed lost. Roberval, who had made it as far as St John's, decided to carry on up the St Lawrence, where he, too, built a *habitation*, for his soldiers and settlers. Their winter experience was even worse than Cartier's, as fifty people died, probably from scurvy. Nor did their explorations make up for the hardships they had suffered. It seems likely that any efforts they made to travel up the Saguenay River were stopped short by the Chicoutimi rapids. Moreover, the very existence of this impassable barrier indicated, as the Lachine rapids on the St Lawrence had, that this was only a river and not an "arm of the sea." By September 1543, Roberval and what was left of his expedition were back in France. The disappointment accompanying the failure of these voyages, combined with the nation's descent into religious civil war (of which Roberval himself became a victim), brought a temporary end to France's active interest in North America. It would not be revived for fifty or more years, at which time Cartier's carefully documented explorations would prove to be of the utmost importance.[25]

Figure 1. The arrival of Jacques Cartier at Québec. Nineteenth-century lithograph attributed to David Lith. (Library and Archives Canada, neg. C-005933)

With the St Lawrence and the Saguenay ruled out as easy routes to the East, explorers turned their attention still farther north. Largely uninvolved in exploration since the days of John and Sebastian Cabot, Britain, by the 1570s, had decided that it needed to re-enter the race for Oriental riches. Britain had a long and distinguished maritime tradition and an impressive number of expert mariners — no part of the country is farther than 70 miles (113 km) from salt water.[26] The Tudors had provided dynastic stability and a measure of national unity and strength that allowed the country to weather the storm of the Reformation without major political upheaval. Their navy, though small, was growing, not the least because England was now a Protestant island surrounded, for the most part, by Catholic enemies. This strategic need was reinforced by an economic one: the English economy was suffering from declining trade, and the country desperately needed to find new sources of wealth.

In this context, it is perhaps not surprising that the English government finally recognized the need to improve the navigational skills of its mariners. It began by enticing Sebastian Cabot away from the Spaniards to train English mariners in the art of celestial navigation and to organize the production of charts and instruments. Armed with this expertise, not to mention Cabot's vast knowledge of Spain's maritime infrastructure, Elizabeth and her government began to pursue a more aggressive mercantile and naval strategy. They sent Francis Drake and Walter Raleigh out to harass the Spanish by disrupting their settlements and trade and raiding their ships. Another group of British mariners renewed the search for a northern passage to the Orient and other potentially lucrative trading regions in the East.[27]

The search began in the northeast around mid-century when a group of English merchants and mariners founded the Muscovy Company and attempted to establish trade routes through and around Russia.[28] By the 1570s, however, focus had shifted to the northwest, fuelled, in part, by the musings of Humphrey Gilbert in his *Discourses*. Gilbert had, in 1566, published what he believed to be all the latest research and evidence "on the possible existence of a north-west passage." He also discussed the possible trade advantages that would result from such a passage and even suggested that Britain should attempt to set up colonies in the New World. Gilbert was well connected in the scientific and mercantile communities; his ideas were widely disseminated and helped to pave the way for a series of northern expeditions approved by the crown and supported by wealthy London merchants.[29]

Martin Frobisher was the first to set out. His voyages of 1576, 1577, and 1578 did not reveal a passage, but neither did they exhaust all the possible locations for it. Unfortunately the "gold" he found and collected turned out to be iron pyrite, and the financial losses his expeditions incurred dampened interest in further explorations until 1585. Even then, John Davis's backers were far less generous than Frobisher's had been, and their caution was justified. Despite extensive explorations far north into what we know as Davis Strait and Cumberland Sound, after three voyages he was no closer to finding the passage than Frobisher, though he had unknowingly approached its entrance at Lancaster Sound.[30]

Twenty years later, still not convinced that the great passage was a myth, another series of British mariners set out for the Arctic. In 1610 to 1611, Henry Hudson sailed through the Hudson Strait and into Hudson and James bays, where he wintered. The winter was very hard and, according to a subsequent investigation, "to save some from Starving," witnesses claimed that Hudson and eight other weakened crew members were cast adrift in a small boat. The remaining crew then made their way back to England.[31] Thomas Button and Robert Bylot went to look for Hudson and the passage the following year, found neither, and declared the wide strait a dead end. In 1616, Bylot and William Baffin, venturing farther north than any other Europeans until 1853, discovered Lancaster Sound, which they named and then declared a dead end. Twenty years later, in 1631, Luke Fox and Thomas James ventured back into Hudson Bay and wintered in James Bay, which took its name from the latter. For all involved, these were hugely discouraging voyages, despite the fact that they greatly increased scientific, geographical, and hydrographical knowledge of the area and gave Britain a preliminary claim to Hudson and James bays. At the time, no one cared to possess ice-strewn waters that led nowhere or a land apparently barren of valuable resources. Only forty years later would two Frenchmen show that Hudson Strait and Bay did, in fact, lead into the heart of a very rich land — the most valuable fur-bearing region of the continent.[32]

By the 1620s, European nations had come to the conclusion that there was no easy way around North America from the east and that the valuable resources that existed there[33] demanded a more systematic and labour-intensive method of exploitation than those of the south. Merchants, mariners, and shipowners involved in the fishery needed to put together ships and men, and enough equipment and supplies for a transatlantic voyage and a lengthy stay in North America. They saw no return on their investment until the catch could be sold months later. For those producing dry cod, there were the added costs of building, maintaining, and protecting land-based infrastructure.[34] The fur trade also seemed to demand "a more complex pattern of exploitation" involving "the year-round presence of settlers,"[35] to set up, inhabit, and operate the network of supply depots and trading posts that stretched deeper and deeper into the rugged interior of the continent.

At the same time, the economic dogma of the day stressed the importance of trade and held that there was a limited amount of trade in the world. Each country could only improve their share at the expense of others. As well, national governments put increasing emphasis on the need to manage trade so that importation of manufactured goods was kept to a minimum while domestic industries were assured of a steady supply of raw materials, from abroad if necessary. This encouraged European monarchs, their agents, and merchants to lay claim to (and maintain their claim to) whatever resources and markets were available by whatever means necessary. Planting colonies in the New World was viewed as one way of accomplishing this. Building large and well-armed navies and merchant fleets was another, something strongly suggested by national and historical examples such as Venice, Holland, and Spain. As a consequence of these and other factors, in northern North America the two hundred years between about 1600 and 1800 were marked by significant, if not extensive, colonial development, substantial growth in trade, frequent military skirmishes, and sometimes outright war.[36]

Initially, France and England were the main claimants to the resources of what is now Canada, though Spain and Portugal both had a significant presence in the fishery, and the former became the major sponsors of colonization projects. Their economic and strategic objectives were often aided by the ongoing religious upheavals of the sixteenth and seventeenth centuries, which created thousands of European refugees willing to go almost anywhere to escape persecution. The English attempted to establish settlements in Newfoundland beginning early in the seventeenth century on the assumption that such settlements would improve the efficiency and profitability of the well-established fishing industries as well as solidify their claim to the area and its rich resources. However, the sponsors eventually found that whatever "marginal advantages" permanent settlements might offer, the cost of maintaining an isolated community with little chance of self-sufficiency was just too high to warrant the continued investment. Though hundreds of fishing crews continued to use coastal bases to process their catches, few people wintered over on a regular basis, preferring to sail across the Atlantic in spring and fall. (On the English shore the number of settlers was "never much more than 2000, while the French around Placentia numbered less than one third that.")[37]

The French, overall, did better than the English in northern North America, not the least because they chose sites that had more potential for agriculture. Their settlement at Québec was also well situated on the major transportation route into the interior. The latter colony was a good staging area for further exploration and for the extensive exploitation of the rich fur-bearing regions to the west. Thus, while these communities remained highly dependent on France for basic support, their existence at least made the growth of a profitable fur trade possible and also established France's claim to a huge area of eastern North America.

Beginning as early as 1603 with Samuel de Champlain's first voyage to Canada, French fur traders and explorers struck out into the interior, following the intricate and, at times, confusing pattern of rivers and lakes that criss-cross the Precambrian Shield. They were searching for more fur — "the major export commodity of New France"[38] — and other natural resources to which France could lay claim, but they were also trying to determine the size of this new continent, probably hoping that they might yet find a practical route through it. By the 1630s Champlain and Etienne Brulé had travelled as far as the western-

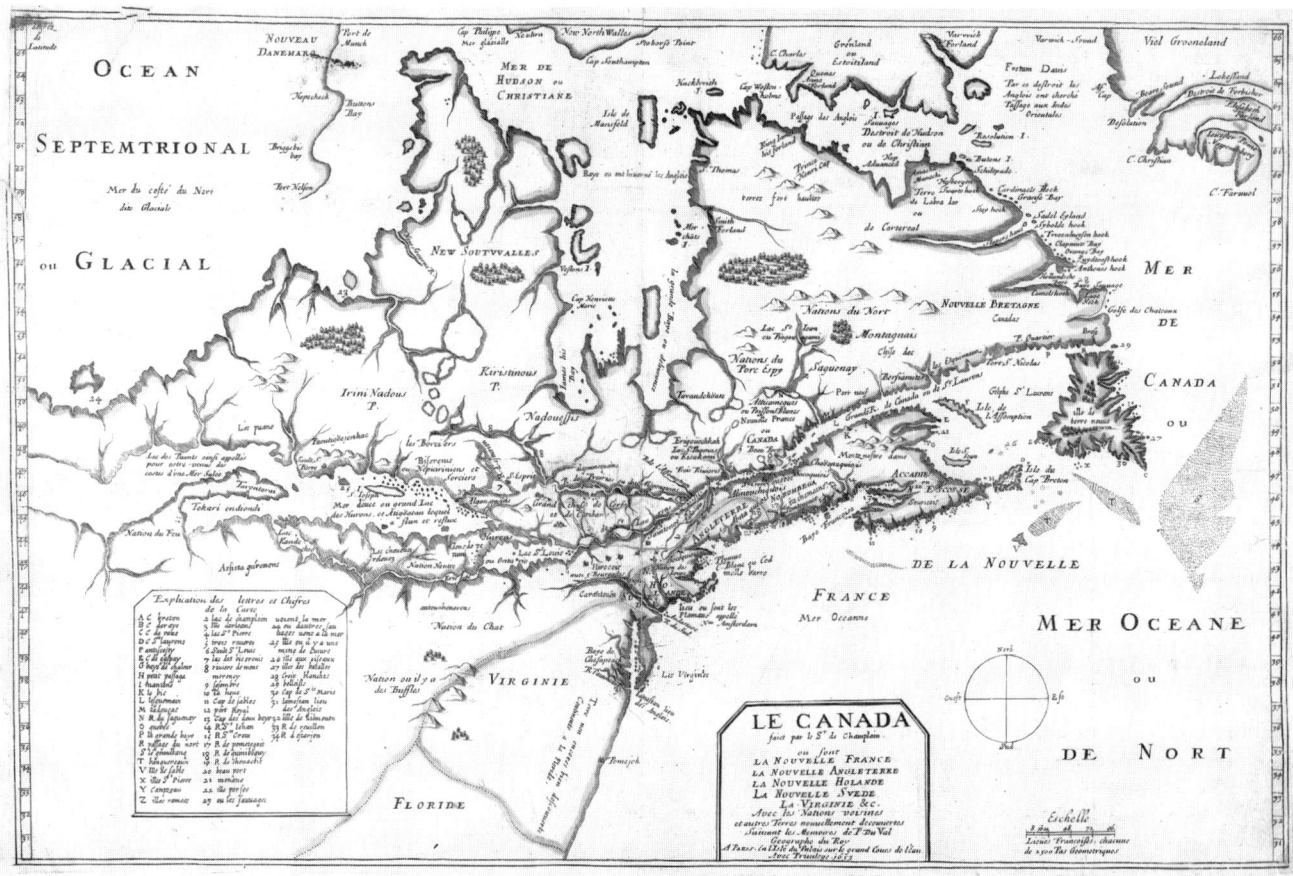

Map 1. *Champlain's map of Canada, 1653. This map depicts the extent of European knowledge of eastern North America in the mid-seventeenth century and is remarkably accurate given the rudimentary surveying instruments available at the time.*
(Library and Archives Canada, neg. NMC-0006333)

most of the Great Lakes. In the 1660s Pierre Esprit Radisson and Médard Chouart Des Groseilliers had ventured far to the north and returned to Québec laden with beaver pelts and promoting a scheme to use Hudson Bay to gain direct access to the rich fur country they had visited. La Salle, meanwhile, went west to the Mississippi and then south to the Gulf of Mexico, claiming all the land for Louis XIV.[39]

Yet while the French would claim dominion over large areas of North America, they found it difficult to sustain these claims. As the century progressed, competition for colonies, trade, and naval supremacy intensified, particularly between Britain and France. In the ensuing wars and skirmishes, Britain established a firm presence in the Northwest through the Hudson's Bay Company, founded by royal charter in 1670, and in the east by gaining title to Newfoundland. France retained fishing rights on the French shore of Newfoundland and its colonies in Acadia and Quebec. It also continued to compete for furs in the west until the eighteenth century, when it lost first Acadia and then, in 1760, Québec itself.[40]

From this point on Britain became the supreme imperial power in North America. Though its northern colonies — in Newfoundland, Nova Scotia, and Quebec — were not very populous or powerful compared to the settlements to the south, they did supply a steady stream of profitable goods including fish and fur. This trade and these colonies became critical after 1775 when the American colonists rebelled against Britain. By the end of the war, the northern settlements, along with the West Indies and a few other small colonies, were all that was left of the British Empire in North America, giving them a renewed and substantial strategic and economic importance.

Around the same time, several other European nations began to stake competing claims to the Pacific coast of North America. Since the seventeenth century no one had shown great interest in the vast and largely unexplored northern reaches of the Pacific, though Spain nevertheless maintained its claim to the whole ocean.[41] Interest in the region was revived, however, by Vitus Bering's explorations of the Alaskan shoreline and Bering Strait in the 1740s, the publication of Samuel Hearne's account of his overland trek from Rupert's Land to the Arctic coast in 1771, and the ongoing military contest for colonial supremacy. It seemed that there might be a western entrance to the Northwest Passage, and whoever found it would have a new and lucrative trade route to the Orient. They would also be able to lay claim to a large part of the North American continent, which, if the rumours of Russian and American trading activity in Alaska were true, might also prove very profitable.[42]

So intense became European interest in the Pacific Northwest that, for twenty years beginning in 1774, the French, British, and Spanish governments equipped and funded several major expeditions to the area, each with an ambitious mandate. They were sent to look for the Northwest Passage; explore and chart the areas they visited; document the land, vegetation, and people they found and any trade opportunities that might exist; and, finally, lay claim to the lands for their sovereigns.[43] Though Juan Perez sailing for Spain in 1774[44] was the first to make his way north to what is now the coast of British Columbia, it was James Cook's voyage in 1776 to 1778 that really began the systematic exploration of the region. Setting sail one year after the British parliament offered a prize for the discovery of the Northwest Passage, Cook travelled extensively in the South Pacific before heading north to B.C. and Alaska, where he not only established Britain's claim but also discovered a rich new resource, sea otter pelts.[45]

Further exploration was postponed by the American War of Independence, in which both France and Spain fought with the colonists against Britain. Shortly after it ended, though, the French sent Jean-François de Lapérouse into the Pacific, perhaps hoping to press the advantage they had won in the war to re-enter North America as a colonial power. This expedition, like

Figure 2. *Captain James Cook.*
(Library and Archives Canada, neg. C-034667)

Cook's, was large, ambitious, well equipped and funded, and expected to cover vast areas of the Pacific from Russia and Alaska to China and Australia. It lasted three years, from 1785 to 1788, and produced much important information about these diverse regions, including more detailed charts of the Pacific coast of North America. Unfortunately, it ended tragically with all ships lost on the reefs of a South Pacific island. By 1789, France was consumed by revolution and thus unable to pursue Lapérouse's work or assert whatever claims he had made in the area.[46]

As a result, the British and Spanish were left to squabble over rights to the region. And squabble they did. In 1790, the Spaniard Esteban José Martinez, surprised by the presence of British traders in Nootka Sound, which Spain claimed, seized them and their ships, causing an international incident. Though Spain backed down on this particular action, it did not relinquish its claim to the whole region. The very next year both countries sent expeditions to the area. George Vancouver was sent out to receive Spain's official reparations for the incident, to reassert Britain's presence on the coast, and, while there, to map and explore the area, looking for an inlet that led to the Northwest Passage. Alejandro Malaspina and Dionisio Alcala Galiano had no overtly political mandate but were also there to "show the flag," to look for a northern route through the continent, and to collect as much useful scientific and other information as they could about the region and its peoples. This they did, though changed political circumstances at home meant that most of their extensive work came to nothing, as Spain more or less abandoned the field to Britain.[47]

Vancouver, on the other hand, spent four and a half years in the Pacific, sailing 65,000 miles (105 000 km) and carrying out a detailed survey of the northern coast, including some of the larger inlets. Though he eliminated these as possible entrances to an ocean passage, he did not extinguish all hope that such a route existed in the Arctic.[48] Of more immediate importance, his work, which he wrote up and published, provided the basis for Britain's claim to the area, a claim that was reinforced by the overland explorations of Alexander Mackenzie. An employee of the North West Company of Montréal, Mackenzie had been sent west to find a more efficient route than the Great Lakes over which to move goods and supplies between Europe and the company's interior fur trade posts. In 1789, he journeyed to the Arctic Ocean via the river that now bears his name and then, in 1793, he made his way across the mountains to the Pacific, missing Vancouver's survey crews by days at the head of North Bentinck Arm. Though he found no supply route comparable to Hudson Bay, he showed just how vast and inhospitable the continent was and demonstrated once and for all that the last hope of getting around it lay in the frozen North.[49]

Out to Sea: Shipboard Navigational Instruments, 1500–1800

Regular oceanic navigation, out of sight of land, began in the mid-fifteenth century with the voyages of Portuguese mariners into the Indian Ocean. When these men set out to find an ocean route to the Indies, they had at their disposal, besides their great practical skill and knowledge, only the basic tools of coastal navigation — the magnetic compass, the sandglass, and a sounding instrument. The compass gave general direction or bearing, which might have been recorded on a traverse board, a circular piece of wood with holes radiating out from the centre following the lines of a compass. The sandglass measured time and thus helped to estimate speed, and the sounding rod or lead and line indicated the depth of the water and provided samples of the seabed. The limitations of these tools and techniques, collectively known as dead reckoning, soon became abundantly clear to mariners. The farther they sailed, the more errors caused by magnetic variation of the compass and the imprecise speed measurement of the sandglass added up, making an accurate estimate of position increasingly difficult. The sounding instrument was of little use except in coastal waters, where it helped warn of the approach of underwater hazards or of land.[50]

As a consequence of these limitations, the Portuguese were forced to consider alternative ways of finding position at sea, and around the mid-fifteenth century mariners began to adopt astronomical navigational techniques, to "steer by the stars," in other words. Astronomers had known since at least Roman times that the positions and movements of celestial bodies could be used to determine one's position on the globe.[51] The simplest astronomical measure to obtain was latitude, that is, one's position north or south of the equator, found by measuring the altitude of Polaris, the Pole Star, or the Sun. This figure was then corrected according to tables that recorded the daily and seasonal changes in the heavens. By the 1470s, astronomers had also devised a formula for converting this angular measure into linear distances, such as miles or leagues.[52]

To use this knowledge, Portuguese mariners adapted existing astronomical instruments. The seaman's quadrant was the first device they applied to oceanic navigation, though it "proved all but impossible to use at sea and the navigator had to go ashore to make any worthwhile observations."[53] The astrolabe was also adapted for maritime use in the fifteenth century by opening up the frame to reduce weight and wind resistance and weighting the bottom to help keep it vertical. This device made it easier to observe the Sun, which was especially important for southern voyages, when Polaris dropped out of sight. It was also better suited to working on a ship's deck but again, was difficult to use properly in rough seas. Moreover, the observer might need an assistant to help him when observing a star or when taking a solar reading in haze. Once he got the reading, the navigator consulted his astronomical tables and conversion formula to interpret it.[54]

These same instruments, tables, and techniques were available to mariners such as Columbus and Cabot when they undertook their first transoceanic voyages. The astronomical devices enabled them to get a fairly accurate fix on their latitude and, based on this, they adopted a method of sailing know as "latitude sailing." The navigator would first set a course to reach the latitude of his desired destination. To do this he used an established rule that told him how far to sail (with progress estimated by dead reckoning) north or south to increase or decrease his latitude by 1 degree. He then plotted a course east or west along that latitude until he reached the set destination, checking (taking a reading of Sun or stars) regularly to make sure he was maintaining his north/south position. As for his east/west position, the best a navigator could do was estimate the ship's speed and keep track of it using sandglass and traverse board, journal, or blank chart to record progress over time.[55]

With all its limitations, latitude sailing was reliable and simple enough to take countless explorers, traders, fishermen, and whalers back and forth across the Atlantic safely. Still, it was far from perfect. And there were great incentives — trade and colonial development and defence — to improve it. Thus in the three hundred years between 1497 and 1800, astronomers, mariners, and instrument makers produced many significant refinements in navigational tools and techniques. These improved mariners' ability to measure latitude, speed, and direction and, ultimately, provided a method for measuring longitude.

As mariners ventured farther away from familiar waters and began to lay claim to newly "discovered" lands, the importance of being able to establish one's position accurately grew. Improving the means of measuring latitude, thus, became a priority. By 1500, literate mariners knew the basic principles of finding position by latitude, and those who had to travel for any distance were gradually adopting the practice. At the same time, it was becoming clear to those who used celestial navigation that the quadrant and the astrolabe were not well suited to shipboard use. As early as 1515 and possibly earlier, the Portuguese had introduced an alternative — also borrowed from the field of astronomy — namely the cross-staff. As its name suggests, this instrument consisted of a straight wooden rod called the staff fitted through the central slot in a shorter wooden crosspiece called the cross. The observer held one end of the staff close to his eye and moved the cross up or down the staff until its ends coincided with the star being "read" and the horizon. The observer could then read the angular measurement from a graduated scale marked on the staff.[56]

The cross-staff had many positive attributes, among them its lightness, ease of manufacture and storage, and versatility in measurement. For many mariners, it quickly became a common tool for measuring the altitude of Polaris and the Sun. Yet it too had severe limitations. It was tricky to use because the observer had to position it very precisely, sight the star or Sun and the horizon at the same time, and hold the instrument completely vertical during the observation. This was difficult enough in calm seas but more or less impossible in rough ones. Moreover, to read the Sun, the navigator had to look directly at it, often for an uncomfortable period of time. Perhaps this is why many navigators continued to use astrolabes, which allowed them to measure the Sun's altitude using the light it cast on the instrument rather than an actual sighting.[57]

Figure 3. *Sixteenth-century illustration showing the instruction of a mariner in the use of the cross-staff.*
(J. Werner and P. Apianus, Introductio geographica Petri Apiani in Doctissimas Verneri annotationes, Inglostadt, 1533)

Figure 4. An English nocturnal, maker unknown. This instrument (1645–1695) is made of pearwood and brass. (CSTM1991.0020)

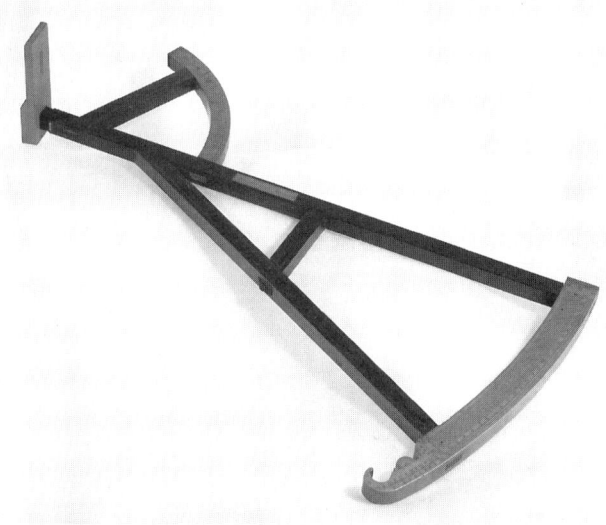

Figure 5. The back-staff or Davis quadrant was invented by John Davis around 1590 and served mariners well for over 150 years until it was gradually supplanted by the octant. This one was made by John Cranevelt of the Netherlands between 1725 and 1775 of mahogany and boxwood. (CSTM1992.0038)

In the early sixteenth century, mariners also began to use an alternative device for reading the sky at night. The nocturnal, as a navigational instrument, was specifically designed to determine the time at night. Usually made of brass or wood, it consisted of two circular plates marked with time scales, an index arm, and a handle that was part of the larger plate. These were held together in the centre by a rivet. The observer held the device at arm's length, sighted the star through the central hole in the rivet, and adjusted the arm until it was aligned with the stars for which the instrument had been calibrated. He could then read from the scale marked on the device to find time quite accurately. This figure could then be used to determine latitude. As with other astronomical navigational instruments, readings had to be corrected to compensate for the constant movement of the Earth around the Sun.[58]

Navigators made do with these four basic instruments until the 1590s, when John Davis, English Arctic explorer and master mariner, introduced the back-staff or Davis quadrant. It has been called "the first truly nautical instrument"[59] because it was the first device designed especially for marine navigation by a mariner. It was not superseded for nearly 150 years. Over that period, the inventor and various instrument makers changed and refined its original form — a staff with a vane, sometimes called a horizon vane, on one end and one movable arc or crosspiece. The observer moved the arc along the staff until its shadow fell on the vane, which was held in line with the horizon. He then consulted the scale for the reading. Later versions included two arcs, allowing for the measurement of larger angles, pinnule sights, and eventually a magnifying glass that cast a beam of light onto the horizon vane or foresight. The back-staff relieved the observer of the unwelcome duty of sighting the Sun directly. It also did not require quite the same skill in sighting two objects at the same time. Once the observer had adjusted the upper arc to get the light from the Sun at about the right angle, he could focus all his effort on bringing "the image cast by the Sun on the vane into line with the direct line of the horizon," using the more precise sight on the lower arc or quadrant. Moreover, the subsequent addition of the magnifying glass concentrated enough light to get a reading even in overcast conditions.[60]

Despite its enduring success, the back-staff, like its predecessors, had limitations. Taking an observation was still a complicated business, even under ideal conditions. As always, on a pitching or rolling deck, it would have been almost pointless. As well, for all its refinements, the back-staff was not significantly more accurate than the cross-staff and almost as awkward to handle. That mariners learned to master this device and make reasonably precise measurements with it much of the time is evidence of their skill, knowledge, and determination. Indeed, some were so familiar with the back-staff and presumably satisfied with its performance that they initially refused to adopt its successor, the octant, when it was finally offered to them.[61]

The octant was so named because its arc was 45 degrees (or half of the 90 degrees marked on its scale), which is 1/8 of a circle. Its operating principle, "using a mirror to bring one target into coincidence with another, and then noting the inclination of the mirror,"[62] was first proposed by Robert Hooke and by Isaac Newton in the late seventeenth century. Yet it was not until the 1730s that scientists actually applied this principle to construction of a device for measuring the altitude of heavenly bodies. Around that time, several individuals, most notably Thomas Godfrey of Philadelphia and John Hadley of London, came up with workable instruments. Though each version was slightly different, the method of operation was essentially the same. The observer held the octant vertically and viewed the horizon "through a pin-hole (later telescopic) sight and the clear portion of a half-silvered mirror, known as the horizon glass." He then moved a second mirror mounted on the index arm until the image of the Sun or star being observed coincided with the horizon. Finally he measured the angle between the two mirrors using the scale provided.[63]

The readings navigators were able to make using the octant were more accurate than those made with either the cross-staff or the back-staff. The device was also more compact and thus easier to handle and store. More importantly, it was better suited to use at sea since "the coincidence of Sun or star and horizon was not affected by the motion of the ship." As a result, it gradually replaced all other altitude measuring navigational instruments.[64]

In 1757, while testing astronomer Tobias Mayer's lunar tables for determining longitude on a voyage to Newfoundland, Captain John Campbell, R.N., found that he needed to measure larger angles than were possible with the octant. He suggested that the arc of the octant be increased from 45 to 60 degrees (1/6 of a circle, hence the name sextant) and commissioned instrument maker John Bird of London to build the instrument for him in 1759.[65]

When first introduced, sextants were expensive and cumbersome devices. Mariners used them exclusively for precision measurement of lunar distances, and they were carried only by the best-equipped ships, usually on government-sponsored expeditions. With the advent of mechanical dividing engines after 1777, however, makers could divide much smaller arcs with the necessary accuracy and

Figure 6. A Hadley's octant manufactured between 1766 and 1782 by English maker Benjamin Cole Jr. The large-radius octant was gradually replaced by the small-radius models made possible by the introduction of mechanical dividing engines. This instrument was owned by a Canadian, G. C. Morrison of Glenholm, Nova Scotia.
(CSTM1992.1569)

Figure 7. The captain of the Finnish barque Passat circa 1947 using a sextant. Invented in the mid-eighteenth century, the sextant became and remained the primary tool for establishing latitude on board ships for more than two hundred years.
(Courtesy Niels Jannasch)

complete the task much more efficiently. Sextants, as a consequence, gradually became smaller and less expensive and eventually emerged as the standard altitude measuring instrument used by navigators.[66]

To go along with these improved navigational devices, mariners also obtained increasingly accurate astronomical tables. Long before 1500, astronomers had been busy accumulating a wealth of information about the behaviour of celestial bodies in relation to the Earth — exactly how much they moved each day and over the course of a year. After 1500, this knowledge was systematically combined with the thousands of observations recorded by mariners voyaging around the world to produce an ever more detailed and precise map of the heavens that navigators could follow.

The increased interest in astronomy during this period was, to a great extent, inspired by the needs of transoceanic navigation and, in particular, the pursuit of a solution to the longitude problem. For although the tools and methods for measuring latitude had steadily improved, little if any progress had been made in determining longitude. Longitude is essentially the difference between the time a celestial object passes an established point and the time it crosses the location being measured. (Today the Greenwich or prime meridian is designated 0 degrees longitude and is therefore the standard reference point.) Four minutes of time equals 1 degree of longitude.

The ideal solution to solving the longitude problem would have been a very precise timekeeping device. In the eighteenth century, however, mechanical timepieces did not work under the harsh conditions at sea. The constant, sometimes violent, motion of ships and the dramatic changes in temperature and atmospheric conditions that were unavoidable on long voyages played havoc with the delicate and carefully balanced inner workings of precision clocks of the era. Researchers, therefore, had to look for other means by which to tell time at sea.

As early as 1514 businessman and amateur astronomer Johannes Werner had suggested using the Moon's motion as a way to tell time at sea. The Moon moves relatively quickly against the background of the stars and appears to the observer on Earth to lag behind the stars by a fixed rate, about half a degree per hour. Werner thought that the distance between the Moon and a given star at any particular time would be the same at different locations and that any change in that distance could, therefore, be used to measure time at a reference point, later designated the prime or Greenwich meridian. Assuming he had a means of predicting the Moon's position in advance and measuring the actual celestial distances accurately, the navigator could then find longitude.

Werner's theory was essentially sound but it was totally impracticable at the time. It did not take into account the effects of refraction on the measurement of celestial bodies at different altitudes or the difference between the observer's position on the Earth's surface and its centre (parallax). Mathematicians and astronomers had to devise elaborate equations to correct for these distortions. Even more significantly, they had to calculate "the precise position of the stars relative to each other" and they had to know enough about the Moon's complex movements to be able to predict its position relative to the stars several years into the future. Finally, instrument makers had to design and build a device or devices that could "take the necessary observations to the required degree of accuracy."[67] It took another two and a half centuries for scientific men to supply these essential prerequisites.

In the meantime, researchers continued to suggest other methods of finding longitude. During the 1570s, some suggested that the measurement of magnetic variation and declination might provide the key to establishing a ship's longitudinal position.[68] Over the next century various distinguished scientists, many of them English, studied the behaviour of the compass and attempted to frame a theory that could predict changes around the globe, allowing mariners to calculate their position accordingly. Mariners, however, saw no predictable pattern in the readings they had been recording for decades, and they were not alone in doubting that the complexities of magnetic variation (which we now know varies with time) could be understood sufficiently to provide the key to measuring longitude.[69]

In the early seventeenth century attention turned back to the heavens as Galileo suggested using "the eclipses and occultations of Jupiter's satellites" to determine time and thereby longitude. A handful of astronomers in England and France pursued this course of investigation in the following decades. Others suggested the simultaneous observation of lunar eclipses as a way to measure east/west position. In 1631 astronomer Henry Gellibrand co-ordinated a lunar experiment with Captain Thomas James. The former observed and measured the lunar eclipse at Gresham College while the latter did the same — following Gellibrand's precise instructions — at Charlton Island, at the south end of James Bay. From James's records, Gellibrand established the precise position of the island at 79 degrees 30 minutes west of Greenwich. Though both of these methods produced promising theoretical results, neither offered a practical solution to telling time at sea, not the least because the celestial events did not occur frequently enough to supply regular readings, typically one to three events per day.[70]

Figure 8. *The Paris observatory, from a nineteenth-century print.* (Courtesy Randall Brooks)

Scientists, mariners, and others concerned with improving navigation, nevertheless, did not give up the quest for a celestial solution to the longitude problem, and by 1670 they had persuaded the governments of both Britain and France that astronomical research needed to be given state support.[71] As a result, both countries established royal observatories and charged their astronomers with a very practical task — studying the movement of the celestial bodies in order to devise a way to measure the east/west position of places and thereby improve navigation. It was during this period that Werner's idea of a lunar method of time measurement was revived, leading astronomers all over Europe to undertake intensive study of the complex motions of the Moon. This was a painstaking and time-consuming process because the Moon's motions relative to the Sun repeat themselves only every 18 years 11.3 days. Researchers, therefore, had to observe and record the Moon's behaviour for a minimum of 18 years to establish a precise pattern. Although its proponents were convinced that this work would eventually yield a sound formula for calculating longitude, by the early eighteenth century there were few concrete results to show for more than thirty years of research.

Facing a rising toll in lost ships and mariners and growing increasingly impatient, the British government established the Board of Longitude in 1714 and offered a prize for the solution of this crucial problem. Two years later France announced a similar prize.[72] By the mid-eighteenth century astronomers and mathematicians in several countries, notably Edmond Halley, Pierre-Charles Lemonnier, Jacques-Dominique Cassini de Thury, L. Euler, Jean d'Alembert, Alexis-Claude Clairaut, and Tobias Mayer, had at last produced a series of formulas and lunar tables that enabled them to predict the Moon's motion accurately and from it calculate longitude. This coincided neatly with the ongoing work of instrument makers who were developing and refining the precision instruments needed to measure lunar distances, namely the octant and, more importantly, the sextant. In 1757 to 1759, John Campbell, navigator and "inventor" of the sextant, tested Mayer's lunar tables and system of measurement at sea with inconclusive results. Astronomer Nevil Maskelyne conducted similar tests in 1761 that proved the method correct within about 1 degree, but only after four hours of calculation to "clear the distance," that is, to compensate for refraction and parallax. Five years later, Maskelyne, now Astronomer Royal, still required an hour to do the calculation.

Clearly the theory was sound, but the technique was impractical for all but the most scientifically inclined navigator and perhaps even for a less-than-inspired astronomer.[73] Anyone interested in using lunar distance to determine longitude also needed the right instrument, preferably a sextant, to make the precise measurements. These were still expensive and uncommon devices aboard most ships. Thus, while all the information needed to use lunar distance effectively to measure longitude based on the Greenwich meridian could be found in Maskelyne's *Nautical Almanac* beginning in 1766, this method does not seem to have won many converts. Not until the nineteenth century, when "a more workable computational scheme" was introduced and when sextants became more affordable and readily available, did measuring lunar distance become a practical method of establishing longitude. After this time, the regularly updated *Almanac* with its detailed lunar tables became an indispensable book for mariners and, as such, continued to be published into the twentieth century.[74]

In the end, the prize for solving longitude (the British one at least) went not to any of the renowned scientists, mathematicians, or astronomers who had contributed to and championed the lunar distance method, but to a clockmaker. In 1735, John Harrison presented his first marine timekeeper or chronometer to the Board of Longitude for testing. He claimed that his device could be set to Greenwich time and would keep that time over the course of a long sea voyage. He had incorporated special features that compensated for the expansion, contraction, and changing elasticity of metal pieces in different temperatures and others

Figure 9. John Harrison's No. 1 chronometer, completed in 1735. This large timekeeper was tested on a short voyage in 1736 and found to keep accurate time at sea. Harrison's No. 4 timekeeper eventually won the Board of Longitude award of £20,000.

(National Maritime Museum, Greenwich, neg. B5157/C)

that prevented the extreme motion of the ship from affecting the working of the clock. Encouraged by the results, he produced a second in 1739 and a third in 1757, all slight improvements on the previous versions.

In 1761 he presented his fourth device to the Board. Although it met all their required performance standards, the board members worried that it was not a "method of common and general Utility" and therefore were hesitant about awarding Harrison the prize. Eventually, in 1764, he was given half the prize, but he had to fight for another nine years and ultimately petition George III and the prime minister before he received the remainder of the £20,000 award and the recognition that went with it. He died within three years of having finally been given the credit he deserved.[75]

As it turned out, however, the Board of Longitude was right to be concerned about the practical utility of Harrison's chronometer because it "did not solve the longitude problem in any realistic or effective sense."[76] His clockmaking techniques, though ingenious, had no lasting impact on the development of practical chronometers. Pierre Le Roy was the man who actually pioneered the route that led to the development of a practical and easily reproduced marine timekeeper.[77]

The chronometer was an incredibly complex and expensive device that, though it solved the problem of longitude in theory, did not become practical for most mariners until the nineteenth century, when makers learned how to produce it in numbers. Until then, and even to some extent after that time, lunar distances measured by sextant was the method of choice for determining longitude. Mariners often compared this reading to that obtained by using a chronometer, if they had one. Eventually, however, the sextant was displaced by the chronometer for measuring longitude and became primarily an instrument for determining latitude.[78]

In addition to the development of instruments and techniques for measuring latitude and longitude, the period between 1497 and 1800 also saw improvements in navigators' ability to judge speed and direction. Until the sixteenth century, mariners had few methods of estimating the speed of their ships. Some used nothing more than their knowledge and experience, while others tossed wood chips over the

Figure 10. Streaming the log to measure the speed of a ship over time was one method mariners used to estimate progress east or west before the invention of the chronometer.

(J. G. Heck, *Complete Encyclopedia of Illustration* [New York: Park Lane, 1979])

bow and used the sandglass to measure how long it took for the chips to float past the ship. Mariners eventually developed the chip method into a more reliable system known as the log, log-line, or log-ship. Though it came in many forms, the log was usually a piece of wood weighted on one side to make it float upright like a buoy and attached to long rope called the log-line. The line was knotted at regular intervals, which had to be in the same proportion to a nautical mile as the number of seconds of the sandglass was to an hour, eventually about 48 feet (15 m) for a 28-second glass. A crewman cast the log out into the water while another held the reel up so the line could run out freely. A third turned the sandglass and when it was empty, stopped the line. As the line was hauled in the knots were counted, giving the ship's speed in knots per hour. Mariners repeated the operation every 30 minutes and this, along with the compass direction, was recorded on a new form of traverse board that had an extra set of holes at the base to accommodate log readings. This method provided only an estimate of speed, albeit a more accurate and consistent one than before, but, until the advent of chronometers and lunar distance measurements, it was the only way navigators had to keep track of their east/west position while at sea.[79]

Direction or bearing was another critical element in determining position at sea. Since about the twelfth century, the magnetic compass had provided European mariners with a practical means of establishing their direction. By the late fifteenth century, however, they had begun to notice that the needle did not point true north — easterly variation had been observed in northwest Europe before Columbus's first transatlantic voyage.[80] In the early sixteenth century, as more and more ships ventured far west into the Atlantic Ocean and navigators witnessed the magnitude of variation and how it changed depending on where they were, it became clear that this posed a significant problem both to direction finding and to chart-making. With potentially important trade routes and land claims at stake, scientists and instrument makers began a systematic study of the phenomenon and tried to develop the means to measure and compensate for it. Their solutions generally required that navigators take readings of Polaris, the Sun, or some other star, which they then compared to the compass reading. The difference gave them the magnetic variation of their location and allowed them to adjust compass bearing accordingly. Apart from this increased understanding of variation and the methods of compensating for it, the work of scientists, instrument makers, and mariners during this period did little to improve the overall performance of the compass.[81]

Where Are You When You Get There? Early Charting and Charts

In the Mediterranean, mariners possessed another important navigational tool by the thirteenth century — the marine chart. Sailors had long been recording their experience in and knowledge of the areas they visited, describing, often in great detail, the characteristics of the waters, winds, skies, and coastal lands. Though sometimes passed on in oral form, increasingly mariners wrote these sailing instructions down in manuscripts known as *portolanos*, rutters, or pilot books, which could be copied, used, and added to by others. Eventually, Italian navigators came up with the idea of producing graphic depictions of routes, coastlines, and harbours to accompany these manuscripts, to help the navigator plot the best course, avoid hazards, and estimate the time required to make his trip from one port to the next. These first sea charts, also known as portolan charts, were based on estimates of distance derived from sailing times from one point to another. Yet, while they lacked a precise scale, they were remarkably accurate guides to the waters of the region and, with the addition of rhumb lines indicating compass direction, they soon became an indispensable tool for navigators.[82]

Transoceanic mariners, of course, had no such tool. Cabot, Columbus, and other European explorers of the New World had clear destinations in mind — Japan, China, the Indies — but only a vague idea of where they were actually going and how far they had travelled. Moreover, once they reached land, they had no idea of the shape or extent of that land or, more importantly, the nature of its coastal waters. Yet in order to exploit their discoveries — to find the route to the Orient, to lay claim to and open up regular trade with the New World, or to establish and support colonies or garrisons — they had to know more about both.

Determining the new continent's precise location in relation to Europe was the more difficult and fortunately the less immediately important of the two problems. Mariners could measure latitude quite accurately, and many were in the habit of comparing the latitudes of the places they visited with those of familiar European locations. John Cabot compared the latitude of Cape Degrat/Cape Bauld, in the Strait of Belle Isle, to that of Dursey Head.[83] Verrazano placed the present site of Newport, Rhode Island, on the same latitude as Rome and was not far off the mark. Cartier did the same for Cape Bonavista, Newfoundland, and St Malo, again with very accurate results. Some mariners even went so far as to estimate their longitudinal position based on their recorded speed and sailing time from home port. In the 1580s, John Davis attempted a longitude of Cape Farewell and was only 3 degrees off, "a remarkably close" estimate based on paying very careful attention to the ship's progress "using his chip log and traverse table." Because of the great distances involved, most such attempts were so inaccurate as to be virtually useless. Moreover, until cartographers produced the first charts or maps of the New World, there was nowhere to locate these points once measured in reference to the known world.[84]

These inadequacies were exacerbated by the difficulties map- and chart-makers had in depicting the Earth's spherical shape on a flat surface.[85] Because of its size and east/west orientation, the convergence of the meridians of longitude toward the poles had no major effect on the depiction of the Mediterranean. The same was not true of the Atlantic and Pacific oceans, where the Earth's shape had to be taken into account in depicting distances. It was not until 1569 that Gerardus Mercator devised a "formula that gradually increased the length of latitudinal degrees from the equator to the North [and South] Pole." This allowed him to depict the "parallels and meridians as straight lines intersecting at right angles to produce at any point a more accurate ratio of latitude to longitude." The practical result of this advance was that map-makers could at last produce charts "with true directions on which a ship's course could be plotted on a straight line."[86]

As with most new techniques, navigators took some time to recognize the importance of the Mercator projection, both because of their skepticism and because Mercator did not publish his formula. Some mariners did manage to get their hands on Mercator's work soon after it was published. Martin Frobisher, for example, had both a world chart and a printed version of Mercator's "Hydrographic" world map when he set off on his Arctic explorations. Ironically, the distortions of this projection are greatest in the high latitudes, so the new map could not have been very useful. As well, even the very latest charts contained little beyond the vaguest, and often only imagined, outlines of Arctic waters and coastlines. And without an accurate longitude measure the Mercator projection, at this early date, could not accurately depict the location of the New World. Thirty years later, Edward Wright explained Mercator's system and transformed it "into a feasible, working navigational aid." From this point on both chart-makers and mariners were in a better position to take advantage of the benefits Mercator projection offered.[87]

By far the most pressing problem facing New World navigators was their ignorance of the extent and nature of the coastlines of North America. Most early explorers were excellent navigators and probably did their best to record the details of their voyages, including sometimes drawing rough charts of the coastlines they saw. But their priority was to show that they had visited a place, establish a claim to it, then get on with the main task of finding a passage to the Orient. Moreover, many of the original documents did not survive long after their creation.[88]

Nevertheless, the map-makers of Europe showed substantial interest in the discoveries of the early explorers, not to mention vivid imagination in depicting them. As early as 1500, Juan de la Cosa produced a world chart that may have reflected knowledge of John Cabot's voyage to Newfoundland.[89] Over the next ten years, various cartographers, including Francesco Rosselli and Martin Waldseemüller, drew maps depicting coastlines that could be interpreted as being part of Newfoundland. The maps of Diego Ribero, dating from 1529 and 1534, incorporated details from the voyages of Verrazano, Gomez, and Fernandez on the northeast coast of the continent, though they still revealed a major gap in European knowledge of the waters between present-day Nova Scotia and Newfoundland.[90]

That gap was soon filled by the explorations of Jacques Cartier. Having decided that this unexplored coast could reveal the opening to a passage east, he set out to discover what lay to the west of Newfoundland. Once he had found the Gulf of St Lawrence, he returned to see if the river beyond it was the passage and to look for the kingdom of Saguenay. In the course of these voyages, he carefully documented his search, producing extensive written descriptions of the waters and coastlines he visited. His work "brought about a revolution in North American cartography" after 1535 as all map-makers began to illustrate the gulf and "Great River of Canada" in significant detail. Cartier's original charts did not survive, and the first maps reflecting his discoveries were produced by Jean Rotz in 1535 and Pierre Desceliers in 1537.[91]

Besides the French, the Dutch also played a significant role in the charting of North American waters. The commercially vibrant society that began to emerge in the Netherlands in the mid-sixteenth century was based largely on seaborne trade with markets all over Europe and around the world. This, combined with the intellectual revolutions of the Renaissance and Reformation, helped to inspire, among many other things, a deep and intense interest in cartography. By the late sixteenth century, the Netherlands, though still ruled by the Hapsburgs, had "established a supremacy...in the production of navigating manuals and atlases."[92] They had also produced a great many distinguished cartographers and geographers, among them Mercator, Abraham Ortelius, and Lucas Janszoon Wagenaer. Many of the maps and charts made by these and other cartographers were published and sold throughout Europe.[93] Thus, in conjunction with the growth of their overseas trading empire, the Netherlands came to dominate the science and business of making, printing, and publishing charts in the late sixteenth and seventeenth centuries.[94]

French and English mariners, who were far more active in North America than their Dutch counterparts, often turned to cartographers and publishers in the Netherlands to supply their needs and record their journeys. Frobisher took a Mercator map on his voyages, while Davis's discoveries were engraved by Jodocus Hondius Sr. on a Molyneux Globe in 1592. A Dutch cartographer also managed to acquire and publish one of the maps made on Hudson's ill-fated final voyage. The results of later English voyages to the north were also illustrated in Dutch publications. French mariners, for their part, were dependent on Dutch charts or *pascaerts* of the St Lawrence River, New France's lifeline, well into the eighteenth century.[95]

Gradually, however, as the governments of England and France began to shift the focus of their maritime policies away from the search for instant riches and toward the longer term exploitation of North America's abundant resources, their interest in the continent's cartography grew. Both nations were heavily involved in the Newfoundland fishery and needed charts of the island, its fishing banks, bays, and harbours, in order to facilitate the activities of their fishermen. The French also needed maps of inland waters to extend their access to furs as well as to reinforce their claim to the territory in competition with the British, who were colonizing to the south. The maps and charts produced in this process were intended not just to make navigation safer and more efficient, but also to provide concrete and well-publicized evidence of each nation's — or, in a few instances, a particular company's — occupation of and sovereignty over a specific region or resource.[96]

In the first half of the seventeenth century, cartographers began to produce a clearer and more detailed outline of the coasts of northern North America. In Newfoundland, a variety of English, French, and Dutch map-makers produced numerous versions of the island's coastlines, gradually, if not steadily, coming to the realization that it was one island. By the 1620s, English cartographer John Mason had created "the prototype for the east and southeast coasts of the island" that, through its influence on W. J. Blaeu, provided the basis for "the series of Dutch marine charts which began to be published about 1630 and which became the most widely-used charts for navigation on the north Atlantic."[97]

Farther west, meanwhile, Champlain had started to map the coastlines, waters, and lands of New France. Over three decades beginning in 1603, he and his men, with the help of local Natives,[98] surveyed and charted the area from the Gulf of St Lawrence west to Georgian Bay on Lake Huron. Though the products of their work were maps rather than true marine charts — they were most concerned about demonstrating the basis for and extent of France's claim to the area — Champlain did produce some drawings specifically for mariners, including charts of Atlantic ports. Moreover, even the maps drawn by him and his men included information useful to mariners. Overall, the products showed a level of accuracy that was remarkable given the techniques and instruments available at the time.

The first map was printed in 1632 and was clearly recognizable as what became eastern Canada. During the next two decades, French cartographers succeeded in outlining much of the continent from the Bay of Fundy to James, Hudson, and Baffin bays.[99]

By the 1670s, with military, commercial, and political competition between England and France growing, safe and efficient navigation, as well as evidence of sovereignty, became more critical than ever. While astronomers at home were charged with the task of finding a way to measure longitude, mercantile and colonial administrators, among other things, expanded their surveying activities. For example, the newly chartered Hudson's Bay Company hired John Thornton to begin to map its massive and largely unknown empire.[100] Around the same time, Louis XIV instructed his colonial officials to improve navigation in New France by setting up classes to teach navigation and pilotage to local mariners and by undertaking a systematic marine survey of colonial waters.[101]

The results of the French policy were mixed. On the positive side, in 1678, authorities published the first charts with soundings for part of the coast of Newfoundland. A similar chart was produced for the Gulf of St Lawrence in 1696. Meanwhile, in 1685 Jean Deshayes, a mathematician and surveyor, was sent out to Québec to chart the St Lawrence River. He conducted a systematic survey of the waterway using all the latest and most accurate instruments and techniques, including determining Québec's longitude by observing a lunar eclipse, a reading so accurate it was still in use fifty years later. He meticulously recorded tides and compass variation and took more than twenty latitudes over several hundred miles of coast. The Deshayes chart was never completely finished and yet "was probably the most advanced hydrographic chart of any region in North America and was the basis for the first printed chart of the river."[102]

Following Deshayes's outstanding example, the French continued their hydrographic surveying work in North America. All French mariners, naval officers, and engineers travelling to and from Canada or stationed there routinely recorded useful navigational information in the form of sailing directions, charts, logs, and journals. Unfortunately, these were not collected, organized, and published consistently and thus seldom reached the people who most needed current navigational information. Until 1699 there was no central authority or archive to handle all the material. Moreover, the official bodies responsible for mapping had a "predilection for theoretical geography that was the nemesis of nautical cartography." Finally, Dutch publishers still had such a firm grip on the market for printed maps and charts that it was hard for their French counterparts to compete, despite the well-known limitations of some Dutch products. Perhaps the most compelling evidence of the failure of French hydrography in this period was the fact that during King William's War (1689 to 1697), more merchant ships were shipwrecked than lost to the enemy in New France.[103]

A minor flurry of charting activity occurred at the end of the War of the Spanish Succession (1701 to 1714), when France lost all but limited fishing and landing rights in Newfoundland and all claim to Acadia. The French government went looking for appropriate new locations for a fortress and bases for the fishery in and around Cape Breton, then set about charting the nearby waters. Also, Deshayes's chart, thoroughly updated and enhanced by information from the journals of Pierre Lemoyne d'Iberville, was reissued. But this was more a reaction to immediate circumstances than part of a coherent plan for the future, and captains of ships travelling to Québec continued to complain about the inadequate charts and poor pilots they had to work with in the New World.[104]

These problems were dramatically highlighted in 1725 when the ship *le Chameau* went down off Cape Breton with 316 including the intendant aboard and the year's money supply for New France. Almost immediately the French navy initiated a systematic program of charting colonial waters. They began with an extensive survey of the Gulf of St Lawrence and St Lawrence River in 1729. Then, in 1750, the navy sent three fully equipped charting expeditions to the colony, resulting in the publication of the first scientific surveys of the coast of Nova Scotia based on astronomical observations. Like Deshayes's seventeenth-century surveys, these were probably "the most accurate hydrographic surveys of any major portion of the North American coastline," and this time the navy saw that they were widely disseminated in France.[105]

In the end, French mariners had only a few years to take advantage of the superior charting work done by the navy. In 1759, Québec fell to the British, who had made their way up the treacherous St Lawrence using a chart hastily constructed by James Cook and Samuel Holland based on published works and their own cursory survey. From this point forward, the British took over responsibility for charting the waters of northern North America.[106] In the aftermath of seven long years of war, and with the specific terms of the Treaty of Paris dealing with French fishing rights in Newfoundland still open to interpretation, that responsibility was a major one.[107]

Much of the exploration and charting work carried out between 1760 and 1800 was done by Royal Navy officers and other military men — men such as J. F. W. DesBarres, Samuel Holland, and Lieutenant Thomas Hurd — under the authority of the British Admiralty. DesBarres not only distinguished himself by crafting highly accurate charts that were not superseded until the 1840s. He also became famous as the "author" of the *Atlantic Neptune*, a collection of all of his own charts of North America's Atlantic coastline and waters as well as those of colleagues including Cook, Holland, Michael Lane, and Hurd. He compiled, edited, and adapted the "existing materials for use by the British Navy during the War of Independence" and in doing so demonstrated his "superb craftsmanship" as a hydrographer. His work, which soon became an indispensable guide to North Atlantic waters, combined a high level of technical precision and informative detail with a "consciously artistic" style.[108]

While working on a survey of Halifax Harbour, DesBarres also trained James Cook in the art of surveying. Cook then went on to make his own distinguished contribution to charting Canada's coastal waters. He was responsible for the first printed chart of Gaspé Bay and harbour in addition to the work he did on the St Lawrence. His best effort, however, was a hydrographic survey of Newfoundland begun around 1763. Though various charts and maps of the island dating from the late seventeenth and early eighteenth centuries existed,[109] none of these provided the level of detail and precision needed to define (and enforce) the new limits of France's fishing rights. Cook was asked to produce charts that would clearly delineate where French vessels could and could not land to process their catches and, at the same time, would improve navigation for British fishermen and identify new areas where they could profitably expand their activities, thereby helping to pre-empt any growth in French fishing in those same areas.[110]

We know very little for certain about Cook's specific survey methods, but based on his previous and subsequent work, the work of his colleagues and teachers, and the final results of his work — that is, the charts themselves — it is clear that his techniques were meticulous and thorough. He established and "applied rigid standards of accuracy," insisting on going ashore in order to make observations from a stable base and surveying mainly from small boats rather than the ship. He used baselines and triangulation to measure precise points along the coast and climbed countless hills in order to get the best view of the rest of the shoreline.[111] His charts were "unparalleled for nautical detail" and, according to a later hydrographer, were the first such surveys that could "with any degree of safety be trusted by the seamen." Sixty years later, Henry Bayfield, another Admiralty hydrographer sent to survey Canadian waters, found the Cook charts he used, like those of Cook's teacher DesBarres, to be "as usual extremely correct."[112]

In 1778 Cook, accompanied by his protégé George Vancouver, undertook another survey, this time of the Pacific coast of northern North America. Though this work was cursory by comparison to his survey of Newfoundland, it and the publication of Cook's journals from the voyage inspired a renewed interest

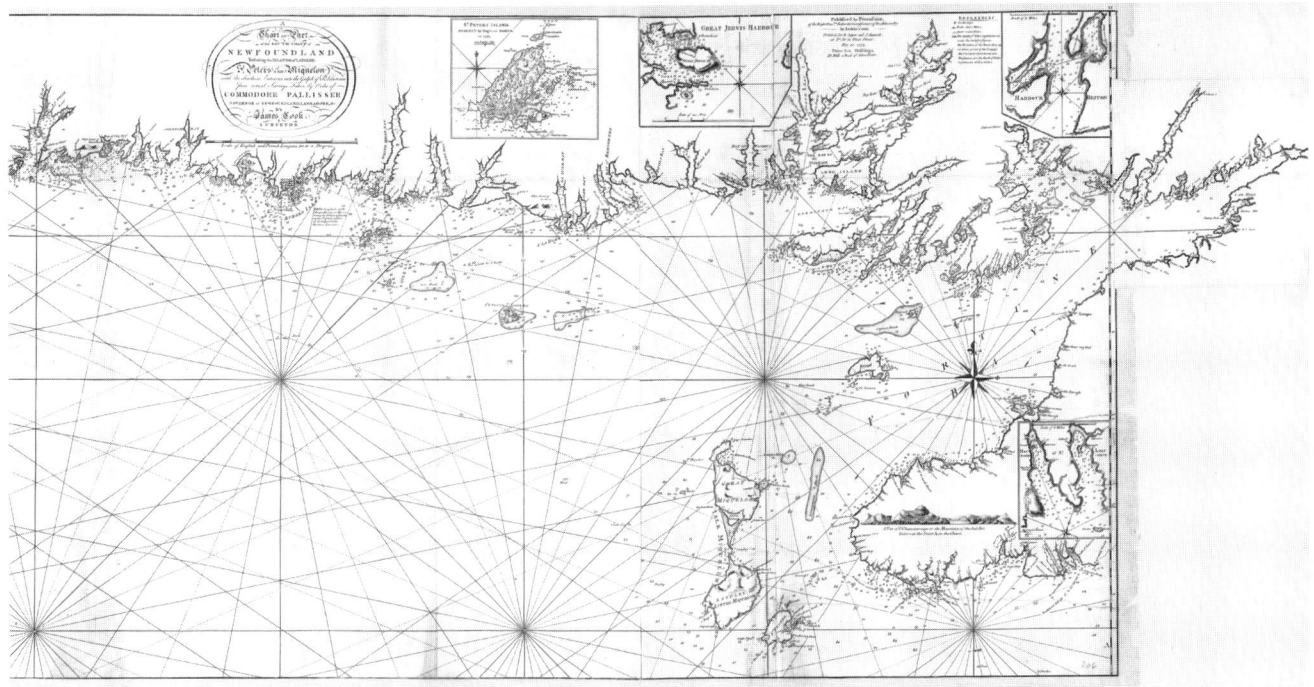

Map 2. *Section 2 of a chart of part of the south coast of Newfoundland by James Cook. Revised version (1774) of the original 1768 chart.*
(Library and Archives Canada, neg. NMC-132320_2)

in the region. In 1786, Lapérouse journeyed to the Pacific and, among other accomplishments, "improved on Cook's highly tentative charts of the coast of British Columbia and south to California."[113] Then, in the 1790s, Malaspina, Galiano, and Vancouver were sent by their governments to explore, to study, and to chart this contested region. The Spaniards, for their part, conducted extensive and intricate surveys, returning to Spain with "hundreds of maps, calculation sheets, logs, and journals," in addition to weather observations and magnetic and gravitational measurements.[114] Unfortunately, Malaspina fell out of favour at court before he could finish and publish his report and findings.[115]

Although he died in 1798, only four years after returning from his great voyage, Vancouver did manage to publish a detailed report of his enterprise, while the Admiralty published the numerous charts resulting from it. Much of the written and cartographic record that Vancouver left behind is a testament to his teacher and mentor, James Cook. Not only was the context of his venture similar to that of Cook in Newfoundland, that is, the acute need for accurate, detailed charts to help identify and establish Britain's claim to the north Pacific coast. In addition, the methods he used and the standards he followed were, to the best of our knowledge, very much the same as those established by Cook in 1763 to 1767.[116]

Vancouver began his task, from Mexico to the Strait of Juan de Fuca, with a running survey carried out from his two ships *Discovery* and *Chatham*. From the strait onward, however, he decided upon a more precise method of charting that would allow him to "trace every foot of the continental shore." The system he implemented was, like Cook's, built around stable land-based readings, in this case taken from temporary observatories, and meticulous measurements carried out carefully and frequently from the ship's boats.[117]

Beginning in the spring of 1792, Vancouver established a daily surveying routine that his men followed for most of the rest of the expedition. The crew anchored the ships in a protected cove and took the boats out, following the shorelines of the many inlets and islands, taking compass bearings of major features and measuring the course and movement of the boat. The officers "went ashore at intervals to take sextant angles of the direction of the coast and tangents to the offshore islands."[118] At the same time, other members of the crew set up a base camp onshore and erected an observatory. This they used to get an accurate latitude reading and for measuring longitude by lunar distance. They also used their chronometers. This enabled them to fix their exact position.[119] Upon returning to the ship, crew members transcribed the recorded information on a plotting sheet. After an area was fully surveyed, the data was recorded on the chart. This process was repeated day after day as the ships inched their way up the coast; it was not uncommon for the crew to spend several days surveying just one or two inlets. They carried on like this until the fall, when the ships sailed south to the Sandwich Islands to be refitted and repaired for the following spring.[120]

Vancouver was well aware that surveying from open boats could be "extremely laborious, and expose those so employed to numberless dangers and unpleasant situations."[121] Apart from boredom and fatigue, his boat crews had to cope with weather that was often rainy and cool, sometimes working for hours in soaking wet clothing. More importantly, they had to face the dangers of sailing along a treacherous coast, most of which was unfamiliar to them. When Vancouver depicted one inlet the expedition visited as "very narrow and intricate," strewn "with rocks above and beneath the surface of the water," and plagued by tides of "great rapidity and irregularity,"[122] he could have been describing any one of hundreds of places along the coast. Perhaps not surprisingly, both of Vancouver's ships ran aground at different times but were lucky to escape without major damage. And even when all was going well with the survey, there was constant concern about the Native population. Vancouver, after all, had been on Cook's final expedition, when Cook was killed by Natives in the Sandwich Islands, and was thus keenly aware of the need to maintain good, if somewhat distant, relations with the peoples of the Pacific Northwest. This was especially important given the length of time the expedition needed to complete its work.[123]

Figure 11. Vancouver's ship Discovery on the rocks in Queen Charlotte's Sound. Surveying unfamiliar waters could be treacherous work. Vancouver ultimately produced the first comprehensive charts of what is now Canada's Pacific coast. (Library and Archives Canada, neg. C-012267)

When Vancouver and his crew returned to Britain after some four and a half years away, they had sailed about 65,000 miles (105 000 km), while the boat crews had covered an additional 10,000 miles (16 000 km) under oars. During this arduous journey, only six of approximately 200 crew had perished. The charts they made traced the coast from what is now California to Cook's Inlet in what is now Alaska, some 5,000 miles (8 000 km) in all. They proved that Vancouver Island was indeed an island and that there was no great strait passing through the continent to the Atlantic Ocean. In addition, the extensive series of charts Vancouver presented to the Admiralty were as detailed and meticulous as anything they had seen before, even from Cook. Moreover, in the Pacific coast charts, the Admiralty had a first-rate survey of a very difficult coastline that, up to that time, had been known to Europeans only in sketchy outline.[124]

The Admiralty was finally coming to see the critical importance of hydrography, in part because of the demands of the war with revolutionary France. It was no longer enough to have an informal approach to charting, where government relied on often isolated sources — private companies and individuals as well as its own officers — to provide essential hydrographical information to the Royal Navy and the merchant marine. Shortly before Vancouver's return in 1795, the Admiralty appointed its first Hydrographer, Alexander Dalrymple, and gave him the task of "selecting and compiling all the existing information and making it available to the Commanders of His Majesty's Ships." Though small and underfunded to begin with, this establishment would play a leading role in producing a coherent, systematic, and reliable hydrographical record of British, including Canadian, waters in the nineteenth and twentieth centuries.[125]

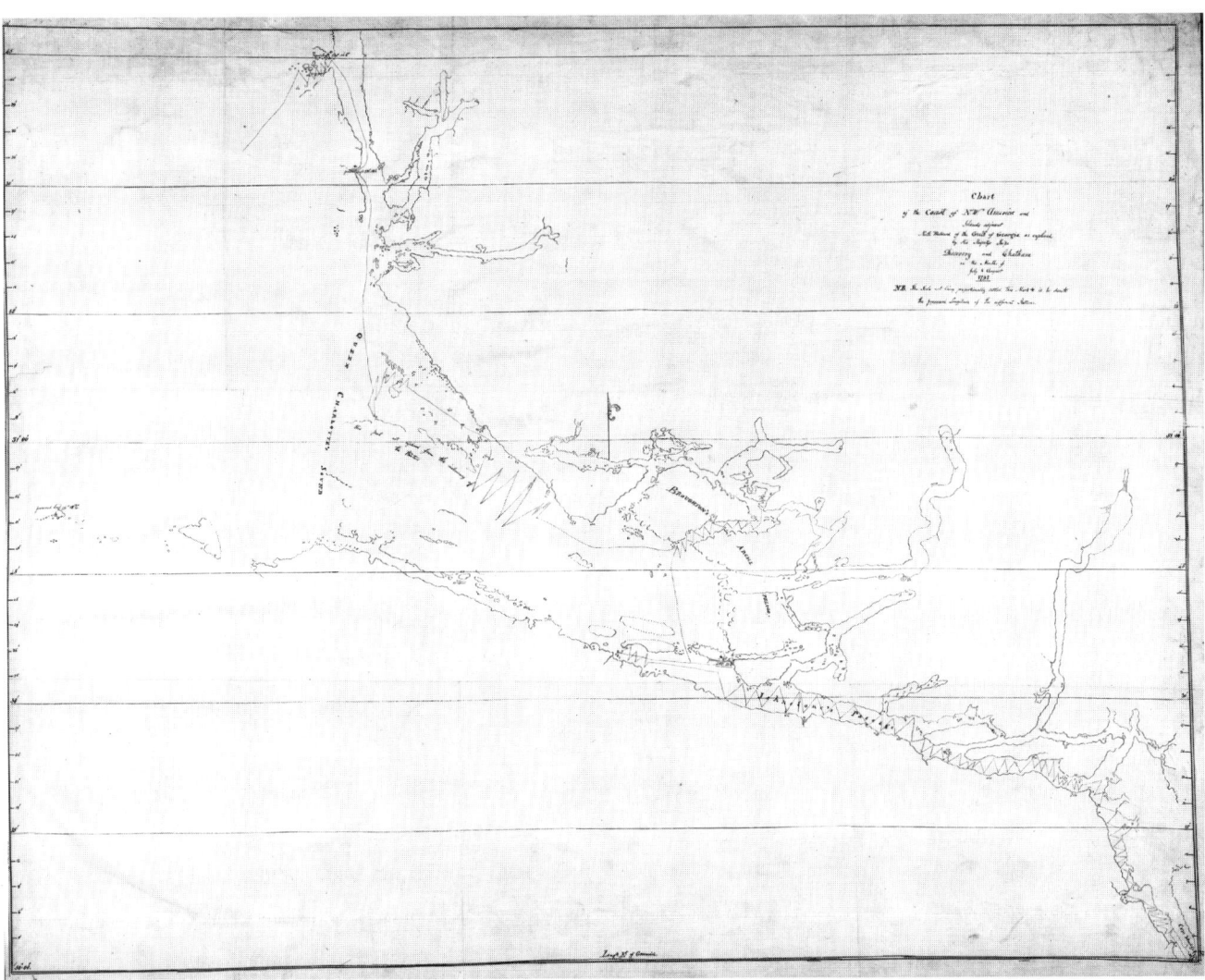

Map 3. *A sample of Vancouver's work: his chart of the coast and islands adjacent to the Gulf of Georgia as surveyed in July and August 1792.*
(Library and Archives Canada, neg. NMC-131751)

A Safe Place to Land: Early Land-Based Aids to Navigation

Coastal waters, with their changing tides, unusual currents, and hidden shoals or rocks, have always been among the most dangerous for mariners. Since antiquity, therefore, maritime and mercantile communities have worked to limit these dangers by marking hazards along important trade and transportation routes. The earliest seamarks, as they have since become known, consisted of both natural and built structures. For example, sailors routinely used prominent coastal features such as hills, cliffs, islets, or rocky outcrops to judge their location and help guide themselves through narrow channels, around shoals, or into a difficult harbour. They or the local inhabitants might also have painted the rocks or otherwise enhanced the visibility of these features. If conspicuous natural features were not available, navigators could also use tall built structures such as church steeples or the towers of a fort to identify a place and obtain an approximate bearing for passage around a hazard. Eventually, the ancients began to build special purpose markers such as cairns, beacons, and towers, some of which were made more visible by the addition of fires. Most of these early marking efforts tended to be dependent on local initiative and resources whenever construction and ongoing maintenance of the site were required.[126]

The first attempts to develop and maintain a system of seamarks were made in the late Middle Ages. With the steady increase in marine trade in both the Mediterranean and northern Europe in the thirteenth century, the need for safe navigation became more pressing than ever before. At the same time that mariners were beginning to adopt the compass, charts, and written sailing instructions, mercantile and trading alliances like the Hanseatic League began to consider establishing a series of fixed navigational aids that would serve the ships of all its member cities. It even developed a system of tolls and taxes to pay for the building and upkeep of the markers. Other cities and states implemented similar policies in an attempt to improve trade in their regions. There was, however, little uniformity in the markers used by the dozens of small states that made up Europe at the time. If they sailed to a number of different ports, mariners either had to have excellent memories or detailed records — on charts or in manuscript sailing instructions — of which marker identified which hazard.[127]

By the time Cabot set sail for the New World, four basic types of seamarks were in common use in Europe: beacons, buoys, leading marks, and fire towers or other crude lights. Beacons were the simplest and therefore probably the most plentiful form of navigational

Figure 12. A simple barrel buoy of the late sixteenth century. This type of buoy, with its symmetrical shape and mooring chain attached to the centre of the barrel, lies flat in the water.

(A. W. Lang, *Geschichte des Seezeichenwesens* [Bonn: Der Bundesminister für Verkehr (Ministry of Transport), 1965])

marker. They came in many forms, from signal poles or cairns to large wood or stone towers, sometimes painted, sometimes not. They were also multi-purpose and could be placed up high on a nearby hill to warn sailors from a distance of their approach to land or placed right in the water to mark a shoal or direct the ship though a safe channel. In their most sophisticated form, beacons could be lit by fire to increase visibility or built in pairs so that navigators could line them up to obtain the proper bearing to enter port or to avoid a hazard.[128]

Buoys are fixed floating markers, and the first written evidence of their use dates from 1295. More complicated to set up and maintain than most beacons, they first were used "chiefly in those places where the depth of water, the strength of the stream, and the variability of deep-water channels precluded the use of fixed beacons or landmarks." Large river channels were one such place, and the first markers used were probably simple timber rafts or floats or even just pieces of wood stuck upright in the mud. These soon lost their flotation and were probably difficult to keep anchored in the heavy river currents. By the mid-fourteenth century, authorities had begun to develop air-filled barrel buoys that, while still difficult to moor securely in some locations, did keep their flotation longer. Gradually, inventors and mechanics refined these barrels into purpose-built devices with a more appropriate shape and sturdier construction, including a built-in structure to secure the anchoring chain. The

Figures 13 and 14. *Late-sixteenth-century conical barrel buoy with its mooring chain linked at the narrow end floats upright in the water.*
(A. W. Lang, *Geschichte des Seezeichenwesens* [Bonn: Der Bundesminister für Verkehr (Ministry of Transport), 1965])

British authorities, however, do not seem to have embraced this method of marking whole-heartedly until the late seventeenth century.[129]

A leading or range mark is a mark either on shore or fixed in shallow water that, "when brought into line with another mark or prominent object ashore, will lead a ship clear of a local danger."[130] The earliest forms of these aids were often as simple as rocks that protruded from the water, small cairns, or islands that could be lined up with a natural landmark or built structure. As with other markers, the growth of maritime trade and traffic encouraged merchants, shipowners, and mariners to adopt a more systematic approach, especially in areas that had low and featureless coastlines. Instead of depending on existing features and structures to provide the necessary back marks, which tended to restrict where they could use this form of aid, they began to erect pairs of marks, one back and one leading, wherever they were thought essential. Thus in the late seventeenth century Yarmouth Roads, "a centre of the North Sea herring industry,"[131] had two lighted towers to guide ships close to the coast, where two more leading marks gave them the right bearing to avoid the Middlefoote Sands, and finally, two more guided them to a safe passage to the southeast.[132]

The use of fire as a signal to navigators is as old as marine transportation itself. From simple bonfires set on coastal hilltops to more elaborate fire towers, light was an obvious way to increase the visibility of a navigational aid. But there were equally obvious problems associated with using fire as a signal. Fire

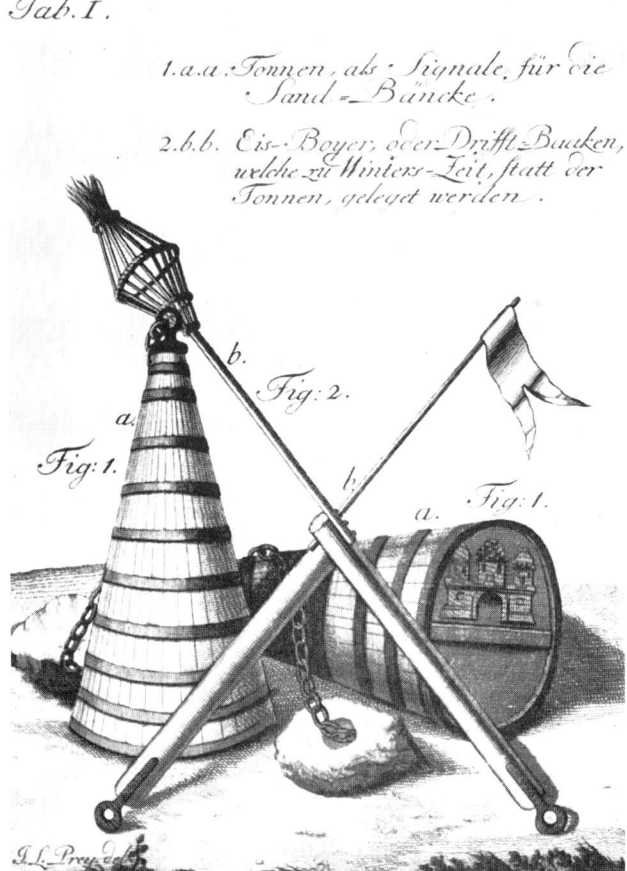

Figure 15. *Conical barrel buoys and beacons from the mid-eighteenth century.*
(A. W. Lang, *Geschichte des Seezeichenwesens* [Bonn: Der Bundesminister für Verkehr (Ministry of Transport), 1965])

had to be maintained and minded, which meant securing a steady fuel supply and maintaining a constant watch. Where towers were used, they had to be repaired regularly. The fact that these navigational aids might also be erected along isolated shorelines only exacerbated these problems. Moreover, fire towers did not give off enough light to do anything more than warn mariners that they were near a coast. Yet these were the immediate precursors of the lighthouses that engineers began to design and build in the seventeenth century.[133]

Needless to say, none of these aids to navigation were available to the first mariners who sailed across the Atlantic to North America. There were no sailing instructions, no charts, and no seamarks to guide them in coastal waters that were completely unfamiliar to them. Thus, having successfully crossed the ocean, they still faced enormous challenges in finding safe places to land and exploring the coastlines of the new continent. With each visit, mariners accumulated more knowledge about the special characteristics of each area — notable coastal features, safe routes and natural harbours, tides and currents, hazards to watch for, including ice. Explorers such as Jacques Cartier kept detailed records of their observations, often including descriptions of natural marks that could be used to help plot a safe course. Some early visitors, notably the many fishing and whaling ships that returned yearly to Newfoundland, Labrador, and the Gulf of St Lawrence, also accumulated a vast amount of information about these coastal waters. They probably enhanced some natural features to act as aids and may even have built some rudimentary markers in or near the seasonal harbours where they processed their catch. Unfortunately, fishing and whaling captains generally kept their navigational knowledge to themselves in order to maintain an advantage over their many competitors.[134]

Like charting, however, real progress in marking the coastal waters of northern North America did not begin until after the age of exploration, when Britain and France began to colonize the region and compete for its resources. With the foundation of a colony at Québec, the French began to make regular voyages up the St Lawrence and soon discovered that this could be every bit as difficult as crossing the Atlantic. The river was dangerous owing to shifting currents that threw ships about, unknown rocks often hidden just below the surface, extensive shoals that shifted each year because of the force of ice moving downstream in spring, dense fog banks from contrary winds, and strange deflections of the compass that are now attributed to the iron ore deposits in Labrador and northern Quebec.[135] At Tadoussac, the river "became considerably more shallow and the shoals more numerous," while the flow from the Saguenay "could turn a ship on its side in the Red Island Channel." Farther upstream there were the hazards of the Gouffre or whirlpool and the Traverse, both of which demanded careful sailing even by captains familiar with the river.[136]

As early as the 1660s, Jean Talon had planned to buoy both the Gouffre and the Traverse, and by the early eighteenth century, these hazards and others along the river were indeed marked. After 1725, the French government took a renewed and more serious interest in improving colonial navigation and ordered a path cut through Isle aux Ruaux and two high markers or towers erected on Ile d'Orléans. At the beginning of each navigation season the towers were whitewashed and the path cleared of any trees that might have sprouted to maintain a clear line of sight for navigators. These markers remained in use up to and after the fall of Québec.[137]

By the mid-eighteenth century, British authorities were also taking a greater interest in navigation, inspired, like the French, by the demands of colonization and war. They began to lay buoys in and around Halifax harbour to mark hazards that often were named after ships that ran aground on them — Litchfield Shoal and Mars Rock, for example. Two charts from the period, one believed to have been drawn by Cook, showed five buoy locations, each probably marked with a large cone-shaped can buoy. In 1784, the Nova Scotia House of Assembly reaffirmed the importance of these aids to navigation when it passed a law to prevent the willful destruction of buoys, seamarks, or beacons placed by the government in its coastal waters.[138]

In the eighteenth century, both governments also undertook the more expensive and difficult task of building lighthouses to mark their major colonial harbours. Since the seventeenth century, European engineers and inventors had worked out some of the major problems of using lighted towers to mark hazards and harbours. English builders, for example, devised methods of building lighthouses on wave-swept offshore rocks. As well, engineers had learned to use a variety of building materials and designs that could be adapted to suit different physical environments as well as available funding.[139]

Inventors also made some important first steps in the development of better lighting techniques. In the seventeenth century, lighthouses were generally lit in one of three ways: by multiple candles, by coal fire, or by fish or whale oil. By the next century, oil had gradually become the most common type of fuel, with a series of wicks being fed from a reservoir. This system had limitations. Most oils became quite thick in cold weather and then did not flow properly into the wicks. More importantly, the wicks of oil-fed lamps produced a lot of smoke, leaving a coating of soot on the lantern and reducing the level of light emitted from the tower. In the early 1780s, inventor Ami Argand introduced "a virtually smokeless oil lamp utilizing a circular sleeve-like wick through and around which was a free circulation of air, much improving combustion."[140]

Argand's improved oil lamp still did not produce as much light as a good coal or wood fire, so designers began to investigate the use of reflection as a means of concentrating light rays to increased the visibility of oil-fuelled lighthouses. In "unassisted" illumination systems, most of the light produced by the fire dissipated and never reached the mariner. The catoptric or reflective method, which had been used by the Swedes as early as 1669, increased the proportion of light energy radiated out to sea. In 1763, Briton William Hutchinson made "the first scientifically designed parabolic reflectors." While these were far from perfect, they did improve the illumination qualities of oil lamps enormously and perhaps inspired inventors to continue the search for more efficient methods of reflection and refraction of light.[141]

The French built the first lighthouse in what is now Canada in 1733 at Louisbourg. Since the loss of Newfoundland, this fortress had become France's "military and economic nerve-centre" in the Atlantic region.[142] With a steady flow of naval and fishing vessels moving in and out of the port there, safe navigation was a priority. Financed by a duty on ocean-going and coastal vessels, the structure, begun in 1731, took two years to complete. It was located "on the rocky promontory at the harbour entrance" and stood some 70 feet (21 m) tall. It was illuminated by a circlet of oil-fed (sperm-whale oil) wicks, and its range "was said to be six leagues (roughly 18 miles [30 km]) in clear weather." This first tower burned down in 1736 and was replaced by a new one in 1738 with a safer lantern design. The authorities upgraded this structure in 1751 by adding reflectors to concentrate the light from the lamp. The Louisbourg lighthouse was seriously damaged in the British siege of 1758 and then allowed to deteriorate.[143]

The Sambro Island lighthouse was built by the colonial government of Nova Scotia between 1758 and 1760. Increased maritime traffic — military and

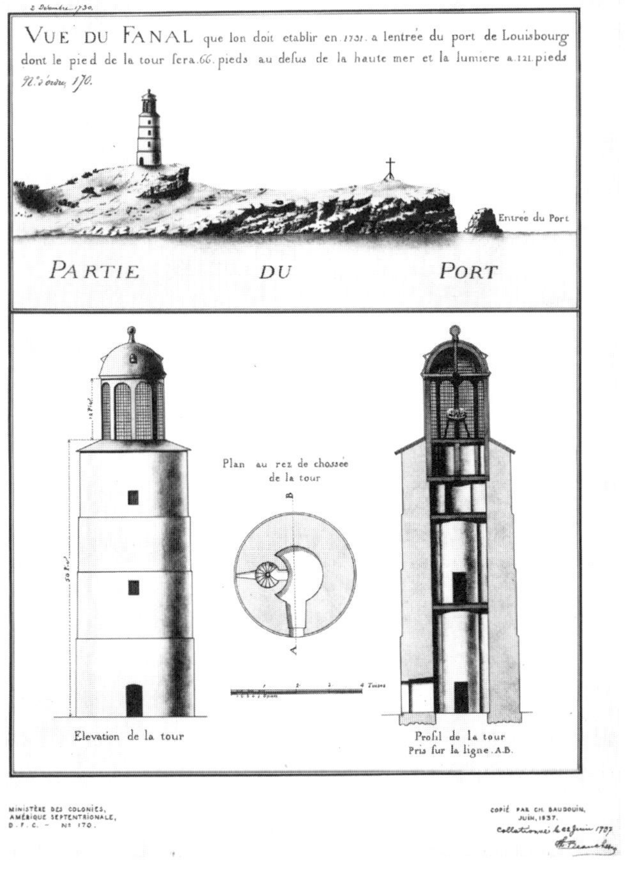

Figure 17. The Sambro Island lighthouse, completed in 1760 near the entrance to Halifax harbour, is the oldest lighthouse remaining in Canada. In 1906 the government increased its height from the original 62 feet to 80 feet (19 m to 24 m). This photograph shows the construction work in progress, including a wooden frame built to hold a temporary light.

(Library and Archives Canada, neg. e003719345)

Figure 16. Plan of the Louisbourg lighthouse, 1730.
(Library and Archives Canada, neg. NMC-0018763)

commercial — resulting from the war probably prompted the construction of this tower. It was located on a rocky island "commanding the outer approaches to Halifax Harbour" and paid for partly by a tax on spirits and partly by a lottery. Like all early oil-fuelled lights, smoke and soot dimmed the Sambro lantern fairly rapidly. Henry Newton, collector of customs and member of His Majesty's Council in Nova Scotia, solved the problem by constructing a series of fountain lamps with flues to divert the smoke away from the glass and improve the overall ventilation of the lantern.[144]

Colonial authorities in British North America built at least two additional lighthouses before the turn of the nineteenth century. The Nova Scotia government built one on McNutt Island, on the colony's outer coast, in 1788. The governor claimed that it was one of the finest yet built on the continent and had been seen some 25 miles (40 km) out to sea. New Brunswick also erected a lighthouse during this era on Partridge Island in Saint John Harbour. Constructed in 1791, it was the first of many built to help mariners find their way along the fog-ridden coasts of the Bay of Fundy.[145]

The placing of these various navigational aids represented only a small beginning in the monumental task of marking the country's long and intricate coastlines. Much more would be accomplished in the nineteenth and twentieth centuries as the British North American colonies grew and their economies developed. As always, trade and transportation went hand in hand, and improved navigation made both more efficient and reliable. After leaving the development and maintenance of navigational aids to local authorities and private groups for many years, governments were finally coming to recognize they had to take a more active role in facilitating safe navigation if their nations were to prosper.

Notes

1. Charles A. Martijn, ed., *Les Micmacs et la mer* (Montréal: Recherches amérindiennes au Québec, 1986). See especially the last three articles in the collection.
2. Robert McGhee, *Canada Rediscovered* (Ottawa: Canadian Museum of Civilization, 1991), 37–70; David B. Quinn, ed., *North American Discovery circa 1000–1612* (Columbia, S.C.: University of South Carolina Press, 1971), 1–2; J. M. Bumsted, *The Peoples of Canada: A Pre-Confederation History* (Toronto: Oxford University Press, 1992), 26–8; Samuel Eliot Morison, *The European Discovery of America: The Northern Voyages, A.D. 500–1600* (New York: Oxford University Press, 1971), 32–80. Birgitta Wallace argues that L'Anse aux Meadows was not a colony but an exploration base. See B. L. Wallace, "The L'Anse aux Meadows Site," in *The Norse Atlantic Saga*, ed. G. Jones, 2nd ed. (Oxford: Oxford University Press, 1986), 285–304.
3. For a discussion of some of the many factors and motives that led Europeans across the Atlantic, see Felipe Fernandez-Armesto, ed., *The European Opportunity*, Expanding World Series, vol. 2 (Aldershot, U.K.: Variorum, 1995).
4. See J. H. Parry, *The Discovery of the Sea* (Berkeley: University of California Press, 1981), 63–79, for a discussion of the importance of eastern trade, and p. 219 for a description of how Columbus "peddled" his project around Europe; also J. H. Parry, *The Establishment of the European Hegemony, 1415–1715* (New York: Harper & Row, 1966), 7–11 and 26–38; Raymonde Litalien, *Les explorateurs de l'Amérique du Nord, 1492–1795* (Sillery, Que.: Les editions du Septentrion, 1993), 19–27; Kenneth Nebenzahl, *Maps from the Age of Discovery: Columbus to Mercator* (London: Time Books, 1990), vi–viii; Morison, *Northern Voyages*, 3; and Kenneth Andrews, *Trade, Plunder and Settlement: Maritime Enterprise and the Genesis of the British Empire, 1480–1630* (Cambridge: Cambridge University Press, 1984), 41–4.
5. Parry, *Discovery of the Sea*, 42–5, 220, and 227; Morison, *Northern Voyages*, 159–60. See also Samuel Eliot Morison, *The European Discovery of America: The Southern Voyages, A.D. 1492–1616* (New York: Oxford University Press, 1974), 3–162, for details of Columbus's voyages.
6. Peter E. Pope, *The Many Landfalls of John Cabot* (Toronto: University of Toronto Press, 1997), 11–42; David B. Quinn, *England and the Discovery of America, 1481–1620* (New York: Alfred A. Knopf, 1974), 72–84; James A. Williamson, *The Cabot Voyages and Bristol Discovery under Henry VII*, Hakluyt Society, 2nd Series, No. 120 (Cambridge: Cambridge University Press, 1962), 42–53; Andrews, *Trade, Plunder and Settlement*, 41–50; Alan F. Williams, *John Cabot and Newfoundland* (St John's: Newfoundland Historical Society, 1996), 3–44; Peter Firstbrook, *The Voyage of the* Matthew: *John Cabot and the Discovery of America* (Toronto: McClelland & Stewart, 1997), 111–2.
7. Williamson, *Cabot Voyages*, 54–116; Williams, *John Cabot*, 3–44; Quinn, *England and the Discovery of America*, 94–111; Bumsted, *The Peoples of Canada: A Pre-Confederation History*, 30–2.
8. See Daniel Vickers, *Farmers and Fishermen: Two Centuries of Work in Essex County, Massachusetts, 1630–1850* (Chapel Hill, N.C.: University of North Carolina Press, 1994), 86–7, and footnotes 3 and 4 for data showing price increases in one region. Ian Cameron has also suggested that the income from the Portuguese Grand Banks fishery far outstripped that from Spain's American enterprises. Ian Cameron, *Lodestone and Evening Star* (New York: E. P. Dutton & Company, 1966), 124.
9. David B. Quinn, ed., *New American World: A Documentary History of North America to 1612*, vol. 4, *Newfoundland from Fishery to Colony: Northwest Passage Searches* (New York: Arno Press, 1979), xix–xx.
10. Vickers, *Farmers and Fishermen*, 87; Peter Pope, "Early Estimates: Assessment of Catches in the Newfoundland Cod Fishery, 1660–1690," in Daniel Vickers, ed., *Marine Resources and Human Societies in the North Atlantic since 1500*, ISER Conference Paper 5 (St John's: Memorial University of Newfoundland, Institute of Social and Economic Research, 1995), 34.
11. Harold Innis, *The Cod Fisheries: The History of an International Economy* (Toronto: University of Toronto Press, 1954), ix–xi, 1–51; Fernand Braudel, *Civilization and Capitalism: 15th–18th Century*, vol. 1, *The Structures of Everyday Life: The Limits of the Possible*, translation from the French, revised by Sian Reynolds (New York: Harper & Row, 1981), 216–20; Parry, *European Hegemony*, 68–70; Quinn, ed., *North American Discovery*, xxxvi–xxxix; Quinn, ed., *New American World*, vol. 4, xix–xx. Innis's book provides a more detailed accounting of both the number and origin of ships fishing in and around

Newfoundland beginning in the sixteenth century, though it is not without serious weaknesses. See also John Gilchrist, "Exploration and Enterprise: The Newfoundland Fishery, c. 1497–1677," in David S. Macmillan, ed., *Canadian Business History Selected Studies, 1497–1971* (Toronto: McClelland & Stewart, 1972), 9, 23.

12. Quoted in Morison, *Southern Voyages*, 154, and Parry, *Discovery of the Sea*, 231–2 and 244–53.
13. Nebenzahl, *Maps from the Age of Discovery*, 80–3; Litalien, *Les explorateurs*, 31–46. For a detailed description of the voyages of Magellan and others see Morison, *Southern Voyages*.
14. Morison, *Northern Voyages*, 210–25, and Parry, *Discovery of the Sea*, 221 and 258.
15. Williamson, *Cabot Voyages*, 145–72; Pope, *Many Landfalls*, 48–50.
16. For a summary of European knowledge of Newfoundland and Labrador before 1530, see David B. Quinn, "Newfoundland in the Consciousness of Europe in the Sixteenth and Early Seventeenth Centuries," in G. M. Story, ed., *Early European Settlement and Exploration in Atlantic Canada* (St John's: Memorial University of Newfoundland, 1982), 9–30. See also Robert Fuson, "The John Cabot Mystique," in Stanley H. Palmer and Dennis Reinhartz, eds., *Essays on the History of North American Discovery and Exploration* (College Station, Tex.: Texas A&M University Press, 1988), 35–51; Nebenzahl, *Maps from the Age of Discovery*, especially reproductions of the charts by Juan de la Cosa (1500), 30–3; Francesco Roselli (1508), 56–9; Juan Vespucci (1526), 84–7; and Diego Ribero (1529), 92–5; Morison, *Northern Voyages*, 186–7, 210–38, and 277–9.
17. Morison, *Northern Voyages*, 430–2; Quinn, *England and the Discovery of America*, 93–4.
18. Quoted in Morison, *Northern Voyages*, 286, from Verrazano's official letter to Francis I.
19. Morison, *Northern Voyages*, 279–82 and 314–6; McGhee, *Canada Rediscovered*, 110–1; Nebenzahl, *Maps from the Age of Discovery*, 88–91.
20. McGhee, *Canada Rediscovered*, 116–20.
21. Quoted in Morison, *Northern Voyages*, 391.
22. Bumsted, *The Peoples of Canada: A Pre-Confederation History*, 49.
23. Ibid., 32–7; Quinn, ed., *North American Discovery*, 96–112; McGhee, *Canada Rediscovered*, 116–26, 128–33; Morison, *Northern Voyages*, 345–424.
24. According to Morison, *Northern Voyages*, 430–2, Francis I saw the Saguenay as the key to re-establishing the balance of power in Europe between Spain, Portugal, and France.
25. McGhee, *Canada Rediscovered*, 136–9; Morison, *Northern Voyages*, 430–54; Quinn, ed., *North American Discovery*, 115–9; Bumsted, *The Peoples of Canada: A Pre-Confederation History*, 37–9.
26. R. K. Webb, *Modern England from the 18th Century to the Present* (New York: Dodd, Mead & Company, 1975), 6.
27. David W. Waters, *The Art of Navigation in England in Elizabethan and Early Stuart Times* (London: Hollis & Carter, 1958), 78–123.
28. Andrews, *Trade, Plunder and Settlement*, 64–75; Waters, *Art of Navigation*, 85–8.
29. David B. Quinn, ed., *The Voyages and Colonising Enterprises of Sir Humphrey Gilbert*, rev. ed. (London: Hakluyt Society, 1940; repr., Nendeln/Liechtenstein: Kraus Reprint, 1967), 8–9. Citations are to the Kraus Reprint edition. Also Andrews, *Trade, Plunder and Settlement*, 183–99.
30. Andrews, *Trade, Plunder and Settlement*, 167–82; McGhee, *Canada Rediscovered*, 155–66; Bumsted, *The Peoples of Canada: A Pre-Confederation History*, 26, 28–30, and 39–43; and Quinn, ed., *North American Discovery*, 211–26. For detailed descriptions of the voyages of Frobisher and Davis, see Morison, *Northern Voyages*, 496–616. For brief summaries and excerpts of contemporary documents relating to these voyages, see Quinn, ed., *New American World*, vol. 4, chapters 80 and 81, 193–251.
31. From the Trinity House inquiry, quoted in Andrews, *Trade, Plunder and Settlement*, 348–9.
32. Andrews, *Trade, Plunder and Settlement*, 341–55; Quinn, ed., *North American Discovery*, 226–7; Bumsted, *The Peoples of Canada: A Pre-Confederation History*, 42–3; and Morison, *Northern Voyages*, 612–3.
33. According to Laurier Turgeon, the volume of trade in the Gulf of St Lawrence in the sixteenth century and early seventeenth century was comparable to that in the Gulf of Mexico. Laurier Turgeon, "Pour redécouvrir notre 16e siècle: Les pêches à Terre-Neuve d'apres les archives notariales de Bordeaux," *Revue d'Histoire de l'Amerique Française* 39 (1986): 523–49. See also Cameron, *Lodestone and Evening Star*, 124, on the comparative value of the fishery.
34. Peter E. Pope, "The South Avalon Planters, 1630 to 1700: Residence, Labour, Demand and Exchange in Seventeenth Century Newfoundland" (DPhil thesis, Memorial University of Newfoundland, 1992); Vickers, *Farmers and Fishermen*, 85–116; Laurier Turgeon, "Le temps des pêches lointaines: Permanences et transformations (vers 1500–vers 1850)," in Michel Mollat, ed., *Histoire de pêches maritimes en France* (Toulouse: Editions Privat, 1987), 133–81.
35. Bumsted, *The Peoples of Canada: A Pre-Confederation History*, 43.
36. Webb, *Modern England*, 15–8; J. F. Bosher, "What Was 'Mercantilism' in the Age of New France?" (forthcoming paper presented at a conference at the University of Ottawa, 3 November 1989). Bosher argues that the term "mercantilism" has been defined so broadly and applied so uncritically by most historians that it has lost all meaning and so is not very useful in understanding the economic systems and policies of the seventeenth and eighteenth centuries.
37. Pope, "The South Avalon Planters," 1; Bumsted, *The Peoples of Canada: A Pre-Confederation History*, 59; Gillian T. Cell, "The Cupids Cove Settlement: A Case Study of the Problems of Colonisation," in Story, ed., *Early European Settlement*, 97–114; Raymond J. Lahey, "Avalon: Lord Baltimore's Colony in Newfoundland," in Story, ed., *Early European Settlement*, 115–38; Quinn, ed., *North American Discovery*, xxxvi–xl. See also Quinn, ed., *New American World*, vol. 4, 129–43, for excerpts of documents relating to the first English settlement on Newfoundland.
38. Bumsted, *The Peoples of Canada: A Pre-Confederation History*, 43; Quinn, ed., *North American Discovery*, xxxvi.
39. Bumsted, *The Peoples of Canada: A Pre-Confederation History*, 43–50.
40. Webb, *Modern England*, 65–69; Bumsted, *The Peoples of Canada: A Pre-Confederation History*, 89–91; Desmond Morton, *A Short History of Canada* (Edmonton: Hurtig Publishers, 1983), 62–5. For a map showing the areas of Newfoundland still open to French fishermen after 1763, see William Whiteley, "James Cook and British Policy in the Newfoundland Fisheries, 1763–7," *Canadian Historical Review* 54, no. 3 (September 1973), 251.
41. Robin Inglis, *The Lost Voyage of Lapérouse* (Vancouver: Vancouver Maritime Museum, 1986), 5–6; John Kendrick and Robin Inglis, *Enlightened Voyages: Malaspina and Galiano on the Northwest Coast, 1791–1792* (Vancouver: Vancouver Maritime Museum, 1991), 7–8; G. S. Ritchie, *The Admiralty Chart: British Naval Hydrography in the Nineteenth Century* (New York: American Elsevier Publishing Company, 1967), 16.
42. Inglis, *Lost Voyage*, 6–9; Kendrick and Inglis, *Enlightened Voyages*, 7–8; Robin Fisher, *Vancouver's Voyage:*

Charting the Northwest Coast, 1791–1795 (Vancouver: Douglas & McIntyre, 1992), 10–11; George Vancouver, *A Voyage of Discovery to the North Pacific Ocean and Round the World, 1791–1795*, vol. 1, edited by W. Kaye Lamb (London: Hakluyt Society, 1984), 6.

43. Alan Frost, "Science for Political Purposes: European Exploration of the Pacific Ocean, 1764–1806," in William K. Storey, ed., *Scientific Aspects of European Exploration*, Expanding World Series, vol. 6 (Aldershot, U.K.: Variorum, 1996), 67; Daniel A. Baugh, "Seapower and Science: The Motives for Pacific Exploration," in Storey, ed., *Scientific Aspects*, 89.

44. For more detailed information on the contribution of Perez and the other Spanish explorers of the North Pacific during this era, see Henry R. Wagner, *Cartography of the Northwest Coast of America to the Year 1800* (Amsterdam: N. Israel, 1968), 172–4 for Perez, 202–5 for Martinez, and 225–30 for Malaspina.

45. Kendrick and Inglis, *Enlightened Voyages*, 8–9; Inglis, *Lost Voyage*, 3–5; Fisher, *Vancouver's Voyage*, 9–11; Frost, "Science for Political Purposes," 73–5; Baugh, "Seapower and Science," 123–6.

46. See Inglis, *Lost Voyage*, 7–33, for a detailed account of the voyage and its accomplishments; Litalien, *Les explorateurs*, 222–6; Frost, "Science for Political Purposes," 75–6; Lamb, ed., *Voyage of Discovery*, 15; Wagner, *Cartography of the Northwest Coast*, 199–201.

47. According to Kendrick and Inglis, *Enlightened Voyages*, 18–19, the Enlightenment ideals that had, in part, inspired these voyages of discovery went out of fashion as a consequence of colonial rebellion in America and revolution in France. With a new monarch in place in Spain, Malaspina's decidedly liberal views and his friendship with the wrong clique at court worked against him. He was imprisoned and the record of his accomplishments buried for many years to come. See also Kendrick and Inglis, 9–20; Fisher, *Vancouver's Voyage*, 11–17; Frost, "Science for Political Purposes," 78–9.

48. Stanley Fillmore and R. W. Sandilands, *The Chartmakers: A History of Nautical Surveying in Canada* (Toronto: NC Press, 1983), 30–3; Inglis, *Lost Voyage*, 21. For a detailed discussion of Vancouver's work, see W. Kaye Lamb's introduction to Vancouver's journal cited above.

49. Ritchie, *Admiralty Chart*, 47.

50. J. E. D. Williams, *From Sails to Satellites: The Origin and Development of Navigational Science* (Oxford: Oxford University Press, 1994), 22–32; J. A. Bennett, *The Divided Circle: A History of Instruments for Astronomy, Navigation and Surveying* (Oxford: Phaidon-Christie's, 1987), 27–31; Jean Randier, *Marine Navigational Instruments*, translated from the French by John E. Powell (London: John Murray, 1980), 7–8, 12; Commander W. E. May, *A History of Marine Navigation* (New York: W. W. Norton & Company, 1973), 8, 10; W. F. J. Mörzer Bruyns, *The Cross-Staff: History and Development of a Navigational Instrument* (Zutphen, Netherlands: Vereeniging Nederlandsch Historisch Scheepvaart Museum, 1994), 13; Waters, *Art of Navigation*, 18–38; E. G. R. Taylor, *The Haven-Finding Art: A History of Navigation from Odysseus to Captain Cook* (New York: Abelard-Schuman, 1957), 215–7, 261; D. W. Waters, "Science and the Techniques of Navigation in the Renaissance," in Charles S. Singleton, ed., *Art, Science, and History in the Renaissance* (Baltimore: Johns Hopkins Press, 1967), 197; Parry, *European Hegemony*, 17–9; Parry, *Discovery of the Sea*, 24–33.

51. Taylor, *Haven-Finding Art*, 46, says that "the first direct evidence we have that the height of the stars was used by sailors to find their position" dates from about A.D. 63–65. See also Waters, "Science and the Techniques of Navigation," 199.

52. Taylor, *Haven-Finding Art*, 44–8, 158–66; Williams, *Sails to Satellites*, 32–5; Randier, *Marine Navigational Instruments*, 76; Bennett, *Divided Circle*, 32–5; Waters, "Science and the Techniques of Navigation," 197–9, 203–5; Waters, *Art of Navigation*, 64–5; Parry, *Discovery of the Sea*, 37–9; Parry, *European Hegemony*, 17–9.

53. Bennett, *Divided Circle*, 33.

54. Alan Stimson, *The Mariner's Astrolabe: A Survey of Known, Surviving Sea Astrolabes* (Utrecht: HES Publishers, 1988). See especially the section entitled "Historical Introduction." See also Francis Maddison, "On the Origin of the Mariner's Astrolabe," *Sphæra*, Occasional Papers 2 (Oxford: Museum of the History of Science, 1997); Taylor, *Haven-Finding Art*, 158–66; Waters, "Science and the Techniques of Navigation," 200, 206; Waters, *Art of Navigation*, 55–7; Bennett, *Divided Circle*, 33–5; Williams, *Sails to Satellites*, 35–7; Randier, *Marine Navigational Instruments*, 83–5; May, *History of Marine Navigation*, 10.

55. Bennett, *Divided Circle*, 37; Taylor, *Haven-Finding Art*, 164–5; Morison, *Northern Voyages*, 170; Firstbrook, *Voyage of the Matthew*, 117.

56. Mörzer Bruyns, *Cross-Staff*, 14–7; Randier, *Marine Navigational Instruments*, 87; Bennett, *Divided Circle*, 35; Taylor, *Haven-Finding Art*, 128–30; Williams, *Sails to Satellites*, 37; May, *History of Marine Navigation*, 10.

57. Bennett, *Divided Circle*, 35; Williams, *Sails to Satellites*, 37; Taylor, *Haven-Finding Art*, 160.

58. Bennett, *Divided Circle*, 77–9, Randier, *Marine Navigational Instruments*, 166–71; Taylor, *Haven-Finding Art*, 145–8.

59. Randier, *Marine Navigational Instruments*, 89; Randall Brooks, "Report on Selected Marine Navigational Instruments," prepared for National Museum of Science and Technology, July 1990, 3.

60. Randier, *Marine Navigational Instruments*, 89–92; Taylor, *Haven-Finding Art*, 220, 255; Bennett, *Divided Circle*, 35–6; Williams, *Sails to Satellites*, 37; May, *History of Marine Navigation*, 125–8; Brooks, "Report," 3.

61. Randier, *Marine Navigational Instruments*, 89.

62. Bennett, *Divided Circle*, 132.

63. Ibid., 130–4; Williams, *Sails to Satellites*, 96–100; Taylor, *Haven-Finding Art*, 256–9; May, *History of Marine Navigation*, 31–2, 256–9; Brooks, "Report," 5–7; Randier, *Marine Navigational Instruments*, 93–104.

64. Bennett, *Divided Circle*, 132–3.

65. Charles H. Cotter, *A History of the Navigator's Sextant* (Glasgow: Brown, Son & Ferguson, 1983), 137–9; Brooks, "Report," 5–8; Eric G. Forbes, *The Birth of Scientific Navigation: The Solving in the 18th Century of the Problem of Finding Longitude at Sea*, Maritime Monographs and Reports Series 10 (Greenwich: National Maritime Museum, 1974), 3–5; Derek Howse, *Greenwich Time and the Discovery of the Longitude* (Oxford: Oxford University Press, 1980), 57–60, 63; Dava Sobel, *Longitude: The True Story of a Lone Genius Who Solved the Greatest Scientific Problem of His Time* (New York: Walker & Company, 1995), 97. Campbell also tested chronometers for the Board of Longitude, including Harrison's H4 in 1764. He served as governor of Newfoundland from 1782 to 1784. Brooks, "Report," 5.

66. Bennett, *Divided Circle*, 130–4, 136–9; Williams, *Sails to Satellites*, 98–100; Brooks, "Report," 5–6.

67. Derek Howse, *Greenwich Time and the Longitude* (London: Philip Wilson Publishers, 1997), 20–1, 183–4; Bennett, *Divided Circle*, 55–7; Randier, *Marine Navigational Instruments*, 123; Williams, *Sails to Satellites*, 87; Sobel, *Longitude*, 21–4.

68. Roger Bacon had noted the existence of magnetic variation, i.e., that a compass needle did not always point true north, in the late thirteenth century. Mariners since at least John Cabot's time had been aware of variation and had devised different methods of compensating for it. See Helen M. Wallis and Arthur H. Robinson, eds., *Cartographical Innovations: An*

International Handbook of Mapping Terms to 1900 (Tring, U.K.: Map Collectors Publication, 1982), 189–90; Taylor, *Haven-Finding Art*, 172–91; and Pope, *Many Landfalls*, 22–4.
69. Bennett, *Divided Circle*, 51–5; Sobel, *Longitude*, 23–4.
70. Bennett, *Divided Circle*, 57–9; Sobel, *Longitude*, 24–7; Saul Moskowitz, "The Method of Lunar Distances and Technological Advance," in *Three Studies in the History of Celestial Navigation* (Marblehead, Mass.: History of Technology Press, 1974), 104.
71. Daniel A. Baugh, "The Sea-Trial of John Harrison's Chronometer, 1736," source unknown. According to Baugh (122), from the 1670s to the 1770s, the British government "showed itself willing to pay lavishly in order to encourage the progress of navigational science" based on the assumption that "human progress and maritime-commercial progress were interdependent."
72. For a discussion of the importance assigned the solution of longitude by various national governments and the encouragement and support they provided to astronomers and others working in the field, see especially Williams, *Sails to Satellites*, 75–83. See also Bennett, *Divided Circle*, 56–8; J. A. Bennett, "Science Lost and Longitude Found: The Tercentenary of John Harrison," *Journal of the History of Astronomy* 24, no. 77 (November 1993): 284; Randier, *Marine Navigational Instruments*, 178; Moskowitz, "Method of Lunar Distances," 105–6.
73. Derek Howse, "The Lunar Distance Method of Measuring Longitude," in W. H. Andrewes, ed., *The Quest for Longitude* (Cambridge, Mass.: Collection of Historical Scientific Instruments, 1996), 149–61; Williams, *Sails to Satellites*, 95–100; Moskowitz, "Method of Lunar Distances," 104–7; Sobel, *Longitude*, 88–99; Bennett, *Divided Circle*, 130–8; Howse, *Greenwich Time and the Longitude*, 65–71.
74. Moskowitz, "Method of Lunar Distances," 104–7; Howse, *Greenwich Time and the Longitude*, 69–71; Sobel, *Longitude*, 166–7; May, *History of Marine Navigation*, 32–6. Howse (70–1) disagrees with Moskowitz on the adoption of the lunar distance method, claiming that by 1766 the calculation time had been reduced to "thirty minutes or so" and that "a very high proportion of the world's deep-sea navigators" had begun to use the system by 1767.
75. F. A. Mercer and Kevin Haydon, "Finding the Longitude: The Trials and Rewards of John Harrison, the Inventor of the Marine Chronometer," *Sea History* 66 (Summer 1993): 22–3.
76. Bennett, "Science Lost," 282.
77. Ibid., and 284–5; Bennett, *Divided Circle*, 59–60, 139–41; Williams, *Sails to Satellites*, 100–4; Randier, *Marine Navigational Instruments*, 173–83; Mercer and Haydon, "Finding the Longitude," 22–3; Ian Jackson, "A Bearing on Good Fortune," *Geographical* (November 1993): 11–2; Taylor, *Haven-Finding Art*, 259–63; Brooks, "Report," 9–12; Baugh, "Sea-Trial," 235–9; Sobel, *Longitude*, 148–9. The standard work on the development of the chronometer is R. T. Gould, *The Marine Chronometer: Its History and Development*, rev. ed. (London, 1923; repr., Woodbridge, U.K.: Antique Collectors Club, 1989).
78. Bennett, *Divided Circle*, 136–41; May, *History of Marine Navigation*, 40.
79. Peter Kemp, ed., *The Oxford Companion to Ships and the Sea* (London: Oxford University Press, 1979), 492–3; A. E. Nicholls, *Nicholls's Seamanship and Viva Voce Guide* (Glasgow: James Brown & Son, 1913), 180–1; Bennett, *Divided Circle*, 31–2; May, *History of Marine Navigation*, 10–1.
80. Helen M. Wallis and Arthur H. Robinson, eds., *Cartographical Innovations: An International Handbook of Mapping Terms to 1900* (Tring, U.K.: Map Collectors Publication, 1982), 190.
81. Williams, *Sails to Satellites*, 26–7; May, *History of Marine Navigation*, 11–4, 164–7; Bennett, *Divided Circle*, 141–2; Taylor, *Haven-Finding Art*, 172–91; Wallis and Robinson, eds., *Cartographical Innovations*, 189–91.
82. Derek Howse and Michael Sanderson, *The Sea Chart: An Historical Survey Based on the Collections in the National Maritime Museum* (Newton Abbot, U.K.: David & Charles, 1973), 9–10.
83. Pope, *Many Landfalls*, 26.
84. Morison, *Northern Voyages*, 307, 346, 588–9, 593.
85. Early cartography was also plagued by inconsistencies and errors of scale arising from "confusion of league types" and "differing assumptions about the length of the meridian degree." Moreover, cartographers had only begun to work on methods of compensating for the distortions caused by magnetic variation. See James E. Kelley Jr., "The Distortions of Sixteenth-Century Maps of America," *Cartographica* 32, no. 4 (Winter 1995): 1–13.
86. Nebenzahl, *Maps from the Age of Discovery*, 126; Taylor, *Haven-Finding Art*, 222–3; Bennett, *Divided Circle*, 60–3; Williams, *Sails to Satellites*, 5–20, 43–7; Kemp, ed., *Oxford Companion*, 157, 539–41.
87. Nebenzahl, *Maps from the Age of Discovery*, 126; Taylor, *Haven-Finding Art*, 206–8, 222–6.
88. N. L. Nicholson and L. M. Sebert, *The Maps of Canada: A Guide to Official Canadian Maps, Charts, Atlases and Gazetteers* (Folkestone, U.K.: Wm. Dawson & Sons, 1981), 2–3.
89. There is a great deal of debate among cartographers and historians about what exactly the Cosa chart does and does not depict. See Fuson, "John Cabot Mystique," 43–7, and Quinn, "Newfoundland in the Consciousness of Europe," 9–13.
90. Nebenzahl, *Maps from the Age of Discovery*, 30, 56, 84–97; Quinn, "Newfoundland in the Consciousness of Europe," 11–3; Kelley, "Distortions of Sixteenth-Century Maps," 7; Nicholson and Sebert, *Maps of Canada*, 2.
91. Morison, *Northern Voyages*, 454; Nicholson and Sebert, *Maps of Canada*, 2.
92. C. R. Boxer, *The Dutch Seaborne Empire, 1600–1800* (London: Hutchinson & Co., 1965), 164–5.
93. J. B. Harley, "Silences and Secrets: The Hidden Agenda of Cartography in Early Modern Europe," in Storey, ed., *Scientific Aspects*, 164–9. According to Harley (167), Dutch merchant companies were, for obvious reasons, often reluctant to share their cartographical knowledge with other interests. They could be especially cautious when it came to distributing charts of newly explored regions and even demanded that some maps intended for publication be censored to remove certain information.
94. Boxer, *Dutch Seaborne Empire*, 164–5; Kemp, ed., *Oxford Companion*, 157–8; James S. Pritchard, "French Charting of the East Coast of Canada," in Derek Howse, ed., *Five Hundred Years of Nautical Science, 1400–1900*, Proceedings of the Third International Reunion for the History of Nautical Science and Hydrography (London: National Maritime Museum, 1981), 119–20.
95. Gunther Schilder, "Development and Achievements of Dutch Northern and Arctic Cartography in the 16th and 17th Centuries," unpublished paper/presentation, 1981, 9–12; Kemp, ed., *Oxford Companion*, 157–8; Boxer, *Dutch Seaborne Empire*, 164–5; Pritchard, "French Charting," 120; Ritchie, *Admiralty Chart*, 3, 21.
96. Fillmore and Sandilands, *Chartmakers*, 9–10.
97. Fabian O'Dea, *The 17th Century Cartography of Newfoundland, Cartographica*, Monograph 1, 1971, 6–20.
98. Louis De Vorsey, "Amerindian Contributions to the Mapping of North America: A Preliminary View," in Storey, ed., *Scientific Aspects*, 211.

99. Fillmore and Sandilands, *Chartmakers*, 9–10; Nicholson and Sebert, *Maps of Canada*, 146; Pritchard, "French Charting," 119–20.
100. William Fisher and John Thornton, *The English Pilot: The Fourth Book*, rev. ed. (London, 1689; repr., Theatrum Orbis Terrarum, 1967), introduction by Coolie Verner, vii.
101. Pritchard, "French Charting," 120; James S. Pritchard, "Ships, Men and Commerce: A Study of Maritime Activity in New France" (PhD thesis, University of Toronto, 1971), 22.
102. Pritchard, "French Charting," 119–20; Fillmore and Sandilands, *Chartmakers*, 13–5.
103. Pritchard, "French Charting," 120.
104. Ibid., 121.
105. Ibid., 122–4. During this period the French also moved north and northwest, mapping the rivers and lakes as they went. In the late 1720s, La Verendrye, relying heavily on Indian descriptions of the region, began mapping the area between Lake Superior and Lake Winnipeg. See G. Malcolm Lewis, "Indicators of Unacknowledged Assimilations from Amerindian Maps on Euro-American Maps of North America: Some General Principles Arising from the Study of La Verendrye's Composite Map, 1728–29," in Storey, ed., *Scientific Aspects*, 219–46.
106. Ritchie, *Admiralty Chart*, 14–5; Fillmore and Sandilands, *Chartmakers*, 17–23.
107. Whiteley, "James Cook," 246.
108. See G. N. D. Evans, *Uncommon Obdurate: The Several Public Careers of J. F. W. DesBarres* (Salem, Mass.: Peabody Museum, 1969), 10–20; and Ritchie, *Admiralty Chart*, 31–4.
109. For a detailed discussion of pre-1760 charts of Newfoundland, see O'Dea, *17th Century Cartography of Newfoundland*, 21–41. For a list of some of these charts, see Fisher and Thornton, *English Pilot*, xix–xx.
110. Whiteley, "James Cook," 246–72; J. C. Beaglehole, *The Life of Captain James Cook* (London: Hakluyt Society, 1974), 62–3.
111. Fillmore and Sandilands, *Chartmakers*, 21–5; Ritchie, *Admiralty Chart*, 15.
112. R. A. Skelton and R. V. Tooley, *The Marine Surveys of James Cook in North America, 1758–1768, Particularly the Survey of Newfoundland: A Bibliography of Printed Charts and Sailing Directions* (London: Map Collectors' Circle, 1967), 177–8; David Andrew, ed., *The Charts and Coastal Views of Captain Cook's Voyages: The Voyages of the Endeavour, 1768–1771* (London: Hakluyt Society, 1988), xxiii, xxxiii; Whiteley, "James Cook," 263–7. Quotations from Skelton and Tooley, 177, and Whiteley, 264, respectively.
113. Inglis, *Lost Voyage*, 21; Wagner, *Cartography of the Northwest Coast*, 199–201. According to Wagner (201): "The long delay in publishing the observations and maps of the voyage was fatal to any chance they might have had of receiving recognition."
114. Kendrick and Inglis, *Enlightened Voyages*, 13–8.
115. Lamb, ed., *Voyage of Discovery*, 15; Kendrick and Inglis, *Enlightened Voyages*, 18–9; Wagner, *Cartography of the Northwest Coast*, 225–30.
116. David Andrew, "Vancouver's Survey Methods and Surveys," in Robin Fisher and Hugh Johnston, eds., *From Maps to Metaphors: The Pacific World of George Vancouver* (Vancouver: UBC Press, 1993), 51–7.
117. Lamb, ed., *Voyage of Discovery*, 79–80; Ritchie, *Admiralty Chart*, 41–2; Andrew, "Vancouver's Survey Methods," 57–64.
118. Fisher, *Vancouver's Voyage*, 27.
119. According to Andrew ("Vancouver's Survey Methods," 64–7), Vancouver's longitudes, unlike his latitudes, were not "very close to modern values," being at different times too far east and too far west. This was due, in part, to "the inherent inaccuracy of lunar distances," where a small error in the distance measured produces a much larger error in the longitude calculation. Moreover, Vancouver's chronometers apparently did not perform all that well either and thus did not provide a precise check on the lunar distance calculations. For a more detailed description of the survey techniques used at the time, see Andrew.
120. Fisher, *Vancouver's Voyage*, 27; Lamb, ed., *Voyage of Discovery*, 46–8; Ritchie, *Admiralty Chart*, 41–7.
121. Quoted in Fisher, *Vancouver's Voyage*, 27.
122. Ibid., photo caption on 37.
123. Ibid., 29, 32, 37, 44; Ritchie, *Admiralty Chart*, 41–4.
124. Ritchie, *Admiralty Chart*, 49; Fisher, *Vancouver's Voyage*, 113–20; Lamb, ed., *Voyage of Discovery*, 48–9. Lamb notes that the survey did have obvious weaknesses, among them the cursory treatment of non-mainland features such as islets, rocks, and islands and the failure to explore certain inlets thoroughly. Vancouver did not try to conceal these failings, convinced that he had made every effort to fulfill the mandate he had been given. Considering that the Admiralty had thought two seasons sufficient to meet their objectives (Lamb, 42), it seems unlikely that they complained too loudly about these limitations.
125. Ritchie, *Admiralty Chart*, 32–4; Fisher, *Vancouver's Voyage*, 114; Fillmore and Sandilands, *Chartmakers*, 32–3.
126. John Naish, *Seamarks: Their History and Development* (London: Stanford Maritime, 1985), 15–24; Douglas B. Hague and Rosemary Christie, *Lighthouses: Their Architecture, History and Archaeology* (Llandysul Dyfed, U.K.: Gomer Press, 1985), 1–14.
127. Naish, *Seamarks*, 25–31.
128. Ibid., 37–45.
129. Ibid., 51 (quote), rest of paragraph 51–7.
130. Kemp, ed., *Oxford Companion*, 472.
131. Naish, *Seamarks*, 74.
132. Ibid., 68–76.
133. Ibid., 79–91; Hague and Christie, *Lighthouses*, 1–24.
134. Morison, *Northern Voyages*, 346, 377, 421; Jean-Pierre Proulx, *Basque Whaling in Labrador in the 16th Century* (Ottawa: Environment Canada, 1992), 15.
135. Pritchard, "Ships, Men and Commerce," 34.
136. Ibid., 35.
137. Ibid., 36; Gilles Proulx, *Between France and New France: Life Aboard the Tall Sailing Ships* (Toronto: Dundurn Press, 1984), 79.
138. Hugh F. Pullen, *The Sea Road to Halifax: Being an Account of the Lights and Buoys of Halifax Harbour*, Occasional Paper 1 (Halifax: Maritime Museum of the Atlantic, 1980), 13–5, 38–9, 42, 49, 53, 54.
139. Edward W. Bush, *The Canadian Lighthouse*, Canadian Historic Sites 9 (Ottawa: Indian and Northern Affairs, 1975), 10–1.
140. Hague and Christie, *Lighthouses*, 153–4; Bush, *Canadian Lighthouse*, 14–5.
141. Hague and Christie, *Lighthouses*, 161–5 (quote from 164); Bush, *Canadian Lighthouse*, 14–5.
142. Bumsted, *The Peoples of Canada: A Pre-Confederation History*, 114–5.
143. Bush, *Canadian Lighthouse*, 32–4.
144. Ibid., 34–5.
145. Ibid., 36–8. See also Pullen, *Sea Road to Halifax*, 20–1, on Sambro Island.

CHAPTER 2

Navigation in the Age of Empire

Navigation in the Age of Empire

At the beginning of the nineteenth century, British North America was a collection of small, scattered, and somewhat tenuous communities dependent on Britain for survival in the face of the emerging military and economic power of the United States. By the end of the century, these colonies had united to form a largely independent and self-sustaining transcontinental nation. Though many factors contributed to this transformation, the steady increase in trade, particularly international trade, was absolutely essential to it. Trade, of course, depended on efficient transportation systems, and transportation by water demanded reliable means of navigation. As traffic increased to accommodate the growth in trade and commerce, effective navigation became even more critical. Throughout the century, therefore, the fundamental problem of navigation in northern North America was no longer finding a way around or through the continent but finding the political will, money, and expertise to improve navigation on existing transportation routes and to establish new ones that would facilitate trade, communication, and defence.

The purpose of this chapter is to describe Canada's development as a maritime trading nation to 1900 and to show how this development necessitated improvement of navigational systems and skills in this country. The first section is an overview of Canadian history that emphasizes the development of the marine transportation systems and infrastructure that made the expansion of colonial trade and commerce possible. Since there were many improvements but few major breakthroughs in shipboard navigational instruments in this period, the second section discusses salient refinements and offers some thoughts on the distribution, sale, and repair of instruments by dealers in Canadian port cities. The third section outlines the extensive charting work done throughout the century, highlighting the contributions of Henry Bayfield and other Royal Navy hydrographers, ending with the creation of a Canadian hydrographic service. A survey of improvements in aids to navigation follows, documenting major technological advances and tracing Canada's extensive use of these devices to mark important transportation routes.

From Sea to Sea to Sea: Building a Maritime Nation

When the dust settled after the American Revolution, Britain was left with what one historian has called "the cold, unprofitable remnants of the continent."[1] By 1790, the settler population of these northern colonies, though swollen by the recent addition of some 40,000 Loyalist refugees, was only about 250,000, and their economies were "extremely limited" and "in considerable disrepair."[2]

Still, the British government had both economic and strategic reasons for maintaining a strong presence in northern North America. It had to be seen to stand by the promises it had made to the Loyalists who had given up everything to live under the crown and who now had to start from scratch clearing and developing the wilderness land they had been granted as compensation. Moreover, British merchants and entrepreneurs had invested a great deal of time, effort, and money in setting up viable and profitable trades in fur, fish, and timber. These reinforced Britain's claim to an ever-widening portion of the continent — fur traders had travelled to both the Pacific and Arctic oceans by 1800 in search of more furs and better supply routes — and helped to provide a financial basis for colonial development. Finally, British North America provided an important base for Royal Navy and British army operations in the New World, where relations with the United States remained tense. When war did come, British North America also proved to be a valuable source of essential resources.[3]

British authorities and colonial governors, merchants and traders knew that in order to exploit the abundant resources of British North America effectively and to secure the economic and political survival of the colonies, transportation systems had to be expanded and improved. Marine transportation was especially important because all transatlantic trade and, until the submarine telegraph cable was laid in 1866, all transatlantic communication depended on it. British North America had an abundance of coastlines and waterways and, by 1800, the Admiralty, mercantile interests, and colonial authorities had already developed some of the more obvious sites along these routes into viable ports — St John's, Halifax, Saint John, Québec, for example. But beyond the eastern fringes of the colonies, little had been done to improve transportation. Montréal, for example, had a port and more than its share of successful merchants and traders. The 11-foot (3.4-m) depth of the natural channel between Montréal and Québec, however, limited the size of vessel that could make the journey,[4] so goods often had to be transferred from ocean-going vessels at Québec before being sent on to Montréal. This added to the cost of goods and the time needed to ship them. Anything travelling to or from the new Loyalist settlements farther upstream, past numerous rapids, shoals, and other obstacles, was that much more costly and time-consuming to move.

Given the colonies' small population base and limited economies, building a viable and efficient transportation system was no small undertaking. Minor improvements such as placing buoys or markers could be carried out by local officials or private individuals, but improving river channels, building canals, constructing harbour installations, and erecting a network of lighthouses were tasks that generally went far beyond the means — financial and physical — of these individuals. For the most part, the colonists and their governments recognized that these major enterprises would have to be carried out gradually, most likely or at least partly as public works, and paid for using both locally raised and imperial funds.

Between 1800 and 1820, the British government, in co-operation with colonial authorities, began to lay both the administrative and structural foundations for improved marine navigation in British North America. In 1803, the government of Upper Canada set up a fund "for the erection and maintaining of lighthouses" and appointed commissioners to carry out the work. They built their first light at Mississauga Point, at the mouth of the Niagara River, in 1804 with the help of British army masons.[5] Two years later the legislative assembly of Lower Canada created Québec Trinity House. This body was modelled after the original British Trinity House, established under Henry VIII in 1512 to assist shipping by building and maintaining lighthouses and other seamarks. Following this example, Québec Trinity House was given general responsibility for making regulations to ensure "the more convenient, safe and easy navigation" of the St Lawrence River from above Montréal to the Gulf. The appointed officials were also responsible for laying down and taking up buoys, erecting lighthouses, beacons, and landmarks, and clearing other hazards such as rocks and sands.[6] They began construction of their first lighthouse in 1806 on Green Island, at the mouth of the Saguenay River, a site recommended for marking as early as 1787 by Peter Fraser, who tried and failed at that time to raise the necessary funds privately to undertake the project. Despite this promising start, the Green Island light, completed in 1809, remained the only lighthouse on the St Lawrence for 21 years.[7] The £1,375 price of the tower, the outbreak of war in 1812, and the cost of rebuilding the colonies afterwards may have prevented the colony from initiating any major building projects. There seems to have been a lapse in activity in the other colonies as well.

The War of 1812, though, did bring a great deal of maritime activity — naval and mercantile — to British North America and, in particular, focused the British Admiralty's attention on the Great Lakes. The maritime colonies, for their part, did a booming business feeding and housing ships' crews and soldiers and supplying and repairing ships. Shipowners and shipbuilders also played a growing role in the West Indian trade.[8] In the Canadas, meanwhile, the demands of war led the Royal Navy to build a naval dockyard and base at Kingston and a base at Penetanguishene on Georgian Bay and to increase shipbuilding capacity generally on the lower lakes, attracting a substantial number of skilled labourers to the area in the process.[9]

The war also highlighted the poor state of hydrographical knowledge of the St Lawrence–Great Lakes waterway, a grave weakness given that these waters were a critical boundary with a hostile country. Immediately following the war, with naval buildup continuing on both sides, the Admiralty made charting a major priority. Accurate surveys were necessary to equip British diplomats to address outstanding disputes over the location of the border and to prepare British mariners to defend that border against possible U.S. attack. Though priorities and the level of urgency changed after Britain and the United States signed the Rush-Bagot Treaty in 1817, strictly limiting the number of armed ships allowed on the lakes and river, the British Admiralty continued to chart these waters, recognizing their great importance for the commercial development of Upper Canada. By 1820, Admiralty hydrographers, led by Henry Bayfield, had surveyed Lakes Ontario and Erie and had begun the arduous task of charting the complex coastlines and channels of Lake Huron.[10]

The Napoleonic Wars and their aftermath also prompted the British government to reconsider its existing policy of discouraging (or at least not encouraging) emigration to the colonies. High levels of postwar unemployment and "a new round of industrialization and agricultural rationalization" following the depression "left many without work in their traditional occupations and places of residence" and threatened to cause widespread social unrest across Britain.[11] At the same time, the North American timber trade was flourishing, with colonial merchants supplying fully 21 percent of British demand in 1820.[12] As shipping interests on both sides of the Atlantic built more and more vessels to accommodate these bulky but essential cargoes, the cost of passage to North America fell. Shipowners preferred to fill their westbound ships with any paying cargo, including emigrants, rather than send them back empty.[13]

As a result of these factors, a steady and growing stream of Britons made their way to North America after

1820. By 1845, some 700,000 had arrived, augmenting the rising native-born population significantly. Between the mid-1820s and 1851, the number of residents of the maritime colonies grew from about 200,000 to about 500,000 while, during the same period, Lower Canada's population nearly doubled, from 480,000 to 890,000. The most dramatic increase, though, was in Upper Canada, where the number of inhabitants rose dramatically, from 158,000 in 1825 to 952,000 in 1851. By 1850, newcomers had extended the band of cleared, cultivated land back fifty kilometres from the shores of the Great Lakes and St Lawrence River.[14]

Much of this immigration was unassisted, since neither the colonial nor the imperial government had a systematic land and settlement policy, but the British North American colonies managed reasonably well with the human and natural resources available to them. Between 1820 and 1850, the colonists built "a very active, even vibrant, commercial economy," based mainly on fish, timber, and grain. Although the Atlantic cod fishery did not grow significantly after 1815, it continued to be an important export trade and gave great impetus to the shipping and ship-building industries of the region.[15] Indeed, in 1850, Newfoundland, whose economy was almost entirely based on the fishery, was the only British North American colony that exported more than it imported.[16] The timber trade, supported by imperial preference and the flourishing British economy, which needed more ships to carry its goods to the world, accounted for 40 percent of all British North American exports in the 1830s and 1840s. By 1850, exports of forest products to Britain totalled £1,164,624.[17]

During this period, the hard work of Canadian farmers also began to pay off. After long years spent clearing and cultivating the land, they began producing significant quantities of wheat. Like timber, grain production benefited both from imperial preference and from rising demand that Britain itself could not supply. In 1835, exports from the Great Lakes region totalled 543,815 bushels of wheat and flour. Though 1837 was a bad year due to heavy rains, financial instability in the United States, worldwide depression, and colonial rebellion, just three years later, the Canadas accounted for more than 1.7 million bushels of wheat and flour, most of which went to Britain. Over

Figure 18. Kingston, Canada West from Fort Henry, 1855, by Edwin Whitefield.
(W. D. Jordan Special Collections and Music Library, Queen's University, Kingston, no neg. no.)

the next decade, farmers expanded and intensified their exploitation of the soil, especially in Upper Canada. By 1851, wheat exports from farms around the Great Lakes had risen to 12,193,202 bushels.[18]

Both transatlantic trade and the British economy generally did well between 1820 and 1845, and, as a result, shipowners and merchants needed more vessels. The link between the demand for timber and the colonial shipbuilding industry became even stronger as shipbuilders in both the Maritimes and Lower Canada produced an increasing number of vessels just to carry timber across the Atlantic. Some timber barons even began building their own carriers to transport their products to market. By the 1830s, for example, the Pollack, Gilmour partnership owned about one hundred timber ships, making it "one of the largest merchant navies under the British flag."[19] Other colonial builders made vessels specifically for the market in Britain, since builders there simply could not keep up with demand. By 1846, "almost 20 per cent of all tonnage on registry in Britain had been built in the colonies," and the major colonial suppliers by far were Lower Canada and the Maritimes.[20]

As the population and commercial activity of British North America grew, so did the need for transportation infrastructure. In addition to higher levels of all kinds of marine traffic, the advent and gradual adoption of steam propulsion after 1830 was increasing the speed of ships and extending their range and frequency of travel up rivers like the St Lawrence. Not surprisingly, with more ships moving more quickly around the world, the number of shipwrecks rose dramatically. By 1836, when the British parliament established a committee to investigate the causes of and possible solutions to this growing problem, "about nine hundred men and £2.8 million worth of property were being lost at sea each year."[21]

With the British Admiralty[22] and imperial and local mercantile interests to remind them, colonial officials became increasingly aware of the need to address the problems of navigating northern North America's coastal and inland waters. Bayfield's ongoing surveys of the Great Lakes, St Lawrence, and east coast in the 1830s and 1840s mapped and described countless navigable channels and hazards. Though these were drawn on charts and published in sailing instructions, this was just the first step. To make navigation safer and more efficient, all or most of these features would eventually have to be marked. Fortunately, in the 1830s, increasing urgency coincided with increasing prosperity, and the various governments seem to have undertaken significant programs of seamarking, including lighthouse construction.[23]

Colonial governments took the task of building lighthouses very seriously because, by the standards of the day, these were significant public works. They were expensive to build and maintain, and officials had to make difficult decisions about where the installations would be of the greatest value. They also needed expert advice on precise position and what type of building construction and light fixture would be most suitable. In 1829, faced with a petition from "Merchants, Shipowners, Masters of Vessels and Pilots" asking it to enquire into "the expediency of erecting Light-Houses on the St. Lawrence," the House of Assembly of Lower Canada called a special committee. The members called expert witnesses including John Lambly, harbour-master at Québec, Captain Bayfield, and J. L. Marett, all of whom had extensive knowledge of the St Lawrence. Though their recommendations differed in detail — east versus southwest end of Anticosti Island, for example — the information they provided helped the government determine its priorities for placing lights, for which there was an increasing demand all along the river and gulf. The committee also produced cost estimates for construction, equipment, and maintenance of the proposed installations. The government responded by appropriating £12,000 in the 1828 to 1829 session and £25,212 in 1831, which was used to build three lighthouses and to contribute to two others, at Cape Ray, Newfoundland, and on St Paul Island, marking the way for mariners passing through the Cabot Strait to the Gulf.[24]

The other colonies were also becoming more actively involved in improving navigation. By the 1830s, Montréal had its own Trinity House to manage marine traffic and seamarking on the upper St Lawrence. Newfoundland appointed its first Lighthouse Board in 1834, and Upper Canada, Nova Scotia, and New Brunswick had well-established lighthouse commissions that fulfilled similar tasks. They undertook a variety of navigation-related projects and duties, not the least of which was building a series of lighthouses that stretched from the west end of Lake Erie to Cape Bonavista, at the eastern extremity of Newfoundland.[25]

Colonial authorities maintained their leading role in enhancing marine navigation despite political upheaval in the Canadas in the late 1830s and the end of protective imperial tariffs and onset of worldwide economic depression in 1846. Politicians, merchants, farmers, and most other residents of British North America did not need to be reminded that without efficient shipping, there would be little trade of any type, preferential or free. This stark reality and the concerted lobbying efforts of business groups such as the Montréal Board of Trade persuaded governments to keep investing their scarce resources in navigational aids and improvements. Thus, after 1837 colonial engineers built a number of new lighthouses, a few of them major installations. Between 1846 and 1849, authorities across British North America added thirteen new lights to the Admiralty lists.[26]

In addition to promoting the improvement of natural waterways, colonial merchants and shipping interests also began to lobby for the construction of canals to bypass the many rapids and falls that prevented direct communication between the communities of the upper St Lawrence–Great Lakes system and the Atlantic seaports. Between 1821 and 1825 the Lachine Canal was completed, providing a partial bypass of the Lachine rapids. The Welland Canal took four years to build, though when it opened in 1829, according to Bliss, it was just barely operable and certainly no competition for the Erie Canal, completed in 1825. Builders began work on the Chambly Canal around rapids on the Richelieu River in 1833. Finally, in the late 1840s, the Province of Canada completed the Laurentian canals, making it possible for "shallow-drafted steamers" to journey to Lake Ontario and, once extensive and expensive renovations to the Welland Canal were undertaken in the 1840s, into Lake Erie.[27]

Unlike navigational aids, these major marine transportation projects were often not initiated or fully funded by colonial governments. Canal-building was too expensive and too controversial — canals often seemed designed to benefit specific private interests and communities more than the colony as a whole — to be readily embraced by local officials, especially in the 1820s and 1830s. Ultimately, though, most of the canal projects became public works after private funding failed (as in the case of the Welland Canal), when imperial funding was available, or when prosperity and the promise of increased traffic made the required investment seem worthwhile (as in the case of the Laurentian canals).[28]

Other forms of transportation also received government attention. The British military had established a backbone of main roads for strategic purposes, for example, Yonge and Dundas streets and the track linking New Brunswick and Quebec. As towns grew, their inhabitants added to the network, and farmers cleared tracks to connect with whatever network existed in their areas. Private entrepreneurs and landowners also constructed roads, in the hope that it would make their land more valuable and attract more settlers and commerce to the area. They sometimes charged tolls to recover some of their construction costs.[29]

Also, the first Canadian rail line, the Champlain and St Lawrence Railroad, was opened in 1836. The brainchild of Jason A. Pierce, a Richelieu Valley merchant, it was privately financed by a group of Montréal merchants including the Molsons. The 14-mile (22.5-km) line linked the south shore community of La Prairie with Saint-Jean on the Richelieu River, thereby eliminating 145 kilometres of river travel and providing an important connection to the American ports to the south. This small success fuelled an intense but short-lived "railway euphoria," as promoters scrambled to obtain charters, financial backing, and government support for their projects.[30]

Yet, despite these promising additions to colonial land transportation systems and the general excitement over emerging railway technology, development was minimal. Private entrepreneurs and local community groups lost interest in these projects after 1837, when political turmoil made investing in them too risky. With the end of imperial preference and the onset of depression in the late 1840s, funds dried up completely. Colonial governments, for their part, seemed to view roads and railways as secondary, a way to meet local needs or to move goods from inland farms and communities to port facilities. They therefore did not take a leading role in promoting or funding these projects. Even in the Canadas, where settlement had penetrated well into the interior by the 1840s, there was no systematic program of road building similar to that which existed for navigational aids until the early 1850s.[31]

In the 1850s, the world entered an era of fundamental economic, political, social, and technological change. After the crisis of the late 1840s, Britain and Europe settled into a period of dramatic economic growth fuelled, in large part, by the spread of British industrial technology and technique. Factories demanded an ever-increasing supply of raw materials, which often had to come from abroad, and though workers were generally recruited locally or regionally, domestic farmers could no longer be expected to supply all the food needed to sustain them. As production grew, industrialists also sought new markets for their goods in countries that could not supply their own needs. Because of this, and Britain's decision to end protection and adopt free trade, international trade grew by leaps and bounds after 1850. With it grew the demand for ships and the amount of shipping traffic in the world's ports. At the same time, shipbuilders had improved the design and construction of steam vessels to a point where they were viable transoceanic carriers. Regularly scheduled steamships had begun to transport the mails, passengers, and other high-value, low-volume commodities across the Atlantic in the 1840s, and from that point on their presence steadily increased. These vessels added a new dimension — and new speed — to shipping and placed special demands on crews as well as on marine authorities and infrastructure.

In British North America, the economic boom brought unprecedented prosperity and growth which, in turn, laid the foundation for the political consolidation of the

Figure 19. *Cape Cove Shipyard near Québec, circa 1865. Note the ships waiting to be loaded with lumber.*
(Library and Archives Canada, neg. PA 103102)

colonies and their gradual expansion into a transcontinental nation-state. As in the first half of the century, colonial development after 1850 remained almost completely dependent on international trade. Between 1850 and 1891, overall imports tripled, to reach a value of about $94 million, while exports quadrupled, to $75 million. Most of the goods imported by colonial merchants were manufactured goods, including the machinery needed to exploit natural resources and to set up factories. Exports were still overwhelmingly staples such as wood, wheat, and other agricultural products and fish, though minerals were emerging as another important raw material export.[32]

The sources of this wealth were spread throughout the colonies. As settlers moved out from the lower Great Lakes and into Lake Huron and beyond, newly cleared land yielded a steady supply of surplus timber and, later, agricultural products, especially wheat. The same was true of the upper Ottawa Valley. The east coast fishery remained a steady source of trade, with Newfoundland alone producing close to $5 million worth of fish products for export in 1874, while Canada accounted for about $4.3 million. There were also mineral resources like iron ore and nickel throughout the east, though entrepreneurs did not begin to exploit them to any great extent until the late 1890s.[33]

Confederation and the addition of vast new territories to the new dominion brought valuable new resources into the economy. The new province of British Columbia had been formed out of the two colonial outposts — Vancouver Island and British Columbia — planted by the British to prevent American annexation of the area in the 1840s and 1850s. With a naval base at Esquimalt to protect them, these small communities had lived mainly off the trade in fish, fur, and timber. The discovery of gold, first along the Fraser and Thompson rivers in 1857 and then in the Cariboo in the early 1860s, however, brought rapid change to the region.[34] People poured into these isolated colonies to seek their fortunes and, when the gold ran out, many stayed on to settle and to develop the region's more enduring natural resources. Between 1871, when the recently united Colony of British Columbia joined Confederation, and 1910, the west coast timber industry increased its production from 350 million to 4.5 billion board feet. The new province also boasted a thriving fishery that in 1879 was worth more than $600,000. Three years earlier, it had opened its first salmon cannery; within twenty years it had forty-seven and overall production "had increased fifty-nine times over."[35]

In Rupert's Land, which the Canadian government had bought in 1869 from the Hudson's Bay Company, agricultural land was the most valuable natural resource. Prosperity in the east had contributed to a significant increase in population, both native-born and immigrant, which had, in turn, put intense pressure on the land in the Maritimes, Quebec, and Ontario. This, combined with concerns about American expansionism, encouraged the Canadian government to acquire and settle the prairie west as quickly as possible. Its precipitous actions caused the local inhabitants to rebel in 1869–70, but federal authorities did succeed in opening up the easternmost regions to farming so that, by 1883, the best agricultural land in Manitoba was already largely occupied. Though the next decade was marred by severe depression, the near collapse of the Canadian Pacific Railway, and another, bloodier rebellion, all of which brought agricultural development to a halt, by the mid-1890s demand for wheat was such that settlers began to fill the remaining arable land. Once there, they turned thousands of acres of prairie into productive wheat-growing land, with yields rising from 29 million bushels in 1896 to 209 million by 1911.[36]

This expansion of settlement and trade produced a comparable increase in shipping. Vessels were needed both to carry exports and imports to their markets and to serve local commercial and transportation needs, especially before the spread of railways and roads. On the Great Lakes, for example, ships not only transported wood and wheat to the east for export to Britain, but also carried American iron ore and coal from one lakeside port to another.[37] Passenger vessels also plied the lakes in large numbers, especially in regions such as Georgian Bay and Lake Superior, where many of the coastal and inland communities were not linked to a reliable land transportation network.

On the Pacific coast, the gold rushes brought a sharp rise in maritime traffic of all kinds as well as an increased demand for inland transportation, most of which, at least initially, was by water. During the Cariboo gold rush in 1860, the British Columbia and Victoria Steam Navigation Co. provided steamer service up the Fraser River as far as Yale. By 1866 there were also steamers plying the Thompson River, serving the southeastern districts of the colony.[38] The Hudson's Bay Company operated vessels in the region, in part to service their coal mines on Vancouver Island. Cannery and sawmill owners also needed ships to move their products, and sometimes bought and operated their own vessels to control their transportation costs.[39]

Even prairie wheat, which was transported long distances by rail, eventually ended up on ships on the east or west coast, bound for markets in Britain and elsewhere. Moreover, since, for prairie farmers, "the land provided nothing but a cash crop,"[40] they had to buy almost all their essential supplies from outside the region. Profits from wheat therefore fuelled demand for both domestic and imported goods, which were usually transported at least part of the way to consumers by ship.

Settlement and development created a steady, if not constant, increase in the demand for shipping after 1850, which had several important repercussions in Canada. First of all, it had a direct impact on the shipbuilding and shipping industries, especially on the east coast. Although the gradual reduction of timber duties, the repeal of the Navigation Acts, and the economic crisis of the late 1840s had seriously undermined the shipbuilding industry, it was rejuvenated by the gold rushes in California and Australia and then by the Crimean War in 1854. The increased demand for tonnage resulting from these factors was not only reinforced by burgeoning trade, but also coincided with a gradual rise in freight rates and a relative decline in U.S. shipbuilding, particularly after the outbreak of the Civil War.[41] Shipbuilders in the Maritimes and Quebec had access to the natural and human resources needed to construct large sailing vessels and, as a result, were generally able to produce wooden ships that cost half or less than half as much as comparable iron-hulled steamers. By 1867, these and other factors had helped to make Canada, "by tonnage, the third largest shipping nation in the world."[42] Though the Canadian shipping industry began to decline soon after this impressive statistic was recorded, the nation's reliance on ship-borne trade and commerce remained high, as did the level of traffic clearing Canadian ports.[43]

As shipping traffic, both steam and sail, grew, government officials had to devote more and more attention to marine matters. By the late 1850s, the reports of the Commissioners of Public Works for the united province of Canada had become much longer and more detailed documents, with extensive sections relating to canals, harbours, lighthouses, and other navigational works.[44] At the same time, both Trinity Houses retained their duties, and a variety of harbour commissions were added to the bureaucratic reporting structure. In 1855, the Newfoundland government placed its lighthouse commissioners under the authority of a new Board of Works made up of some of the most powerful colonial officials. When four of the British North American colonies united to form Canada in 1867, the negotiators decided that the sea coasts and navigable inland waters of the new nation were so "valuable to our people" and so "essential to the national well-being" that they should be the responsibility of the federal government.[45] After the first election, the government created the Department of Marine and Fisheries, which, among other things, was responsible for operating and maintaining lighthouses and other seamarks, inspecting steamships, administering the laws relating to shipping, and carrying out meteorological observations to assist shipping. Within a few years the department took over lighthouse construction from Public Works.[46]

Under this new centralized system, improved navigation continued to be a major priority. Reports of the department reflect an almost constant expansion and upgrading process in aids. For example, between 1867 and 1872, 93 new lights and 10 new fog whistles were added to the existing system, while 43 lighthouses and light beacons were under construction. At the same time, officials reported that they were either in the process of upgrading or had already upgraded many of the existing lights.[47] When a committee of the London Trinity House visited Canada in 1872 to assess its system of aids, they were greatly impressed by what had been accomplished in such a new country, with limited financial resources and seemingly unlimited coastlines to mark. Though the technology was seldom the latest, Canadian marine officials managed to get the most out of it and, with "commendable zeal," had enhanced the safety and efficiency of travel in their waters.[48]

Shipping safety also demanded, in the view of the British government, new regulations requiring the certification of masters and mates of "foreign-going" British vessels. Part of legislation known as the Mercantile Marine Act (1850), these certification clauses grew out of concerns over the competency of British mariners. With the high loss rates recorded earlier by a parliamentary committee, the government was worried that, in the absence of the Navigation Acts that once protected them, "British shipowners might lose freights to foreign fleets if their merchant marine had a reputation for excessive risk-taking and incompetence in officers and masters." Forcing them to take exams that demonstrated their knowledge of navigation, among other things, would show the world that Britain's mariners were still the very best.

Though shipowners opposed the legislation, it was passed into law. It was not applied retroactively, but it did apply to all British mariners who wished to qualify as masters or mates of British ships in the international trade from that time forward. The act set high standards that many mariners would have found it hard to meet without instruction and study. For example, a second mate had to "understand the first five rules of arithmetic" and be able "to correct the course steered for variation in the compass bearing, make observations with sextant, find the latitude from the meridian altitude of the Sun, and answer questions about rigging, stowage, the log-line, and the rule of road for ships." A first mate had to know all this and "be able to observe and compute azimuths, use chronometers, use and adjust the sextant." Masters were expected to have spent at least a year as mate with all that entailed as well as be able "to navigate along any coast, by drawing on a chart the courses and distance he would run, with bearings corrected for variation." He also "had to know the method of determining the effect of iron in a vessel on the ship's compass."[49]

In itself this law posed no great or immediate threat to colonial mariners, but it seems to have coincided with and reinforced a growing concern in the colonies about the lack of sound navigational training for local mariners. According to Appleton, in 1851, a Mr. Joseph Hamel, Esq., suggested setting up a school of navigation at Québec to the board of Québec Trinity House. They supported his idea and managed to convince the colonial government to do the same, offering a British institution, the Royal Hospital School at Greenwich, as a model.[50]

The government school of navigation opened in 1853 under the direction of George Kingston, formerly on the staff of Royal Naval Hospital at Plymouth, England. The school was land-based and gave bilingual instruction. Its primary objects were as follows:

 I.   — *To instruct in the scientific parts of their profession persons already occupied in a sea-faring life.*

 II.   — *To train for the position of officers young men or boys who have not served at sea.*

 III.   — *To rear up working seamen.*[51]

The curriculum was heavily oriented toward scientific studies, stressing pure mathematics and its application "to navigation and practical astronomy with special reference to nautical purposes and Geodesy." For those students "designed for the sea," Kingston also intended to give instruction in "the art of rigging and managing a boat."[52]

The school was an ambitious, even visionary, institution for what was still a very practically oriented colonial community. After only two years, Kingston was defending the school and its curriculum against complaints from mariners and questions from the government. For their part, many serving mariners

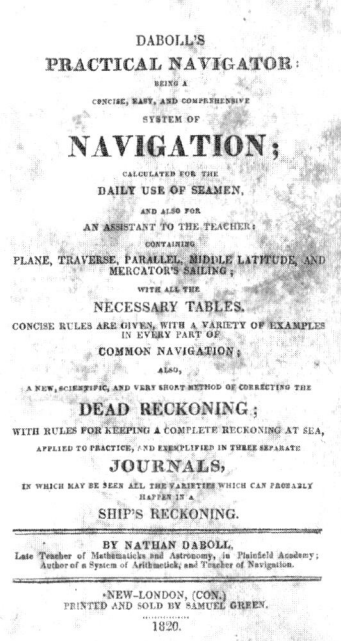

Figure 20. Title page and front plate from Daboll's Practical Navigator, *by Nathan Daboll (New London, Conn.: Samuel Green, 1820).*

believed that the subjects being taught were "too hard." The government, meanwhile, was anxious to see clear and immediate results for its investment. It wanted to know the number of students who had received instruction at the school to date and how many of these had entered the institution "with the avowed intention of going to sea." According to the principal, since 1853, thirty-five students had attended, of which twelve had, before or since their enrollment, "been engaged in the sea life," though he could not say for certain how many of these came to the school with that "avowed intention."[53]

Kingston defended the school, arguing that he could not, in good conscience, change the curriculum in order to attract more of those students who only wanted to acquire those navigational skills that "the British Legislature has made great effort to uproot" and which, in his view, perpetuated an approach to seamanship that was "destructive to life and property." Moreover, he claimed, even with its low enrollments, the school's "advantage is altogether out of proportion to its expense." Despite the passage in Britain of another Merchant Shipping Act in 1854 that extended certification requirements for master and mates to colonial vessels entering British ports, the government did not agree. In 1855, it closed the navigational school. A disappointed George Kingston moved on to a position at the University of Toronto.[54]

For the next fourteen years, a British North American mariner wishing to work as master or mate on a foreign-going vessel had to produce a certificate of service demonstrating that he had been acting as an officer in good standing at the time the Merchant Shipping Act was passed or had to take the appropriate tests administered by a local marine board in Britain. If, as seems likely, he needed instruction in order to pass the test, he would either have had to seek out a private teacher in a colonial port city — individuals occasionally listed themselves as nautical teachers in city directories of the time — or go to Britain.[55]

Though these regulations may, in the long run, have enhanced the level of navigational knowledge and skill of professional mariners, in the short term, they threatened to marginalize a colonial merchant marine already, according to some, suffering from a lack of formal education.[56] They certainly placed a major impediment in the path of young colonial mariners hoping to work their way up the ranks to take charge of a foreign-going ship. They would also have been a serious disincentive to many ambitious young men who might have been thinking about joining the merchant marine. Moreover, experienced masters or mates without the proper certificates, knowing that they could be relieved of command if they sailed into a British port, were probably inclined to remain in the home trade (covering the coast from Newfoundland to the West Indies) and avoid the insult, not to mention the expense and inconvenience, of finding another, lower-ranking position to get them home.[57]

Despite "growing demands that the colonies establish their own examination and certification procedures," nothing was done until after Confederation. In 1869 the British government passed the Merchant Shipping (Colonial) Act, which gave colonial governments the power to set up their own certification systems. These qualifications would be accepted in Britain as long as "the Board of Trade was satisfied that examinations met the appropriate standards." The Canadian government, just two years old, acted quickly, passing enabling legislation and setting up its system of certification, including instituting examinations the following year. Also, "to ensure the success of the scheme while starting," the recently created Department of Marine and Fisheries granted "a subsidy to instructors at each of the ports" where the six-hour written examinations were to be given — Halifax, Saint John, and Québec. The first master's certificate was awarded on 16 September 1871, and between that date and 31 December 1872, a total of 235 were given out. Of these, Halifax accounted for 68, Saint John, 144, and Québec, 23.

At the same time, 46 mates were certified: 4 at Halifax, 5 at Saint John, and 37 at Quebec.[58]

As with the British examinations, the Canadian tests were quite rigorous. A mate had to

> *understand the first rules of arithmetic and the use of logarithms...be able to work a day's work complete, including the bearings and distance of the port he is bound to, by Mercator's method; to correct the sun's declination for longitude, find his latitude by the meridian altitude of the sun, and by single altitude of the same body off the meridian...to observe and compute the variation of the compass from azimuths and amplitudes; be able to compare chronometers and keep their rates...be able to find the longitude by them from an observation of the sun by the usual methods...be able to lay off the place of ship on the chart, both by the bearings of known objects, and by latitude and longitude...be able to determine the error of the sextant, and to adjust it; also to find the time of high water from the known time at full and change.*[59]

The master candidate had to meet the mate's qualifications as well as "be able to find the latitude by a star" and answer questions about "the nature of the attraction of the ship's iron upon the compass" and how to determine it. He was also examined on "the laws of the tides" in order to show that he could "shape a course, and...compare his soundings with the depths marked on the charts."[60] We do not know for certain what form instruction took — how much time was spent in a classroom, how much, if any, on board a ship — and what the balance was between practical and theoretical content. The textbook prepared for candidates instructed them in specific skills such as how to adjust and use a sextant, without going into the theoretical basis of angular measurement of altitude as a way of determining position.[61]

Until 1883, this certification process only applied to officers destined for ocean-going ships. At that time it was extended to include Canadian vessels plying inland waters,[62] perhaps indicating the government's belief that certification had improved safety and efficiency in the ocean trade and, as a result, was seen as a possible remedy to growing problems with traffic inland, especially on the Great Lakes. It is even possible that the loss of the steamer *Asia* with about 120 people in Georgian Bay the previous year had something to do with the timing of this extension.

Although it did not provide any indication of where the examinations were given and on what subjects the candidates were tested, the departmental report of Marine and Fisheries for 1883 to 1884 indicated that mariners could be awarded either certificates of service or certificates of competency. The former cost less and many more were awarded, but it seems that candidates were tested in some way, which was not the case with certificates of service for ocean-going vessels. During this fiscal year, the department awarded 661 inland and coasting masters' certificates of service, 83 certificates of competency, 443 mates' certificates of service, and 13 certificates of competency. In the final category, 18 candidates failed. During the same period, 65 candidates for ocean-going masters' certificates of competency were tested, of whom 56 passed, and of the 127 applicants for mates' certificates of competency, 74 passed. Certificates of service in this category were issued to 14 masters and 12 mates who were "unable or unwilling to undergo examination for certificates of competency," but who had "held situations as masters and mates previous to 1st January, 1870" and could "produce certificates of experience and general good conduct."[63]

Instruments of the Trade: Navigational Instruments, 1800–1900

Technical Advances

With the invention and successful application of the sextant and chronometer in the late eighteenth century, mariners finally had basic solutions to the problem of finding their precise position at sea. Designers, makers, and engineers, therefore, increasingly turned their attention to refining these devices and producing them in larger numbers. They also began to consider the limitations of the navigator's other and much older tools — the compass, log, and lead-line — with a view to improving their performance.

Throughout the nineteenth century there were "no generally adopted changes in principle" in the sextant. Most instrument makers had settled on the vernier scale reader device, which gave more precise readings than the diagonal scale. They gradually reduced the size of sextants "to a frame radius of around 20 cm." As new metals became available, instrument makers began to test different alloys and frame designs to see if they could achieve a better combination of lightness and strength. Among the most popular designs were the lattice frame, modified lattice frame, and "triple circle" frame. Most of the other "innumerable variations in detail" had little or no lasting impact on the device. The same was true of the octant, except that nineteenth-century makers introduced brace frames, which gradually replaced ebony ones.[64]

Like the sextant, the marine chronometer was invented in the mid-eighteenth century but had to be simplified and standardized before it could be made in large numbers and at a cost that made it affordable to most mariners. Various makers contributed to this process of refinement. Pierre Le Roy's work was especially important because he, unlike Harrison, who invented the device, "obtained results not by nullifying defects, but by eliminating them" and reducing the device to its bare essentials. He invented the compensation balance and the first detached escapement.[65]

Englishman Thomas Earnshaw is generally credited with inventing the "spring detent" escapement, though others, including John Arnold, also claimed this achievement. Earnshaw's version of this device survived the test of time. According to Gould, "In spite of all the attempts made by hundreds of highly skilled horologists to devise a better escapement and balance," as late as the 1920s, chronometers with identical escapements and balances were still being made.[66]

The simplification and standardization of chronometer design, along with improved engineering and manufacturing techniques, allowed makers such as Earnshaw and Arnold in the U.K. and Abraham-Louis Breguet and Louis Berthoud in France to produce these devices in significant quantities. This led to a reduction in their high cost and gradually made them more practical instruments for general use at sea.[67] During the nineteenth century, the chronometer and sextant became standard equipment on virtually all ocean-going vessels.

Instrument makers also worked to improve the chronometer's ability to perform in extreme temperatures, which greatly affected the elasticity of the spring mechanism that governed the period of oscillation. Though Earnshaw had included a basic compensation balance in his design, neither it nor those developed by other makers provided "complete temperature compensation." By mid-century, instrument makers had come up with a variety of discontinuous and continuous auxiliary compensation balances that made chronometers run more accurately and thus remain reliable in hot and cold climates.[68]

In the nineteenth century, scientists and instrument makers also finally began to focus serious attention on the problems of determining direction and speed and measuring depth at sea. Mariners had long been aware of the limitations of the tools they routinely used for dead reckoning. The log and sandglass gave only an estimate of speed, and the higher the seas, the more imprecise the measure. Also, two or three crew members had to carry out the task. The first inventors who attempted to improve on this simple method tried to solve both problems at once. They developed

Figure 21. A chronometer representative of those made in the late eighteenth and throughout the nineteenth century. This particular device was made by John Fletcher of London, England, and dates from 1830.
(CSTM1976.0708)

Figure 22. This taffrail log was manufactured by Thomas Walker probably around the mid-nineteenth century. Known as a harpoon log, it was one of many that incorporated improvements on the first mechanical log introduced by Edward Massey, Walker's uncle, in 1802.
(CSTM1977.0392)

a free-running rotator device activated by the motion of the ship through the water and attached to an on-board register that translated the rotations into linear distance. The problem with these instruments was that the wheelwork in the on-board registers did not run freely and so produced inaccurate readings. Inventors, therefore, temporarily gave up the idea of on-board registers in favour of devices in which the register was either linked directly to or made part of the rotator mechanism. This meant that the log still had to be pulled in to be read, but the readings were much more reliable than with earlier designs. Edward Massey introduced the "first commercially successful mechanical log in 1802."[69] It had a separate rotator and register that counted ⅛ of a mile, miles, tens of miles, and, in its final version, hundreds of miles. This type of log, which provided "impressively accurate" readings, was popular with mariners throughout the century,[70] and Massey's basic design was copied and improved by a variety of makers including his nephew Thomas Walker. Walker's harpoon log of 1861 was a one-unit device in which the register and dials were part of an outer casing that covered the rotator.[71]

By the late 1870s, "engineering development had reached the stage where revolutions of the rotator astern could be transmitted accurately to a register inboard without distortion by friction."[72] As a consequence, makers began to introduce the first logs that could be read without hauling the rotator in from the water. In 1878, Thomas Ferdinand Walker, son of Thomas Walker, produced his taffrail log, which had its register mounted on the stern of the ship. He followed this up with several other models, many of which became very popular in Britain. Other makers in Britain, Europe, and the United States contributed similar devices that both improved the accuracy of speed measurement and reduced the resources required and the risk involved in carrying out the measurement.[73]

The lead and line, the oldest of all navigational devices, gave a reasonably accurate depth reading, but the process of throwing it, hauling it in, and reading the depth off the line was time-consuming, and the ship had to stop for the duration of the operation. In an attempt to solve these problems, inventors developed two main types of mechanical sounding devices in the nineteenth century. The first functioned like the mechanical log, with a rotator and counting mechanism that registered the distance the lead fell through the water. Edward Massey once again was one of the first makers to enter the field, patenting a mechanical sounder in 1802 in which the lead, rotator, and counter were all connected directly together. Other makers improved on this design by, among other things, separating the sounding device from the lead and locking the rotator when it was being hauled in to maintain the accuracy of the measurement. There were also sounders that measured depth as they were hauled in. With all of these, crewmen had to ensure that they followed as straight a course as possible to the bottom in order to obtain an accurate depth reading.

Later in the century, inventors introduced devices that used water pressure as a means of measuring depth. In most of these devices, the first of which was patented in 1835 by the American John Ericsson, water was forced into a glass tube as the mechanism descended through the water. In some, like the Ericsson sounder, the level of water forced into the tube against the pressure of the air gave the necessary measurement.[74] In a later version invented by William Thomson in 1876, the tube was coated with a chemical that discoloured as the water came in contact with it. The length of discolouration was then compared to a boxwood scale that gave the corresponding depth in fathoms.[75] Other models used a ground glass tube that became clear when wet. One significant advantage of these sounders was that, unlike earlier mechanical sounders that measured depth by the distance the device travelled through the water, the path of descent of the instrument had no impact on the reading because it was based on the measurement of water pressure. Various versions of these pressure-activated sounders became popular by the late nineteenth century — the Royal Navy favoured the Thomson device while the U.S. Navy used one made by Tanner-Bilsch — and remained in use until the development and adoption of echo sounding techniques after 1900.[76]

Mariners had been using the magnetic compass since about the thirteenth century and had gradually become aware of its limitations. Although they had found ways of compensating for the effects of magnetic variation, a new problem — magnetic deviation — arose with the increasing use of iron and steel in shipbuilding. In the early years of the nineteenth century, Matthew Flinders found that even the ironwork in a wooden ship could exert enough attractive force to throw off the ship's compass. To neutralize this force he placed an unmagnetized iron rod — a Flinders Bar — in a vertical position near the compass. Neutralizing iron- and steel-hulled ships, as G. B. Airy demonstrated, demanded not just Flinders Bars but a series of magnets and unmagnetized iron positioned near the compass. This principle was carried further by William Thomson, who in the 1870s designed a binnacle to which all the correcting magnets and iron could be attached in a permanent but adjustable manner. This binnacle was "the ancestor of all well-designed binnacles" that followed it.[77]

A second problem that had long plagued mariners was how to keep the compass stable long enough to get an accurate reading. Suspending the device in gimbals had helped, but there was still room for improvement.

William Thomson's answer to the problem was a dry card compass made with thin rice paper secured to an aluminum ring. Though light, it was larger in diameter than the existing Admiralty standard and thus had "a large amount of inertia about its vibration," making it a steady card.[78] Thomson's device was popular with British mariners in both the Royal Navy and the merchant service and was "still favoured" at the end of the nineteenth century.[79] It was not without competition, however, from the liquid compass. In these devices the card was immersed in a liquid, usually a combination of alcohol and water, making both the card and the needle buoyant and "damping down the swing of the card." First introduced in Britain and the United States around mid-century, liquid compasses were generally steadier than their dry counterparts, especially in rough weather, and were not nearly as susceptible to such disturbances as engine vibration, weapon firing, and high-speed buffeting. They were, however, more difficult to maintain than dry card compasses.[80]

The Instrument Trade in Canada

With marine trade and traffic growing steadily in Canada over the course of the nineteenth century, it seems reasonable to assume that there was a corresponding increase in demand for navigational instruments. Evidence of this increase, however, is difficult to find. There seem to be few, if any, records showing how mariners or shipping companies equipped their vessels or where they purchased the necessary devices. The only information we have that offers some indication of the level of demand for shipboard navigational devices is the existence of instrument dealers in Canadian port cities. But even this evidence is far from complete or conclusive.

Instrument dealers would seem to be a natural outgrowth of the shipping economy and, thus, a predictable fixture in any active port city. The more active the port, the more likely there would be a thriving trade in nautical devices. This, however, does not seem to have been the case. Based on information found — and not found — in the Atlantic Canada Newspaper Survey and a variety of city and provincial directories, instrument dealers do not appear to have played a prominent role in port economies during the nineteenth century.[81] Although there were instrument dealers in cities such as Halifax, Saint John, St John's, Québec, Montréal, and Toronto, there is little reliable evidence to suggest that their numbers or their trade grew along with the level of shipping activity.

According to the sources, there was no marked increase in the number of businesses listed as selling nautical equipment in any of the cities in question. Halifax had the largest and most consistent list of businesses dealing in navigational instruments, with entries from the 1860s to the 1890s and a high number of six separate enterprises under the heading "Nautical Instruments." Several of these same businesses were also listed as "Chronometer Raters." Saint John had a smaller number of similar businesses listed between 1857 and 1881 and at least one clock and watchmaker who "repaired and warranted" nautical instruments. But by 1891 there was no longer a category for chronometer raters or nautical instruments.

In Québec, the first specifically nautical entry appeared in 1857. Robert Neill was listed under "Chronometer Depot," and he advertised that he would clean, repair, and rate chronometers by astronomical observations and a transit clock. His shop also boasted "a well-assorted stock of nautical instruments." By 1872–73 there were two different businesses listed under the "Chronometer Depot" heading, and in 1882–83 and 1889–90 just one, owned by Archibald McCallum, who, in addition to handling chronometers, sold maps, charts, and nautical books. In Montréal, meanwhile, the closest category to these was "Mathematical Instruments," which appeared in 1872–73 and 1892–93. Only one business, Hearn and Harrison, was listed in both years, and they are known to have dealt in navigational instruments.

There were not many directories available for St John's, Newfoundland, and there was only one listing in 1890 that suggested nautical equipment sales. It was for M. Fenelon & Co., a firm that sold maps and charts and was also listed under the heading "Watches, Clocks and Jewellery." Toronto had a few entries under "Mathematical Instruments" in 1856, 1874, and 1896, including Hearn and Potter. Yarmouth, Kingston, and Victoria listings had no separate headings for nautical or mathematical instruments. For all of these centres, there were many more names included under such categories as jewellers and watch and clockmakers, but it is hard to tell how many, if any, might have been involved in the instrument trade.

We also know very little about how much trade these various enterprises did or how successful they were over the long term. Halifax and Saint John seemed to support a least a few businesses through several decades — Cogswell, Cornelius and Creighton in Halifax and Hutchinson and Mills in Saint John.[82] According to at least one source, Charles Potter of Toronto enjoyed a growing demand for the instruments and Admiralty charts he sold in the late 1860s.[83] Yet even the more prosperous and enduring instrument dealers could not make a living working in this specialized trade. They all seem to have had other lines of work and other merchandise for sale, usually, but not exclusively, watches, clocks, and jewellery, surveying or other precision devices, maps, charts, stationery, and nautical books. The Atlantic Canada Newspaper Survey confirms this basic assertion. The vast majority of entries dealing with navigational instruments and devices appear in notices of, or advertisements for, sales of the contents of various ships, usually originating in Britain. Here, compasses, sextants, and quadrants are sold along with the rest of the ship's equipment — such things as sails, anchors, ropes, boats — or as part of its cargo, which might include dry goods, fish, liquor, silver plate, or stationery.[84]

Moreover, even among businesses involved specifically in the instrument trade, only one or two are known to have manufactured some of their own products. Richard Upham Marsters (1787 to 1845) of Halifax was the first "Canadian" to build "the most complex and delicate" of navigational instruments, a marine chronometer. Shortly after accomplishing this "considerable" feat, he set up a transit observatory so he could rate chronometers, which were becoming increasingly common.[85] By this time, Royal Navy ships were carrying two chronometers each, and larger and better-equipped merchant vessels generally had at least one. Charles Potter also seems to have made instruments in Toronto between the 1850s and the 1890s, although the compasses and sextants he offered for sale were probably only assembled, finished, and adjusted, not actually made by him. Similarly, Gustav Schulze (late Schulz) of Halifax was listed in city directories as a watch and chronometer maker in 1888–89 but was most likely "assembling imported parts or making replacement parts for instruments he was repairing." Most of the other entrepreneurs who offered navigational instruments for sale, and even some who claimed to be makers, were, at most, assembling their devices from imported parts. It seems likely that many were not even doing that but instead were ordering their goods wholesale from established English or European makers and attaching their own company label to them.[86]

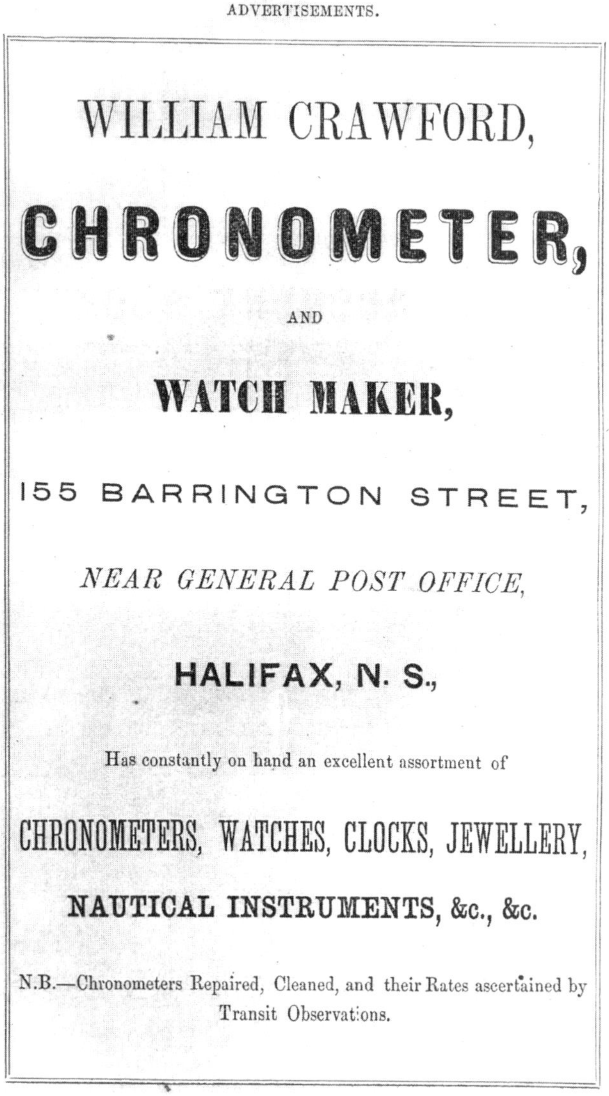
ADVERTISEMENTS.

WILLIAM CRAWFORD,

CHRONOMETER,

AND

WATCH MAKER,

155 BARRINGTON STREET,

NEAR GENERAL POST OFFICE,

HALIFAX, N. S.,

Has constantly on hand an excellent assortment of

CHRONOMETERS, WATCHES, CLOCKS, JEWELLERY,

NAUTICAL INSTRUMENTS, &c., &c.

N.B.—Chronometers Repaired, Cleaned, and their Rates ascertained by Transit Observations.

Figure 23. *An advertisement from* Hutchinson's Nova Scotia Directory for 1864–65 *for William Crawford, a chronometer maker and dealer in nautical instruments in Halifax.*

We can only speculate about why the instrument trade was so marginal in the major ports and shipbuilding centres of British North America and Canada. One obvious factor was the easy access Canadian mariners had to British instruments. London was the uncontested centre of the international instrument trade and as such offered a large supply of the latest and best equipment at competitive prices. Canadian precision manufacturing capacity, on the other hand, was very limited, and the few dealers who were building instruments would no doubt have found it hard to make a name for themselves in the business. Many mariners engaged in the transatlantic trade probably chose to buy their navigational devices in Britain, and if they were making regular trips, they may also have had them repaired and maintained there whenever possible. Committed customers of London makers might only have turned to Canadian dealers for emergency repairs or rating.

British North American shipping companies, though, were also deeply involved in coastal and West Indian trade, and the captains and owners of these ships would not have had such easy access to the British instrument market. Yet they do not seem to have relied heavily on Canadian dealers to supply their needs. It is possible that they bought their instruments and had them serviced in major American ports such as Boston and New York, which had developed a thriving domestic instrument-making industry as a result of trade barriers that restricted access to British goods. The dealers in these cities perhaps offered greater selection, more competitive prices, and easier access than the scattered handful of generalist tradesmen based in British North America's ports.

Although Canadian maritime trade and shipbuilding grew enormously over the century, the nation's close links with Britain seem to have made it unnecessary and uneconomic for domestic entrepreneurs to provide certain specialized types of infrastructure. Thus, while a port like Yarmouth, Nova Scotia, which produced hundreds of ships, could and did support countless shipbuilding-related businesses, in 1868–69 there was not one instrument dealer listed in the local directory. The same was true of Kingston, Ontario, in 1862–63, despite the presence of a variety of shipbuilding enterprises in the area.[87]

Finding the Way to Market: Charting Canada's Primary Shipping Routes

Because Canada has the longest coastline and most fresh water of any country in the world, charting her navigable waters in the nineteenth century was an enormous and costly task. Prior to 1800, only a few areas had been systematically surveyed by the Royal Navy — places the British government regarded as important, either strategically or commercially. During and immediately after the Napoleonic Wars and the War of 1812, however, Canada's waters suddenly became more interesting to Britain. Its interest was partly the result of legitimate concerns about American expansionist intentions toward Canada. British claims on the west coast and in the north were not internationally recognized, and the United States maintained a significant armed presence on the Great Lakes and St Lawrence. As well, the east coast fishery was a frequent source of Anglo-American tension. At the same time, the cessation of hostilities in Europe left the Royal Navy with a wartime complement of ships, officers, and men without much to do. Talented and ambitious officers, in particular, needed to find new ways to demonstrate their skills in order to gain promotion.[88] Hydrography, which had brought Cook, Vancouver, and others to the attention of superior officers and for which many naval officers were at least partially trained, was one obvious outlet for those seeking ships to command.

Canadian hydrography benefited greatly from this coincidence of factors. The governments of the British North American colonies and, later, Canada understood the critical importance of charting. They knew that ongoing settlement and trade were largely dependent on safe marine transportation and that this required a systematic approach to navigational aids. They all had made some effort to mark coastal hazards and regulate pilotage, even before the turn of the century. But charting was another matter altogether. Professional hydrographical mapping required a high level of scientific knowledge and skill, precision surveying equipment, well-manned and -equipped vessels, and a great deal of time, especially given the short working season in much of the country. With limited funds and expertise at their disposal, the colonies could not have undertaken such a massive survey themselves.

Prior to 1800, marine surveying and chart-making was a less-than-systematic discipline. The standards that governed it were essentially those established by the collective experience and work of previous generations of mariners, hydrographers, and chartmakers. Mariners prized thoroughness and accuracy — in general, the more plentiful and closely spaced the soundings, the more accurate the chart was judged to be — but they also demanded clarity and did not want non-essential information cluttering up the document. When approaching shore or entering harbour, they needed large-scale charts that depicted small areas in great detail and, to ensure effective use of all their charts, they wanted sheets that fit easily on their chart tables. As a result, certain sizes became most common, if not exactly standard, notably 38 × 25 inches (96.5 × 63.5 cm) for large charts and half that size for smaller ones. This standardization also made life easier for the engravers and printers of charts, who could work with a few basic sizes of plates and paper.[89] Other than these practical requirements, and the long-standing procedures for the proper and precise use of the marine surveyor's instruments, there seem to have been few hard and fast rules about how to make a good chart.

These conventions, for the most part, remained in place throughout the nineteenth century but were gradually refined and adapted to suit the changing needs of mariners. During this period, the hydrographical services of nations such as Britain, France, and the United States began to take a more systematic approach to charting. They collected and organized existing charts, commissioned new surveys of uncharted or poorly charted waters, and published information to supplement or update that included on existing charts. The British Admiralty took a leading role in this process and by 1850 was responsible for producing, revising, reproducing, and publishing hundreds of charts of waters around the world as well as the *Nautical Magazine*, *Notices to Mariners*, and the *Admiralty Manual of Scientific Enquiry*, a navigational guide for naval officers and travellers that included a "Plate to illustrate Hydrographic delineation."[90]

This work and the work of other national hydrographical authorities was complemented by the compilation and publication of sailing directions and coastal guides for many of the world's shorelines and harbours. Throughout the nineteenth century, authors Edmund March Blunt, James Imray, and John Nories, to mention only a few, produced guides to the waters of much of North America. Like the pilot books of earlier centuries, these publications were filled with detailed descriptions of local coasts and waters and information about unique local conditions and traditions that might have an impact on navigation. In addition, these modern versions contained valuable scientific data — tide and astronomical tables, for example — as well as general advice on the use of instruments and on sound navigational practice. They also explained the variations in chart symbols and in seamarking from country to country, which helped mariners interpret unfamiliar charts and coastal markers more effectively. Whether he wanted to know about the local tidal flow or the meaning of a particular light, the mariner could turn to a good coastal pilot book for the area for the necessary details. Judging by the number of editions published just by the authors mentioned, these books were in great demand for many years.[91]

All this charting and charting-related activity, however, did not produce uniform standards, formats, or practices in chart-making. In the decades before and after 1800, certain nautical symbols had come into common use on British and European charts, and many of these were adopted by other nations when they established hydrographic services over the course of the century. During this same period, though, French hydrographers adopted a new measurement scheme — the metric system (1840) — and Hugh Godfray introduced a new projection — the gnomic projection (1858) — which was especially useful in depicting the polar regions that were so badly distorted by Mercator's projection. Similarly, as demand for "modestly priced" charts increased, the British Admiralty decided to abandon the traditional but time-consuming practice of using colour to give depth and dimension to chart features, replacing it with "varying styles of engraved lines" to add shading, contouring, and detail.[92]

Moreover, over the course of the nineteenth century, established notions of thoroughness and accuracy gradually gave way to more exacting standards. For example, as more and more shipping companies adopted steam-propelled vessels, mariners were encouraged to take advantage of the flexibility this form of propulsion offered to shorten their runs. They travelled closer to shore and often cut corners along routes originally established for much less manoeuvrable sailing vessels. Most charts, however, were drawn with sail in mind and did not include many details of the depths and hazards nearer to shore. A number of steamships were grounded or wrecked on uncharted rocks or shoals before hydrographers revised their methods to accommodate steam navigation.

Though the British Admiralty began systematic hydrographical work in what is now Canada in the eighteenth century and only carried out its last survey off Labrador in the 1930s, its most significant contributions were made between about 1815 and 1870. During this period, Royal Navy expeditions surveyed and, in some cases, re-surveyed the Atlantic coast and Newfoundland, the St Lawrence River and Gulf, the four Canadian Great Lakes, the Pacific coast, and a large portion of the Arctic archipelago as well as numerous colonial harbours. In each of these areas, the Admiralty and the colonial and British governments had a variety of motivations and objectives, but their primary concerns tended to be strategic and commercial.

The first series of hydrographical surveys actually began before 1815, when Francis Owen charted St John's and other coastal areas of eastern Newfoundland in 1800 to 1801. This work was carried on after the war by George Holbrook (1814 to 1820), John Hose (1821 to 1823), and Frederick Bullock (1823 to 1826), who by 1827 had completed an extensive survey of most of the east coast of the island. Newfoundland also received some attention from Henry Bayfield's staff, who at the time were working on a survey of the Gulf of St Lawrence. Between 1852 and 1864, John Orlebar surveyed a large portion of the south coast and Avalon Peninsula. The following year, the Admiralty ordered a "thorough resurvey" of Newfoundland and placed James Kerr and, later, William Maxwell in charge of it. When William Tooker relieved Maxwell in 1891, he focused his attention on the west and Labrador coasts. The Admiralty also sent a surveyor, Anthony Lockwood, to Nova Scotia in 1813, and he spent about five years completing his work on the colony's coastal waters. In 1818 he published a book of charts for Nova Scotia ports and a chart for New Brunswick.[93]

Perhaps the most ambitious hydrographical project initiated by the Admiralty in the immediate aftermath of the War of 1812 was the Great Lakes and St Lawrence survey. The survey was started as part of a British government strategy to deal with the pressing problems of boundary disputes and American military buildup on the Great Lakes. After just two years, though, it was transformed into a long-term scheme to help ensure safe and efficient commercial shipping in British North America.

In 1815, the Admiralty sent William Fitzwilliam Owen to the Canadas to carry out several "urgent tasks," among them identifying a suitable site for a naval base and researching and locating the site of the international boundary at various places along the waterway. He followed up this preliminary work by establishing a plan for the "deliberate scientific surveying of the St Lawrence River and the Great Lakes."[94] Despite Owen's arrest and detention at Detroit, that survey began in February 1816. Working for the first two months in harsh winter conditions, the teams nevertheless completed their work on Lake Ontario and down the St Lawrence to Prescott by the fall of that year. In 1817, Owen and his men completed their survey of the Niagara River and were about to begin charting Lake Erie when the Admiralty's priorities suddenly changed. In late April the British and American governments signed the Rush-Bagot Treaty, which brought an end to the armed buildup by strictly limiting the number of ships each country could have on the lakes. Owen was recalled to London in June, and the hydrographical establishment was severely reduced and placed under the direction of one of Owen's promising young assistants, the twenty-two-year-old Henry Wolsey Bayfield.[95]

Bayfield soon distinguished himself as a dedicated, determined, and meticulously professional hydrographer. Though strategic concerns had fallen into the background and the Admiralty no longer saw the lakes as a major priority, Bayfield took his new appointment very seriously. He knew that the need for charts of the upper Great Lakes was acute and would only increase with immigration and settlement. He therefore threw himself into his work, completing the survey of Lake Erie in one season (1817–18) using just two boats and with the help of one inexperienced assistant, Philip Collins. In 1819 he moved on to Lake Huron, where he and Collins spent four seasons charting the intricate and island-strewn coastlines. Living under the very roughest conditions, they carefully recorded twenty thousand islands and many more rocks, shoals, and other hazards as well as countless coves and inlets. The following season, 1823, they entered Lake Superior, set up a winter base at Fort William, and began the arduous task of circumnavigating the largest freshwater lake in the world. Over the course of three more fly- and mosquito-infested summers, the two men surveyed the whole shoreline of the huge lake, including "all its bays and coastal islands." Returning to England in 1825, Bayfield "spent nearly two years completing the charts of the three lakes, annotating them with comments on coastal features and geological formations." He then constructed additional charts of the waters connecting the lakes as well as some harbours.[96]

Bayfield also found time to convince the Admiralty that the existing surveys of the St Lawrence River and Gulf made by DesBarres and Holland in the 1770s were inadequate to present-day needs. He argued that they contained errors that "had led to numerous shipwrecks with great loss of life,"[97] and that the advent of steamships and general increase in traffic to and from the colonies only added to the dangers of this treacherous route. Bayfield was appointed superintendent of the St Lawrence survey and spent the next fourteen years charting the river, gulf, and surrounding areas, including the whole north shore, Lac Saint-Pierre, Québec and Montréal harbours, the Belle Isle coasts of both Labrador and Newfoundland as well as the Strait itself, various St Lawrence islands, the New Brunswick coast of Northumberland Strait, three New Brunswick rivers, and many harbours along all these coasts. Bayfield also set a demanding standard for plotting and recording all this data before sending it to Britain to be engraved and printed.[98]

Bayfield had a larger and better-equipped establishment for the St Lawrence survey. As with his earlier projects, though, he and his men had to work long hours in harsh conditions to compete their task. They were plagued by bugs and inclement weather and were even stranded for five days by a storm. The greatest hardship they endured, however, was the tragic drowning death of Lieutenant Collins while surveying Îles de la Madeleine in 1835.[99]

Figure 24. *Henry Wolsey Bayfield, Royal Navy hydrographer. Bayfield spent most of his distinguished career in Canada and was responsible for surveying and charting all the Canadian Great Lakes as well as the St Lawrence River.* (Library and Archives Canada, neg. C-001228)

Bayfield moved his headquarters from Québec to Charlottetown in 1841 to work on the coastlines of Prince Edward Island and Nova Scotia. By the mid-1850s, he and his staff of three assistants had surveyed all of P.E.I.'s complex coastline, the coasts and harbours of Cape Breton Island, and much of the coast of Nova Scotia, including Halifax Harbour. He also confirmed the precise position of Sable Island for the Admiralty and advised them on the placement of a lighthouse there to mark it. He worked with Owen, who was then charting the Bay of Fundy, to connect their respective surveys, using rockets to measure distance across the Nova Scotia isthmus, and still managed to revise and prepare for publication several instalments of his *Sailing Directions for the Gulf and River of St. Lawrence*. These were later published in their entirety as *The St. Lawrence Pilot*. He followed this up with *The Nova Scotia Pilot*, which was published in two parts in 1856 and 1860.[100]

When he was finally forced to retire due to ill health in 1856, Henry Bayfield knew more about the navigable waters and coastlines of British North America than most Canadians will ever know. And he did more than anyone to make that knowledge available to the people who most needed it. Over 50 percent of the

Map 4. *A map of Lake Huron made from a survey by Henry Bayfield in 1819, 1820, and 1822. Though not an actual chart, this map gives a good indication of how accurate Bayfield's surveys were.*
(Library and Archives Canada, neg. NMC 0021705)

total number of pre-1867 Admiralty charts of Canadian waters were either entirely or partly attributed to Bayfield. There were, in fact, "few sections along the main steamer routes between Halifax, N.S. and Fort William in Lake Superior that he had not had a hand in charting."[101]

By modern standards, Bayfield's hydrographical instruments and techniques were primitive. He used chronometers and a sextant to take longitude and latitude,[102] a lead and line to sound inshore areas, and a patent sounding machine in deeper offshore areas. To measure coastal features he employed triangulation and the theodolite, much as Vancouver had done sixty years earlier on the west coast. Yet Bayfield's surveys and charts, for all their limitations, served mariners well for over half a century. They not only "guided innumerable ships through the treacherous waters of the St. Lawrence system," but also laid a solid foundation for his Canadian successors.[103]

The Admiralty's second and much less pressing strategic concern in North America after 1815 was the Arctic. British interest in the region dated back to the sixteenth and seventeenth centuries, when a series of English explorers had laid claim to much of the eastern Arctic while pursuing the search for the Northwest Passage. Since the eighteenth century, though, apart from the presence of the Hudson's Bay Company and Cook's landing in the far west, Britain had done little to assert her claims to the region. With the demobilization of the navy and the apparent interest of Russia and the United States in the western Arctic, the Admiralty was convinced to renew a search that many felt had never really been completed. If the Northwest Passage existed, it was clearly in Britain's strategic and commercial interests to find it, chart it, and exploit it before someone else did. With the help of the Royal Society, the Admiralty even persuaded Parliament in 1818 that Arctic exploration — for the passage and the North Pole — was important enough to warrant the "offering of substantial rewards."[104]

Over the next ten years the Royal Navy mounted a series of Arctic expeditions aimed at exploring and charting the Arctic Archipelago. Despite the hardships of northern travel, the navy had no trouble finding officers to lead these voyages, since some of its most accomplished mariners were also ambitious men who welcomed any opportunity to distinguish themselves and to command ships and men. John Ross, Edward Parry, John Franklin, and Frederick Beechey were among the many British officers who left their names and their mark on Canada's north. Their strategy was to work from the known coastlines of the Arctic — Baffin Bay and Hudson Strait in the east, the Coppermine and Mackenzie rivers in the south, and the Bering Strait in the west — filling in the gaps and, eventually, tracing a route across from Atlantic to Pacific.[105]

Although these voyages added important pieces to the Arctic coastline puzzle,[106] recorded a vast amount of navigational information such as currents, tides, ice formations, and magnetic variation, and developed some important new techniques for navigating in icy waters, they all failed to reach their objectives. The going was much harder and the progress much slower than anyone had anticipated, all of which seemed to demonstrate that any passage that might be found would be too inaccessible and treacherous to be viable. Given this realization and the apparent decline of Russian ambitions in the north, both the Admiralty and the government lost interest in the quest. In 1828 the prizes for Arctic discovery were cancelled.[107]

Arctic exploration, however, did not end. British mariners funded by private individuals and companies or other organizations continued the search. Increasingly that search focused on the Boothia Peninsula region. Beginning in 1829, John Ross and his nephew James Clark Ross spent four years exploring the area and recorded some important firsts. They were the first to use steam propulsion in the Arctic, and the first to abandon it. They identified the location of the north magnetic pole and made the first mainland landfall. John Ross produced a chart based on this journey which indicated that Boothia (named in honour of the voyage's patron, Felix Booth) was indeed a peninsula.

George Back, meanwhile, travelled overland, eventually journeying down and mapping the river that now bears his name. Upon reaching the coast, Back emerged just west of the Boothia Peninsula and thus added another critical point of reference to the Arctic shoreline. He proved that the river route to the area was faster than the ocean passage, but, unfortunately, perpetuated and reinforced the erroneous belief that Boothia was an island with a passable strait at its base. Thomas Simpson of the Hudson's Bay Company, who had earlier traced the mainland coastline of the Beaufort Sea from Cape Barrow to Cape Bathurst,[108] made his way to Boothia from the western Arctic via boat and coastal lands in 1838–39, adding significant detail to the existing maps of the area.[109]

Convinced that British mariners had now accumulated enough knowledge and expertise to make the final step through the passage a "simple" one, the Admiralty decided to mount one more elaborate deep-sea expedition.[110] Commanded by the sixty-year-old Franklin, the 1845 expedition ended in tragic failure, but in twenty-five searches for the lost ships and men, British explorers filled in many of the remaining gaps in the intricate and ice-covered coastline of the archipelago. William Pullen, for example, completed

Map 5. *This Gall and Inglis map of the Canadian Arctic shows how much explorers had accomplished by 1850 and how much territory remained partially or totally uncharted.*

(Library and Archives Canada, neg. NMC 0044425)

"the British survey of the western part of Canada's northern coast" when he reached the Mackenzie River via the Alaskan coast in 1849, and George Richards, in the winter of 1852, "made an epic 95-day sledge journey to search and survey the islands and channels to the north of Melville Sound."[111] In 1853 the Northwest Passage was completed when Henry Kellet, approaching from the Pacific, met Robert M'Clure, who had come via the Atlantic, at Mercy Bay.[112] By 1859, searchers had collected enough physical and oral evidence to determine definitively the fate of the Franklin expedition. Of more lasting importance, they had mapped most of the coastlines and islands except those in the very far north and northwest and had learned about and documented many of the problems associated with navigating in the Arctic environment.[113]

The last major focus of Admiralty hydrographers was the Pacific coast of British North America. Like the Arctic and the Great Lakes, the original impetus was strategic. Until the 1840s, the British had seen no need to redo Vancouver's surveys, especially since, besides the Hudson's Bay Company and its employees, there were as yet very few settlers and little commercial activity in the region. When the Americans began making noises about taking control of the whole Pacific coast in 1844, Britain sent a naval force to the area to secure her interests and then to identify and survey the border. Two of the six ships were survey vessels, and their commanders, Henry Kellett and James Wood, were ordered in 1846 to chart the border area including the Strait of Juan de Fuca, Victoria and Esquimalt harbours, and anchorages at Fort San Juan,

Neah Bay, Port Townsend, and Becher, Pedder and Cordova bays.[114]

As on the Great Lakes, the immediate danger passed quickly, as a boundary settlement was reached later in 1846, but tensions, fuelled in part by competition for fur and other resources, remained high. The Royal Navy therefore maintained a noticeable presence in the tiny colony of Vancouver Island and, as part of their duties, the officers began re-surveying the intricate coastline. When gold was discovered in the Queen Charlotte Islands in 1853–54, they focused their attention there while, at the same time, the Hudson's Bay Company began work around Nanaimo and Departure Bay to facilitate movement of the coal that had been found there.

In 1857, a new crisis threatened to erupt over a controversial section of the international border running through the San Juan Islands. The ongoing dispute was particularly worrying given the fact that the gold rush in the southern interior of British Columbia was attracting hundreds of American prospectors. As part of the work of the Boundary Commission, George Richards undertook a thorough survey of all the coastlines and channels in the vicinity of the disputed islands. Unfortunately, expert hydrography by itself could not solve the problem, and the two parties had to refer the decision to a non-expert outsider, Kaiser Wilhelm of Germany, who, in 1872, upheld the American claim.[115]

Once the boundary project was finished, the Royal Navy shifted its priorities. In 1859, it sent Richards and his ships to the Fraser River as a show of force to keep the American "invaders" in line. This allowed the officers to map much of the river, but it delayed the start of their assigned work, which was a "survey of the Gulf of Georgia and the harbours of Vancouver's Island according to their importance."[116] This they finally began in 1860, and by 1863 they had completed the survey of Vancouver Island and parts of the mainland coast. For the next eight years, Daniel Pender, who had succeeded Richards, worked to complete the survey of the remaining coasts, including the islands north of the main island and "the inner ship-channels of communication as far as the northern boundary of British Columbia." He also completed "many large scale surveys of anchorages."[117]

Canada took control of its coasts and waterways at the time of Confederation, and the newly formed Department of Marine and Fisheries was given responsibility for most matters relating to oceans, waterways, marine transportation, and fisheries. Its mandate, however, did not extend to hydrography, which the federal government felt ill-equipped to handle and did not see as a priority in any case. After all, the Admiralty had done an expert job surveying all the major transportation routes and publishing the necessary charts, the latest of which were just ten years old. Moreover, Britain, with its strong belief in naval supremacy, was anxious — at least in theory — to retain responsibility for surveying the waters off its dominions and colonies,[118] so there seemed no good reason to build a separate hydrographic establishment.

By the 1880s, however, it was becoming clear that existing Admiralty charts were no longer sufficient to ensure safe and reliable marine transportation. The advent and gradual adoption of steam propulsion and the propeller by shipbuilders and owners had profoundly altered shipping. Nowhere was this change more noticeable than on the Great Lakes and St Lawrence system, where by the 1870s larger iron-hulled freighters and carriers of deep draft proliferated along with settlement, commercial development, and trade. Under most conditions, these steam-driven vessels were faster than sailing ships. They were also easier to control, so mariners could and did manoeuvre them closer to shore. According to one informed observer, since the "paying capabilities" of these ships depended on their getting quickly from port to port, the captains were all too willing to "take every practicable shortcut that offers, and shave round capes and corners in a manner much to be deprecated, but which will continue as long as utility is the object."[119]

The problems posed by steam navigation became tragically apparent in 1882 when the passenger steamer *Asia* sank in a storm in Georgian Bay, claiming 150 people. Preceded by numerous much smaller mishaps in the area, this wreck received such wide public attention that, like the *Titanic* disaster thirty years later, it helped to prod the government into immediate action. Though the ship did not founder on an uncharted shoal, as the company had tried to claim, the investigation into its loss made it clear that there were many such shoals and other hazards that did not appear on the Bayfield charts. Either they were deemed to be too close to shore to warrant inclusion on charts intended mainly for sailing ships or they were simply overlooked. In any event, in 1883, the federal government decided that the area needed to be re-surveyed and created the Georgian Bay Survey, precursor to the Canadian Hydrographic Service, to carry out the task. In the absence of any suitably skilled Canadian candidates, the government, on the advice of the Admiralty, appointed Staff Commander John George Boulton, RN, to lead the Georgian Bay Survey. He had extensive hydrographical experience, having worked in Australian and South African waters before spending nine years (1872 to 1881) as assistant to W. F. Maxwell on the Newfoundland Survey. Unhappy with the English posting that followed, he asked repeatedly to be sent back to Canada, and in July 1883, based on Maxwell's recommendation, he was seconded to the Canadian government.[120]

Boulton's mandate was to survey the primary steamship routes between Owen Sound and Sault Sainte Marie and, secondarily, to recruit Canadians and train them as hydrographers. Despite meagre support from the government — he was originally told to reuse parts of Bayfield's charts probably to save money and had to charter his own ship — he managed to accomplish both parts of his mandate. The survey itself took eleven years to complete and cost $250,000, producing thirteen charts and a book of sailing instructions. Fortunately the high cost did not put the government off hydrography, at least in part because they were persuaded that the most difficult and time-consuming work was behind the team. In 1895 they approved the next stage, the Great Lakes Survey, which was directed by the first Canadian chief hydrographer, William Stewart, who had been selected and trained by Boulton. In 1891, Stewart had conducted the first saltwater survey in the history of the Canadian service when he re-surveyed Burrard Inlet and Vancouver harbour after a CPR steamer "touched" an uncharted shoal there. The Canadian government had asked the Admiralty to look into the mishap but they had been too busy to see to it immediately and so, almost inadvertently, Canadians began to assume full control of their coastlines and waters.[121]

The Longest Coastline: Marking Canada's Coastal and Inland Waters

At the turn of the nineteenth century, British North America had only a handful of navigational aids marking its extensive coastal and inland waterways. The Royal Navy had placed some of these aids, and each of the colonies, often with the navy's advice and assistance, had marked a few important locations and notable hazards. But these were token efforts at best, and became increasingly inadequate as settlement and trade expanded and demands for marine transportation grew. Recognizing the need for a more systematic and coherent approach, the colonial governments each set up administrative bodies to develop and maintain a network of navigational aids in their coastal waters. It was these bodies, and later the federal government, that had to decide where markers were needed most and what kind of equipment was required to perform each task. The officials who made these decisions had to consider factors including performance standards, suitability to the local climate, and cost of purchase, installation, and maintenance. With meagre funds at their disposal and a monumental task to complete, they often could not afford to use the latest technology or the most elaborate structures to house it. Instead, the marine authorities tried to find a balance that allowed them to provide sufficient and reliable, if not the very best available, coverage of as many navigable waterways as possible. Once the basic framework of navigational aids was in place, they could then focus more money and attention on upgrading and improving it.

Technological Advances in Navigational Aids

The primary purpose of land-based and coastal aids to navigation is to tell the mariner where he is so that he can adjust his course to make port, avoid a hazard, or find a navigable channel. The mariner has to be able to see the lighthouse, buoy, or range mark, to distinguish it from other similar ones, and to inter-

Figure 25. Bateau Rock, Ontario, late nineteenth century. The survey team have set up a transit on shore to fix the position of the boat while the crew measure the depth of water in each location.
(Library and Archives Canada, neg. e003719335)

pret its meaning. These seamarks also have to be positioned accurately to do their jobs properly and, once in place, have to be monitored and maintained to ensure, among other things, that lamps are lit and visible and buoys remain moored in the correct position. Throughout the nineteenth century, most of the inventive energy of engineers and designers working in this field was, therefore, focused on improving the visibility and versatility of lights for use in lighthouses, lightships, and eventually buoys. They also made progress in enhancing the durability of beacons and buoys and their moorings, and developed fog alarms for use in thick weather when lights could not be seen for any distance. Finally, officials began to consider ways to standardize signals and markings so that mariners knew what they were looking at, even in unfamiliar waters.

Some of the most notable advances in navigational aid technology after 1800 came in the area of lighting. Inventors, especially in France, continued to investigate methods of intensifying, concentrating, and aiming the light given off by oil lamps. In the early years of the century, J. A. Bordier-Marcet developed two reflective or catoptric systems to enhance the capabilities of the simple Argand lamp. The first employed two parabolic reflectors that focused the light of two Argand lamps into a beam that could be seen over a greater distance than an unassisted open light. As a result, this device "won general favour in the French lighthouse service by 1819." Bordier-Marcet's second device, known as "the *fanal sidéral* or star-lantern, utilized two circular reflecting plates, one above and one below the flame, projecting the light in a parabolic curve horizontally."[122] This system "increased the candlepower of an ordinary Argand lamp from 10 to 70 candlepower."[123]

These advances in catoptric or reflective lighting systems, though significant, were gradually superseded by the development of dioptric lenses. Made up of "concentric rings of glass prisms," these precisely cut and ground lenses refracted and bent the light rays from a lantern on "the desired focal plane."[124] In 1823 Augustin Fresnel, another Frenchman, introduced the first such device in a lighthouse at the mouth of the Gironde River. Authorities soon determined that a "dioptric apparatus emitted a light five times the strength of a catoptric" for the same oil consumption and that a much greater proportion of the light reached out to sea.[125] Also, while catoptric devices needed multiple lamps, the new refractive devices used only one light source. Thus, despite the high initial expense of purchasing the precision Fresnel lenses, by the 1850s, countries such as Britain and the United States were following France's lead and installing dioptric lights in many of their lighthouses. By this time they also had a third lighting option, the catadioptric system, in which the refractive

Figure 26. *This wick-type lantern and 24-inch reflector were the front part of a range marker. Ranges consisted of two lights that, when lined up by a ship's navigator, indicated a safe course.*
(Library and Archives Canada, neg. e003719346)

capabilities of dioptric lenses was combined with and enhanced by the use of parabolic reflectors similar to those used in simple catoptric lights.[126]

Authorities categorized dioptric lights according to their size, which also determined how far out to sea they could be seen. The British ranked their lights in six orders while the French used four, with the first order being the largest and most powerful. These lights measured 6 feet (1.8 m) in diameter or had a focal distance of 92 centimetres (half the diameter, or 3 ft) and were generally used for landfall lights. Second-order lights were about 57 inches (1.5 m) across, while third-order lights could be either 39.4 or 29.5 inches (100 or 75 cm) across. The last three orders were just under 20, 15, and 12 inches (50, 40, and 30 cm) in diameter, respectively. The smallest of these lights tended to be harbour lights.[127] There was no specific range assigned to each order, because this varied with the type of lantern and illuminant used and the height and position of the tower in which the light was housed. For example, a very tall first-order light could have a range of as much as 30 miles (48 km), but 15 to 20 miles (24 to 32 km) was a much more common range for these lights. Some second-order lights reached as far as twenty miles out to sea, while many others had ranges of between 12 and 15 miles (19 to 24 km). Similarly, sixth-order lights could have a range anywhere between 4 and 9 miles (6 to 14.5 km).[128]

Inventors also increased the visibility of lighthouses by experimenting with new types of fuels and methods of illumination. In the early years of the century, animal oils such as whale, porpoise, and fish were still commonly used to fuel lanterns. Of these, sperm-whale oil was often preferred because "it burned evenly with a bright light," though if it was "too old or too thick" it gave "a smoky, poor quality flame."[129] Compared to other animal and vegetable oils, however, it became increasingly costly as intense hunting reduced the supply of whales. Some lighthouse authorities therefore chose less expensive alternatives. The French, for example, began using colza or rape-seed oil[130] in the 1840s, which cost about half the price of sperm oil. Though lamps had to burn more of this vegetable oil to achieve "an equivalent effect," as long as they did not need twice as much, it remained the cheaper fuel. After 1845, the British also began to favour this fuel over the brighter burning but more expensive sperm oil.[131]

Another alternative to animal and vegetable fuel was mineral oil. In 1846, Nova Scotian Abraham Gesner devised a method of distilling kerosene from coal. Also known as coal oil or paraffin, this fuel could be produced from oil or bituminous shale and was both cheap and plentiful in North America, especially after the 1859 oil strike in Pennsylvania. It was more volatile than previous fuels and thus required no preheating equipment or pumps to assist capillary action from reservoir to wick. In tests along the St Lawrence River in the early 1860s, Canadian officials found that coal oil provided a much brighter light than sperm oil and was less expensive to use than colza oil. Kerosene, though, needed "much more air to effect proper combustion," and so, initially, was not well suited to use in multi-burner, dioptric lights.[132] Inventors on both sides of the Atlantic came up with various solutions to this problem by 1870, notably flat-wick lamps. These made it possible for lighthouse authorities to convert even dioptric lights to use kerosene, though, according to Canadian instructions to lightkeepers, special care still had to be taken when tending dioptric kerosene lamps.[133]

In the latter half of the nineteenth century, engineers began experimenting with the "incandescent oil vapour" or gas mantle light.[134] Invented by Carl Auer von Welbach in 1885, the incandescent mantle was a fine mesh of cloth that provided a surface upon which vaporized fuel burned, causing it to glow brightly. A variety of European and American inventors improved on this basic principle over the next two decades. In 1898, tests at France's L'Île Penfret lighthouse demonstrated that the gas mantle lamp installed there was significantly more powerful than the wick it had replaced. Improvements continued into the early twentieth century, when this lamp, "the final step in the refinement of the flame," enjoyed its widest application.[135]

During the same period some engineers attempted to use flames from gas jets to illuminate lighthouses. Some significant experiments were conducted after mid-century, including those of John Wigham of Dublin. In 1885 to 1887 he installed a device at Tory Island, Donegal, Ireland, that had a total of 324 gas jets, the light from which was concentrated into a beam every minute by a series of lenses. The apparatus could also give "group flashes" via a mechanism that turned gas on and off continuously. The problem with this and other gas-fuelled lights was the cost of supplying the necessary fuel where there was no local town

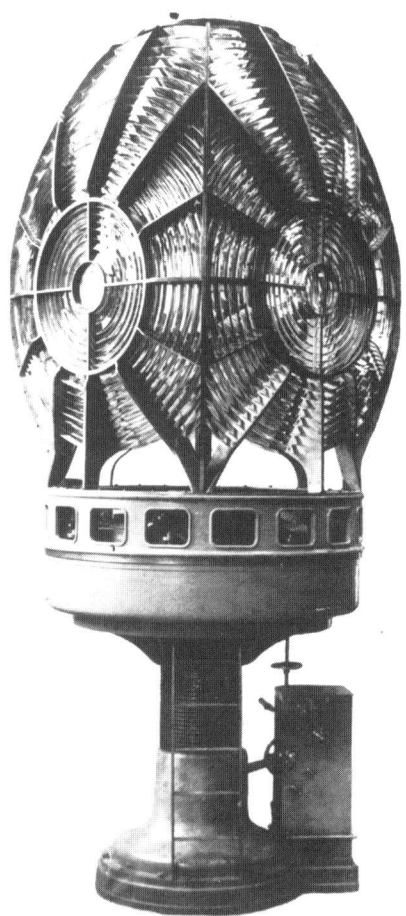

Figure 27. First-order Fresnel lens and single flashing apparatus, Langara Island light, B.C.
(Library and Archives Canada, neg. PA 121757)

supply from which to draw. The fuelling method simply was not cost-effective for most locations in Britain. And even where there was a public supply of fuel, the lighthouse often had to compete with local demand and sometimes the level of illumination suffered as a result.[136]

There were also some attempts to use electric lights and power to illuminate lighthouses in the latter half of the nineteenth century. The basic configuration was electric arc lights powered by either a magneto-electric machine or, later, an electric dynamo. British lighthouse authorities conducted tests in the 1870s to establish which dynamo was best suited to their needs and eventually electrified a few of their stations. The new lights far exceeded all others in brilliance but, like gas installations, the cost of generating the electricity — in equipment, manpower, and fuel to run the steam-driven dynamos — was simply too high to justify widespread application. This did not change until the development of electrical power grids and local power mains in the twentieth century.[137]

With the proliferation of lighthouses and other lights after 1800, marine authorities became increasingly concerned about how to identify them and distinguish one from another. As early as the seventeenth century, some governing bodies began to use multiple lights to set certain towers apart from the standard single fixed white light that was most commonly used. By the mid-eighteenth century, Swedish engineers were experimenting with clockwork mechanisms to make lanterns oscillate according to a recognizable pattern. In 1781, one of these men, Jonas Norberg, "installed the first revolving light in the world at Carlsten on the west coast of Sweden." Within ten years both the British and French lighthouse authorities had adopted revolving lights for many of their more important sites. In these installations, the lanterns were turned by weight-driven rotary gearing systems, and the period of rotation could be adjusted to help distinguish one revolving light from another. After 1800, engineers refined and enhanced this basic system, developing different gearing mechanisms and offering a variety of light sequences — flashing lights displayed longer periods of darkness than light and occulting lights the opposite — to identify specific lighthouses.[138]

The primary problem with the various revolving light systems was the buildup of friction between the rollers on which the lanterns were mounted and the raceway around which these rollers moved. This limited both the size of the lights that could be made to rotate and the speed at which they could turn. Larger lights thus generally remained fixed, while smaller ones in the area would be identified by different flashing or occulting sequences. Restrictions on speed of rotation, however, also placed limits on the number of different on and off sequences that could be offered, making it hard for officials to give unique signals to every closely spaced lighthouse in high-traffic areas. In an attempt to remedy this situation, some designers worked out alternative means of varying lights, including using shutters, blinds, and other devices to mask the light at regular intervals. Though some of these were adopted by marine authorities, they were abandoned after 1890 when Bourdelle invented a method of "floating the whole [lantern] assembly, weighing several tons, in an annular bath of mercury." His system reduced friction to such a low level that even the largest lights "could be revolved by the touch of a finger."[139] The mercury bath also permitted much greater speeds of rotation so that groups of up to five flashes could be produced, adding to and diversifying the flash patterns available to lighthouse designers.[140]

Engineers also used colour to identify specific lights. In 1806, a lighthouse off the coast of Yorkshire in Britain was fitted with a device that produced a periodic red beam followed by the standard white light. Designed by Benjamin Milne, it had parabolic reflectors mounted on a three-sided rotating frame, one side of which was covered in red glass. Marine authorities in Britain and elsewhere also incorporated fixed coloured lights in some of their light stations to help distinguish them from others nearby, though white remained the preferred colour because of its greater range and visibility.[141]

Many of these lighting advances were also applied to lightships. Though first used in the mid-eighteenth century, these floating lights became an increasingly important navigational aid after 1900. The first lightships were not purpose-built vessels but simple sailing ships adapted by, among other things, adding baskets or cages to each masthead to hold the lanterns. They were usually moored over major shoals or banks that could not support a lighthouse "because of the distance from the shore or constructional difficulties," but which warranted a more significant mark than a buoy.[142] Authorities also used lightships as temporary markers while lighthouses were under construction.[143]

The use of lightships posed many of the same challenges that had long been associated with supplying and maintaining lighthouses and their keepers. But keeping this technology functional and improving its performance over time also gave rise to some new problems. For example, the motion of the ships caused lamps to sway, reducing their visibility and risking oil spillage and fire. For this reason, masters often "preferred to use the less volatile colza and sperm oil and even olive oil than the more dangerous paraffin," even though the light then was not as bright. In an effort to reduce the sway, designers also began mounting lightship lanterns in gimbals.[144]

Nor could early lightships accommodate the elaborate and heavy lighting fixtures used in many lighthouses. The size, design, and position of the masts of many of these vessels precluded the use of dioptric lenses for many years and made it difficult to mount revolving apparatus. Inventors were thus forced to use simpler methods of increasing lighting capacity and distinguishing one ship from another. One English company developed "a twelve-lamp kerosene lantern backed by twelve parabolic reflectors" that sold widely until mid-century,[145] and Scottish engineer and lighthouse builder Robert Stevenson "developed some very advanced designs for the display of lights around the whole horizon," which allowed for various numbers and configurations of lights.[146]

Mooring was also a serious problem. The first lightships were secured much as any ship at anchor would have been, by heavy hemp rope and a traditional anchor. But because these vessels were often positioned in very exposed locations, it was not unusual for them to be torn lose from their moorings in bad weather. Over the course of the century authorities began to introduce chain cables and heavy mushroom anchors that provided more secure footings. Engineers also added adjustable mooring mechanisms to some lightships, allowing them to maintain a fairly precise position using a short cable in good weather or at low tide, and lengthen it when the tide came in or when the seas turned rough.[147]

Many of these problems were also addressed when marine officials began to develop purpose-built vessels. Engineers not only began to build ships out of iron but also experimented with hull shape, mooring fixtures, and support structures for lanterns in an attempt to make lightships more stable and secure and better suited to carrying sophisticated lights. For example, by the 1870s, they had devised several methods of supporting — usually a metal latticework tower in place of the mast — and operating revolving dioptric light assemblies on lightships. In some countries, lightship designers were also responsible for developing propulsion systems for the vessels, so that their crews could navigate to and from their position at the beginning and end of the season (rather than being towed) and could offer help or take shelter in emergencies.[148] Even with these advances and careful attention to maintenance, lightships and their crews were often cast adrift, severely damaged and sometimes lost entirely.[149]

Less sophisticated seamark technology such as buoys and beacons also received the attention of inventors and engineers. Here again, their concern was how to make these markers more visible, identifiable, and durable and how to ensure they were positioned correctly and remained that way. As late as the 1830s, wood was still the primary material used to construct buoys. Though builders had improved the design of these devices over the years and offered several different shapes and sizes — can, cone, spar, and nun among them[150] — to meet various marking needs, wooden buoys were not very durable and were frequently damaged or lost. Engineers, therefore, were more than willing to take advantage of steady advances in iron and metalworking technology in an attempt to improve on existing buoy design and construction. By the 1860s, they were building both combination wood and iron buoys and buoys made of riveted wrought iron and steel. These large markers often weighed more than three tons, but because they were built with "horizontal and vertical bulkheads," were fully watertight, and were securely moored, they "could be laid in deep and stormy channels with some certainty of their remaining on station and intact." Thus, while iron buoys were first used mainly to mark wrecks, authorities gradually extended their application to channels to warn of deep shoals that, with the increasing draft of ships, had become real hazards to mariners.[151]

Beginning in the 1860s, engineers also began to include sound and light devices on buoys to alert ships to their presence. The earliest sound-makers they used were simple bells that rang whenever wind or waves made the buoy move. The sound from these bells, however, did not travel very far and so inventors continued to look for ways to make buoys audible. By 1880 they had developed whistle buoys that used either compressed gas or wave motion to actuate a whistle mechanism built into the buoy. This created "a high-pitched moan" that mariners could hear "upwards of 3 miles in quiet conditions." During the same period, engineers also added lights to buoys. In 1879 Pintsch introduced the first lighting system for buoys. It used a reservoir or cylinders of compressed gas to fuel the lantern. From this time forward, lights became an increasingly common feature of buoys, especially those located in high-traffic areas or otherwise dangerous waters. With this proliferation of lighted buoys, differentiation became a problem — buoys with fixed white lights could not only be mistaken for one another but also for ships' lights. Engineers found that the flashing-light mechanisms designed for lighthouses were much harder to adapt to small, unattended devices, but by the 1880s they had developed a workable system of discontinuous buoy lights.[152]

Beacon construction also profited from the introduction of metal structures and lighting. Like buoys, metal beacons and range marks were more durable than wooden ones and thus more likely to stay in place despite constant exposure to the elements. Lighting, of course, made them more visible in poor weather and in the dark and, in some areas, could be used to help differentiate between marks.[153]

Despite these important advances, mariners still had to deal with a growing problem of identification of beacons and buoys. As the simplest and cheapest form of seamark, these devices had proliferated with the growth of international maritime trade and traffic and the introduction of larger and faster ships. Though marine authorities in most countries had developed some basic rules for interpreting markers, there were numerous inconsistencies and contradictions, which were often complicated by the introduction of new forms of technology. For example, large iron buoys were durable enough to be placed well out to sea, "where their identity and significance" was not necessarily clear to the "mariner approaching from seaward."

Beginning in the eighteenth century, topmarks and colours had been used extensively to identify buoys. Though this information was generally included on local charts, there was no uniformity in the use of symbols or colours from one country to the next.

Figure 28. *Pintsch gas-buoys were first used in Canada in the 1880s. They were superseded by the automatic acetylene buoys manufactured by Canadian Thomas Willson beginning in 1904.*
(Library and Archives Canada, neg. e003719363)

Certain conventions evolved, such as the use of pointed-topped buoys on the right-hand side leading into port and flat-topped ones on the left. Buoys with round superstructure, horizontal bands, and a round topmark were for "middle-ground shoals and mid-channel use." Also, concerned mariners, hydrographers, and others in the field did their best to compile and publish current information about markings in and around major shipping lanes and ports. Still, as late as the 1880s, international authorities could not agree on several important issues, including which colour of buoy should indicate which side of a channel, whether the lateral system of buoyage should be replaced by a cardinal system that provided more options for marking hazards as well as channels, and which flash sequences ought to be applied to port and starboard light buoys.[154]

Finally, in 1889, at the International Maritime Conference in Washington, the various national delegations were forced to accept that, as traffic levels and speed continued to increase, there was an urgent need to move toward uniformity in marking sea lanes. After much negotiation, officials agreed on some basic standards for channel and wreck buoys and accepted that there should be both a lateral and a cardinal system of buoyage. More importantly, participants seemed to recognize that the process of making seamarks more consistent and comprehensible worldwide would be a continuous process. Not only did some fundamental issues remain unresolved after the conference — the colour of port and starboard buoys, for one — but new ones were bound to arise with every technological advance in the field. In order to deal with this ongoing problem, marine officials from around the world created the Permanent International Association of Navigation Conferences in 1889.[155]

One other development in seamark technology deserves mention in this section — fog alarms. Over the centuries, coastal communities and maritime authorities used a variety of sound signals to try to warn ships of hazards in foggy weather. Guns, bells, and whistles, some of which operated automatically using clockwork mechanisms, were among the most common noisemakers used up to and during the nineteenth century. As the century progressed, however, a number of inventors and engineers began to study the peculiar behaviour of sound waves over water and to experiment with the application of steam and other forms of power to produce sounds. After 1850 several fog trumpet, siren, or horn devices were introduced by American, Italian, and English makers. Most of these devices were powered by compressed air or steam. One, Giovanni Amadi's fog trumpet, could be heard twenty-four kilometres away and could send Morse code messages as far as nine kilometres.[156] Another interesting device was designed and built by Robert Foulis of Nova Scotia. We know little for certain about Foulis's steam foghorn, other than that it was activated by releasing steam through a large horn, that it was said to have sounded automatically in foggy weather, and that its signal could be heard many miles out to sea.[157] Though all of these fog signals were subject to deflection and echo and, thus, sometimes gave false bearings to ships,[158] mariners, governments, and shipping interests generally supported their use. As a result, after mid-century, they were increasingly incorporated into lighthouses, lightships, and buoys, and engineers continued to work on enhancing their performance.

Canadian Aids to Navigation

In British North America and Canada, establishing a reliable system of aids to navigation presented an enormous physical and financial challenge. With long, often uninhabited coastlines to mark and limited funds with which to do it, colonial officials moved relatively slowly and deliberately in deciding what sort of aid was required and where and when to build it. They sought the technical advice and opinions of experts from the Admiralty and other maritime authorities and from commercial and shipping concerns. They also talked to mariners with experience in the area and to members of the local communities. All this information, along with cost estimates, had to be considered before any major decision could be made.

Lighthouses were by far the most prominent and expensive navigational aids built in what is now Canada in the nineteenth century. Because of their cost, very few were built in the early decades of the century, when the population of the colonies was small and scattered and their economic prospects uncertain. Between about 1804 and 1817, authorities put fewer than ten lighthouses into operation, which could, at best, fulfill only local needs. These, along with the two or three surviving from the eighteenth century, had to serve mariners travelling to and from the colonies for another decade or more.[159]

With the 1830s came a steady rise in population, trade, and commerce that highlighted the grave inadequacies of colonial navigational aids. British Admiralty hydrographers working in British North America charted many of the most obvious hazards and added their voices to calls for a more systematic approach to marking. The various governments responded by undertaking significant building programs over the next forty years. In the 1830s alone, they erected close to twenty lighthouses on some of the most treacherous stretches of water around the port of St John's, Newfoundland, on the Bay of Fundy, through the Cabot Strait, into the lower St Lawrence, and on Lakes Ontario and Erie. Through the forties

Figure 29. *The Green Island light, built in 1809, was the first light on the St Lawrence and remained the only light on the river until 1830.*
(Library and Archives Canada, neg. PA 203341)

and fifties, the various lighthouse authorities expanded coverage of these areas. The Commissioners of Public Works for the Province of Canada (so-called 1841–67) were particularly active, adding at least eight lights along the lower St Lawrence and Gulf, including the Strait of Belle Isle. They also extended their network into the upper St Lawrence, where, in 1856, they placed nine small lights to mark a safe route through the Thousand Islands from Brockville to Kingston, and into Lake Huron and Georgian Bay, where they erected six major lights, known as imperial towers, in 1858–59.[160] Nova Scotia officials, meanwhile, constructed fourteen lights on their Atlantic shores and inlets and several along the Bay of Fundy. By 1868, the four colonies that made up the new dominion of Canada together reported no fewer than 227 lights, grouped into 198 light stations. When British Columbia joined Confederation in 1871, it brought two additional lighthouses with it. The following year the Department of Marine and Fisheries reported a total of 314 lighthouses.[161]

In the years after Confederation, the federal Department of Marine and Fisheries consolidated and expanded the network of lighthouses. In addition to renovating and upgrading many existing structures, the department added new lighthouses at an average rate of between 15 and 30 per year. By 1884, there were 507 light stations in Canada with a total of 597 lights shown, including a few in Newfoundland for which Canadian authorities had responsibility. Twelve years later the network had grown to include 616 light stations, and in 1905, the government reported more than 1,000, though this latter total included pole lights, which had previously been counted separately (136 in 1896). The network reached as far inshore as Manitoba, where, by 1884, the federal government had built the first two lighthouses on Lake Winnipeg.[162]

Figure 30. The Red Islet lighthouse east of Québec around 1898. Built in 1848, this 52-foot (16-m) stone tower still exists today and was one of only two with the unusual and entirely decorative design feature of three raised horizontal bands of brick.
(Library and Archives Canada, neg. PA 164482)

In building this network of lighthouses, the colonial and Canadian governments had a variety of construction techniques from which to choose. Many factors influenced their decisions. European and, especially, British experience in designing and building reliable structures to suit even the most difficult locations had an obvious impact, not the least because the imperial government often helped to fund and build colonial lights. They tended to favour stone as the most durable form of construction and later promoted cast-iron structures as a cost-effective, low-maintenance, and durable alternative. Wood they saw as a last resort or a temporary solution to an immediate problem.[163]

Canadian authorities, though, had other issues to consider. Of these, cost was perhaps the most important. In order to keep costs down, colonial governments often built lighthouses from materials that were available locally or relatively inexpensive to buy and transport. Thus the lighthouses along the lower St Lawrence tended to be stone towers built using the abundant limestone and sand of the region. In one instance, the first lighthouse on Anticosti Island (1831), proximity of building resources actually entered into the decision to locate the light on the southwest point rather than the west point of the island.[164] In Nova Scotia and New Brunswick, on the other hand, good wood was readily available, so many of the lighthouses along these coasts were frame buildings. The same was true in British Columbia, where large, plentiful trees and numerous sawmill operations made timber the obvious construction material, even for important landfall lights such as Carmanah Point (1891), on the southwest coast of Vancouver Island.[165]

In some isolated locations — St Paul Island (1839), Bird Rocks (1870) in the Gulf of St Lawrence, the Strait of Belle Isle (1858) — where building resources were scarce or inferior, some, if not all, construction materials had to be brought in from outside the immediate area. In the latter two instances they also had to be landed in extremely difficult waters and then hauled up steep shores. At Bird Rocks, ships could only approach the site in July and August, and engineers had to build a special landing stage and trestle to receive the necessary stores and move them up the steep cliffs. Yet, because these lights marked the southern and northern routes into the Gulf of St Lawrence, the colonial and Canadian governments determined that the high cost of building and maintaining them was clearly warranted.[166]

In Newfoundland, imperial authorities advocated the widespread use of cast-iron towers. The first of these were built at Cape Pine (1851), marking the southern tip of the Avalon Peninsula, and Cape Race (1855), at its southeastern extremity. Initial experience with these structures was not good — the damp climate caused hoarfrost and condensation to form on the inside of the towers, making them "uninhabitable" — and local authorities complained that, in this case, British experience was not applicable in the Newfoundland context. They suggested alternatives such as the American technique of lining a brick structure with Portland cement.[167] Yet after 1875 Newfoundland authorities adopted cast-iron construction for a number of their new lighthouses.[168]

The height of lighthouses and the strength of their lights depended on their purpose. The tallest towers and most powerful lights were generally reserved for landfall stations such as Cape Race and Belle Isle, where the lighthouses warned incoming ships of their approach to land and gave outgoing ships their first bearing. Often as tall as 200 feet (60 m), they were usually equipped with large catoptric or dioptric fixtures that mariners could see for about twenty nautical miles out to sea. Major coastal lights such as those on Georgian Bay, along the lower St Lawrence, and at St Paul and Seal islands, were almost always less than 150 feet (45 m), with slightly less powerful lights. After these came secondary coastal lights, such as those marking the upper St Lawrence between Brockville and Kingston, which could be seen from 6 to 10 miles (10 to 16 km), and harbour lights such as those maintained at Oshawa Port and Whitby Harbour on Lake Ontario.[169]

The vast majority of these lighthouses were equipped with catoptric lanterns, usually Argand lamps with multiple reflectors fuelled by animal or mineral oil. Though less efficient than the dioptric lights preferred in Britain and the United States, these lights provided a cost-effective solution for small colonial budgets. According to the Trinity House committee sent from Britain to inspect and report on the lights in 1872, Canadian authorities got the most out of the less sophisticated reflective technology by taking advantage of low-maintenance and high-illuminating-power catoptric lamps fuelled by mineral oil, which was cheap and plentiful in Canada.[170]

Figure 31. The tower pictured here was originally erected at Cape Race, Newfoundland, in 1855. Built of prefabricated cast-iron plates manufactured in the U.K., it was disassembled and moved to the location in the photograph, Cape North, Nova Scotia, in 1906. It was moved again around 1980 to its present location in front of the Canada Science and Technology Museum in Ottawa. (Library and Archives Canada, neg. e003719338)

Lighthouse authorities installed the first dioptric light fixtures in British North America at Seal Island (1830) and Gannet Rock (1831). Both were second-order lights. Newfoundland's first dioptric fixture replaced the original (1813) catoptric light at Fort Amherst in 1852. The Belle Isle and Cape Rosier houses, built by the Canadian government in 1858, were equipped with the earliest first-order dioptric lights in the colonies. Four Georgian Bay towers, built around the same time, also showed dioptric lights, though of the second, third, and fourth order. Fisgard and Race Rocks in British Columbia had dioptric lights of the fourth and second order, respectively. By 1872, there were 25 lighthouses throughout Canada equipped with dioptric apparatus out of a total of 314. Though the 1884 report of Marine and Fisheries did not include a detailed list, the use of dioptric fixtures seems to have increased such that even pole lights and the little lighthouse at Beren's River on Lake Winnipeg were being equipped with dioptric apparatus.[171]

Because the making of dioptric lenses required such specialized knowledge, skill, and equipment, only a handful of companies were capable of producing them. In the early years of the nineteenth century, France was the primary source of what were called Fresnel lenses, though few sources specify that this was a company name. In the mid-1850s, the government of Canada West ordered the lenses for its imperial towers from Fresnel and had to wait until 1858 for them to arrive due to heavy demand for lenses from the United States. When they came, they were delivered and installed by specially trained French technicians.[172]

After 1830, other suppliers began to emerge, often supported by experts who had worked with or for Fresnel. Chance Brothers of Birmingham, England, obtained the expertise of two French craftsmen who had fled to England during the revolution in 1848, and within a few years they were making lenses "on a par with that of their French forerunners and future competitors." According to Bush, this firm "supplied a large portion of Canada's requirements" prior to the advent of the Dominion Lighthouse Depot in the early twentieth century. A second French company, Letourneau and Lepaute of Paris, also began to make and export lenses.[173]

As the network of lighthouses grew, colonial governments also had to pay increasing attention to distinguishing lights from one another. Canadian authorities built the first revolving light on Anticosti Island in 1831. In 1839, the Admiralty "insisted" that one of the two lights being built at its expense at either end of St Paul Island be made to flash or revolve so that there would be no chance of mariners confusing the two.[174] During the next decade, three more revolving lights were installed — at Point Prim, Prince Edward Island; Cape Bonavista, Newfoundland; and at Bicquette Island and the South Traverse on the lower St Lawrence. By 1872 Canada boasted no fewer than forty-three flashing or revolving lights, some of which showed more than one colour. The department continued to expand its use of these distinguishing features into the 1880s and beyond.[175]

Figure 32. Cove Island's lighthouse, near the entrance to Georgian Bay, was one of six stone towers completed in 1859 along the shores of Lake Huron and Georgian Bay. Known as the "imperial towers," these elegant structures were, with one exception, over 85 feet (26 m) in height, and all were equipped with the latest in dioptric lighting apparatus.
(Library and Archives Canada, neg. PA 188330)

Figure 33. The Fisgard lighthouse dates from 1860 and, along with the Race Rocks light, was the first on Canada's Pacific coast. The 56-foot (17-m) brick tower underwent extensive renovation in 1872 to counteract the deterioration caused by the use of poor-quality bricks in the original.
(Library and Archives Canada, neg. C 20072)

Colonial and Canadian governments also used a variety of other seamarks to improve navigation in their waters. Lightships seem to have been used sparingly in Canada, with just twelve in operation in 1872. By 1884, the number was still about twelve, with Quebec accounting for eight, New Brunswick two, and Nova Scotia and Ontario one each, though Ontario may have had more than this. In 1904, the government reported just fifteen lightships under its jurisdiction. Beyond these and any other numbers that can be gleaned from the annual reports of the Department of Marine and Fisheries, we know very little for certain about these vessels and how they were used. Throughout the nineteenth century, marine authorities often used vessels that were converted wooden schooners purchased at home or abroad.[176] They also began to order purpose-built vessels such as those placed on the Manicouagan Shoal and on Red Island in 1872 and the iron lightship proposed for Halifax Harbour in the same year.[177] These light vessels were sometimes used as temporary lights and eventually replaced by lighthouses, as was the case with the lightship at the mouth of the Fraser River in British Columbia, which was taken out of service when the Sand Heads lighthouse was completed in 1884.[178]

Anecdotal evidence suggests two further, if tentative, generalizations. It seems likely that, as with lighthouses, there was a gradual evolution in lighting technology in Canadian lightships from catoptric to dioptric and from fixed white to various forms of coloured and flashing lights, though these details are seldom mentioned with any consistency. It is also safe to assume that the Canadian climate was especially hard on lightships, which, at the best of times, were exposed to great wear and tear from the elements. The addition of ice, snow, and cold to the usual hazards of wind, water, and wayward ships meant that Canadian lightships were probably more often damaged and lost than those moored in ice-free, temperate waters. In the extreme ice conditions of 1871, several St Lawrence lightships were damaged, including the Red Island vessel, which lost its Trotman patent anchor and forty-five fathoms of cable.[179]

The story of buoys, beacons, and range marks is similar. The few government documents and specialist publications that mention these devices in any detail seem to suggest that, as with lighthouses and lightships, colonial authorities adopted the most cost-effective method of marking channels and hazards. This usually meant making do with older technologies and gradually replacing them with improved devices, beginning with the most critical sites. Thus, as late as 1871, the government was testing "new wooden buoys" that were "lighter and less expensive" than the "large iron buoys" then marking Lake St Peter in the St Lawrence River.[180] As well, in 1878, all the buoys in Halifax Harbour were wooden except the two marking the Thrum Cap and Rock Head shoals, which were iron can devices. Some of these probably had bells attached to provide an audible signal.[181]

By 1884, the government had begun to introduce new buoy technologies to Canadian waters. In that year, for example, the Nova Scotia division of Marine and Fisheries gave a detailed breakdown of its buoyage, reporting 7 automatic signal buoys, 5 iron bell buoys, 71 iron can buoys, and 420 spar and other small buoys. New Brunswick authorities also placed an automatic buoy off Point Lepreau. Meanwhile, Ontario reported 216 buoys and Quebec 91, two of which seem to have been the first Pintsch gas buoys used in Canada.[182]

Whatever technology the government adopted, however, as always, general wear and tear and the Canadian climate took their toll. In 1872, the Marine and Fisheries agent for British Columbia complained, among other things, about the "worm-eaten" state of the wooden buoys and the "corroded and worn" condition of the small iron buoys in use on the Pacific coast.[183] Quebec officials, at the same time, reported on the wholesale loss of much of their buoyage, which could not be retrieved before an unusually early freeze-up on the St Lawrence.[184] In Nova Scotia, various iron buoys were torn loose in gales, most notably the one marking Roaring Bull Rock near Cape Canso, which was moored with an 1,800-pound (816-kg) mushroom anchor.[185] Marine and Fisheries workers, like many of their counterparts around the world, thus had to carry on an almost constant retrieval and repair service. They also had the much less common and frequently onerous task of removing hundreds of buoys and their moorings every fall, refurbishing them, and laying them again each spring.

Marine and Fisheries annual reports provide very little information on the use of colour or shapes and symbols to distinguish buoys. Although it seems likely that Canadian officials took their lead from Britain in this as in so many maritime matters, the fact that Britain itself was divided over colour and shape codes complicates the issue. And what details are available only partially clarify Canada's policy. For example, in his 1872 report, the agent for Marine and Fisheries at Québec noted that along the St Lawrence River "all the black buoys are on the south side of the channel" and must, with three exceptions, be passed on the north side. The red buoys, meanwhile, were located on the north side, to be passed to the south. In general "white and chequered buoys indicate rocks or ends of shoals which can be passed on either side," with the exception of those "off the Saguenay, which are to be left to the north." Wrecks were marked by green buoys.[186] This meant that ships entering the channel from seaward and moving up the St Lawrence kept the red buoys to starboard and black to port. The reverse would have been true moving downstream. In Halifax, meanwhile, where the Admiralty system prevailed, ships coming into harbour kept red buoys to starboard and white ones to port.[187]

By 1875, the federal government had implemented a more coherent system that reflected the continental standard: for ships approaching from seaward, all starboard-side buoys were to be red, all port-side ones black. Those that could be passed on both sides were to be black and red horizontal stripes or black and white vertical stripes, and wrecks were to be marked by green buoys. This policy was eventually applied throughout the dominion, including Halifax Harbour after the Admiralty relinquished control of buoyage there to Marine and Fisheries in 1875. It is not clear how long it took the government to make the necessary changes or if they extended to other Admiralty spheres such as Esquimalt, British Columbia.[188]

Government sources contain even less information on beacons and range marks. They were routinely mentioned by Marine and Fisheries officials and a basic description of their character — beacon, pole light, range mark, or light — and position provided from time to time, especially if they were new or had been altered in some way. But the documents do not provide any lists of the different types used, how they were constructed, or what system of symbols was used to differentiate one from another. Based on what little information was reported, we know that, like buoys and lightships, these seamarks sometimes had to be removed or repositioned to accommodate new needs, to deal with shifting shorelines, sandbars, or repeated weather damage, and to take into account the concerns and complaints of mariners. It also is apparent that beacons and range marks were gradually upgraded to include lights. By 1896 the government reported 136 pole lights, many of which seem to have had distinguishing colour or flash characteristics.[189]

Colonial and Canadian authorities used various types of fog alarms probably from the early years of the century, to supplement visual seamarks. Cannon, bells, gongs, and other manual noisemaking devices were common additions to lighthouses in fog-prone regions. As with other aids to navigation, governments often used fairly basic and inexpensive technologies to fill an immediate need and, when funds became available, replaced these with more sophisticated devices. Thus, in their 1857 report, the Commissioners of Public Works for the united provinces of Canada announced that the lighthouses below Québec had each been equipped with a nine-pounder gun and ammunition to signal ships in thick weather. At the same time, they stated that "the engineer had been directed to make arrangements for having an air or fog whistle at each place by September next."[190] This technological improvement, however, was apparently not accomplished for some time, since in 1872, just two of these stations had steam fog whistles, while at least five still relied on fog guns. And even when, by 1884, the Canadian government had placed about thirty fog alarms along its coasts, it continued to employ much simpler devices, equipping the new lighthouse at the mouth of the Fraser River and the existing station on Bunker's Island in Yarmouth Harbour with fog bells. The Nova Scotia division alone reported that, along with 12 steam fog alarms, they had 2 fog bells, 3 signal gun, and 6 hand fog-alarm stations in operation.[191]

Colonial authorities — in this case the government of New Brunswick — probably installed British North America's first steam fog whistle in 1860, on Partridge Island in Saint John Harbour. According to some sources, the Partridge Island site was equipped with the device invented by Robert Foulis.[192] Bush, who did not specify which individual or company provided the apparatus, described the alarm as being powered by an 8-horsepower engine that produced 100 pounds per square inch of pressure. It was controlled by a clockwork mechanism that triggered it to sound for ten seconds of every minute and could be heard for about 10 miles (16 km).[193]

Figure 34. *New Brunswick's Partridge Island steam fog alarm was probably one of the first in British North America. It may have been the type invented by Canadian Robert Foulis.*

(New Brunswick Museum, Saint John, N.B., John Clarence Webster Canadiana Collection, neg. W.4389)

Mariners welcomed this first fog alarm, but at a cost of £350 or about $1,700, colonial governments seem to have been a little reluctant to install the devices elsewhere. The year after Confederation, there were just two such fog whistles in service, and the ones planned for three Gulf of St Lawrence lighthouses in 1858 had still not been installed in 1872, despite the fact that the fog gun at Belle Isle was so worn from overuse that it had become dangerous to fire. Instead of replacing it with a steam fog whistle, which by this time would have cost $1,900 not including the buildings and auxiliary machinery — the budget that year for all aids below Québec was less than $42,000 — the federal government ordered a new gun for the site.[194] Ten years after Confederation, there were just 25 fog whistles in operation at the 416 government light stations in the dominion.[195]

In 1877, the federal government began to introduce a new form of fog alarm, the automatic foghorn. Divisional agents of Marine and Fisheries mentioned at least two different brand names: the Neptune, made by the Neptune Fog-Horn Company of Québec and costing $2,118, and the Champion fog alarm, which cost $2,169.60. In 1884, two horns of the former type were installed in Ontario at Isle of Coves, Georgian Bay, and Gibraltar Point. In both cases buildings had to be erected to house the devices, adding $850 and $1,100, respectively, to the cost of the equipment. The Nova Scotia government also procured a Neptune foghorn for the lighthouse on McNutt's Island, which was described as being operated "by air through a reed trumpet" and which sounded "a blast of 10 seconds duration with intervals of 110 seconds between the blasts." Meanwhile, officials in New Brunswick chose an "improved Champion fog-horn" for their facility at Martin Head on the Bay of Fundy and had contracted for the construction of a $3,330 building to house the apparatus. Apart from this, the annual reports contain little technical information describing how these devices functioned and who originally invented or patented them.

By the close of the century, the government had also set up its first fog sirens on Belle Isle and at Louisbourg and Father Point. The Belle Isle device was English-made and powered by compressed air. A water wheel supplied the power to drive the compressor. The whole unit cost over $20,000. The other two sites were equipped with "Scotch sirens," also made in Britain. These devices, according to Bush, "gave the best results" of all the fog alarms then invented. Given the price of these devices, though, the government probably used them sparingly to mark only the most important and fog-prone shipping lanes, while continuing to rely on a variety of simpler manual and automatic alarms to serve less crucial coastlines.[196]

Notes

1. Desmond Morton, *A Short History of Canada* (Edmonton: Hurtig Publishers, 1983), 29.
2. J. M. Bumsted, *The Peoples of Canada: A Pre-Confederation History* (Toronto: Oxford University Press, 1992), 166, 178–9, 198.
3. Morton, *Short History*, 32–3.
4. Captain Ernest J. Chambers, *The Canadian Marine: A History of the Department of Marine and Fisheries* (Toronto: Canadian Marine and Fisheries History, 1905), 24–9.
5. Edward W. Bush, *The Canadian Lighthouse*, Canadian Historic Sites 9 (Ottawa: Indian and Northern Affairs, 1975), 61–2.
6. Lower Canada, *Statutes*, 45 Geo. III, cap. 12, quoted in Bush, *Canadian Lighthouse*, 26; Chambers, *Canadian Marine*, 33n1.
7. Bush, *Canadian Lighthouse*, 56–8.
8. Eric W. Sager and Gerald E. Panting, *Maritime Capital: The Shipping Industry in Atlantic Canada, 1820–1914* (Montréal and Kingston: McGill-Queen's University Press, 1990), 24–6; Morton, *Short History*, 56–7; Michael Bliss, *Northern Enterprise: Five Centuries of Canadian Business* (Toronto: McClelland & Stewart, 1987), 137–9.
9. Garth Wilson, *A History of Shipbuilding and Naval Architecture in Canada*, Transformation Series 4 (Ottawa: National Museum of Science and Technology, 1994), 30.
10. Paul G. Cornell, "Owen, William Fitzwilliam," *Dictionary of Canadian Biography*, vol. 8 (Toronto: University of Toronto Press, 1985), 669–70; Ruth McKenzie, "Bayfield, Henry Wolsey," *Dictionary of Canadian Biography*, vol. 11, *1881 to 1890* (Toronto: University of Toronto Press, 1982), 54–5; R. W. Sandilands, "Hydrographic Surveying in the Great Lakes during the Nineteenth Century," *The Canadian Surveyor* 36, no. 2 (June 1982): 139–46; Rear Admiral D. W. Haslam, "The British Contribution to the Hydrography of Canada" (unpublished and unpaginated paper provided by Ed Dahl). See section entitled "East Coast." Although this paper has no notes, it does include a bibliography for each of the four sections.
11. Bumsted, *The Peoples of Canada: A Pre-Confederation History*, 186.
12. Brian S. Osborne, "Expanding Economies," in R. Louis Gentilcore, ed., *The Historical Atlas of Canada*, vol. 2, *The Land Transformed, 1800–1891* (Toronto: University of Toronto Press, 1993), 33.
13. Bliss, *Northern Enterprise*, 131, 136; Bumsted, *The Peoples of Canada: A Pre-Confederation History*, 180–1, 186, 207.
14. Gentilcore, ed., *Historical Atlas*, see Plate 10, "Population in the Canadas and the Maritimes to 1851," and Plate 14, "A New Agriculture: Upper Canada to 1851."
15. Bumsted, *The Peoples of Canada: A Pre-Confederation History*, 201; Osborne, "Expanding Economies," 33–5.
16. Gentilcore, ed., *Historical Atlas*, see Plate 15, "Trade to Mid-Century."
17. Ibid., see Plate 11, "Timber Production and Trade to 1850."
18. Bumsted, *The Peoples of Canada: A Pre-Confederation History*, 209, 301; Wilson, *History of Shipbuilding*, 30; see also Gentilcore, ed., *Historical Atlas*, Plate 13, "An Established Agriculture: Lower Canada to 1851," and Plate 14.

19. Bliss, *Northern Enterprise*, 130–2.
20. Sager and Panting, *Maritime Capital*, 31–3; see also Gentilcore, ed., *Historical Atlas*, Plate 16, "By Hand and By Water: Manufacturing to 1851."
21. Eric W. Sager, *Seafaring Labour: The Merchant Marine of Atlantic Canada, 1820–1914* (Kingston: McGill-Queen's University Press, 1989), 94.
22. See Bush, *Canadian Lighthouse*, 53–4, for the opinions of two Royal Navy officers about the problems caused by the lack of lights on the coasts of the St Lawrence River and Gulf before 1830.
23. See Canada, Marine and Fisheries, *Annual Report of the Department of Marine and Fisheries for the Year Ending the 30th of June, 1872* (Ottawa: Government of Canada, 1873), app. 35, 314–45. This chart lists all the lights under the jurisdiction of the federal government and includes the year that each was lighted.
24. Lower Canada, *Report of the Special Committee of the House of Assembly of Lower-Canada on the Petition of the Merchants, Ship-owners, Masters of Vessels and Pilots, with an instruction to enquire in the expediency of erecting Light-houses on the St. Lawrence* (Québec: House of Assembly, 1829), no page number; Bush, *Canadian Lighthouse*, 54. Bayfield also advised on the location of the St Paul Island lights in 1837. See Bush, 40.
25. Bush, *Canadian Lighthouse*, 26–7, 36–70; see also *Annual Report...1872*, 314–45.
26. The lighthouse chart in the departmental report for 1872, again, gives an indication of activity during this period. One possible casualty of the depression was the plan to deepen the St Lawrence channel between Québec and Montréal. Work began in 1844 but was suspended and then cancelled in 1846–47. Chambers, *Canadian Marine*, 25–8.
27. Bliss, *Northern Enterprise*, 167–72; Bumsted, *The Peoples of Canada: A Pre-Confederation History*, 215; W. A. Mackintosh, "Economic Factors in Canadian History," in W. T. Easterbrook and M. H. Watkins, eds., *Approaches to Canadian Economic History* (Toronto: Macmillan Company of Canada, 1978), 7; Morton, *Short History*, 45; see also Gentilcore, ed., *Historical Atlas*, Plate 25, "Emergence of a Transportation System, 1837–1852"; Chambers, *Canadian Marine*, 21–4.
28. Bliss, *Northern Enterprise*, 167–72; Chambers, *Canadian Marine*, 18–24.
29. Bliss, *Northern Enterprise*, 169; Bumsted, *The Peoples of Canada: A Pre-Confederation History*, 215; see also Gentilcore, ed., *Historical Atlas*, Plate 25.
30. Bliss, *Northern Enterprise*, 178; see also Gentilcore, ed., *Historical Atlas*, Plate 26, "The Railway Age, 1834–1891."
31. Morris Zaslow, *The Opening of the Canadian North, 1870–1914* (Toronto: McClelland & Stewart, 1971), 12; Bliss, *Northern Enterprise*, 172–9; Morton, *Short History*, 48; Bumsted, *The Peoples of Canada: A Pre-Confederation History*, 293. According to the latter three sources there were between 50 and 60 miles (80 to 100 km) of railway in British North America in 1849–50. See also Gentilcore, ed., *Historical Atlas*, Plates 25 and 26.
32. C. Grant Head, "Economies in Transition," in Gentilcore, ed., *Historical Atlas*, 95–7; also Plate 43, "International Trade to 1891."
33. Gentilcore, ed., *Historical Atlas*, Plate 37, "Canadian Fisheries, 1850–1900"; Zaslow, *Opening of the Canadian North*, 40–6; J. M. Bumsted, *The Peoples of Canada: A Post-Confederation History* (Toronto: Oxford University Press, 1992), 48, 50; Bliss, *Northern Enterprise*, 314–24.
34. Gentilcore, ed., *Historical Atlas*, Plate 36, "The Gold Rushes in British Columbia, 1858–1881."
35. Zaslow, *Opening of the Canadian North*, 40–3; Bumsted, *The Peoples of Canada: A Post-Confederation History*, 50; Bliss, *Northern Enterprise*, 321–4; see also Gentilcore, ed., *Historical Atlas*, Plate 37, "Canadian Fisheries, 1850–1900."
36. Zaslow, *Opening of the Canadian North*, 2–3 and 40–3; Bumsted, *The Peoples of Canada: A Pre-Confederation History*, 305–10; Bumsted, *The Peoples of Canada: A Post-Confederation History*, 50; Bliss, *Northern Enterprise*, 321–4. See also Gentilcore, ed., *Historical Atlas*, Plate 42, "Homesteading and Agriculture in the West, 1872–1891."
37. Wilson, *History of Shipbuilding*, 31–2.
38. Bumsted, *The Peoples of Canada: A Pre-Confederation History*, 310–4; Zaslow, *Opening of the Canadian North*, 48–9.
39. David Farrell, "Keeping the Local Economy Afloat: Canadian Pacific Navigation and Shipowning in Victoria, 1883–1901," *The Northern Mariner* 6, no. 1 (January 1996): 31, 40–1.
40. Morton, *Short History*, 123.
41. Wilson, *History of Shipbuilding*, 27–8.
42. Ibid., 34; Sager and Panting, *Maritime Capital*, 88–127, especially 97–103; Frederick William Wallace, *Wooden Ships and Iron Men* (Belleville, Ont.: Mika Publishing Company, 1976), 42–88; Bumsted, *The Peoples of Canada: A Pre-Confederation History*, 290–1; Morton, *Short History*, 94. See also Gentilcore, ed., *Historical Atlas*, Plate 39, "Ships and Shipping, 1863–1914."
43. See Gentilcore, ed., *Historical Atlas*, Plate 39.
44. See, for example, Canada, *Journals of the Legislative Assembly of the Province of Canada 1857*, app. 19, General Report of the Commissioners of Public Works.
45. Chambers, *Canadian Marine*, preface.
46. Canada, *Annual Report...1872*, 1–5.
47. Ibid., 346–8. The details of upgrades and renovations are contained in the various reports and statements of expenditure of the regional agents, found mostly between pages 6 and 114.
48. Ibid., 361.
49. Sager, *Seafaring Labour*, 93–6.
50. Thomas E. Appleton, *Usque ad Mare: A History of the Canadian Coast Guard and Marine Services* (Ottawa: Department of Transport, 1968), 265–6.
51. Canada, *Journals of the House of Assembly of the Province of Canada, 1858*, app. 38, Return to an Address from the Legislative Assembly of the 19th April, 1858, for copies of documents relative to closing of School of Navigation, established in Quebec, no page numbers, see first page of return.
52. Ibid., see "Advertisement" on fifth page of return.
53. Ibid., see correspondence between the ninth and eleventh pages of return.
54. Ibid., see correspondence between the ninth and sixteenth pages of return.
55. Sager, *Seafaring Labour*, 95, 98; Canada, *Annual Report...1872*, 2–3.
56. In the correspondence relating to the closing of the nautical school at Québec was included a new plan for a school of navigation on board the fisheries schooner *La Canadienne*. In his proposal P. Fortin laments the fact that a "want of educated seamen in Canada" confined Canadian vessels mainly to the coastal and West Indian trade.
57. Canada, *Annual Report...1872*, 2–3.
58. Sager, *Seafaring Labour*, 97–8; Canada, *Annual Report...1872*, 43–4.
59. Canada, *Annual Report...1872*, 263.
60. Ibid., 264.

61. See John St Vincent McNally, *Seamanship Examiner and Instructor of Masters and Mates for the Marine Board Examination in Canada* (Saint John, N.B.: Barnes & Company, 1873).
62. Sager, *Seafaring Labour*, 97.
63. Canada, Marine and Fisheries, *Annual Report of the Department of Marine and Fisheries for the Fiscal Year Ended 30th June, 1884* (Ottawa: Government of Canada, 1885), xlii–xliii.
64. J. A. Bennett, *The Divided Circle: A History of Instruments for Astronomy, Navigation and Surveying* (Oxford: Phaidon-Christie's, 1987), 179–84; Jean Randier, *Marine Navigational Instruments*, translated from the French by John E. Powell (London: John Murray, 1980), 93–115; and Peter Ifland, *Taking the Stars: Celestial Navigation from Argonauts to Astronauts* (Malabar, Fla.: Krieger Publishing Company, 1998), 54–8. See also Charles H. Cotter, *A History of the Navigator's Sextant* (Glasgow: Brown, Son & Ferguson, 1983).
65. R. T. Gould, *The Marine Chronometer: Its History and Development*, rev. ed. (London, 1923; repr., Woodbridge, U.K.: Antique Collectors Club, 1989), 134, 137, and 144.
66. Ibid., 189 and 192–3.
67. Bennett, *Divided Circle*, 184–6; Randier, *Marine Navigational Instruments*, 183–9; and Gould, *Marine Chronometer*, 188.
68. Bennett, *Divided Circle*, 186.
69. Ibid., 190–1; Peter Kemp, ed., *The Oxford Companion to Ships and the Sea* (London: Oxford University Press, 1979), 493.
70. Kemp, ed., *Oxford Companion*, 493.
71. Bennett, *Divided Circle*, 190–1; Kemp, ed., *Oxford Companion*, 493; Randier, *Marine Navigational Instruments*, 50–5.
72. Kemp, ed., *Oxford Companion*, 493.
73. Bennett, *Divided Circle*, 190–1; Kemp, ed., *Oxford Companion*, 493; Randier, *Marine Navigational Instruments*, 50–5.
74. Based on Boyle's Law, the volume of the air in the tube decreased as the water pressure increased so that penetration of water into the tube was "directly related to the depth to which the tube has descended." The navigator could then compare the water level to a special scale to arrive at an actual depth measurement. Kemp, ed., *Oxford Companion*, 817–8.
75. Thomson's device was also based on Boyle's Law, so that measuring the discolouration also provided an accurate measure of water pressure and therefore depth. Kemp, ed., *Oxford Companion*, 817–8.
76. Bennett, *Divided Circle*, 191–3; Kemp, ed., *Oxford Companion*, 817–8; Randier, *Marine Navigational Instruments*, 68–72.
77. J. E. D. Williams, *From Sails to Satellites: The Origin and Development of Navigational Science* (Oxford: Oxford University Press, 1994), 135–7; Bennett, *Divided Circle*, 187–8; Kemp, ed., *Oxford Companion*, 189–90, 244, 908; Randier, *Marine Navigational Instruments*, 18–20. Researchers also discovered, "purely by chance," that needles arranged underneath the compass card to stop the main needle from swinging when the ship rolled "also corrected for deviation." Alan Gurney, *Compass: A Story of Exploration and Innovation* (New York: W. W. Norton & Company, 2004), 206–10.
78. Kemp, ed., *Oxford Companion*, 190.
79. Williams, *Sails to Satellites*, 136.
80. Kemp, ed., *Oxford Companion*, 190; Williams, *Sails to Satellites*, 136–7; Bennett, *Divided Circle*, 188–90.
81. The Atlantic Canada Newspaper Survey was never completed. For some cities in some time periods it is fairly comprehensive while for others it is not. For more information, see "What Is the Atlantic Canada Newspaper Survey?" on the website of the Canadian Museum of Civilization at Civilization.ca. I consulted the National Library's collection of city directories for the centres and years mentioned.
82. Miscellaneous Halifax and Saint John directories.
83. Julian A. Smith, "Charles Potter, Optician and Instrument Maker," *Journal of the Royal Astronomical Society of Canada* 87, no. 1 (February 1993): 21. Smith's assertion is based on the fact that Potter moved his family out of the combined shop into a separate home.
84. Here I have consulted the results of the database search conducted by Randall Brooks using the names of various navigational instruments as keywords.
85. Randall C. Brooks, "Nautical Instrument-Makers in Atlantic Canada," *Nova Scotia Historical Review* 6, no. 2 (1986): 45–6.
86. Ibid., 45–53, and comments on draft manuscript.
87. Ibid., 53–4.
88. Trevor H. Levere, *Science and the Canadian Arctic: A Century of Exploration, 1818–1918* (Cambridge: Cambridge University Press, 1993), 37–9; and Hugh N. Wallace, *The Navy, the Company, and Richard King: British Exploration in the Canadian Arctic, 1829–1860* (Montréal: McGill-Queen's University Press, 1980), 5–6.
89. Kemp, ed., *Oxford Companion*, 160; G. S. Ritchie, "500 Years of Graphical and Symbolic Representation on Marine Charts" (paper presented to International Hydrographic Organization Sixth International Conference on the History of Cartography, 1975), 7–9; and Stanley Fillmore and R. W. Sandilands, *The Chartmakers: A History of Nautical Surveying in Canada* (Toronto: NC Press, 1983), 117–21.
90. Ritchie, "500 Years," 7–9; G. R. Crone, *Maps and Their Makers: An Introduction to the History of Cartography*, 5th ed. (Chatham, U.K.: W. & J. Mackay, 1978), 72–3; and Kemp, ed., *Oxford Companion*, 160–1.
91. Library records show numerous editions of Imray's guides to the west coast of North America and fewer but still plentiful versions of Norie's guides, mainly relating to the east coast. Blunt's guides to the east coast, mainly the United States, are the most numerous of all. Though there seems to have been little written about either Imray or Nories, two works chronicle and celebrate the substantial work of Blunt and his successors: Harold L. Burstyn, *At the Sign of the Quadrant: An Account of the Contributions to American Hydrography Made by Edward March Blunt and his Sons* (Mystic, Conn.: Marine Historical Association, 1957), and John F. Campbell, *History and Bibliography of* The New American Practical Navigator *and* The American Coast Pilot (Salem, Mass.: Peabody Museum, 1964).
92. Ritchie, "500 Years," 7–9; Kemp, ed., *Oxford Companion*, 346; and Crone, *Maps and Their Makers*, 72–3.
93. Haslam, "British Contribution," no page number. See section entitled "East Coast."
94. Cornell, "Owen," 669.
95. Ibid., 669–70; R. W. Sandilands, "Hydrographic Surveying in the Great Lakes,"139–42; Haslam, "British Contribution," no page number, see section entitled "The Great Lakes"; Ritchie, "500 Years," 104
96. McKenzie, "Bayfield," 54–5. Also Ruth McKenzie, *Admiral Bayfield: Pioneer Nautical Surveyor* (Ottawa: Environment Canada, Fisheries and Marine Service, 1976), 2–3; Sandilands, "Hydrographic Surveying in the Great Lakes," 142–6; Fillmore and Sandilands, *Chartmakers*, 38–9.
97. McKenzie, "Bayfield," 56.

98. Ibid., 55; Fillmore and Sandilands, *Chartmakers*, 39; Haslam, "British Contribution," no page number, see sections entitled "The Great Lakes" and "East Coast."
99. McKenzie, "Bayfield," 55.
100. Ibid., 55–6; McKenzie, *Admiral Bayfield*, 4–7; Haslam, "British Contribution," no page number, see section entitled "East Coast."
101. O. M. Meehan, *The Canadian Hydrographic Service: A Chronology of Its Early History between the Years 1883 and 1947* (unpublished manuscript), quoted in Fillmore and Sandilands, *Chartmakers*, 37.
102. The accurate measurement of longitude was critically important to this whole process and especially so in making charts "match up." Hydrographers, therefore, went to great lengths to ensure that their readings for Canadian locations were precise. Owen sailed "back and forth between Halifax, Boston, Quebec and London with a number of chronometers" on board to correct for errors. Bayfield, not convinced of the results obtained by this method, tried using "the explosion of shells to tie Halifax and Quebec." He also recommended that the government establish a transit observatory in Charlottetown. Randall C. Brooks, "Time, Longitude Determination and Public Reliance upon Early Observatories," in Paul A. Bogaard, ed., *Profiles of Science and Society in the Maritimes prior to 1914* (Sackville, N.B.: Acadiensis Press and Centre for Canadian Studies, Mount Allison University, 1990), 179–80.
103. McKenzie, "Bayfield," 56–7.
104. Levere, *Science and the Canadian Arctic*, 44; Wallace, *Navy, the Company*, 5.
105. Wallace, *Navy, the Company*, 9. For additional details on the mapping and charting of the Canadian Arctic in this period, see Don W. Thomson, *Men and Meridians: The History of Surveying and Mapping in Canada*, vol. 1, *Prior to 1867* (Ottawa: Queen's Printer, 1966), 166–9, and *Up North: The Discovery and Mapping of the Canadian Arctic* (Toronto: Royal Ontario Museum, 1958), 10–3.
106. Levere, *Science and the Canadian Arctic*, 122–4, for details of Franklin's survey including a map.
107. Wallace, *Navy, the Company*, 15; Ritchie, "500 Years," 138–56; Levere, *Science and the Canadian Arctic*, 44–63 on Ross, 63–84 on Parry, and 103–25 on Franklin.
108. R. W. Sandilands, "Charting the Beaufort Sea," *Lighthouse*, no. 24 (November 1981): 10.
109. Wallace, *Navy, the Company*, xv and xviii for maps depicting work of these expeditions; and 13–9, 28 on Ross; 19, 24–5, 28–30 on Back; and 38–43, 46 on Simpson; Levere, *Science and the Canadian Arctic*, 192–3, on Simpson; Ritchie, "500 Years," 256–66.
110. Wallace, *Navy, the Company*, 49.
111. Haslam, "British Contribution," no page number, see section entitled "The North Coasts."
112. Wallace, *Navy, the Company*, 9, 132–8; Haslam, "British Contribution," no page number, see section entitled "The North Coasts"; Ritchie, "500 Years," 258–66.
113. Levere, *Science and the Canadian Arctic*, 207; Ritchie, "500 Years," 258–66. The knowledge gained in the first half of the nineteenth century was expanded and supplemented by the Hudson's Bay Company expedition of 1884. Commissioned by the federal department of Marine and Fisheries and led by Royal Navy lieutenant Andrew Gordon, this expedition helped to establish Canada's claim to lands recently ceded to her by Britain. It also collected a vast amount of scientific and cultural information about the region and its peoples and included a section on navigation in the Arctic. The expedition's report can be found in Sessional Papers (no. 9), 1885, app. 30, beginning on 189.
114. Haslam, "British Contribution," no page number, see section entitled "British Columbia"; R. W. Sandilands, "The History of Hydrographic Surveying in British Columbia," *The Canadian Cartographer* 7, no. 2 (December, 1970): 108–9; Fillmore and Sandilands, *Chartmakers*, 35.
115. Haslam, "British Contribution," no page number, see section entitled "British Columbia"; Sandilands, "Hydrographic Surveying in British Columbia," 109–10; William Glover, "The Challenge of Navigation to Hydrography on the British Columbia Coast, 1850–1930," *The Northern Mariner* 6, no. 4 (October 1996): 3.
116. Quoted from the Admiralty's instructions to Richards in Glover, "Challenge of Navigation," 3.
117. Haslam, "British Contribution," no page number, see section entitled "British Columbia"; Sandilands, "Hydrographic Surveying in British Columbia," 112; Fillmore and Sandilands, *Chartmakers*, 37.
118. Fillmore and Sandilands, *Chartmakers*, 62.
119. Quoted from Rear Admiral Sir William Wharton, *Hydrographical Surveying: A Description of the Means and Methods Employed in Constructing Marine Charts*, 2nd rev. ed. (London: John Murray, 1898), 75, in Glover, "Challenge of Navigation," 6. Glover (5–7) also deals with some of the other technological improvements that had an impact on charting, such as improved compasses.
120. M. J. Casey, "The *Asia* Tragedy," *Lighthouse*, no volume, no number, no date, published in Burlington, Ont., by the Canadian Hydrographers' Association; Fillmore and Sandilands, *Chartmakers*, 57–9; Sandilands, "Hydrographic Surveying in the Great Lakes," 155–6.
121. Fillmore and Sandilands, *Chartmakers*, 62–7.
122. Bush, *Canadian Lighthouse*, 15.
123. Ibid.; Douglas B. Hague and Rosemary Christie, *Lighthouses: Their Architecture, History and Archaeology* (Llandysul Dyfed, U.K.: Gomer Press, 1985), 165. Quotation is from Bush.
124. Bush, *Canadian Lighthouse*, 15.
125. Ibid., 16; Andre Gutsche, Barbara Chisholm, and Russel Floren, *Alone in the Night: Lighthouses of Georgian Bay, Manitoulin Island and the North Channel* (Toronto: Lynx Images, 1996), 36–7.
126. Bush, *Canadian Lighthouse*, 15–6; Hague and Christie, *Lighthouses*, 166–72; John Naish, *Seamarks: Their History and Development* (London: Stanford Maritime, 1985), 130–2; Gutsche et al., *Alone in the Night*, 31–2.
127. Hague and Christie, *Lighthouses*, 170; Alexander Findlay, *A Description and List of the Lighthouses of the World, 1861* (London: Richard Holmes Laurie, 1861), 25–6.
128. These figures are taken from Findlay's 1861 list of lighthouses, *Description and List*, 32–142.
129. Francis Ross Holland Jr., *America's Lighthouses: Their Illustrated History since 1716* (Brattleboro, Vt.: Stephen Greene Press, 1972), 23
130. While most sources including the OED equate colza with rape-seed oil, Gutsche et al., *Alone in the Night*, claimed that "it was manufactured from a variety of Swedish turnip" (32).
131. Bush, *Canadian Lighthouse*, 17–8; Hague and Christie, *Lighthouses*, 153–4; and Findlay, *Description and List*, 10–1. According to one, undocumented source, lightkeepers "actually preferred it [colza oil] because of its relatively flicker-free flame and non-clogging properties." Gutsche et al., *Alone in the Night*, 32.
132. Hague and Christie, *Lighthouses*, 154–6; Bush, *Canadian Lighthouse*, 18.
133. Hague and Christie, *Lighthouses*, 154–6; Bush, *Canadian Lighthouse*, 18. Gutsche et al., *Alone in the Night*, 32, quote an 1875 document that instructed lightkeepers to filter any unused oil before returning it to dioptric

lamps. This was apparently not required for catoptric lights.
134. Bush, *Canadian Lighthouse*, 18.
135. Hague and Christie, *Lighthouses*, 156–7; Bush, *Canadian Lighthouse*, 18; Holland, *America's Lighthouses*, 23. Few sources are specific about exactly how much more powerful gas mantle lamps were compared to wick types. Bush (18) claimed that the gas mantle was responsible for "trebling the power of all former wick lamps," while Holland (23) quoted a writer who maintained that "the candle power and brilliance are increased many fold as compared with the wick type, with no increase in the actual fuel consumption."
136. Hague and Christie, *Lighthouses*, 157–9.
137. Ibid., 159–61.
138. Ibid., 176–8.
139. Naish, *Seamarks*, 132–3.
140. Ibid.; Bush, *Canadian Lighthouse*, 19–20.
141. Bush, *Canadian Lighthouse*, 20; Naish, *Seamarks*, 131–2.
142. Kemp, ed., *Oxford Companion*, 484.
143. Hague and Christie, *Lighthouses*, 199.
144. Ibid., 201.
145. Naish, *Seamarks*, 111.
146. Ibid., 110–1; Hague and Christie, *Lighthouses*, 202–3.
147. Hague and Christie, *Lighthouses*, 196–7.
148. Naish, *Seamarks*, 110–1; Hague and Christie, *Lighthouses*, 202–3.
149. Hague and Christie, *Lighthouses*, 195–7; Naish, *Seamarks*, 107–11.
150. Initially spar buoys were made from simple lengths of squared and painted timber with anchors attached to one end so that they floated upright in the water. Later spar buoys, also known as pillar buoys, were fabricated from iron and steel. The nun buoy is a double cone shape — the widest part of the cones meeting in the centre — which evolved from the simple cone form. Its longer shape made the nun buoy more visible than the cone. Naish, *Seamarks*, 52–3, 58–60; Kemp, ed., *Oxford Companion*, 820; and Holland, *America's Lighthouses*, 206–8.
151. Naish, *Seamarks*, 68–9.
152. Ibid., 60, 142.
153. Ibid., 45–7, 76–7.
154. Ibid., 140–3.
155. Ibid., 143–4.
156. Hague and Christie, *Lighthouses*, 188–92.
157. David Walker, "A Survey of Major Technological Developments in Canadian Marine Transportation from the Earliest Times to the Present" (unpublished research report for Curator of Marine Transportation and Forestry, National Museum of Science and Technology, circa 1990), 38–42.
158. Bush, *Canadian Lighthouse*, 23.
159. Canada, *Annual Report...1872*, 314–45.
160. For a detailed description of these towers, their construction and operation see Gutsche et al., *Alone in the Night*.
161. Canada, *Annual Report...1872*, 314–45; Bush, *Canadian Lighthouse*, 36–72.
162. Canada, *Annual Report...1884*, x, xiii; Chambers, *Canadian Marine*, 51.
163. Bush, *Canadian Lighthouse*, 8–13.
164. Ibid., 54.
165. Ibid., 36–44, 79; Canada, *Annual Report...1872*, 314–45.
166. Bush, *Canadian Lighthouse*, 39–42, 51–3; Canada, *Annual Report...1872*, 15, for details on the difficulties and additional costs of building on Bird Rocks.
167. Bush, *Canadian Lighthouse*, 12.
168. David J. Molloy, *The First Landfall: Historic Lighthouses of Newfoundland and Labrador* (St John's: Breakwater, 1994), 14.
169. Bush, *Canadian Lighthouse*, 8; Canada, *Annual Report...1872*, 314–45.
170. Canada, *Annual Report...1872*, 361.
171. Bush, *Canadian Lighthouse*, 36–9, 45, 51, 55, 71–3, 77; Canada, *Annual Report...1872*, 314–45; Canada, *Annual Report...1884*, xiii.
172. Bush, *Canadian Lighthouse*, 15–16; Gutsche et al., *Alone in the Night*, 5–8.
173. Bush, *Canadian Lighthouse*, 15–16; Naish, *Seamarks*, 131–2.
174. Bush, *Canadian Lighthouse*, 40.
175. Canada, *Annual Report...1872*, 6–24, 314–45; Canada, *Annual Report...1884*, x–xxxii; Bush, *Canadian Lighthouse*, 46, 54–5, 59.
176. Appleton, *Usque ad Mare*, 116.
177. Canada, *Annual Report...1872*, 16, 20.
178. Canada, *Annual Report...1884*, xxxi–xxxii; Bush, *Canadian Lighthouse*, 79.
179. Canada, *Annual Report...1872*, 32. See Appleton, *Usque ad Mare*, 116–21, for a description of life on board Canada's lightships during this period.
180. Canada, *Annual Report...1872*, app. 2, 7.
181. Hugh F. Pullen, *The Sea Road to Halifax: Being an Account of the Lights and Buoys of Halifax Harbour*, Occasional Paper 1 (Halifax: Maritime Museum of the Atlantic, 1980), 14.
182. Canada, *Annual Report...1884*, x, xiv, xvii, xviii, xxvii.
183. Canada, *Annual Report...1872*, app. 7, 92.
184. Ibid., app. 2, 7, app. 4, 36.
185. Ibid., app. 5, 65.
186. Ibid., app. 4, 36.
187. Pullen, *Sea Road to Halifax*, 14.
188. Ibid.; Naish, *Seamarks*, 140–3.
189. Chambers, *Canadian Marine*, 51; see also any departmental annual report from the period, where the agents for each region sometimes mention repositioning, repairs, and upgrades of different beacons and range marks.
190. Canada, *Journals*, no page number, under heading "Light-Houses Below Quebec" and in app. H.
191. Canada, *Annual Report...1872*, app. 4, 30–5; Canada, *Annual Report...1884*, xviii, xxi, xxxi.
192. Walker, "Survey," 39–41.
193. Bush, *Canadian Lighthouse*, 23–4.
194. Ibid.; Canada, *Annual Report...1872*, 18, 35.
195. Canada, *Annual Report...1884*, x. Description of McNutt's Island foghorn, xx–xii, and Martin Head foghorn, xxvi.
196. Bush, *Canadian Lighthouse*, 24.

CHAPTER 3

Navigation in the Age of Electronics

Navigation in the Age of Electronics

Canada had one of the world's fastest-growing economies after 1891. This growth was fuelled by "a combination of dramatic urban-industrial development along with a great expansion of the natural resource–based economy."[1] Though an increasing amount of this trade was conducted over land with the United States, much Canadian commerce continued to depend on water-borne transport. In 1989, for example, marine carriers handled more exports by value than either rail or air, and of the $36 billion worth of Canadian exports destined for non-U.S. markets, $28 billion were transported by water.[2] Moreover, while the number of vessels clearing in and out of Canadian ports declined over the decades, the registered tonnage and total amount of cargo carried has increased, making Canada "one of the major deep-sea trading nations of the world."[3] This level of trade and traffic, combined with advances in ship design and performance, increases in the size of vessels, and improvements in the efficiency of port and cargo-handling facilities, has, over the decades, placed almost constant pressure on navigational infrastructure. Along with other factors such as war-related demands, these developments have inspired scientists and engineers to design more efficient and accurate instruments and systems for determining direction, speed, and position and avoiding hazards such as collisions and groundings.

This chapter describes some of the major advances in navigational technologies in the twentieth century, focusing on how these devices and systems have improved the safety and efficiency of shipping in an era when the number and size of ships and the level of competition in shipping grew dramatically. The first section is a brief overview of some of the political, social, and economic events that had a significant impact on marine navigation in Canada after 1900. This is followed by a description of advances in shipboard navigational instruments. The third section concentrates on those navigational systems that rely on interaction between shipboard and shore-based installations, including charts — paper and electronic — radio, and electronic positioning instruments. The focus of the fourth section is land-based aids to navigation, including traffic management systems in ports and high-traffic channels.

An Economy Afloat: Marine Transportation in Canada since 1900

Though the twentieth century was marked by two hugely destructive world wars, profound social and political turmoil, and periods of great economic distress, worldwide productive capacity has, nonetheless, grown steadily since 1900. With it have grown the volume and variety of world trade and the demand for vehicles, including ships, to carry it. At the same time, international competition among trading and shipping nations has intensified as more and more countries entered the international economy. To competition for trade was added competition among the various forms of transport, which became especially intense with the dramatic rise of trucking and aviation after 1945. Also, within the shipping industry itself, companies vied with one another to attract and hold those clients who continued to use water-borne transport.

In order to survive and prosper in this increasingly competitive environment, shipping had to become more efficient. Essentially, this meant that the shipping industry — shipbuilders, shipowners, mariners, port and harbour authorities, and related business enterprises and government institutions — had to move more goods more quickly while at the same time reducing costs, especially those for labour. The industry accomplished this goal by various means. First of all, shipbuilders, inspired in part by competitive pressures, introduced a number of important technological improvements in shipbuilding techniques and materials, propulsion systems, and cargo-handling equipment. By 1900, builders were making ships out of steel, which was both lighter and more flexible than the iron it replaced. Marine engineers, having perfected the triple-expansion engine in the late nineteenth century, went on to develop the steam turbine and internal combustion engines as alternative forms of propulsion. The latter, in the form of the diesel engine, gradually became the preferred form of propulsion for most vessels. Even the largest liners and tankers, which had used steam turbine or geared turbine engines into the 1960s and beyond, began to adopt diesel-electric engines when speed became less important than other considerations such as fuel efficiency, particularly after the rise in oil prices caused by the embargo of 1973–74.[4] Combined with other advances, these improvements made it possible and practical for builders to construct larger and faster ships.[5]

The growing volume of trade in certain commodities also encouraged shipping companies and builders to develop a variety of specialized vessels. For example, in the twentieth century oil gradually eclipsed coal as the fuel of choice for most industrial and domestic applications. Since most of the world's reserves were concentrated in a few locations, oil companies needed increasingly large fleets of tankers to carry their product from the fields to refineries and markets. Similarly, growing European demand for imported agricultural products contributed to the introduction (in the late nineteenth century) and subsequent refinement of refrigerated cargo ships that could carry meat, fruit, vegetables, and other perishable goods from suppliers located as far away as North and South America, Australia, and New Zealand.[6] Also, over the course of the twentieth century shipbuilders developed larger dry bulk carriers to transport materials such as iron ore, coal, and grain and combination carriers called OBOs because they can handle oil and ore, bulk, or ore. This latter design addressed the basic inefficiency of specialized oil tankers, which almost always travelled in ballast back to their loading ports.[7]

Beginning in the 1950s there was also a major shift in the demand for passenger transport. By 1958, more people were crossing the Atlantic by air than by ship, and within a decade, "the jet airliner had all but cornered the market,"[8] leaving only the relatively small and specialized niche of cruise vacations to the shipping companies. Yet while the number of luxury liners steadily declined, increasing automobile use produced a significant rise in the need for car ferries to bridge the gaps in expanding road networks. Car ferries were designed so that motor vehicles could drive on and off them using ramps and, eventually, were built to accommodate not only cars and their passengers but also larger vehicles like transport trucks and buses.[9] In many busy shipping areas, the advent of regularly scheduled car ferries added significantly to existing traffic levels.

Also in the 1950s, as a result of a steady rise in labour costs both on ship and at cargo-handling facilities in port and the demand for faster turnaround times in port, shipping companies and shipbuilders began to adopt more efficient methods of handling cargo. Perhaps the most notable innovation, introduced in the mid-1950s in North America, was containerization — "the development of a standardized box to carry the myriad of commodities referred to as general cargo (shoes, books, clothes, electronic goods) on a standardized ship."[10] There are competing claims regarding the first experiments with container shipping. Several Canadian writers give credit for the first use of standardized containers (1953) and the first purpose-built container ship (*Clifford J. Roger*, 1955) to the White Pass & Yukon Route, a company that operated ship, rail, and road services connecting Vancouver and Whitehorse, Yukon. Sidney Gilman, writing for *Conway's History of the Ship* series, calls Matson Navigation Company's converted cargo vessel *Hawaiian Merchant* the first "containership." It sailed from San Francisco to Honolulu in August 1958.[11]

Once established, the concept of containerization spread rapidly. The industry worked out a series of standard sizes and types of containers that could be accommodated by specially adapted or purpose-built transport trucks, railcars, and ships. Port authorities built facilities specifically to handle containers, making it possible to streamline the transfer from road or rail to ship and back again. This method of shipment was particularly important in the movement of general cargo, the volume and variety of which has grown dramatically along with demand for consumer goods since the Second World War.[12]

Shipbuilders have made other notable improvements to cargo-handling techniques. Self-unloading equipment, which has been around in one form or another since the 1920s, became more common, more fully automated, and more efficient after 1960. With it, ships could unload bulk cargoes more quickly. In addition,

Figure 35. Bridge of the ice-breaking ferry Abegweit circa 1970. This highly innovative vessel was designed and built in Canada for service across the Northumberland Strait. (CSTM/CN000222)

they could deposit their loads closer to the locations where they were being used and where it was not necessarily economical to build elaborate port facilities.[13] All of these improvements in cargo-handling have increased the speed and ease with which goods can be loaded and off-loaded and thereby reduced layover time in port as well as the number of shore workers required to do the work.[14]

In its search for greater efficiency, the shipping industry also turned its attention to port facilities and their supporting infrastructure. As shippers adopted larger, faster, and more sophisticated vessels, ports had to be modernized and expanded to accommodate them. For example, only the very largest and deepest harbours could safely receive very large crude carriers (VLCCs) and ultra large crude carriers (ULCCs), and even then they demanded special off-loading equipment and storage tanks. Similarly, as container shipping became more and more important, the industry developed special highly automated container ports that could handle thousands of containers each day. Often these modern facilities were built separate from existing ports, necessitating the construction of new infrastructure such as ship channels, piers, navigational markers, rail lines, roads, and storage and administrative buildings.

The shipping industry has also found ways to reduce labour costs. The steady increase in the size and level of automation of many types of vessels has made it possible to reduce the number of crew needed to operate them. This is especially evident with tankers, where the size of crew needed "is independent of the ship's size."[15] As a consequence, in the years after the Second World War and especially after 1960, while the overall tonnage of commercial shipping grew enormously, the number of personnel employed in operating these vessels declined dramatically.[16] Today, some of the most automated ships boast what is called a "one-man bridge," that is, a bridge that can be controlled by a single officer[17] whose watch-keeping duties, in the most advanced examples, need not even be interrupted by the call of nature, since his specialized monitoring equipment includes a glass-enclosed toilet.[18]

As shipbuilders have incorporated more and more sophisticated technology into ships' operating and navigational systems, skill requirements have also changed significantly. Increasingly, small cadres of highly skilled mariners are responsible for operating most large vessels. Although they are trained to interpret and act upon the outputs of all the automated systems that monitor what is happening throughout the ship and how well it is progressing to its destination, the ships' crews tend to be made up of workers from developing nations, many of whom have little professional training or education. This approach to manning ships has been made possible not just by technological advances but also by the rise of "flag of convenience" nations. These countries have very minimal regulations governing the manning, wages, working conditions, insurance, maintenance and repair, and safety standards of commercial vessels as well as very low corporate taxes, all of which has made it very attractive for shipowners from other nations with stricter regulations to register their ships there.[19]

The pressure on the shipping industry to move more goods more quickly and efficiently continues today. With the revolution in communications, businesses can and often expect to be able to carry out complex commercial transactions in a matter of seconds; the actual movement of the goods is seen as the slow link in the chain, and transportation companies are under constant pressure to speed up the process. The growing interdependence of separate and often distant economies only adds to the pressure as nations become increasingly reliant on one another for essential materials and products as well as for markets. Moreover, as the world moves toward more open trade and increasing numbers of formerly isolated or underdeveloped nations enter the international economy, the level of integration is likely to grow, and with it our dependence on and demand for efficient transportation.

The expansion of shipping and especially the growth of trade in dangerous materials such as oil, gas, and chemicals in large quantities and the constant pressure to operate more efficiently have had certain negative side effects. Although the risk of accidents may not have increased significantly, the potential for damage has. Despite regular upgrades of channels and ports to accommodate larger and faster vessels, the natural barriers that exist in and around harbours and their approaches place definite limitations on how much space can be made available to ships. Even with all the latest automatic steering and navigating equipment, mariners and pilots make mistakes that are sometimes hard to identify let alone correct in the time it takes to stop or turn a massive vehicle like an oil tanker.

This issue first came to prominence in the 1960s with the dramatic increase in the size and number of oil tankers travelling long distances through international waters. Even though the rate of tanker accidents did not increase markedly, "the sheer volume of oil being transported by sea meant that the probability of accidents was greater."[20] At the same time, in the western industrialized nations, the public was becoming aware of the problem of environmental pollution. This awareness was heightened by a number of very high-profile oil spills beginning in 1967, when the *Torrey Canyon* ran aground on the southwest coast of the United Kingdom and released thousands of gallons of crude oil into the ocean. In the aftermath of this accident, international regulators and national governments instituted a series of regulations making specific navigational equipment mandatory on ships of a certain size. Subsequent spills — the *Arrow* in Nova Scotia's Chedabucto Bay in 1970, the *Amoco Cadiz* off Brittany's coast in 1978 (spilling a record 220,000 gallons [833 000 L] of oil), the *Kurdistan* off Cape Breton in 1979, and, in 1989, the *Exxon Valdez* in Alaska — have, however, made it clear that regulation can go only so far toward reducing the risks associated with enormous vessels filled with dangerous cargoes transiting through treacherous waters. Even the new double-hull requirements for tankers being phased in by the U.S. and Canadian governments cannot eliminate the risk of oil spills.[21]

Regulation, nevertheless, has become a fact of life for the whole shipping industry. Beginning late in the nineteenth century, shipping and trading nations worldwide began to recognize a need for international standards and rules to improve the safety and efficiency of shipping. Representatives from various countries began to meet and form specialized groups to discuss such issues as the unification of marine law and practice, standardization and improvement of aids to navigation and marine charts, and the need to establish some basic rules for the safe operation of vessels and for the safety of passengers and crew. Though most of these groups were not formalized until after the formation of the United Nations, they did produce important regulations. For example, the International Convention for the Safety of Life at Sea laid down regulations for everything from the construction and stability of vessels to required life-saving equipment and rules for preventing collisions, navigating in ice, and issuing safety certificates. Also, by 1934, there were, on the books, an International Load Line Convention and a series of conventions protecting the rights of seamen and restricting the employment of children.[22]

In the decades after 1945, many of the ad hoc groups formed to improve international shipping were formalized and have since taken on important and active roles in monitoring and regulating the development of the industry. The leading organization is the International Maritime Organization or IMO (1948), the goal of which is to promote "the adoption of the highest practicable standards in matters concerning maritime safety and efficiency of navigation."[23] The International Association of Lighthouse Authorities (IALA, 1965) oversees the development and use of aids to navigation, while the International Hydrographic Organization (IHO, 1970) seeks to establish uniform standards for paper and electronic charts. INMARSAT, or the International Maritime Satellite Organization, was formed to make provision for the use of satellite communication systems to help take the pressure off overused radio channels and to help extend coverage. These latter groups all have technical and analytical roles, that is, they study and assess the usefulness of various systems, devices, and procedures, but they also play an important role in setting the rules for when and how these will be applied worldwide.[24]

Although many governments are loath to intervene in certain aspects of shipping — flag of convenience registration, for example — and are striving to reduce restrictions on international trade and commerce, most have implemented legislation to comply with important international conventions. In addition, many national governments had established their own, often stricter, rules governing vessels registered by them or that travel in their waters. These deal with any number of issues, from minimum crew levels and insurance coverage to types of radio systems and emergency safety equipment required on board. Many regulations at both the national and international levels relate to mandatory minimum standards for navigational equipment, its use and performance. Only in rare instances do regulatory bodies demand immediate and absolute compliance with new regulations, choosing instead to phase in most changes to limit the sometimes onerous costs of conversion, their impact on shipping charges, and, ultimately, on the price of goods traded on the world market.[25]

All of these events and trends in world trade and shipping have had a profound impact in Canada. Like the international economy, Canada's has grown substantially since 1900, despite suffering severe setbacks in the early decades of the century. Fuelled by substantial population growth (post–Second World War immigration and the baby boom especially), the industrial requirements of two world wars, and the post-1945 rise in demand for consumer goods, Canadian productive capacity has risen dramatically since 1900. In 1890, per capita gross domestic product (GDP) was just $700; by 1926 it had risen to about $1,200; and by 1960 it was well over $2,000 per capita, or more than $13.5 billion in total. In particular, there has been an enormous expansion in agricultural production and in the production of various minerals, coal, and forest products. And, since Canada has such a small domestic market, most of these goods have been destined for foreign markets. Over the course of the twentieth century Canadians "came to supply one-sixth of world wheat and flour exports and large shares of newsprint, lumber, and copper." At the same time, the country became a major importer of machinery to equip its factories and to help extract and process its natural resources.[26] By the 1990s, Canadians numbered more than 27 million and were producing and consuming more goods and services than ever before. In 1995, Canada's total GDP was $694 billion, placing the nation thirteenth in the world, while per capita production was $24,400, or fifth overall.[27]

Figure 36. Churchill, Manitoba, shown here in August 1959, was one of two major ports built by the Canadian government in the twentieth century to expedite the shipment of prairie grain around the world.
(Library and Archives Canada, neg. e003719359)

With increased trade came substantial growth in shipping. In 1920, there were 7,904 vessels registered in Canada, with a net tonnage of more than 1.15 billion. By 1931 the number of vessels had risen to 8,905 and their combined tonnage to 1.4 billion.[28] These totals fell back somewhat as a result of the Depression, but with the outbreak of war in 1939 Canadian shipyards became important suppliers of military and merchant vessels. When the war ended, Canada had the ninth largest tonnage of merchant vessels in the world. The country did not retain this high ranking for long, falling to sixteenth position by 1960 and thirty-second by 1988. Yet while the number of ships on the Canadian registry books declined, the total tonnage continued to rise, at approximately the same rate as the world fleet.[29]

The worldwide increase in tonnage was felt strongly in Canada's ports, where trading activity grew steadily after the Second World War. In 1946, more than 64.5 million tons (58.6 million tonnes) of shipping — inland and sea-going but excluding coastal vessels — arrived at and departed from Canada's many ports. At eight of the ports handling incoming or outgoing foreign cargo, over 25 million tons (22.7 million tonnes) were loaded and unloaded. Fourteen years later, the tonnage of vessels entering and leaving Canadian ports had grown to more than 152 million (138 million tonnes), excluding coastal vessels, which accounted for an additional 173 million tons (157.3 million tonnes). The cargo carried by these ships totalled 118.3 million tonnes. In 1988, Canada's water-borne trade reached an all-time high when Canadian ports handled 320 million tonnes of cargo, 250 of which was international. By 1989, the registered tonnage of vessels calling at Canadian ports had risen to 521.2 million. Though the recession of the early 1990s caused a serious decline in trade, by 1995 markets had recovered sufficiently to support movement of 310.2 million tonnes of cargo through Canadian ports.[30]

Canada has also felt the impact of specialization and automation. For example, on the Great Lakes, shipping companies began adopting self-unloading technology as early as the 1920s. Especially well-suited to cargoes such as coal, sand, rock, and grain, self-loading vessels became increasingly common in the 1960s, by which time the most advanced versions could unload as much as 3,000 tons (2 700 tonnes) of cargo per hour, compared to the 600 ton per hour (545.5 tonne per hour) rate of the 1920s models. By 1988, "31 of the 81 dry bulk carriers operating in the Great Lakes were self-unloaders," compared to just 16 out of 186 in 1960.[31]

The 1950s and 1960s also witnessed a major expansion of passenger and automobile ferry services in Canada, especially on the east and west coasts. Between 1952 and 1960, the vessels travelling on just one major route, that between Port aux Basques and North Sydney, more than doubled their passenger load (31,000 to 67,000), tripled their freight load (86,908 to 257,429 tons [79 000 to 234 000 tonnes]), and began to carry a significant number of vehicles for the first time (negligible to 18,000). This was four years before the opening of the Trans-Canada Highway across Newfoundland and eight years before it was paved. By 1990, the ferries on this route were making 1,689 single crossings each year, carrying 362,350 passengers and more than 172,000 commercial and passenger-related vehicles. That same year, the sixteen ships of CN's Marine Atlantic fleet ferried 2.5 million passengers and 1.2 million vehicles across the waterways of the east coast.[32] The story of the British Columbia Ferry Corporation's rise is no less impressive. When it was founded in 1960, the B.C. Ferry Authority had just 2 vessels and 191 employees, but by 1966, the fleet had grown to include 24 vessels and several new or upgraded terminal facilities. Today, BC Ferries has a fleet of 39 vessels operating out of 43 terminals along 26 routes. In the 1997–98 fiscal year, these vessels carried 22 million passengers and 8 million vehicles.[33] Throughout Canada, in 1993, members of the Canadian Ferry Operators' Association, who account for more than 95 percent of domestic ferry traffic, operated a total of 158 vessels on which they moved more than 41 million passengers and about 16 million vehicles.[34]

In the late 1960s, the Canadian shipping industry began to take its first systematic steps toward full containerization. In 1968, the port of Montréal opened Canada's first container terminal, which authorities expanded in 1970 and then supplemented with a second terminal in 1972. By this time other ports had adopted this new approach to cargo-handling, notably Halifax, Québec, Saint John, Toronto, and Vancouver. In 1972, Montréal alone handled more than 800,000 tons (727 000 tonnes) of containerized cargo, while Québec and Halifax were expecting to process 950,000 and 800,000, respectively. All of these figures represented impressive increases over the previous year's totals.[35] By 1980, the port facility at Halifax was handling more than 2 million tonnes of containerized cargo, and within nine years that total had nearly doubled, to 4 million tonnes. Montréal, meanwhile, experienced a similarly dramatic increase in container trade, with 1989 totals reaching 5.5 million tonnes.[36]

Ferries and container carriers, like many other specialized vessels and their cargoes, required specialized terminal facilities to service them. These facilities were especially important in Canada, where producers and shippers often spent much time, effort, and money moving commodities such as wheat and minerals from distant and sometimes isolated regions to tidewater ports. Any savings they could make in cargo-handling helped to keep them competitive. Thus, throughout the twentieth century, the Canadian government and the shipping industry attempted to create and improve the system of ports in order to smooth and speed the transfer of cargo from one means of transportation to another. One of the earliest efforts in this area was the creation and augmentation of grain-handling capacity. Beginning before the First World War, the Canadian government built major grain terminals at the Lakehead and at various points along the Great Lakes/St Lawrence route. By the 1930s, they had added facilities on the west coast at Vancouver and Prince Rupert, British Columbia, and in the north at Churchill, Manitoba.[37]

Later, in the 1960s and 1970s, governments and port authorities also had to respond to the development and deployment of increasingly large oil tankers that carried much of eastern Canada's supply of imported oil. As crude oil came in from abroad, it had to be distributed to the various refineries along the Atlantic coast and as far upstream as Montréal.[38] Tankers, of course, needed special off-loading and storage installations, and for the very large crude carriers that became common after 1967, harbours and channels had to be deepened and enlarged.[39] Today, east coast ports are also handling a significant amount of oil bound from Europe and the Middle East to the United States but which must be "transhipped from very large crude carriers to smaller tankers which comply with the U.S. Oil Pollution Prevention Act of 1990."[40]

Although port expansion and development could help to reduce the time and labour needed to move goods to market, it could do only so much for inland traffic, because the canals and channels of the Great Lakes/St Lawrence system restricted the size of vessels that could move inland and the speed with which they could travel safely. These restrictions were especially significant because, among other products, they affected the shipment of wheat and iron ore, two very important export commodities. Thus, in addition to upgrading port facilities, Canadian officials had to invest in expensive improvements to the complex of channels and canals that linked the Great Lakes and upper St Lawrence to ocean-going ports. These improvements culminated in the construction of the St Lawrence Seaway in the late 1950s, an enormous and controversial project that eventually involved both the U.S. and Canadian governments. Its Canadian promoters saw it as a way to promote trade in bulk goods like grain and iron ore by removing the bottleneck between Montréal and Lake Ontario that permitted only relatively small-capacity canallers (1 000 tonnes capacity) to pass. The seaway opened up the channel to vessels that could carry up to 9 000 tonnes of cargo, making it possible for ocean-going ships to travel all the way from the Atlantic Ocean to the head of Lake Superior.[41]

Canadian trade, especially inland trade, was also impeded by the harsh climate. Except during abnormally mild winters, the Canadian ports of the St Lawrence and Great Lakes system freeze up. Historically this meant that businesses wishing to move bulk goods to the east and on to Europe or elsewhere had to use more expensive land transportation to get them to the all-season ports of the Atlantic coast, bypassing, in the process, the ports of Montréal and Québec. In the late 1950s, probably as an adjunct to the construction of the seaway, winter navigation was gradually extended through the Gulf of St Lawrence and upriver to Québec and finally to Montréal. Any ships that ventured upriver required icebreaker support from the Canadian Coast Guard, and at first service was irregular. In 1964 there was just one line offering regular sailings to Montréal. Within three years, however, "at least ten lines were advertising regular Montreal service."[42] By the early 1970s, shipping industry interests were also discussing the possibility of extending the navigation season of the whole seaway using a combination of icebreaker support, "a comprehensive ice reconnaissance programme and an extensive vessel information system." Proponents of this plan believed "that the potential benefits likely to result from even a short extension of the navigation season on the Great Lakes are significant enough to justify the allocation of additional resources towards research in this area."[43]

In addition to the growth in commercial and ferry traffic and the development of infrastructure and services to support them, Canadian authorities had to cope with the increasing demands of fishermen and pleasure boaters, especially after 1945. Though the major Canadian fisheries had faced many difficult years after a brief post–First World War boom,[44] the Second World War ushered in a new era of expansion. The combination of high demand for fish and the introduction of larger, more mechanized vessels and new navigational technologies such as sonar both encouraged and enabled Canadian fishermen to catch more fish more quickly than ever before. Moreover, on the Atlantic coast, provincial and federal government policies reinforced these trends by, among other things, providing generous subsidies to fishermen to help them build new vessels and modernize their existing fleets. As a result, the number of "larger fishing vessels in the Canadian fleet multiplied fivefold between 1959 and 1974."[45] By 1988, the Coast Guard reported that there were some 39,500 fishing vessels in Canada manned by 95,600 fishermen. Since that year — a peak year for water-borne trade generally in Canada[46] — numbers have declined to 36,500 vessels in 1993 and 21,367 as of 1 January 1997. Of these vessels, over two-thirds were based in Newfoundland and the Maritimes.[47]

The post–Second World War period also marked the beginning of a dramatic rise in the number of small vessels owned and operated by Canadians. These vessels, which were exempt from registry but were licensed by the Department of Transport at least until the late 1960s, were first mentioned as a category of vessel in the late 1940s. Though departmental reports do not specify what sort of vessels fell into this category or how many of them were recreational craft, it seems safe to assume that a large proportion of them were pleasure boats, since part of the government's response to the increase in this type of vessel was to send representatives to various harbour commissions and yacht clubs to explain the regulations. In 1951–52, the government implemented a new set of regulations governing the licensing of small vessels, the numbers of which by this time were increasing by about 50,000 a year. By 1958–59, more than 251,000 small vessels had been licensed in Canada, and by 1965–66, the total had risen to 619,205. According to Statistics Canada, Canadians owned about 2 million pleasure craft by the early 1990s, and a more recent survey by a boating publication puts the number even higher, at 2.4 million.[48]

Though fishermen and pleasure boaters have different needs than those of the commercial shipping industry and ferry services, they all create traffic and they all place pressure on the systems, institutions, and individuals charged with ensuring safe and efficient navigation in Canadian waters. Canada has responded to this pressure in much the same way as other developed nations: by expanding government's operational and legislative/regulatory presence in marine transportation. Continuing the traditions and precedents of the nineteenth century, the federal government has committed substantial resources to safeguarding shipping in Canadian waters.[49]

On the operational side, it maintained and extended the network of existing navigational aids — buoys, beacons, and lights — integrating improvements as they became available and establishing the Dominion Lighthouse Depot as early as 1903 to do research and development work on aids. Depot staff experimented with "all types of burners, lanterns, illuminants and lenses" under harsh Canadian conditions, developed and tested new tower designs, and also manufactured equipment, helping to free the government of its complete dependence on foreign makers.[50] By 1904, the Department of Marine had established a total of 1,027 lights — 826 light stations, 15 lightships, and 186 pole lights — and 4,200 buoys. Ten years later, the number of lights stood at 1,400.[51] In 1988, the Canadian Coast Guard was responsible for installing and servicing some 13,000 buoys and 10,000 land-based aids, 266 of which were major lights.[52]

Over the years, department employees have also had to keep pace with new navigational instruments and systems — radio is one obvious example — and analyse them to determine whether they were appropriate for use in the Canadian context and how they could best be applied to Canada's marine needs. After the Second World War and especially since the 1960s, the rapid pace of technological change and the complexity of new inventions such as vessel traffic and satellite positioning systems have made this role an increasingly important and demanding one.

With more navigational aids, waterways, and marine infrastructure to maintain and more vessels travelling through Canadian waters, the government also needed more vessels. Over the course of the century, it not only significantly augmented its fleet, but also gradually moved away from its practice of adapting existing vessels to meet many, often diverse, requirements and began to commission purpose-built ships specifically designed to withstand harsh Canadian conditions and to carry out specialized tasks. These included buoy tenders to lay and take up markers, dredgers and icebreakers to maintain channels and harbours, and supply and cargo vessels to service light, radio, and meteorological stations. Officially named the Canadian Coast Guard in 1962, the fleet operates out of several regional bases and, in addition to its work in facilitating navigation, it provides search and rescue services, undertakes fisheries protection, and resupplies isolated northern communities. It is also responsible for inspecting Canadian-registered vessels and any vessels travelling through Canadian waters to make certain that they meet safety and other standards laid down in the Canada Shipping Act.[53]

The government also needed many more personnel to fulfill its expanding role in marine transportation. Until the advent of automation, additional light stations demanded additional keepers. More shipping traffic and more compulsory pilotage zones required more pilots to assist vessels moving through these restricted areas. As the government fleet and its responsibilities grew, crew numbers expanded to keep pace. And in addition to these traditional occupations, authorities created and filled new positions such as radio and radio direction finding operators and, later, harbour radar and vessel traffic systems technicians.

In order to finance this steady expansion, the federal government increased the budget of the departments responsible for marine transportation significantly over the decades. Between 1868 and 1905, departmental expenditures rose from $371,070 to $5,727,000. By mid-century, the Marine Services division of the Department of Transport required some $17 million to carry out its varied duties, not including those related to radio communication and radio aids to navigation.

Figure 37. The bustling port of Montréal with a variety of ships docked, circa 1955. (CSTM/CN002160)

In 1966, expenditure rose to a new high of just under $45 million, of which more than half was spent by the operations branch.[54] By 1988, the Coast Guard alone had a total budget of $700 million.[55]

The era of expansion came to an end in the late 1980s and the 1990s when the federal government began to make deep cuts to departmental budgets and to review the cost and effectiveness of the programs and services it provided. This, combined with a long-term policy of fiscal restraint, has forced marine authorities to reduce or eliminate certain services or tasks. For example, light stations are gradually being automated, thereby eliminating the first line of emergency assistance and shelter for stranded fishermen, pleasure boaters, or other coastal mariners. Marine authorities have also had to consider privatizing or instituting cost-recovery schemes for services and tasks such as ports, dredging, ice breaking, and pilotage. Although technological advances in navigation have made some of these services less essential, many are too critical to Canadian trade for the government to abandon them altogether. Indeed, in 1995, Parliament's Standing Committee on Transport submitted a series of recommendations that reiterated the need for a strong federal presence in marine affairs. Though the committee suggested the thorough review of many departmental operations and services and the possible "commercialization" of some, it also stressed the need for Canada's marine infrastructure to continue to meet basic standards of safe and efficient navigation.[56] There is, of course, much disagreement within the shipping industry about what exactly is required to do this.

In addition to carrying out its multi-faceted operational responsibilities, the government, over the course of the twentieth century, has also adopted an increasingly active legislative and regulatory role to help it deal with the rising volume of water-borne trade and traffic. The British North America Act of 1867 gave the Canadian government "the power to legislate generally with respect to navigation and shipping (BNA Act, Section 10) including navigational aids (Section 9)."[57] Prior to 1906, however, shipping in Canada was largely governed by British legislation — the Merchant Shipping Act (1854) and the Merchant Shipping (Colonial) Act (1869) — which, among other things, laid down the rules for ship registry and inspection, certification and employment of mariners, and provision for sick and distressed mariners. Subsequent governments added sections to address new or newly recognized problems such as load lines (1876) and the special risks of operating steam engines and boilers. Successive British governments passed these acts to ensure that British ships and mariners maintained high standards of safety and efficiency so that they could compete effectively with other shipping nations.[58] At the same time, Canadian officials enacted laws to cover coastal shipping and otherwise give specific meaning and force to the general principles laid down in the British legislation.[59]

When the Canadian government passed the first Canada Shipping Act in 1906, it essentially followed the British example, using the act to establish rules for Canadian-registered ships or for ships operating in Canadian waters. It set similar safety, registry, and certification standards as well as the procedures for inspecting ships to ensure that they complied with those standards. Other sections of the act dealt with issues such as wrecks and salvage, lights and buoys, harbours and harbourmasters, pilotage, navigation, collisions, liability, and legal proceedings. This legislation was revised several times after 1906 and supplemented by other laws that provide standards and rules for new technologies. For example, following an international conference on radiotelegraphy held in 1912, Canada passed its first Radiotelegraph Act, which laid down the basic requirements for the proper and lawful use of shipboard radio. Similarly, the adoption of radar for civilian use after 1945 eventually led to the development of specific regulations governing its use.

New social, economic, and political circumstances also inspired the Canadian government to enact new and more comprehensive regulations. The 1934 version of the Canada Shipping Act, for example, contained three draft international conventions limiting the employment of children and establishing certain rights of seafaring labourers. It also contained the 1929 International Convention for the Safety of Life at Sea (SOLAS) and the international load line convention of 1930.[60] Both of these reflected a growing recognition that, in an increasingly competitive industry, shipowners had to be compelled to meet certain safety standards in the day-to-day operation and maintenance of their vessels as well as in the provision of emergency equipment and procedures.

Beginning in 1956, the Canada Shipping Act also included the International Convention for the Prevention of Pollution of the Sea by Oil, 1954, which sought to address the risks posed by increased tanker traffic around the world. Later the federal government passed its own legislation in response to specific pollution concerns. After the test voyage of the tanker *Manhattan* through the Northwest Passage in 1969, it passed the Arctic Waters Pollution Prevention Act. This legislation restricted the type, schedules, and routes of vessels travelling through certain designated shipping safety control zones. The very next year the sinking of the tanker *Arrow* in Chedabucto Bay, Nova Scotia, prompted the government to establish a traffic separation zone

(IMO recognized) to control the movement of vessels into and out of the area.[61]

The Canadian government has also followed the lead of the international maritime community in establishing and enforcing standards for the certification of mariners. Originally implemented in 1869, the standards for certificates of competency were intended to ensure that mariners had certain basic skills that would help to make shipping safer and more efficient. The goal of ensuring the competency of mariners did not change in the twentieth century, but the knowledge mariners needed to meet the standards did. As the international economy grew, shipping increased to accommodate it. Naval architects, engineers, and scientists developed new ship and engine designs and new navigational and other technologies to increase the capacity, speed, and efficiency of shipping.

All of these changes had an impact on the content and level of knowledge required to operate vessels effectively. Though regulation often lagged well behind the introduction of these new technologies, legislators eventually responded by revising and updating the requirements for certification. Beginning with the introduction of radio in the early years of the century, certification standards have grown to include operational knowledge of complex systems such as the gyrocompass, radar and automatic radar plotting aids (ARPA), sonar, radio- and satellite-based positioning systems, sophisticated communications systems and protocols, electronic charts, and integrated bridge systems. Mariners must also understand and apply an increasingly elaborate set of rules and regulations controlling navigation through congested, constricted, or fragile marine environments.

As the requirements for certification increased, mariners found it more and more difficult to acquire the necessary knowledge in the traditional manner, that is, by combining their practical shipboard experience with a minimal amount of pre-examination tutoring and cramming. Since they were responsible for certification, national governments had to take an interest in education that supported the process. In Canada, there was no system of marine education in place at the turn of the twentieth century, due, in part, to the country's historic reliance on Britain for so much of its marine infrastructure. As that reliance decreased following Confederation, the Canadian government had to take over many new responsibilities, including making an effort to offer some kind of vocational instruction to Canadian mariners.

The government's initial efforts in the marine education field were far from ambitious. In 1902, the Department of Marine and Fisheries provided a subsidy of $500 to a private school in Montréal. It took over that facility the next year and set up four additional schools in Halifax, Saint John, Yarmouth, and Victoria. Funding was not generous, with just $3,000 provided to cover all costs for the five schools, including the meagre $250 retainer paid to instructors (who were the certification examiners in these cities). According to the department's own description, the "subjects taught were of an elementary nature principally on seamanship, [and] navigational problems were in some instances lightly touch upon."[62]

Over the next forty years, the government gradually expanded the system of schools both by funding private schools and setting up more of its own. Yet although the annual reports of the department for these decades often provide a list of schools and their locations and tell us where examinations for masters' and mates' certificates were held, how many people took the exams, and how many certificates were issued, they are, for the most part, silent on the content of the courses offered. For example, in 1936 the government announced significant revisions to the 1919 regulations relating to examinations for certificates of competency,[63] but there is no mention in the report for that year of these changes or if and how the navigation schools responded to them. Appleton states that, in the early years of the century at least, the government kept educational standards at "the simplest level commensurate with the demands of safety and existing legislation."[64] There is little evidence to suggest that this policy changed significantly until the outbreak of war in 1939.

During the Second World War, the demand for trained seamen rose dramatically as Allied Merchant Navies became "the main artery of freedom," ferrying essential supplies to an otherwise isolated Britain. The existing marine infrastructure could not supply the trained manpower needed to fulfill this requirement, so the federal government extended the responsibilities of Director of Merchant Seamen, Department of Transport to include the recruitment and training of "officers and seamen for the Canadian Merchant Navy by the establishment of Training Centres and the extension of Nautical Schools." The government's new educational scheme was aimed at producing a full range of merchant mariners, including junior ordinary seamen, cadet officers, engineering ratings, wireless operators, and ship's cooks. It also provided opportunities for experienced seamen to upgrade their credentials by offering preparatory instruction for certificates of competency as navigating officers (first and second mates and masters). To implement this scheme, the government set up two new schools: St Margaret's Sea Training School at Hubbards, Nova Scotia, and the Marine Engineering Instructional School at Prescott, Ontario. The former was set up to train men aged seventeen to twenty-two to become junior ordinary seamen, "with opportunities for a few of the more apt trainees to secure immediate appointment as Cadet Officers." The syllabus included classroom instruction in elementary navigation, mathematics, English, meteorology, and "kindred subjects." The school also had special equipment, including a facsimile of a deck and other critical parts of a ship to assist in teaching basic skills including compass work and steering, watches, lead lines, signals, knots and hitches, and cargo and lifeboat handling. Special attention was given to steering and lifeboat handling. The duration of the course was thirteen weeks.[65]

The government also began to offer special training to experienced seamen to enable them to become navigating officers. This training was delivered at government nautical schools including St Margaret's and was specifically designed to prepare candidates to sit for certification exams for second mate, first mate, and master. The government provided those with the requisite sea experience free tuition, room and board, and pay at the rate of their last sea position for a maximum of six weeks. Graduates of the courses at St Margaret's and the other schools would either be enrolled in the manning pools or appointed to new ships.[66] It is worth noting that despite these educational efforts, the Canadian Merchant Navy suffered from a chronic shortage of certificated navigating officers and marine engineers throughout the war and had to "borrow" officers from the United Kingdom to crew some of their ships.[67]

When the war ended, Canada had a surplus of experienced mariners, and the government seems to have reverted to its limited pre-war educational objective of providing instruction at its navigation schools to mariners to prepare them for certification exams.[68] During the 1950s, due to a shortage of marine engineers, federal officials assigned engineering instructors to its schools at Toronto, Montréal, Halifax, and St John's, and its schools at Rimouski and St John's carried out "pre-sea training" for newcomers to the marine profession.[69] But these were exceptions to the general trend that saw the Canadian government gradually transfer responsibility for nautical education of civilian mariners to local authorities.[70] It maintained its central role in enforcing national and international certification standards by setting exams and issuing certificates.[71]

Federal officials noted two important developments that influenced their decision. They pointed to the introduction of new navigational technologies such as radar and to the general broadening range of instruction in all educational fields as an indication that the structure of navigational instruction had to change. The new and emerging demands of the shipping industry required a more comprehensive, flexible, and rigorous approach to navigational education,[72] and local authorities, with more direct access to the educational and maritime resources of the region, were in a much better position to provide this.

By the mid-1960s, navigational instruction in Canada had changed noticeably. Some independent schools of navigation remained in place and continued to offer certification-oriented courses to experienced mariners. As the requirements for good seamanship and certification changed to include new technologies and shipping regulations, these schools introduced new courses and training aids to stay current. In 1964, for example, the Nova Scotia Marine Navigation School in Halifax announced the introduction of a course using a radar simulator to train students to deal with "unexpected traffic situations." Successful completion of the course could be noted on their master's or mate's certificates.[73]

Around the same time, many provinces began to increase their commitment to post-secondary education, including setting up institutes, colleges, and other facilities to address the need for technical education. Some of these began to offer marine education programs as part of their trades-based curricula. These programs had the same long-term goal as earlier schools — to help graduates qualify for various certificates of competency — but their approach was different. For example, in 1965 Ontario's Department of Education, Technological and Trades Training Branch, announced the creation of four-year courses for deck officers and marine engineers. The course was aimed at newcomers to the field and was intended to augment the ranks of well-trained and certified Great Lakes mariners. The course for deck officers (up to level of First Mate, Home Trade) was made up of twenty months of academic study and twenty-four months of sea time, for which arrangements were being made with several Great Lakes companies. Depending on their specific course selection, students could expect to work with many of the latest navigational technologies, including Decca Navigator, gyrocompasses, echo sounders, radar, and LORAN. The branch also offered upgrading courses for experienced mariners in the off-season, carrying on the work started by the Dominion Marine Association in 1946 and maintained by the federal government until 1959.[74]

It is also worth noting that, despite its almost complete withdrawal from the civilian marine education field, in 1964 the federal government established its own specialized marine school, the Canadian Coast Guard College in North Sydney, Nova Scotia, which held its first classes in September 1965. The goal of this institution was "to provide full professional training in navigation and engineering to meet the needs of an expanding fleet of sophisticated ships and the demands of the new age in mercantile shipping."[75] The college offered "a four-year course covering academic and practical subjects to the standard of the examinations for master, foreign-going, and engineer first class." Until 1982, however, only graduates of the engineering program received commercially recognized certificates. The college issued navigation graduates who had successfully completed nine months sea time and an oral examination a Coast Guard Watchkeeping Certificate valid only in the CCG. Then, in 1982, the college established a "sandwich" program whereby graduates were able to accumulate enough sea time during the training program to qualify to sit the exams for Watchkeeping Mate. Coast Guard students could reach senior and command positions in the fleet by additional sea service and training.[76]

Today, navigational education still reflects this dual approach to instruction. A few institutions, such as Camosun College in B.C., cater mainly to professional mariners who want to upgrade their qualifications and certification. Most others, including the British Columbia Institute of Technology (Marine Campus, North Vancouver), the Nautical Institute of Nova Scotia Community College, and Memorial University of Newfoundland (MUN), offer both certification-oriented courses and entry-level professional programs. The Nautical Institute's "New Entry Seaperson" course is eighteen weeks in duration including an eight-week work placement, and its "Basic Marine Navigation Cadet" program lasts ten months. The programs at the other colleges consist of three or four years of combined study and sea time. With the successful completion of all required courses and sea time, graduates (with the exception of the Navigation Cadet group) are awarded a number of Transport Canada–approved qualifications and are eligible to take the certification exams for Bridge Watchkeeping (rating) or, in the case of BCIT's four-year program, will receive a Watchkeeping Mate Unrestricted Certificate of Competency. The Institut maritime du Québec at Rimouski offers a four-year navigation course that includes a maximum of six terms of theoretical study combined with six to twelve months of training at sea, qualifying graduates to write Transport Canada's examinations for certification at various levels.[77]

Although the fundamental structure of the nautical training system has not changed significantly since the 1960s, the content of the courses and the methods of teaching have. These changes reflect the recent evolution of the shipping industry, where crews are smaller and more likely to be from developing countries, officers are fewer, and ships are larger, faster, and more complex. International regulators have recognized that these developments pose a potential threat to safety and have produced a steady stream of regulations that attempt to balance the drive for efficiency with the need to protect mariners and the environment. As crewing levels have fallen, some shipping companies have introduced sophisticated navigational and communications systems that are intended to automate bridge operations so that fewer officers can manage the ship effectively. Regulators have also made the adoption of certain technologies mandatory for various classes of vessels. The responsibility for understanding and operating these systems properly has, of course, fallen on the shoulders of the remaining deck officers.[78]

As a consequence of these developments, deck officers must now learn to use a number of complex systems not only to gain certification but also to feel confident and be competent at the helm. This is clearly reflected in the curricula of the various nautical programs. For example, the deck officers course at MUN (targeted to certification candidates) not only includes the basics of astro-navigation, chart work, electricity, and radio, but also covers electronic navigation systems, integrated bridge systems, voyage management systems, electronic chart systems, and dynamic positioning systems. The four-year BCIT diploma program in nautical sciences includes even more technical content, including courses on the Global Maritime Distress and Safety System (GMDSS) and applied mathematics and computer studies. In each year, students take one or two in a series of progressive navigation courses as well as related classes in communications, collision regulations–navigation safety, and meteorology.[79]

Another major innovation — perhaps *the* major innovation — in nautical education has been the use of simulators. First introduced in the 1960s, simulators began as stand-alone units that could re-create only simple scenarios, a radar screen display, for example. With the introduction of semiconductors and integrated circuits, engineers were able to create more and more elaborate simulation programs, first running off large, main-frame computers and now based on personal computers with software that can be changed and refined to meet very specific needs. Today, nautical institutions rely heavily on electronic navigation simulators that re-create the integrated operation of positioning systems like GPS, depth and speed indicators, radar systems, and electronic chart information. The software allows the instructors to change the exercises to reflect the level and specific content required for each course. Some schools also have what are known as full mission ship's bridge simulators that, like sophisticated flight-training simulators, put students in "virtual" control of a modern ship in a variety of situations.[80]

According to instructors and others within the industry, simulators that produce realistic and complex scenarios provide students with a preliminary practical awareness of what a bridge looks like, how ships move, and how that movement must be monitored and controlled by them. Simulators can also be used to fabricate emergency situations to help students learn how to cope with unforeseen problems and react quickly and effectively to solve them. They are, of course, no substitute for actual experience at the helm of a ship and, like many sophisticated technologies, can cause problems when relied upon too heavily to solve complex training problems. There can be no doubt, however, that when used as part of a well-rounded educational program, they do impart critical knowledge and experience and can significantly reduce the level of intimidation that inexperienced students naturally feel when first placed in front of the controls of a real ship.

In February of 2002, the International Marine Organization's latest upgrade to the International Convention on Standards of Training, Certification and Watchkeeping for Seafarers (STCW-95) came into force. Canadian-trained mariners and the Canadian system of nautical education should have no trouble meeting this new standard. The Canadian system produces well-trained seafarers who are respected throughout the industry. The biggest problem confronting both Canadian schools and their graduates seems to be the lack of good jobs within the industry. For those who do manage to find a decent position, there are other challenges. Increased regulation of shipping and seafarers has not eliminated the dangers of life on board ship, and some critics argue that these have increased in spite of regulation. In addition to the increased responsibilities of managing a ship that probably has been crewed in the cheapest possible fashion, deck officers must also monitor all of the automatic systems and alarms that are constantly providing new and possibly important navigational information. Add to this the mountain of paperwork now required to meet IMO regulations, and the job of master or mate begins to look less attractive even, one can imagine, to the most devoted mariner.[81]

A New Direction: Shipboard Navigational Advances

After 1900 the requirements of shipboard navigation remained essentially the same as in the sixteenth century. Mariners still needed to know how fast they were going and in what direction, where exactly they were on the Earth's surface, and whether or not they were in danger of running aground or colliding with another vessel. What changed — apart from the size and speed of ships — were the devices that navigators had available to them to obtain this information and the level of precision these tools offered. During the twentieth century, engineers and scientists introduced important new navigational devices and also produced improved versions of existing ones. Among the most important additions to existing shipboard instruments were the gyroscopic compass and echo-sounders.

The gyroscopic compass was first introduced by Dr. Hermann Anschütz-Kaempfer in 1908. This device "seeks out and indicates true geographic north"[82] and is in no way influenced by the magnetic field of the Earth or any metal or magnetic material built into or carried on board the ship. The function of the gyrocompass is based on two properties that influence the behaviour of spinning bodies. Gyroscopic inertia describes the tendency of a spinning body "to maintain its axis and plane of rotation relative to space."[83] The second property, precession, is the tendency of a spinning body to react to disturbing force or torque by slowly rotating, or precessing, in a direction at right angles to the direction of the impressed force.[84] In a gyrocompass, a metal wheel or gyro rotor is mounted in frictionless bearings so that it can spin as freely as possible. Its axis of spin is set to indicate true north, and the gyro is kept spinning at a steady rate by an electric motor. During the course of operation, the Earth's rotation causes the gyro to tilt and rotate with respect to the Earth. The tilt effect is actually used by the gyrocompass to maintain an accurate setting. Its instrumentation "is so arranged that the gyro is automatically precessed" according to the planet's motion to stay in the north-south plane. Rotation, on the other hand, combined with the effects of the ship's speed especially if it is travelling north or south, causes the gyro to wander from its set direction. This

Figure 38. The gyrocompass, which became widely available for civilian use after 1945, not only eliminated the problems of magnetic variation and deviation that plagued the magnetic compass. It is also very stable, accurate, and reliable, even in rough seas.
(CSTM1999.0051)

drift must be corrected by a special gravity control that precesses the gyro just enough to ensure that it continues to indicate true north.[85]

Because it is not influenced by the magnetic field of the Earth, the gyrocompass eliminated the problem of magnetic variation, making it a very reliable indicator of direction even in high latitudes where the magnetic compass was almost useless. Moreover, it did not have to be corrected for deviation resulting from the presence of magnetic metals in the ship.[86] But, like most new inventions, the gyrocompass was not without problems. The earliest versions (circa 1908 to 1916) were plagued by a problem known as "intercardinal error," caused by the pitching and rolling of the ship. In heavy seas, British battleship crews had noted errors of as much as 40 percent in their readings from devices made by Anschütz and by American Elmer Sperry. With Europe's navies locked in a massive military conflict since 1914, this level of accuracy was unacceptable. The problem was solved around 1916 when Englishman S. G. Brown devised his "mercury control" method of damping the compass.[87]

With this major improvement and many smaller refinements, the gyrocompass became not only a very accurate instrument, capable of identifying true north "within a small fraction of one degree," but also reliable and stable even in very rough seas due to "the inherent rigidity of plane of the gyroscope" and the successful damping devices incorporated in it.[88] In addition to its superior directional properties, the gyrocompass provided information that could be "transmitted electrically to remote locations" and used to operate repeater compasses in the chart room, steering stations, and the captain's cabin.[89]

Though the designers of advanced warships were quick to take advantage of the gyrocompass — it was used for controlling weapons as well as for finding direction — merchant shippers did not embrace the technology in any numbers until after the Second World War.[90] By this time, engineers had introduced course recorders and the first automatic helmsman devices, both of which functioned using data transmitted from the gyrocompass. The course recorder produced a printed chart of a ship's course changes and the time of each change. Though traditional charts and course-keeping remained essential to routine navigation, the records from course recorders became increasingly important in investigating accidents, especially collisions, where the memories of the ships' officers, which could not always be trusted to be accurate, were all investigators had as evidence.[91] In the automatic helmsman or autopilot, the gyrocompass readings were used to detect any deviations from the set course. When these occurred, the device activated "the rudder-turning engine for a period proportional to the error," thereby correcting the ship's course.[92]

A second important advance in shipboard navigational equipment after 1900 was the echo-sounder. These devices, also known as depth-sounders or *sound navigation and ranging* (hence sonar), employ high-frequency or ultrasonic sound waves to measure the distance between the ship's hull and the seabed or other submerged objects. A transducer that converts electrical energy into sound energy is placed at the bottom of a ship's hull. From there, the sound waves are transmitted down until they reach the ocean floor, at which point they are reflected back toward the ship. Here, another transducer converts them back into electrical impulses and measures the time elapsed between transmission and reception. This time measurement is then translated into a distance figure.[93]

Like Brown's "mercury control," the echo-sounding technology was a product of war-related research and development. The first system, Asdic (Allied Submarine Detection Investigation Committee), was mainly conceived by French experts, then developed in co-operation with English authorities in 1918. As its name indicates, it was intended to determine the range and bearing of enemy submarines, rather than the depth of the water through which a ship was travelling.[94] But soon after the war, this sounding technique was adapted to both marine surveying and general navigation purposes. It was much easier to use than the traditional leads and lines, which, despite the number of crew and time needed to manipulate them, did not always provide accurate readings. When the ship was making good speed or when seas were rough, mariners had an

Figure 39. *Sonar equipment, HMCS Rimouski, 1943. Naval vessels were always among the first to be equipped with new technologies.*
(Library and Archives Canada, neg. PA 139916)

even harder time obtaining an accurate reading from the lead and line. By contrast, the echo-sounder was both simple and accurate, in addition to being much less susceptible to distortion caused by the motion of the ship. As a consequence, the echo-sounder gradually displaced other, mechanical methods of sounding, though many ships continued to carry a traditional sounding device as a backup instrument.

Growing use of echo-sounding technology by mariners and navies encouraged engineers to refine and enhance it. By 1940, makers were building systems that produced a continuous record in the form of an inked line that reflected the contour of the seabed beneath the ship.[95] Other systems could be set to give a warning alarm when the depth of water approached a critical level.[96] In more recent years, engineers have developed echo-sounding apparatus that can give bearing and direction, the latter using the Doppler effect.[97]

During the twentieth century, inventors also made some progress in addressing the difficult problem of determining a ship's speed. Calculating average speed over the course of a day posed few problems for mariners, who simply measured the distance covered and divided by the time it took to cover it. But this provided "only historical information" and not the speed of the ship "at any given moment."[98] To find this value, instrument makers had to find a way to improve on the many different varieties of mechanical logs. For ships driven by propellers, engineers devised an arithmetic formula for calculating speed based on the pitch or forward movement of the propeller and the number of revolutions per minute. Counting devices attached to each propeller shaft automatically registered each and every complete turn of the propellers. A master counter then averaged the totals and from this, the crew could establish current speed. Later versions of these counters monitored engine rather than propeller revolutions and became known as tachometers.[99]

Inventors also introduced a number of bottom logs which, instead of being towed behind the ship as most nineteenth-century logs were, protruded from its hull. The pitometer, based on the pioneering eighteenth-century work of Henry Pitot, was a tube positioned so that water was forced into it by the forward motion of the ship. The distance the water travelled into the tube depended on the speed of the ship through the water. What in essence was an indication of pressure was then translated into a measure of speed. Captain Chernikeeff, a Russian naval officer, introduced another type of bottom log around 1917. His version consisted of an impeller or rotator enclosed in a retractable tube that was lowered a few feet below the hull of the ship "through a watertight gland and sluice valve." When it turned, "the impeller made electrical contacts which registered as speed and distance on the bridge."

As with many new navigational devices, both of these instruments were first used on naval ships during the Second World War and were not introduced on merchant vessels until later.[100]

Since the 1970s, inventors developed a third type of bottom log, using electromagnetism to measure speed. In this instrument, an electromagnet produces a magnetic field. The movement of the water relative to that field generates an electric potential difference that is picked up by two electrodes lowered beneath the hull of the ship. The signals from these electrodes are then converted to give a speed measurement. After some refinement, this electromagnetic system was "found to be accurate, economic, and simple, and [was] widely fitted to ships."[101]

These new types of devices eliminated some of the most obvious problems associated with even the best towed logs. They were much less likely to be torn from the ship in turbulent water or caught up in weeds or other debris. Without the long trailing line, there was less likelihood of the mechanism slipping, and the ship's manoeuvrability astern was not restricted even for a brief period of time. But there was one problem that these new measuring instruments did not solve. They, like the mechanical logs of the nineteenth century, were only capable of determining speed through water, which is itself constantly moving. Changing tides and currents had an obvious impact on the flow of water through or around the different measuring instruments. As well, the pitch and roll of the ship could increase the level of distortion in the readings. Although experienced mariners learned to correct their calculations to account for these variables, the results were not necessarily precise and, in unfamiliar waters, must often have amounted to little more than "inspired guesswork."[102]

When scientists introduced Doppler sonar after 1960, they provided at least a partial solution to the problem of accurate speed determination. This system uses ultrasonic waves, like those used in echo- or depth-sounding, and a phenomenon known as the Doppler shift to measure a ship's speed. Transducers aim four relatively narrow beams of waves out from the vessel — forward, aft, and to each side — then measure the difference "between the frequencies of the transmitted and received waves in each beam." This difference is the Doppler shift and "is in direct proportion to the ship's speed, and the vectorial summation of the Doppler shifts in the four beams enables both the fore- and aft- and thwartship (sideways) components of the ship's speed to be found." In "relatively shallow" waters, where the ultrasonic beams bounce directly off the seabed, Doppler sonar actually measures a ship's speed over the Earth's surface rather than through water. In very deep waters, though, even Doppler sonar can only give the ship's speed relative to the sea mass itself, since the ultrasonic waves do not travel far enough to produce echoes off the bottom.[103]

Sources disagree on the extent to which Doppler sonar or Doppler logs are installed on merchant ships in general,[104] despite their superior accuracy. They do agree, however, that one important and widespread application of this technology is to help the navigators of big vessels such as very large crude carriers (VLCCs).[105] Often "over a quarter of a mile long and with hundreds of thousands of tons of inertia," these ships challenge the abilities of even the most experienced mariners to judge speed, distance, and bearing when docking. The fact that they carry millions of gallons of dangerous cargo makes the need for precision that much more acute. Doppler sonar docking aids allow the navigator to track the forward or aft speed of the ship as well as "the separate sideways velocity of the bow and stern." This data is then displayed digitally in units of about one foot per minute. These readings, though, can be distorted by water turbulence resulting from the motion of the propellers in the confined area of a harbour and must be interpreted and used with care.[106]

From Ship to Shore and Shore to Ship: Two-Way Aids to Navigation

Perhaps the most important navigational development of the twentieth century was the introduction, refinement, and dissemination of electronic communication, navigation, and positioning systems. Until the advent of radio around 1900, mariners who were out of sight of land had to rely on their shipboard instruments to tell them where they were and warn them when they were nearing land. When confronted by unforeseen circumstances — bad weather, dangerous ice conditions, or an accident — they had only luck and their skill, experience, and instincts to fall back on. Electronic communication, while it did not eliminate navigational errors or the inherent dangers of seafaring, did provide mariners with another tool that could help to reduce them.

All electronic navigational systems and devices that depend on intercommunication among ships and between ships and shore installations are based on radio technology of one form or another. In general terms, radio is the radiation and detection of signals propagated through space as electromagnetic waves to convey information. Signals carried in this manner do not need wires to convey them to the intended recipient, which is what makes radio so indispensable for communicating with distant and moving vehicles such as ships. Radio waves vary in frequency from a low of 3 kilohertz to a high of 300 gigahertz, and these different frequencies possess different propagation and reception characteristics and different information-carrying capacities. Very long or very low frequency (VLF) waves, for example, can travel great distances because they tend to follow the Earth's surface rather than travelling up into the ionosphere or in a direct, line-of-sight path away from the transmitting antenna, as higher-frequency waves do. Higher frequencies, though, can accommodate many more users and much more information than lower ones. Marine navigation systems use a wide range of frequencies from very low (VLF) to super high (SHF) to meet the diverse communications and positioning requirements of international shipping.

Radio Communication

The first application of radio technology was basic marine communication. Before radio, maritime interests had no way of communicating with their ships once they were out of sight, short of sending a message via a faster ship. This had long been an accepted risk of travel and transportation on the high seas, but as European powers became increasingly caught up in intense military, political, and commercial competition after 1900, authorities began to perceive this lack of communication as a serious weakness. Thus, when Guglielmo Marconi introduced one of the first working wireless or radiotelegraph systems in 1897, the Admiralty, Lloyd's, and the shipping industry embraced the new technology and began to use it almost immediately.

In general, mariners and the shipping industry used radio for "commercial, strategic and tactical communications."[107] For naval authorities, it became another tool in the battle to rule the seas, helping to extend and strengthen the lines of communication and thus the command and control of huge fleets of vessels stationed around the world. In the mercantile world, it made possible the passage of important and timely navigational information such as weather reports, ice conditions, new hazards, and, perhaps most important, accurate time signals by which mariners could set their chronometers. All these data helped the master decide when to adjust his course or schedule. And in emergencies, the ship's radio operator sent out distress signals that alerted other ships or coastal stations within range and advised them of the ship's position and status. Merchant ships also exchanged time-sensitive commercial information with shore stations — current prices for their cargoes, locations of buyers or return cargoes, and any changes in schedule or ports of call that might result from these. For early radio-equipped passenger vessels, the system was also often used for more frivolous purposes, such as obtaining the latest news and sending passengers' greetings to friends and family ashore.

Canadian authorities were quick to embrace radio as an aid to marine navigation. The government established five coastal stations in Newfoundland, Labrador, and the Gulf of St Lawrence in 1904. By the end of 1907, the east coast–St Lawrence network included 15 stations, 9 high powered and 6 low powered. The first stations on Canada's Pacific coast opened in 1908, and by 1913 the government had constructed a total of 23 coastal stations. These stations communicated with the growing number of radio-equipped vessels plying Canadian waters and calling at Canadian ports. The easternmost high-powered stations also routinely interacted with vessels transiting the North Atlantic from the United Kingdom to the United States. It was the operator at the Cape Race station that received and relayed the *Titanic*'s distress signals in April 1912.[108]

Despite its obvious usefulness as an all-purpose communications tool and its rapid and widespread adoption by maritime interests, radio, in its initial, rudimentary form, had severe limitations. Its range was limited. In Canada, for example, the highest-powered shore stations could normally reach about 125 miles (200 km) out to sea, while low-powered stations could reach only 60 miles (96.5 km).[109] Much of the experimental work done by Marconi and others was aimed at improving this performance, but as long as spark technology was the norm, these improvements were incremental at best. Spark sets produced oscillations by generating an electrical spark across a gap. They

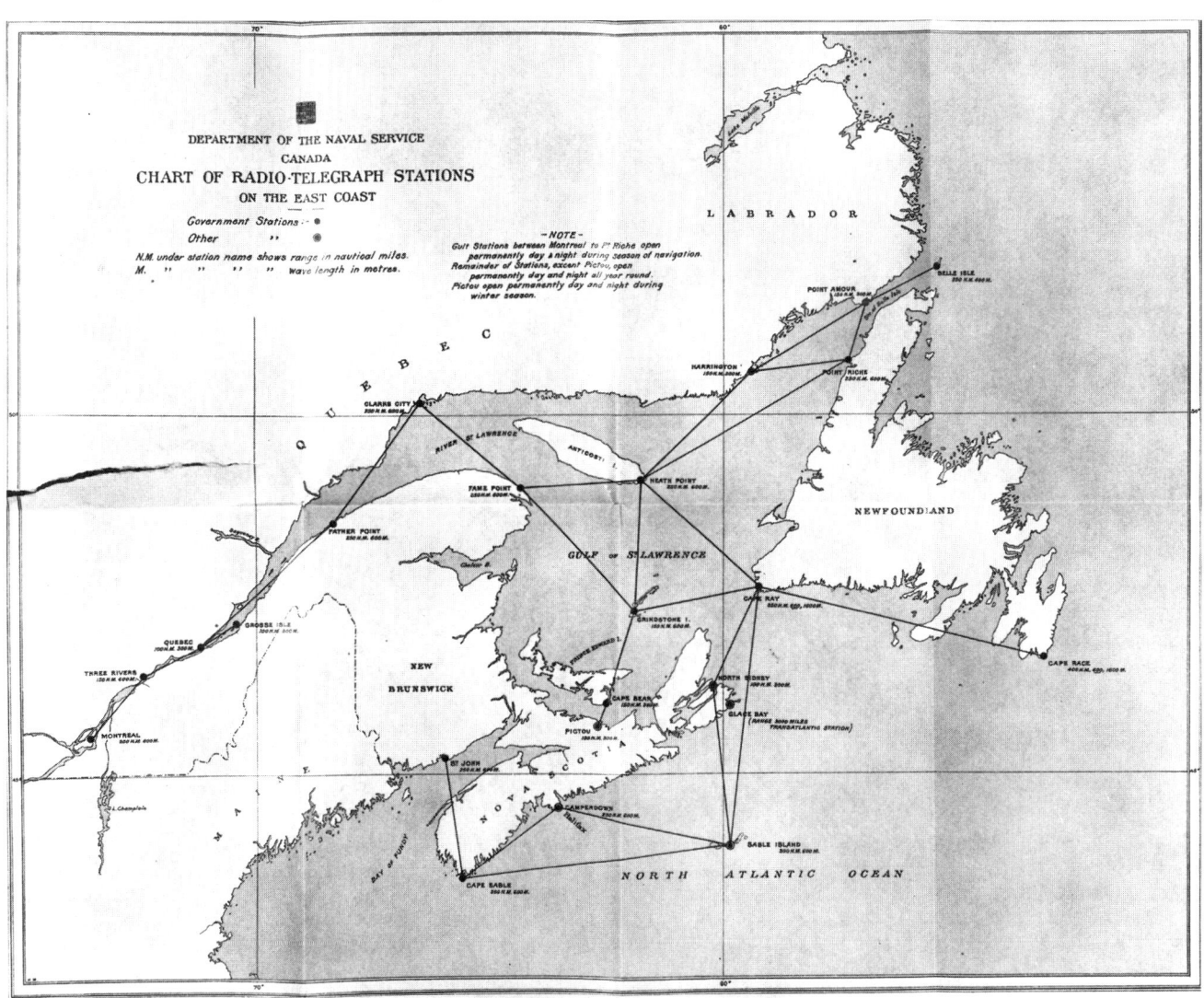

Map 6. *This map shows Canada's network of marine radio, then called wireless telegraph, stations on the east coast in 1912, including their operating frequencies and ranges.*
(Department of the Naval Service, *Annual Report* for 1912–1913)

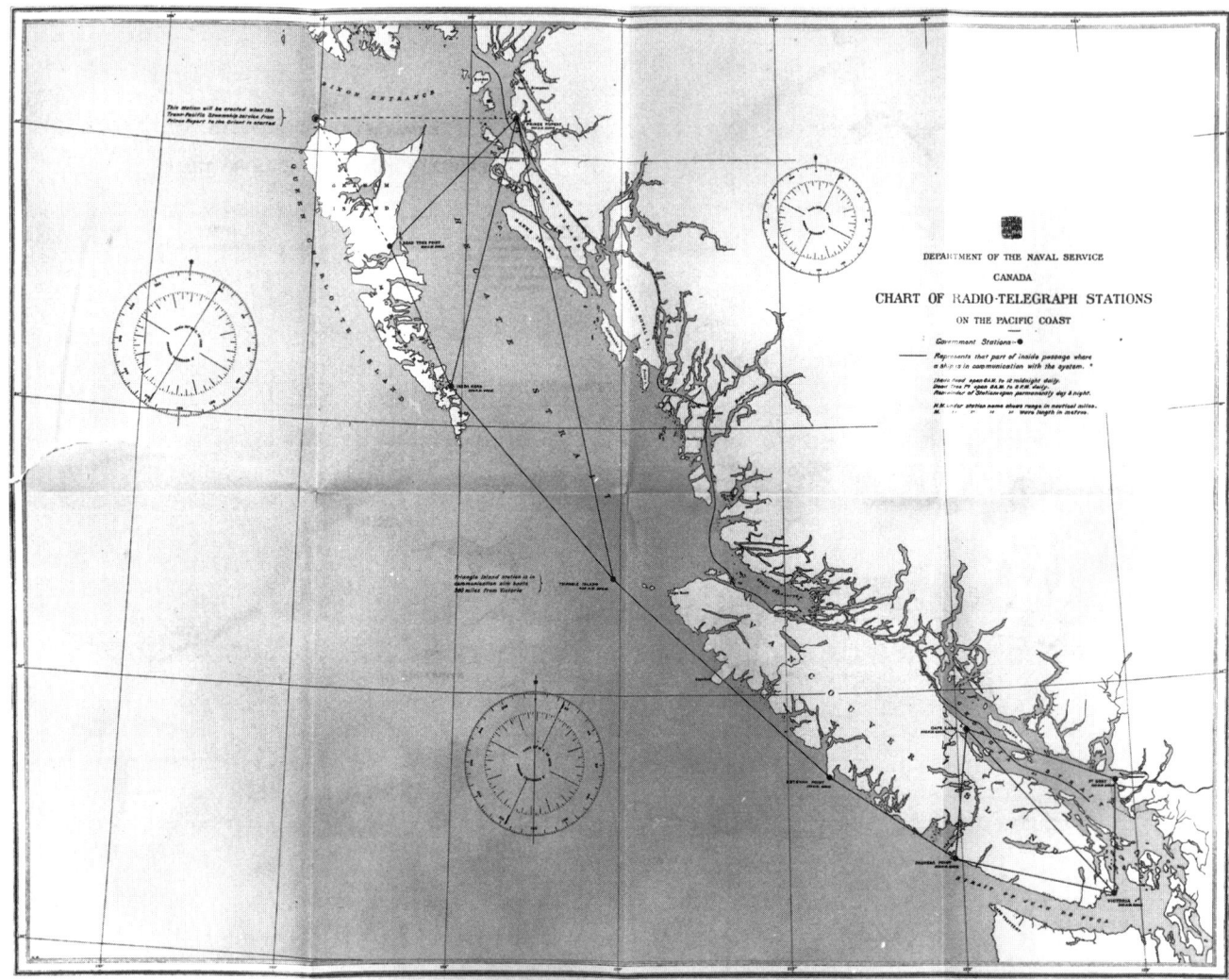

Map 7. Canada's west coast marine radio stations in 1912. The government also had stations on the Great Lakes by this time. (Department of the Naval Service, *Annual Report* for 1912–1913)

produced pulses of energy that began strongly and then quickly faded away, as did the radio waves they generated. This meant that radio transmitters and receivers could not be precisely tuned to one frequency but dissipated their transmission power by spreading it over a broad band of frequencies. They also created a great deal of interference, which made clear reception of signals difficult even when other conditions were favourable. Moreover, early radios could only be operated by specially trained individuals who knew telegraphic code and how to adjust the often temperamental equipment.[110] And, as with most new communications technologies, there were problems with compatibility, protocol, and regulation: which, if any, ships ought to have sets; during which hours should they operate; did ships equipped with one system have to communicate with those using another in non-emergency situations and, if so, how would compatibility be achieved?

By 1920, engineers, the shipping industry, and international regulators had addressed many if not all of these problems. The sinking of the *Titanic* had forced governments around the world to frame a series of radio regulations that would ensure more systematic monitoring of shipboard radio sets for distress and other critical signals. Around the same time, inventors, prompted in part by the demands of the First World War, were perfecting the vacuum tube and applying it to the development of reliable continuous-wave (CW) radio systems that not only allowed for precise tuning, but could carry voice in addition to the dots and dashes of telegraphic code.

In the years after the war, the Canadian government did not greatly expand its coastal radio network. In 1919 there were 47 coastal stations, and by 1936 there were just 30. Because war-related research had improved radio's coverage and capabilities so dramatically, fewer stations were needed to fulfill the government's growing requirements. Officials gradually replaced spark systems with continuous-wave sets that were more efficient and reliable at all distances. They also took advantage of the voice capabilities of CW radio to extend its reach to smaller vessels that did not employ radio officers. In 1924, marine authorities initiated an experiment on the west coast in which a number of tugs and other small craft were equipped with what were then called radiotelephone systems. The success of this program prompted officials to extend the experiment to fishing vessels on the east coast using the Louisbourg station, which could reach fishing boats as far away as the Grand Banks.[111] Voice radio systems were used to broadcast critical information such as weather reports and ice conditions. These first experiments in voice radio laid the groundwork for what became an important and enduring service provided by government radio stations to the operators of small working vessels.[112]

The next major phase of technological change in radio came after the Second World War. Among the most important post-1945 developments have been the steady increase in coverage of long-distance systems and the development of more versatile equipment for both offshore and coastal/harbour communication. From the 1940s until the 1960s, merchant ships relied on medium- and high-frequency radio systems to cover long distances. Of these systems, the radiotelegraph at around 500 kHz (the low end of the medium frequency [MF] band) had the longest reach — about 500 miles (800 km) offshore — but could only be used by ships carrying licensed radio operators who could send and receive in code. Medium-frequency radiotelephone sets became increasingly common in the 1930s and 1940s especially on smaller vessels, but their coverage was more limited, about 150 miles or 240 kilometres.[113]

Beginning in the 1950s, though, engineers began to experiment with the use of higher frequencies and frequency modulation techniques. In 1952, Canada's deputy minister of Transport took part in an experiment using VHF FM radiotelephony on the Great Lakes.[114] By the late 1950s, the International Telecommunication Union had designated specific VHF channels for the maritime mobile FM service. Throughout the 1960s, the Department of Transport undertook a major renovation program that saw the widespread adoption of radiotelephone on Coast Guard vessels and at coastal stations. Most of the installations were VHF/FM systems, though a small number of vessels and launches belonging to larger ships were equipped with HF/AM equipment. Though the VHF/FM systems had a limited range — under 50 nautical miles — and, at least initially, offered simplex (push-to-talk) capabilities, they were invaluable to coastal, fishing, and recreational vessels that did not carry radio operators.[115]

During this same period and as part of the same upgrade program, the Department of Transport introduced another important technical innovation to Canadian marine radio when they began installing single-sideband (SSB) systems in coastal and CCG ship stations. Single sideband is a form of amplitude modulation in which one of two sidebands of the carrier is suppressed prior to transmission. Since both sidebands carry identical modulation data, all the necessary information can be conveyed by one band. As a consequence, SSB systems use less bandwidth, produce better signal-to-noise and signal-to-interference ratios, and use power more economically.[116]

The DOT SSB radiotelephones operated at high frequencies and represented an improvement over existing radiotelegraph and radiotelephone equipment. Because they were voice systems, they eliminated the need for highly trained operators proficient in Morse code. At the same time, SSB techniques dramatically improved the intelligibility of voice communications over long distances, one of the main problems with existing radiotelephone systems. Using this new technology, it became possible, in good transmission conditions, for ships to establish voice contact with shore from almost anywhere on the Atlantic Ocean. In 1964, the Department of Transport began implementing a modernization program that involved the conversion of all medium- and high-frequency installations on Coast Guard ships to single sideband.[117]

There were, however, still significant gaps in the worldwide coverage of marine radio. Engineers began to close these gaps in the 1970s by using newly launched communications satellites to relay radio signals to distant ships. In 1976, the Canadian Coast Guard took part in a trial of the Marisat system, in which telephony, telex, and facsimile messages were sent via satellite to the CCGS *John A. Macdonald*. The system, which also included a channel reserved for distress calls only, proved efficient and reliable, though there were some problems with the quality of communications north of the 80th parallel.[118] The success of this experiment confirmed the great potential of satellite links for marine communication and led to the development of today's Inmarsat satellite network, which provides sophisticated and reliable marine communications for the entire globe, again with the exception of the extreme polar regions.[119]

At the same time that they were working to extend the range of radio, engineers were enhancing its other capabilities and finding new applications for those capabilities. VHF radio, for example, became important inshore where vessel and radio traffic were heavy. The additional space available in this area of the spectrum accommodates many more users than the HF band, so regulators could assign specific channels for different uses. The operators of Vessel Traffic Systems (VTSs) (see page 133 for details) in busy waterways establish contact with approaching ships on one frequency and track them with radar to ensure they are following a safe course at a safe speed. Once in the VTS, however, the master of a vessel may need to establish bridge-to-bridge contact with a nearby ship. This communication would take place on another, separate channel. In the early years of VTS — the first VTS system in Canada was installed at the port of Montréal in 1968 — ships that were not equipped with VHF radio had to rent a portable set from local authorities, which the pilot took out to the vessel when he boarded.[120]

Marine officials also took advantage of the introduction of integrated circuits and microprocessors to improve marine radio. Solid state circuitry consumed less power and was smaller and more robust than vacuum tube systems, which meant that stations required less maintenance. This, along with the processing power of microchips, has allowed engineers to create automated radio networks. In the 1970s, Canadian officials began setting up remote-control systems, with a number of radio installations controlled from one central site. Any signals sent to the unstaffed stations were automatically relayed (by telephone line or radio, depending on location) to the control centre, which responded. The control centre was also equipped to "interrogate" the remote sites to ensure all systems were functioning properly.[121]

In more recent years, the International Maritime Organization has set up a new radio system — Global Marine Distress and Safety System (GMDSS) — to improve safety at sea. Regulators had, in the early decades of radio, established an international distress and calling frequency and had laid out strict rules for its use, including watches to be kept and the level of expertise of the operators. The frequencies and accompanying rules were adapted as new technology became available and a greater variety of ships fell under the regulations. For example, for smaller vessels that did not carry a trained radio operator, the LF frequency signals were useless because they were in telegraphic code. For ships in this category, regulators assigned an MF voice channel using the spoken word "mayday," which had been used to signify a ship in distress since the advent of radiotelephone systems in the 1920s.[122]

GMDSS uses a combination of satellite and VHF/MF/HF radio to extend the reach and reliability of distress alerts. It increases the probability that an alert will be sent when a vessel is in trouble and that it will be received. It also improves the chances of finding survivors and enhances the overall level of communication and co-ordination. Finally, it provides mariners with the most current maritime safety information.

GMDSS is an automated system using a method called digital selective calling (DSC) to allow crews to maintain the required watch on the distress and calling channel without listening constantly. A DSC receiver only responds when one of the worldwide communications centres sends out a message containing its Maritime Mobile Service Identity number or alerting "All Ships" within a given range. The receivers are tuned to two listening frequencies, one in the VHF band and one in the MF band. GMDSS is also equipped to pick up signals from emergency position indicating radio beacons that are supposed to deploy automatically in the event of a sudden accident, providing a position for rescuers even when they have not received a distress call.[123]

In addition to distress alerts and search and rescue data, GMDSS provides other critical information for mariners, including weather warnings and hazards such as ice, malfunctioning markers, or obstacles such as wrecks. These maritime safety information broadcasts are delivered in three different ways to make them as accessible as possible. The NAVTEX system provides an edited series of messages that can be received up to 300 nautical miles offshore and can be printed out on the ship's bridge.[124] Outside of the NAVTEX coverage area, ships equipped with INMARSAT-C terminals[125] can receive the information via Enhanced Group Call-SafetyNET (EGC). Finally, as an alternative to EGC, HF narrow band direct printing receivers can also receive the broadcasts where service is available. Newer receivers (circa late 1990s) combine the GMDSS requirements with regular voice communications requirements, allowing the crew access to radiotelephone communications without interfering with the DSC watch.[126]

Despite this broad accessibility, some significant gaps in GMDSS coverage still exist. First of all, not all ships are required to have the systems. Ships of 300 gross tons (273 tonnes) or more and all passenger ships must be GMDSS equipped, but for all other ships, it is voluntary. In Canada, the Coast Guard will continue to monitor the established distress frequencies until they determine that the service is no longer required — that is, when the new system is fully implemented and covers all service areas and the cost of DSC equipment decreases, making it possible for all or most vessel owners to afford it. Also, as with previous satellite-based systems, GMDSS coverage does not extend to the polar regions of the globe.[127]

Recently, INMARSAT, the worldwide marine satellite communications consortium, launched a third series of satellites, with the intention of extending coverage to a new group of users. Mini-M service relies on concentrated beams of radio signals that can be received reliably by small, light antennas. Unlike previous satellite systems that required large transponders and thus could only be fitted to relatively large vessels, Mini-M can be used on any vessel more than 50 feet (15 m) in length. It provides masters with access to more reliable long-distance voice communication as well as fax and data services. Although the service does not provide anything like global coverage, it is much less expensive, and this, combined with the transponder's small size, should appeal to operators of smaller vessels that travel in the many areas it does service.[128]

Radio Ranging and Positioning Systems

Very soon after the introduction of radiotelegraphy, scientists discovered that radio waves have predictable and measurable directional and reflective properties. In experimenting with these properties, they showed that radio waves could be used to determine the position of distant objects. This information could be used by mariners not only to establish their vessel's position and direction of movement but also to determine the location of other ships or physical obstacles that might be in their way. For mariners, these capabilities promised to provide both a means of checking astronomical observations and calculations based on dead reckoning and a method of finding position and avoiding collisions when the heavens were obscured by fog or cloud.[129]

Radio Direction Finding

Since 1911 when they were first applied to marine navigation, radio's directional properties have formed the basis of virtually all radio navigation systems. The earliest systems were grouped under the label "radio direction finding" or RDF, and these dominated the field until the Second World War. Scientists carrying out war-related research in the 1930s and 1940s introduced the second generation of radio navigation, known as hyperbolic navigation (see pages 105–7). Finally, in the 1960s, the work of space scientists and engineers led to the development of the first satellite systems of radio navigation, which are the foundation of the latest and most precise positioning methods in use today.

Marine authorities in Britain began to establish RDF stations just before the First World War. The war, of course, accelerated both the development of this technology and its adoption worldwide. Initially, the sets were fairly simple radio receivers with specialized loop antennas. Researchers had determined that the loop antenna was highly directional so that when turned on its axis, "there are two points, 180° apart, where the strength of the signal loses volume and fades away." Known as nulls, these points occurred when the loop was positioned at right angles to the transmitting station. This predictable directional behaviour allowed the operator of an RDF station to establish a line of bearing for any radio-equipped ship within range of his installation.[130] Shipboard navigators trying to establish the position of another vessel at sea using RDF needed at least two lines of bearing to establish the actual bearing of the other ship.

Radio research was an active field during this period, not least because of the technology's perceived role in the intense military and commercial rivalry consuming much of the world at the time, and inventors patented a variety of DF systems that fell into three basic categories. The first were shore-based stations, manned by an operator who gave bearings on demand to the masters of radio-equipped ships travelling in the vicinity. The operators of these stations could take a bearing from just one ship at a time. They then sent the recorded position back to the ship in a radiotelegraph message. There were also ship-based DF receivers, the first of which was installed on the liner *Mauritania* in 1911. It allowed the ship's radio officer to take bearings from coastal stations whose locations appeared on the ship's charts or were otherwise known to him as well as from other transmitters including ship-borne ones. The final type of DF system was the directional beacon, "a ground transmitter radiating a directionally differentiated signal so that receivers can identify the radial on which they lie by the signal they receive." The latter two systems could accommodate multiple users and did not require interaction with an operator in the transmitting station to obtain the bearing.[131]

Despite the variety of systems available, most of the earliest DF stations in Britain and Canada were coastal. For all their drawbacks, these manned installations gave the most reliable service because they could serve all radio-equipped ships, not just those with special DF receivers. Any corrections that had to be made to the readings "to compensate for the deviations of incoming signals" and any other "determinable errors" were made by the station operator, who was experienced in making these particular calculations for his location. Once these corrections were made, navigators received a true bearing that they could generally depend on being "accurate to within ±2° for distances under 150 miles." Ship-based systems, on the other hand, provided only relative bearings, that is, relative to the ship's heading, and so the ship's "true heading" had to be established "at the *same instant*" that the bearing was taken in order to prevent the introduction of an error "equal to the amount that the ship has yawed in the interval between taking the bearing and reading the compass." Overall, the accuracy of these bearings was much less certain than those taken from shore and relayed to the ship.[132]

Figure 40. Alexander "Sandy" McLean at Canadian government marine radio station VCM Belle Isle, Newfoundland, winter 1925. McLean sits in front of a Marconi direction finding set. Next to the DF set is a receiver used for conventional radio communication.
(CSTM/Collection of S. G. Roscoe, no neg. no.)

By 1920, partly as a result of war-related research and experience and partly as a result of the application of the vacuum tube and continuous wave technology to radio, which improved both tuning and amplification, shipboard systems became increasingly common. After 1935, all large ships registered in Britain had to carry DF equipment, and although coastal stations continued to provide bearings on demand for a number of years, this service was gradually phased out in many countries as small, reliable ship-borne equipment became more available and affordable.[133] At the same time and in conjunction with this development, governments began to build networks of radio beacons that mariners and their radio operators could use to obtain the necessary bearings when approaching a coast. The most common type of radio beacon before the Second World War was the circular or non-directional beacon, which sent out signals in all directions. Each of these stations had "a simple characteristic signal of dots and dashes" that it transmitted on a set frequency. The signals and frequencies were published along with each beacon's location in various national and international lists of aids to navigation.[134] By 1940, marine authorities were also experimenting with rotating radio beacons, which sent out coded signals that varied "according to the direction of projection." When the constantly revolving beam passed through true north, the beacon emitted "a distinctive all-around signal" that could be picked up by all radio-equipped vessels within range, even those without radio compasses or direction finders on board. The navigator then calculated the interval between this signal and the minimum signal to obtain the bearing of his vessel from the station.[135]

In Canada, the government established the first RDF stations toward the end of the First World War. All of these were located on the east coast, at Chebucto Head, Cape Sable, Canso, and Cape Race. After the war, these stations became the core of Canada's emerging RDF network, which grew to 7 stations by 1924, including the first west coast station, at Pachena Point, B.C. By 1929, Canadian RDF stations numbered 12, of which 7 were on the east coast, 4 on the Arctic route through Hudson Strait and Hudson Bay, and 1 on the west coast. These stations provided bearings to all radio-equipped ships requesting them, and in this early period they provided an essential service to the many vessels passing within range of their signals.

The important pioneering role of the government's coastal RDF stations, though, was quickly eclipsed by the development and deployment of RDF beacons. As early as 1923, the government announced plans to set up two experimental radio beacon stations on the east coast. These beacons, which were "specially designed and built by the department," were "so arranged that when the ordinary fog alarm machinery is started up, the radio alarm signal automatically operates and continues until the plant is shut down." With a range of about 50 miles (80 km), these signals could be received and used by any ship carrying an RDF set to establish bearings. Officials noted that if this new technology proved to be useful, its use would be extended considerably.[136] And so it was. By 1928 there were 8 beacons operating: 6 on the east coast, 1 on the Great Lakes at South East Shoal, Lake Erie, and 1 on the west coast at Race Rocks, B.C.

The great success of this first generation of radio beacons prompted the government to buy and install a new type of beacon that operated continuously regardless of whether the fog alarm was activated or not and had a longer range, about 75 miles (120 km). The "result of several years' experience in beacon operation," these new devices became the standard for the department. In 1929, officials took delivery of 6 from the Marconi Company and announced plans to install 10 more across the country during the year.[137] By 1952, there were some 52 radio beacons, while the number of RDF stations had levelled off at 12. In the early 1960s, Department of Transport (DOT) officials began working with their U.S. counterparts to coordinate the radio beacon system in border areas. By 1965 the plan had been completed on the west coast and Great Lakes and was nearing completion on the east coast.[138] The radio beacons remained in service until the mid-1990s, when the government began phasing them out.[139]

Radar

War-related research, this time before and during the Second World War, also gave mariners *ra*dio *d*irection *a*nd *r*anging, or radar, which allowed them to "see" objects through darkness, fog, and haze. Radar is based on the special characteristics of certain radio frequency electromagnetic waves, which easily penetrate and travel through the Earth's atmosphere at the speed of light but are reflected by solid masses such as land, buildings, ships, and seamarks. In simple terms, a radar set consists of a transmitter that generates short pulses of high-frequency electromagnetic waves (microwaves) and radiates them from a directional antenna or scanner toward specified target areas. When these waves, which tend to travel in straight lines, strike an object, some of them are reflected back toward the scanner, which channels them through a receiver, where they are amplified. The radar set then measures the time difference between transmission of the signal and reception of the reflected or echo signal and identifies the direction from which the signal was received. These distance and bearing data are then displayed on the face of a cathode ray tube, where objects show up as points of light or a blip on the screen.[140] If the object is stationary, a coastal feature for instance, the mariner can adjust his course to avoid it. If it is moving, as another vessel might be, the navigator can combine the radar position reading with careful plotting to help establish the approximate course and speed of the other ship, which will help him to prevent a possible collision.

Scientists had known about radio's reflective capabilities since Heinrich Hertz's original experiments in the 1880s. As early as 1904, Christian Hülsmeyer had proposed that radio waves could be used to "give warning of the presence of a metallic body, such as a ship or a train in the line of projection of such waves."[141] But it was not until the 1930s, long after they had made radio communication and radio direction finding reliable technologies, that engineers introduced the first radar systems. As the European powers began their descent into war, radar suddenly became an immediate priority. In 1935, engineers equipped the new French liner *Normandie* with a UHF (ultra high frequency) system, which the owners publicized as a new method of detecting deadly icebergs on the transatlantic run. The following year, German and British naval authorities installed radar sets on two battleships. Test results from all three systems, however, were disappointing. Within five years, though, scientists had developed a wide variety of radars that could, among other things, detect the presence of enemy ships and aircraft, aim naval guns and anti-aircraft artillery, guide bombers to their targets, and identify signals from friendly vessels and distinguish them from those of the enemy (identification friend or foe, or IFF). Many of these systems were built around the cavity magnetron, a vacuum tube that produced the centimetric radio waves, more commonly known as microwaves, needed to identify small and fast-moving objects.[142]

When the war ended, "marine radar was immediately the most important peaceful application of radar."[143] Many in the shipping industry, not known for its willingness to embrace expensive new technologies, welcomed it as "the conqueror of fog," the enemy that was responsible for many costly delays and losses at sea. Enthusiastic about the prospect of getting their cargoes to market more quickly and safely, shipowners began to install systems in increasing numbers of their vessels.[144] In 1953, there were 2,800 radar-equipped vessels registered in Britain and no doubt many more in the United States, Europe, and the Far East.[145]

Like many new and promising technologies, radar's capabilities were much touted while its limitations were ignored or misunderstood. As a result, some of its promoters and users relied too heavily on its apparent infallibility, believing that radar-equipped ships could maintain full speed even in conditions of low visibility. In the absence of systematic training, it was not always clear to navigators that, although the radar screen could give the position of an object relative to their vessel at a particular moment, it gave no information about the course or speed of another moving object, such as a ship. To obtain this crucial data, mariners had to plot and analyse the readings over time, and even this technique could not be relied upon if the other vessel was changing course. In this context, radar could not possibly provide enough information to allow a ship to speed through fog safely. In the 1950s, a series of accidents that became known as "radar-assisted collisions" proved to all but the most skeptical observers that radar was no substitute for good seamanship.[146]

The court cases that arose out of these collisions highlighted the limitations of radar technology, including the lack of guidelines for its proper use. The courts filled this regulatory gap with their rulings. In an early U.S. case, a court ruled that even though no law required vessels to carry radar, a radar-equipped vessel that did not use its system was at fault for causing a collision. The Supreme Court of Canada went even further in a 1951 ruling, arguing that to realize its potential as a navigational aid, radar and "the report which it brings must be interpreted by active and constant intelligence on the part of the operator." Thus, the officers of radar-equipped vessels were obligated not only to use their radar, but to use it diligently and monitor it constantly.[147]

These rulings, combined with the realization that, despite radar's limitations, more and more shipping companies were installing it on their vessels, forced international regulators to produce new rules governing the use of radar for the avoidance of collisions. In 1960, they added a Radar Annex to the International Regulations for Preventing Collisions at Sea, also known as the "rules of the road" or COLREGS. Though this annex did not mention plotting the courses of target vessels in the area, it did warn mariners that "assumptions" based on "scanty information may be dangerous and should be avoided." The implication was that mariners should be undertaking and recording a series of systematic observations of targets rather than making decisions on the basis of casual observation of a blip on the screen.[148] Regulators revised the COLREGS again in 1972, further defining the role and appropriate use of radar in collision prevention.[149]

In the 1950s and 1960s, manufacturers of radar equipment were also working to improve the capabilities and the general application of radar. In the 1960s, they produced the first "true motion" plan position indicator (PPI) radar. The earliest sets had relative motion displays, which placed your vessel's heading at the top of the screen while the land and other vessels or targets rotated whenever the vessel changed course. When connected to a gyrocompass, the PPI became relative motion, stabilized, which provided a "north up" display with the heading marker indicating the true course on the scale around the edge of the PPI. During a course alteration, the heading marker swings around to the new course indication but the picture stays aligned in the same position. No blurring takes place and the bearings are true. Finally, true motion displays the point representing the ship's position moving across the PPI, showing the movement of targets in relation to your vessel.[150]

Although the true motion PPI made the actual vessel positions clearer, it did not solve the problem of determining the course and speed of nearby ships. Initially, manual plotting was the only way to accomplish this. It was a "tedious and time-consuming" task and was not much help when a quick response was needed. Reflector plotters made the job somewhat easier by allowing the plot to be made in erasable marker on a transparent screen positioned directly over the PPI. But this was only an interim solution.

Throughout the 1960s, manufacturers concentrated on solving the plotting problem, and by the early

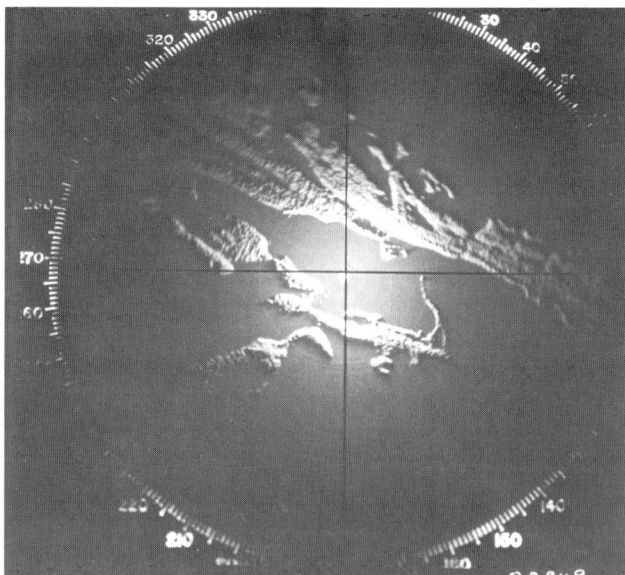

Figure 41. This photograph of a Sperry Position Plan Indicator display shows a radar scan of an anchorage at Gaspé Bay, 12 July 1953.
(Library and Archives Canada, neg. PA 137937)

1970s they had introduced what they called collision avoidance systems. These relied on microprocessors that took the data from the radar receiver and calculated the course and speed of all the targets on the PPI. Using this information, these systems could also tell the navigator the time and distance to closest approach and inform any decision regarding avoidance. Some systems included collision risk alarms to warn of an approaching vessel.[151]

Taking advantage of rapid progress in computing technology through the 1980s and 1990s, manufacturers steadily enhanced the capabilities of collision avoidance systems, which by this time had become known as automatic radar plotting aids, or ARPAs. These systems can now provide "own vessel's" speed and course instantaneously and determine its position in the future based on that course. They can establish "the location and future activity of all acquired targets [vessels picked up by the radar] for continuous observation" as well as identify "any or all stationary targets for continuous reference."[152]

These technical advances gradually made their way into the regulatory international framework beginning in the mid-1970s when the IMO's predecessor, IMCO, made installation of radar sets compulsory on ships larger than 1,600 gross tons (1 454 tonnes). By the 1980s, the largest vessels, over 10,000 gross tons (9 090 tonnes), had to have two sets. Currently, it is mandatory for every ship over 500 gross registered tons (g.r.t.) (455 tonnes) to have radar and for every vessel over 10,000 g.r.t. to have two radar sets in addition to a specified form of automatic radar plotting aid (ARPA).[153]

Over the same period, the institutions responsible for training mariners began to take radar instruction more seriously, and their efforts to improve training were helped by the introduction of radar simulators. Gradually, enhanced instruction combined with more extensive shipboard experience to produce a new, radar-literate generation of mariners.[154] Yet a thorough understanding of the technology still entails knowing not only how and when to use it, but also what it can and cannot tell you about a potentially dangerous situation and what action is required to avoid it.

In Canada, marine authorities and the shipping industry were quick to recognize the importance of radar for navigation. In 1952, Department of Transport officials reported that equipping merchant ships with radar "has become general practice." Moreover, by this time the department had installed radar sets on a "considerable number" of its own ships and was working to enhance the usefulness of ship-borne radar in coastal regions by adding radar reflectors to many of its buoys.[155] (See page 131 for details.) As manufacturers have developed new and more sophisticated radar systems and as regulators have introduced increasingly stringent rules regarding the installation and use of radar, Canadian shipping companies have gradually upgraded their systems to meet the new standards. For example, in 1983, Canadian Pacific ordered £750,000 worth of radar equipment from Krupp Atlas-Elektronik as part of its upgrading program to meet "IMO and USCG requirements and specifications." As part of this enhancement, it planned to install dual sets on its two newest ships under construction in Denmark and Atlas ARPA 8500 A/CAS units on its tankers and VLCCs.[156]

Hyperbolic Navigation Systems

Hyperbolic navigation systems are based on two important characteristics of radio waves: radio waves "travel in curves known mathematically as hyperbolae and navigationally as great circles" and "they all travel at the same speed." Because of this predictable behaviour, a navigator can take signals from two stations, measure the difference in reception time between them, and "plot the requisite curve on the chart," to represent his ship's position line in relation to the stations. By taking a reading from a third station and comparing it to one of the first two, he can plot a second hyperbolic curve. The intersection of these two curves represents the actual position of his vessel. This process, which would be laborious and time-consuming if done manually, is carried out automatically by electronic receivers that "simultaneously and continuously" take readings from a number of stations along the ship's course. The navigator plots this information using special charts and tables overlaid with lattice patterns that allow him to identify the point of intersection quickly and precisely.[157]

Like radar, hyperbolic navigation was largely a product of the Second World War. Because the number, variety, range, and speed of ships and aircraft had increased so dramatically since 1918, military authorities needed faster and more versatile and precise position-finding devices to help track and deploy their fleets. Enhanced positioning capabilities could also help defenders prepare more effectively for an imminent attack. Working in the late 1930s and early 1940s, engineers and scientists in Britain, Germany, and the United States came up with a number of different systems using the hyperbolic principle. They fell into two basic categories: phase comparison and pulse comparison. The former type — systems such as Sonne or Consol, Decca, and, later, Omega — used another characteristic of radio waves, phase, as a way to measure distance. When two stations transmit in phase, they generate signals that are at precisely the same point in the wave cycle. But because their signals travel different distances before they reach a ship at sea, they will be out of phase when picked up by the shipboard receiver. The phase difference, "(expressed as a fraction of a cycle) times the wavelength" between the two sets of signals provides the basis for calculating the difference in the distance of the two stations from the ship.[158]

The Sonne/Consol system — the first is the German name, the second is British — was the simplest, requiring only a radio receiver to read signals from the transmitting stations, each of which consisted of an array of three aerials. The navigator plotted the signals using a Consol lattice chart or tables to obtain bearing and position. Despite its simplicity, Consol achieved daytime ranges of up to 1,200 nautical miles and 1,500 n.m. at night. It was also surprisingly accurate; under good conditions and for ranges up to 1,000 n.m., the error of the position line could be less than 0.4°.[159] Initially employed by U-boats and the RAF in the Second World War, Consol was adopted after 1945 by various users including fishermen. The system was still operational in the 1970s, though it is not much in evidence now.[160]

During the war, the Decca Navigator Company also introduced a phase comparison positioning system, known simply as Decca or Decca Navigator. A Decca chain is made up of one "master" and three "slave" stations, which transmit continuous signals. A navigator reads signals from the master and the slave stations using a visual display receiver known as a decometer, which shows the phase difference between them. He then plots this information on a Decca chart. Essentially a coastal fixing system, Decca's effective coverage is limited to around 300 n.m. but offers greater accuracy than Consol within that range — between 0.2 and 2.0 n.m. to a range of about 240 miles (385 km). The three slave stations are necessary because at close range the angle of intersection of position lines from any two slaves may be too acute to be useful.[161]

First used on a large scale during the Normandy landings, Decca became an important navigation system soon after the war. Authorities found that by building "a sufficient density of Decca chains" along coastlines, they could provide mariners with fixes of "unprecedented accuracy" at a time when the increasing density of traffic was demanding more accurate and disciplined navigation. Decca coverage was concentrated around northwestern Europe, the Persian Gulf, Japan, southern Africa, and northeastern North America. In northern North America, it was used mainly by Canadian vessels; the Americans preferred LORAN, even for inshore work. Decca was the only example of "a widespread fixing system provided by private enterprise." It was phased out in most areas between 1980 and 1984 and replaced by Loran C.[162]

Beginning in the 1950s, professor J. A. Pierce, the Decca Navigator Company, and the United States Navy all contributed to the development of a very low frequency (VLF) phase comparison positioning system that eventually became known as Omega. Researchers had known since before the First World War that VLF waves travel very long distances using the space between the ionosphere and the Earth's surface as a wave guide and that "their propagation characteristics are relatively stable and reliable." After the war, engineers and scientists devised a method of transmitting and receiving "on very narrow frequency bands, drastically reducing background noise and eliminating the need for very powerful transmitters." By the 1970s, the Omega system was up and running — the eighth and last station was not operational until the 1980s — and providing global coverage.[163]

Like Consol, Omega initially used "relatively simple" electronic equipment, charts marked with Omega position lines, and tables to correct for propagation errors. Designers also added devices such as lane counters and recorders to help mitigate or eliminate some of the ambiguities and inaccuracies inherent in these long-distance readings. Using this system, a skilled navigator could obtain a position fix within 2 n.m. of his actual position during most times of the day or night and from most locations around the world. Signals travelling over ice caps, however, could be subject to considerable distortion. Omega was decommissioned in August 1998, having been superseded by satellite communications systems.[164]

Pulse comparison of radio signals provided a second method of measuring distance and fixing position. In such systems, a pulse generator converts radio waves into pulses, which the transmitter then sends out "in the form of small discrete packets of radio waves," as opposed to the long chain of continuous waves generated by phase comparison transmitters. The navigator then measures the time between reception of pulses from different stations to establish his position. The first practical version of such a system was Gee (operational in 1942), which the RAF developed to try to improve their success rate in night bombing over Germany and which, like Decca, was employed by the Allies during the Normandy landings. Though it proved useful in some limited roles, authorities decided not to develop it any further after the war.[165]

Another war-inspired system, this time developed by the Americans to assist them in the Pacific theatre, did outlive the hostilities and eventually became an important component of the international system of electronic aids to navigation. Loran or long-range navigation (which later became known as Loran A or Standard Loran to distinguish it from later forms), as its name implies, was intended for long-range position-fixing over water by both ships and aircraft. Its creators chose a radio frequency of 2 MHz in order to allow transmission by ground wave and by ionospheric reflection, which would extend the range of coverage significantly. The system, operated in master-slave pairs each with its own "pulse recurrence or repetition frequency," or PRF. By day over water, navigators could receive reliable ground-wave signals up to about 700 n.m. from the stations, while signals bouncing once off the E layer of the ionosphere were useable at twice that distance, though sky-wave correction formula had to be applied to the readings. They could also cross-match ground and sky waves using specially developed tables. Users of Loran A, depending on their ship's position "relative to the geometry of the chain," could expect their fixes to be accurate within about 1 n.m. for ground-wave and 10 n.m. for sky-wave readings.

Loran A coverage expanded rapidly during and immediately following the war, taking in large parts of the eastern Pacific and western Atlantic oceans. Later forms of the receiving equipment were semi-automated, "with digital read-out and automatic tracking."[166] Loran receivers were relatively expensive, and this limited adoption of the positioning aid to those shipping companies whose ships travelled regularly within the coverage areas. Nevertheless, the system remained operative until the early 1980s, when, like Decca, it was phased out to make way for the more versatile Loran C network.[167]

Loran C is a combined pulse/phase comparison positioning system, that is, it works by comparing the phase of pulses of radio waves. A chain is made up of a master and as many as four slave stations, each of which transmits a train of eight pulses, some of which are phase coded. Using the different phase code to distinguish the signals, the receiver compares the phase of the third cycle of each of the eight pulses from a given slave station with its counterpart from the master. This technique allows a navigator at a range of 800 to 1,000 n.m. from the transmitters to identify his ship's position to within 50 to 1,500 feet (15 to 450 m) of its actual location. Strong ground-wave signals were the most reliable; sky-wave readings were less accurate and carried more risk of error. Early receivers had digital readout, and some were also equipped with visual monitors that allowed the skilled navigator to interpret and therefore use sky-wave signals more effectively. Later equipment was fully automated. The first Loran C installation began operation in 1957, and over the next two decades the system gradually spread around the world, eventually supplanting both Decca and Loran A for most users, including many small craft such as fishing boats and yachts. There are, however, gaps in Loran C coverage — most notably significant stretches of the Pacific Ocean — and now that there are satellite-based systems that can cover all the world's major waters with great accuracy and reliability, marine authorities are seriously considering abandoning the last and most sophisticated of the terrestrial hyperbolic positioning systems.[168]

Canada took full advantage of developments in hyperbolic navigation. In 1948–49, Department of Transport officials reported that they had set up three Loran stations, at Deming and Baccaro, N.S., and Spring Island, B.C. These used the Loran A system and operated in conjunction with the stations at Port aux Basques, Newfoundland, Siasconet and Point Grenville, U.S.A., respectively, providing coverage for both the Atlantic and Pacific coasts as well as Davis Strait and Baffin Bay. In 1957, DOT set up two Decca stations with three satellites each in Halifax and Quebec "to determine user interest in the system." The evaluations were favourable and in 1960, the DOT set up four chains. By 1962, after the relocation of two of the chains to improve coverage of the Gulf and the Cabot Strait, the east coast had full Decca coverage. This system was never used on the west coast.[169]

In 1965, Canada's first Loran C station was built at Cape Race. Funded by the U.S. government, it was part of their military network though it was built by the Canadian government. As this new system proved its value as a navigational aid, the department set up additional stations to expand coverage. To provide coverage on the west coast, it established a station at Williams Lake, B.C., in 1977 and another in 1980 at Port Hardy on Vancouver Island. By 1982, both the east coast and the Great Lakes had full coverage, though in the latter case provided by a United States Coast Guard chain. The following year, the government closed the last Loran A station in Canada.[170]

Canadian transportation officials also experimented with the Omega system. In 1968, the government began an Omega monitoring program in the Canadian Arctic to "determine the amount of correction necessary in readings at various points in the Canadian North." The results of the study were sent to "the U.S. Naval Electronics Laboratory for inclusion in the Skywave Prediction Tables provided to users of the system." Fourteen years later, the Canadian Coast Guard carried out a study of differential Omega in the Gulf of St Lawrence. The system was discontinued in 1998.[171]

Satellite Positioning Systems

In satellite navigation systems, the basic principle is the same as in land-based ones: the time difference in reception of two or more sets of signals is used to establish the difference in distances between the receiver and the transmitters, which then allows the navigator to identify a hyperbolic position line. By repeating the process, he can establish a series of position lines that will give his ship's position. With satellite fixing systems the stations are located in the heavens rather than on land and are in continual motion as they orbit the planet. Because of this, they must transmit orbital information detailing their exact position along with the basic radio signals used to measure time differences. The ship's velocity must also be accounted for in the calculations. As well, because the Earth's atmosphere refracts and delays the passage of electromagnetic waves of various frequencies, satellite transmitters send two sets of signals at different frequencies. This allows the receiver to measure precisely the refraction error in the primary positioning signals.[172]

Like hyperbolic systems, satellite navigation grew out of war, in this instance the Cold War. During this period, the Soviets and the Americans invested huge amounts of money in military research and development that led to the deployment of the first satellites as well as highly specialized guidance systems for military vehicles and the weapons they carried. It was in this context that, in 1964, the U.S. Navy introduced the first satellite navigation system, Transit. The system was originally intended for use by the navy's submarines, but by 1967 the navy had made it available for general use by navigators.[173]

Transit consisted of four or five satellites in polar orbits at a height of about 600 n.m. above the Earth. Every two minutes, each satellite transmitted its position information (updated regularly by ground stations) as well as its navigational signal broadcast as a continuous tone. On board vessels, the receiver measured the Doppler shift, that is, the difference between the known or actual frequency of the satellite's signals and that of the signals received. By taking readings from several successive transmissions as the satellite moved through its orbit, the navigator could establish a series of hyperbolic position lines that indicated his ship's location. A teleprinter printed out the position in longitude and latitude, thereby eliminating the need for special charts and tables. Though mariners could not observe the satellites continuously, they could get accurate fixes every hour or two just about anywhere in the world "except for small areas near the geographical poles." In its earliest forms, Transit could, "on 95 per cent of occasions," provide a position within 1 n.m. of the vessel's actual position. Later versions of the system improved this level of accuracy to 0.25 n.m.[174]

Obtaining a position from Transit, however, required a great many complex calculations that could not be done practically without the aid of a computer.[175] The first such computerized receiver, used on Polaris submarines, took up "three metres of large racks."

Designers gradually improved Transit receivers, taking advantage of rapid developments in computing technology and electronic circuitry, to reduce both their size and cost. With a price tag of about $20,000 in the late 1970s, it was not a system that many smaller marine firms could readily adopt, but it did enjoy widespread use within the commercial shipping industry. The U.S. government officially ended Transit service in December 1996.[176]

The Americans replaced Transit with a much more sophisticated system called the Navstar Global Positioning System, or GPS. First proposed by officials in the Defense Department in 1973, the system took twenty years to build and bring into operation. In 1998, it consisted of twenty-four satellites spaced out in a symmetrical pattern and travelling high above the Earth (20 200 km) in elliptical orbits. The GPS receiver uses radio signals to measure the distance of each satellite from the vessel. The satellites transmit their signals, including location information, at pre-arranged and precise times. The receiver generates an "identical signal controlled by its own atomic frequency standard," then measures the difference in phase of the two signals to calculate distance.[177] The information places the observer "on the surface of an imaginary sphere with the satellite at its centre and its radius equal to the distance of the satellite from the observer." As with hyperbolic navigation, additional readings provide more position information — in this case in the form of the intersections of the imaginary spheres — but GPS greatly increases the extent and precision of that information. For example, by reading three satellites, a navigator can establish his vessel's longitude and latitude, while signals from four will give him latitude, longitude, and altitude above the Earth's surface as well as a correction for his clock. By monitoring the Doppler shift of the transmissions, he can also determine his ship's velocity.

Because GPS was developed for use by the military, Defense Department officials originally degraded the accuracy of GPS signals to 25 to 100 metres to limit its value to America's enemies.[178] In response to this, marine authorities concerned with safe transportation, including the U.S. Coast Guard, introduced Differential GPS, or DGPS, to enhance the level of accuracy of signals available to general users. Differential GPS uses a series of land-based reference stations, which, because their exact locations are known and unchanging, can measure the precise position of the satellites at a given instant. The reference receiver processes this data and produces a correction estimate, which is then broadcast by a network of marine radio beacons to users at sea. Shipboard receivers automatically apply these corrections to the "raw GPS position calculations" taken directly from the satellite, eliminating the errors introduced by the Department of Defense and bringing "the accuracy back to within 10 metres, 95% of the time."[179]

Although the GPS system was based entirely on the constellation of U.S.-owned satellites, DGPS relied on ground-base stations to transmit corrections. The Canadian Coast Guard set up a number of these DGPS installations, some of them at former medium frequency direction finding sites, and began test transmissions in 1995. By 1998, DGPS corrections were available on both coasts and the Great Lakes.[180]

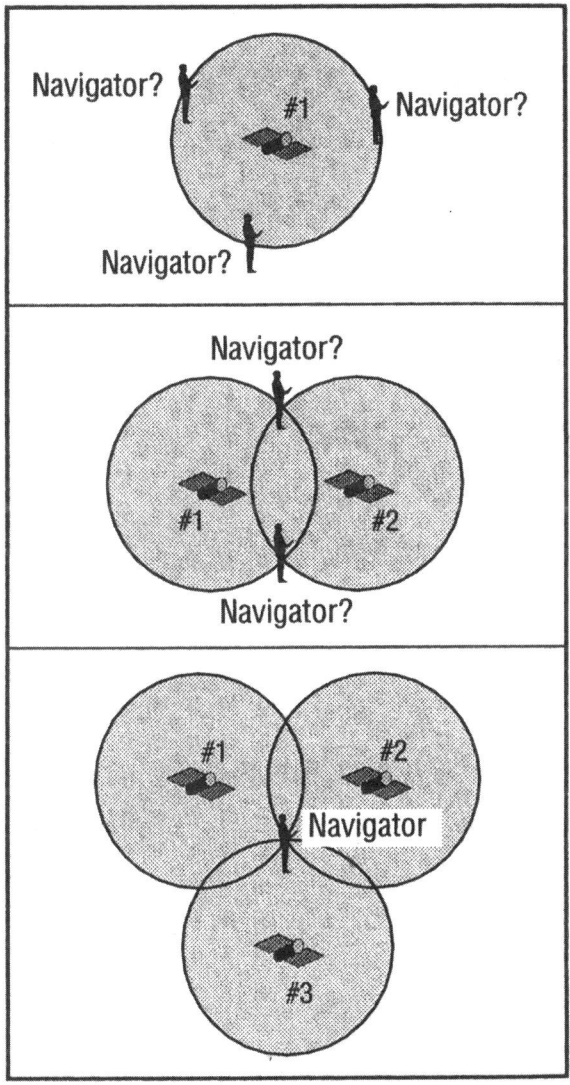

Figure 42. This simple diagram shows how a navigator interacts with the global positioning system (GPS) satellites. A reading from one satellite provides the navigator with a simple distance measurement along the circumference of an imaginary circle. A reading from a second satellite narrows down the position to where the two circles intersect. A third satellite gives a precise position as the three circles intersect at only one point.
(Lawrence Letham, *GPS Made Easy* [Calgary: Rocky Mountain Books, 2002])

Charts and Integrated Navigational Systems

The Canadian government assumed financial responsibility for charting its own waters beginning in 1883 with the creation of the Georgian Bay Survey under Royal Navy staff commander John George Boulton. In 1904, it created the Hydrographic Survey of Canada (renamed Canadian Hydrographic Service in 1928) by amalgamating the hydrographic operations of the Department of Public Works, the Department of Railways and Canals, and the Ministry of Marine and Fisheries. By this time, most of the primary coastlines along the east and west coasts and along the St Lawrence River and Great Lakes had been charted. But there was still an enormous amount of work to be done surveying countless navigable inland waterways and the long and intricate Arctic coastlines. Also, there was a constant requirement to re-survey areas in order to upgrade older charts.[181]

Like many of the essential tools of marine navigation, the nautical chart underwent a dramatic transformation in the twentieth century. At the centre of that transformation has been the application of electronic and digital systems first to surveying and eventually to the collection, processing, and display of survey data. This process, which began in the 1960s, ultimately resulted in the development of electronic navigational charts (ENCs). These charts are part of an elaborate information processing system that integrates data from all of the ship's navigational tools and displays the ship's actual position at that instant in relation to both its planned course and its surroundings on a computer monitor. Using this new technology, mariners no longer need to spend precious time transferring their position readings onto a paper chart to tell them where they are or, more precisely, where they were at the time they took the reading. Access to instantaneous position information is especially important in high-traffic areas or dangerous waters.

From Paper to Pixels: Marine Charting since 1900

The technical evolution of charts and charting since 1900 follows much the same course as that of navigational instruments. Prior to the 1930s, the hydrographer's survey tools were, with the exception of the theodolite, the same tools used by mariners to find their way at sea. The sextant was used mainly for measuring latitude, the chronometer, longitude, and the lead and line, the water's depth. Hydrographers used the theodolite to establish baselines on land from which to begin their survey of the water. It was labour-intensive and painstaking work, involving thousands of measurements and soundings for every new chart. The level of precision that could be achieved, even by the most meticulous surveyor, was limited by the nature of the instruments.

Beginning in the 1930s, hydrographers were able to take advantage of several important advances in navigational science. Early in the century researchers had developed the first gyrocompasses, and during the First World War they introduced echo-sounders[182] as a means of tracking the movement of submarines. Both of these innovations, after some refinement,[183] were gradually adopted by the commercial shipping industry. Hydrographers also embraced them and adapted them to their specialized needs. The echo-sounder not only significantly reduced the time and energy required to take soundings — especially in deep or rough waters — but it also improved the overall accuracy of the measurements. The gyrocompass also provided a more precise and reliable indication of true north. This capability was especially important to Canadian chart-makers who had to work in the Arctic, where the magnetic compass was "virtually useless" because of proximity to the magnetic north pole.[184]

In 1928–29, the Canadian Hydrographic Service installed a gyrocompass and an echo-sounder on the survey ship *Acadia*. Despite the high cost of the devices and despite the limitations of the echo-sounder — it was designed to perform best in deep water — the service was very pleased with the results. By 1934 they had installed gyrocompasses on three of their ships, and one year later, "all major CHS ships, plus their auxiliary survey launches were equipped with echo-sounders." The latter devices, called magneto-striction transducer recording sounders, were a refined form of the original type. They could measure both shallow and deep waters accurately and automatically recorded the soundings at a rate of four per second on a roll of paper. According to Canada's chief hydrographer at the time, echo-sounding increased the efficiency of deep-water sounding significantly.[185]

By 1945, Canadian hydrographers, like their counterparts in other countries, were taking the vast majority of their depth measurements with echo-sounders. This trend continued after the war, when researchers introduced important new forms of echo-sounding. Sonar was the first advance and then, in the 1960s, military scientists in the United States introduced multi-beam sonar systems. Made available for civilian applications in the 1970s as Sea Beam, these devices sent out twenty sound beams instead of one. A sophisticated receiver then sorted through the return signals, which, taken together, gave a clear depiction of the dominant features of the seabed. Using this method, hydrographers "could map about 450 square miles [1 150 sq km] of sea floor per day at a contour interval of thirty to sixty feet [9 to 18 m]." A more sophisticated version of the system that could cover three times this area became available in the 1990s.[186] Today, the Canadian Hydrographic Service uses a version of this technology, which it calls multi-beam echo-sounders, in its work.[187]

In the post-war period, surveyors also adapted advances in radio-based technologies for use in charting. Mariners had been using radio to establish position since the First World War, and it made sense that the same basic principle could be used for locating control points, coastal features, and offshore soundings. In the 1930s, the U.S. Coast Guard began experimenting with a system called radio acoustic

Figure 43. GGS *Quadra around 1900. Before the advent of sonar in the 1930s, mariners and hydrographers measured the water's depth and mapped the sea bottom using a lead line like the one in this photograph. This ancient tool had changed little over the course of many centuries.*
(Library and Archives Canada, neg. e003719355)

ranging for fixing offshore soundings. The Canadian government followed their example and also began to test this system.

Following the war, a variety of new radio-positioning technologies became available. The tellurometer (circa 1956) measured distance by sending and timing the return of microwave radio signals and could measure accurately distances greater than thirty kilometres even over rugged terrain, in darkness, or in bad weather. Decca Navigator was also applied to surveying and led to the introduction of a number of similar positioning systems designed specifically for surveying, including ARGO, Hydrodist, Hi-Fix, and MRS. Loran-C and GPS are also used by hydrographers to measure distances across land and water accurately.

The application of radio-based positioning systems to hydrography significantly increased the accuracy of the surveys. These technologies also relieved surveyors of the time-consuming work of measuring out baselines, setting up triangulation networks, and fixing the positions of the survey vessels and soundings using sextants. This gave them more time to do their soundings, which meant that they could accomplish more in the short season available for hydrographic work in Canada.

The work of the field hydrographer was also made easier by the development of computerized systems for collecting and recording data. By the early 1980s, equipment was already in place that allowed surveyors to input and store their measurements and soundings in digital form on magnetic tape or disk. Though they still often drew field sheets recording and depicting their work, the digitization of their data was a crucial first step in the movement toward computerized chart construction.

In the past twenty years, scientists and engineers have produced increasingly powerful microprocessors and ever more sophisticated software programs for compiling, sorting, and arranging data. These advances, combined with the development of computerized positioning systems such as GPS, have increased the accuracy of data as well as the precision and speed with which it is collected, recorded, sorted, and compiled. Equally important, the digitization of data has made it possible for the results of fieldwork to be transferred easily to the chart production facilities, where computers can interrogate and manipulate it to produce different charts in a variety of formats.

The process of transforming field data into a useful chart has also changed significantly in the twentieth century. Up to the 1950s, chart-makers relied on long-established methods of hand-drafting to create their charts. Their painstaking drawings were made on paper and then engraved onto copper plates, which became the template for printing multiple copies of the charts or, in more advanced systems, for creating photographic negatives, which then were transferred onto printing plates. Corrections or changes could either be added to the plate (once a sufficient number had been collected to make a reprint worthwhile) or published in notices to mariners and added to the charts by the navigators themselves.

Some charts were also produced using a less expensive alternative to engraving. In 1903, Canadian hydrographers produced the first all-Canadian chart (a colour chart of Lake Winnipeg) using a new process called photolithography. Though this method provided less fine detail and a lower overall resolution than engraving, it was an important short-term alternative for the fledgling Canadian Hydrographic Service, which had just begun to take over responsibility for charting and chart production from the British Admiralty. In 1909, the first two Canadian-engraved charts were offered for sale by the government, marking "the beginning of organized chart distribution by the CHS."[188]

Copper engraving remained the standard for chart production for many years because of the fine detail that could be rendered using this technique. Gradually, though, as printing technology improved, the hydrographic service adopted new forms of reproduction. The CHS played a pioneering role in the introduction of negative engraving on plastic. In this process, the "data are scribed (engraved) in negative form on an emulsion-coated polyester carrier, rather than drafted on paper." Since the originals are actually the negatives in this process, the intermediate photographic stages usually required to produce printing plates are eliminated. The first chart in the world using this technique was issued by the Canadian Hydrographic Service in 1953.[189] This process is still used, though the negatives are based on drawings done by computer.[190]

The CHS began work on a computer-assisted drawing system around 1967. The goal of these systems was to reduce the increasingly time-consuming process of hand-drafting charts. The adoption of new navigational systems such as Decca and Loran-C had made it necessary for hydrographers to add new overlays of information to help mariners transfer readings from their instruments onto their charts. With the integration of major advances in processing power and software design, hydrographers had at their disposal sophisticated digital systems that can transform data into precise, detailed, and clear colour charts in a fraction of the time it would take to draw a chart by hand.[191]

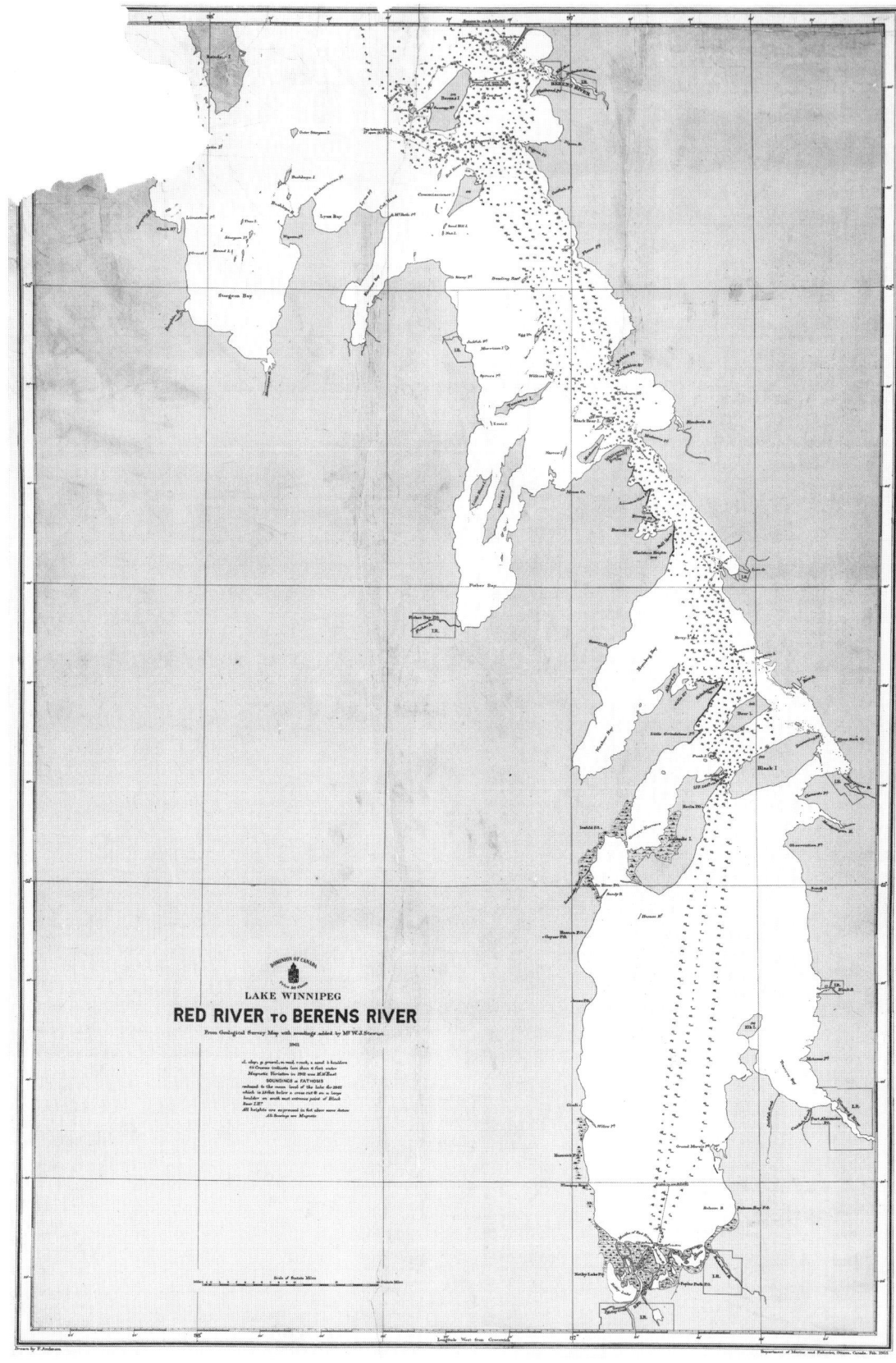

Map 8. *William Stewart's 1903 chart of the southern portions of Lake Winnipeg was the first produced using Canadian surveys and printed in Canada using a new photolithographic process.*
(Library and Archives Canada, neg. NMC 0043301)

The digitization of the charting process has, in recent years, made possible the creation of electronic charts. Electronic charts are essentially charts created from a digital database and displayed on a computer monitor. There are two basic types: the raster chart and the vector chart. Raster charts are created by scanning a paper chart so that each tiny segment of the drawing is converted into a pixel or picture element. Together these thousands of pixels form what is known as a fixed bitmap, which the computer displays as a picture but cannot interpret. Vector charts,[192] on the other hand, exist "as collections of data that can be searched, rearranged, turned on and off, and so on." By searching the database, the computer is capable of identifying a buoy as a buoy, providing its characteristics, and distinguishing it from other markers. Mariners can, therefore, tailor vector charts to meet their specific needs. If, for example, a mariner does not need deep-sea soundings on his chart, he can tell the computer to turn this element off. Vector charts can also be edited and updated more easily than raster charts because all the hydrographer needs to do is edit the data set. To edit a raster chart requires that the hydrographer design a "patch" made up of a new arrangement of pixels corresponding to a specific marker, feature, or sounding and distribute this to chart owners.[193]

Electronic Chart Display Information System

Electronic charts, particularly in the vector format, are attractive to hydrographers, mariners, and the shipping industry for a number of reasons. On a purely practical level, they are seen as a viable replacement for paper charts, which are expensive to construct, produce, distribute, and buy and rather awkward to handle and to keep up to date. Far more important than these cost considerations, though, was the realization that electronic charts could work with other navigational and communications instruments to create a fully integrated navigational system providing instantaneous and complete position information on the chart display.

These integrated chart systems, which the international maritime and hydrographic organizations (IMO and IHO) now refer to overall as the Electronic Chart Display Information System, or ECDIS, have been under development since the early 1980s. The first systems were tested in the late 1980s and were called automatic radar positioning systems because they were built around networks of radar installations covering busy coastal waterways and harbours. These systems took speed and heading information from the ship's sensors, combined it with a Loran-C fix, and downloaded this location data into a special computer. The computer then activated a radar system that took

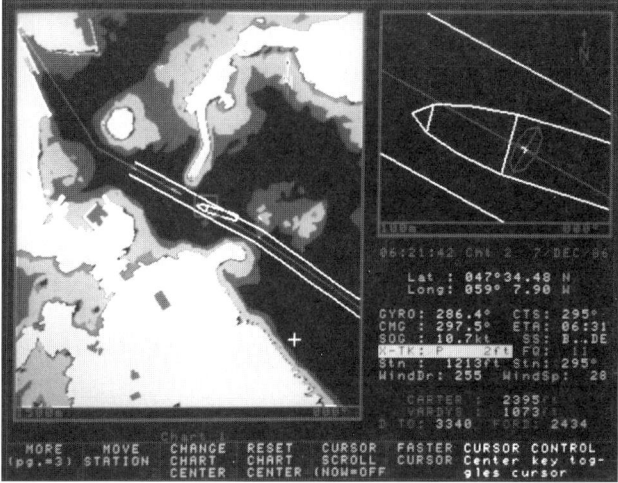

Figure 44. *A two-window display on the* PINS *monitor showing the route of the Marine Atlantic ferry* MV Caribou. *The white lines indicate the route pre-set by the computer. Water depth is indicated by colours ranging from light blue (shallowest) to black (deepest). This is the reverse of how water depth is depicted on conventional paper charts. The right window shows detail from the left.*
(Offshore Systems Limited, Vancouver, no neg. no.)

Figure 45. *Control console of the* MV Caribou *showing* PINS *video display terminal in left foreground.*
(Offshore Systems Limited, Vancouver, no neg. no.)

readings from shore installations, which provided a more precise and current position fix. This information was then displayed on an electronic chart.

These systems were designed primarily to help mariners navigating in coastal or inshore areas where Loran-C fixes were not accurate enough to ensure safe navigation and where the time lag between taking a position reading and plotting it on a paper chart could negate the benefits of even the most accurate fix. Companies that offered this technology, such as Offshore Systems Limited (OSL) of Vancouver, had to set up their own private networks of radar reflectors to supply ships with the position information required to make the system work.[194]

The main drawback of these early systems was that they were available only in those areas where companies like OSL had set up the necessary radar reflector networks. Moreover, because the networks were privately owned and operated, mariners could not count on having access to the position data supplied by a competing network even if the systems were compatible. This severely limited the level of coverage of automatic radar positioning systems and thus restricted the market to shipping companies that operated mainly in areas that had appropriate coverage.

Despite this limitation, many in the shipping industry saw these enhanced navigational systems as a great advance in electronic navigation. By 1989, for example, OSL had sold its Precise Integrated Navigation System 9000 (PINS 9000) to several Canadian and U.S. customers including the Department of National Defence, the Canadian Coast Guard, the ferry service Marine Atlantic, Chevron International Shipping Co., and the U.S. Navy. PINS 9000, the successor to their original automatic radar positioning system, consisted of a computer equipped with colour monitor and loaded with specially designed and patented navigational software and stored electronic charts. The computer processed all information available from the onboard instruments and from coastal installations to obtain a precise, current position and displayed it as it changed on the relevant chart. The system also displayed the ship's intended course with reference to all major coastal features and markers. The navigator could change the scale of the chart to get a more detailed perspective as needed, and could set the system to warn him when the ship was departing from its course or when it was getting too close to a hazard. In 1990, PINS 9000, which was perhaps the most sophisticated system of its kind in the world, cost about CAN$75,000.[195]

In the years since the introduction of PINS 9000, electronic chart display and information systems have gained substantial technological momentum and much wider acceptance within the shipping industry. Much of the technological momentum has come from the development and deployment of DGPS. This system is much more precise than Loran-C and therefore can be relied upon to provide position fixes accurate enough to be used even in confined waters. Equally important, the system delivers signals via a uniform, U.S. government–maintained system of satellites and shore installations, so that coverage is very nearly global (the polar regions are the main exception) and access is not limited by proprietary ownership of infrastructure.[196] This, combined with dramatic advances in the capacity of microprocessors and the versatility of computer software, has made ECDIS a viable and affordable addition to the standard set of navigational equipment and tools used by mariners. In 1995, the IMO issued performance standards for ECDIS that "define requirements for an ECDIS installation that would allow a vessel to do without paper charts."[197] Four years later, in 1999, Transas Marine received official approval for its ECDIS system Marine Navi-Sailor.[198]

For all this progress, though, ECDIS still faces technical, regulatory, and other obstacles. In order to meet the performance standards established by the

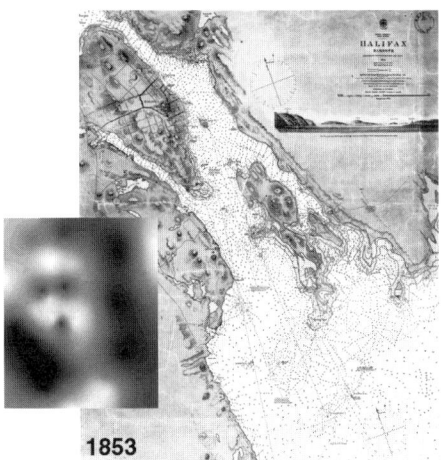

Figure 46. These images of Halifax Harbour demonstrate how charts have changed over the past 150 years. The newer chart clearly provides a more complete and accurate image of both the coastlines and of the seabed. This has been made possible, in part, by greatly improved resolution, demonstrated by the reproductions of the Mona Lisa.
(© 2006 Canadian Hydrographic Service/Nautical Data International, www.digitalocean.ca)

IMO, equipment manufacturers, chart-makers, and others involved in the development and deployment of the system must establish a series of precise technical standards. For example, each ECDIS manufacturer has their own method for displaying the electronic navigation charts (ENCs) created by national and international hydrographic organizations. Companies must therefore convert the ENCs into what are called system electronic navigation charts, or SENCs. In order to minimize conversion errors, the IHO has had to develop a common transfer standard for digital hydrographic data. This standard — IHO S-57 — ensures that all systems will "speak the same language" and thus can use any chart based on these specifications. There is also an IHO standard (IHO S-52) for chart content and display, including information relating to the means and process of updating charts and the colours and symbols to be used on them. These standards, which in some cases have taken years to develop, are still being revised as engineers and hydrographers refine and improve the technology and the data and as testing, analysis, and practical experience reveal potential flaws or weaknesses.[199]

A second obstacle standing in the way of rapid adoption of ECDIS is the lack of digital charts. The introduction of electronic charts and integrated navigational systems coincided with major staff and resource reductions at hydrographic establishments in Canada and in most western nations. National governments retained their wide-ranging responsibilities for chart-making and distribution — paper and electronic versions — but the amount of work that could be accomplished declined significantly. The impact was obvious. Fewer staff produced fewer new charts and fewer upgraded versions of existing charts. This has meant, among other things, that the advances in accurate positioning made possible by DGPS are only gradually being reflected in Canadian charts. As a consequence, though many older charts have been converted to electronic vector format, the position data on these are not as precise as the fixes that mariners can obtain from their DGPS sets, leading to discrepancies between actual position and the position shown on the chart.[200] Also, because the Canadian Hydrographic Service began converting its paper charts to digital format before the IHO had established its S-57 data transfer standard, there are also a number of digital CHS charts that use an interim data format called NTX. These charts also have to be converted to meet the new standard.[201]

In an attempt to address the problem of digital chart production and distribution, the Canadian Hydrographic Service entered into a partnership with a private company called Nautical Data International in 1993. NDI has essentially taken over responsibility for marketing and distribution of CHS electronic charts, allowing the service to concentrate on conducting its surveys and constructing new charts. NDI is also assisting the CHS in development of an electronic chart updating service that will provide users with recent changes to charts such as wrecks, new markers, special traffic restrictions, or other useful navigational information. This service must be compliant with the same S-57 standard established for all ECDIS data transfer.[202]

Another major challenge that the industry and regulatory agencies must address is training. This is a requirement for all new technologies, but it is especially important in the case of ECDIS. With all of its sophisticated information processing and display capacities, it poses two major risks for deck officers. First, its enormous capabilities can lead to overconfidence in the reliability of the readings and images. Although all good mariners know they should never rely on one navigational device to determine position, it can be tempting to see ECDIS as an exception because it incorporates and constantly updates information from so many different sensors.

Like all technological systems, though, ECDIS is not infallible. As noted above, there remain technical problems and inconsistencies in the overall ECDIS framework. Even assuming these are overcome, however, the system can still produce inaccurate readings. Something as simple as the placement of the GPS antenna in relation to the pivot point of a ship and the radar antenna, for example, will often produce discrepancies between the two sets of readings. Also, a minor GPS signal dropout such as might occur while passing under a bridge can have a major impact on position information. Moreover, while the radar overlay on ECDIS is very useful, experts recommend that the automatic radar plotting aid — these became standard equipment after the limitations of simple radar displays became evident in the aftermath of a number of "radar-assisted collisions" — remain the primary device for target tracking and collision avoidance.[203]

The second risk posed by ECDIS is system complexity. Mariners who are inexperienced with the system can easily spend too much time looking at the monitor — working through the menu structure; planning, monitoring, and revising their route; setting up the necessary charts; adjusting safety settings and alarms; and testing various functions — and too little time attending to other critical duties such as maintaining a visual lookout and monitoring readings from other navigational systems. Moreover, in certain situations, even experienced ECDIS operators may find the system confusing. In times of stress when decisions must be made quickly to avoid a possible mishap, when various alarms are going off to warn of potential problems, or when the ECDIS operator is also responsible for navigating the ship, it becomes more of a challenge to remember how to retrieve the information you need promptly, let alone interpret and act upon it.

The industry has recognized that, even though ECDIS is still evolving and is not likely to be made mandatory in the near future, the widespread use of this complex technology has created a need for systematic training. As early as 1996, when ECDIS was still relatively new, Det Norske Veritas, a Norway-based international organization, advocated a comprehensive approach that included "both the technical and functional capabilities and limitations of the system and its subsystems." The author of the report, Olaf Gundersrud, placed special emphasis on the challenges posed by the current state of available electronic charts and the need for mariners to know what they were dealing with — type and accuracy of technical data, the maker, etc. — when they used a particular chart. He also stressed the need for manufacturers "to provide a full training package" for operators who would be using their particular systems.[204]

In more recent years, both international and national regulators have become involved in ECDIS training. The IMO has developed a framework for a "model course on the operational use of ECDIS" and has also issued specific guidelines for training with ECDIS simulators that include "simulation of live data streams, as well as ARPA and AIS [automatic identification system] target information."[205] In Canada, the Marine Safety Directorate of Transport Canada has had an ECDIS course standard in place as part of its Simulated Electronic Navigation courses since at least 2000. Details of the course content, goals, and objectives run more than ten pages and specify the minimum amount of time that must be spent on each subject, divided between practical training and lectures. The course must include at least twenty-four hours in total of instruction and training, with a maximum of two students per ECDIS simulator and eight students per instructor.[206]

According to one experienced analyst, the most successful approach to ECDIS training is one that balances generalized instruction on the system and knowledge of its characteristics "with the mastering of one specific type of ECDIS." Also, a good course should present topics in "a navigational context" that makes them "meaningful" for students and should be "tightly structured" to prevent students from trying "to learn the entire system all at once." Most importantly, trainees, instructors, regulators, equipment manufacturers, and shipping companies must recognize that courses are only the first stage in training — that the mariner must continue to learn how to use ECDIS effectively on board a ship.[207] Used properly, ECDIS is clearly an incredibly powerful navigational tool and an important new aid to the mariner's navigational judgment.

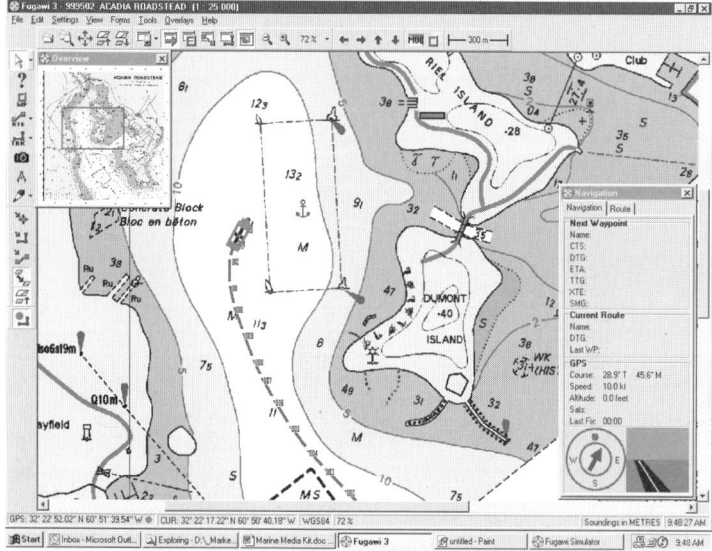

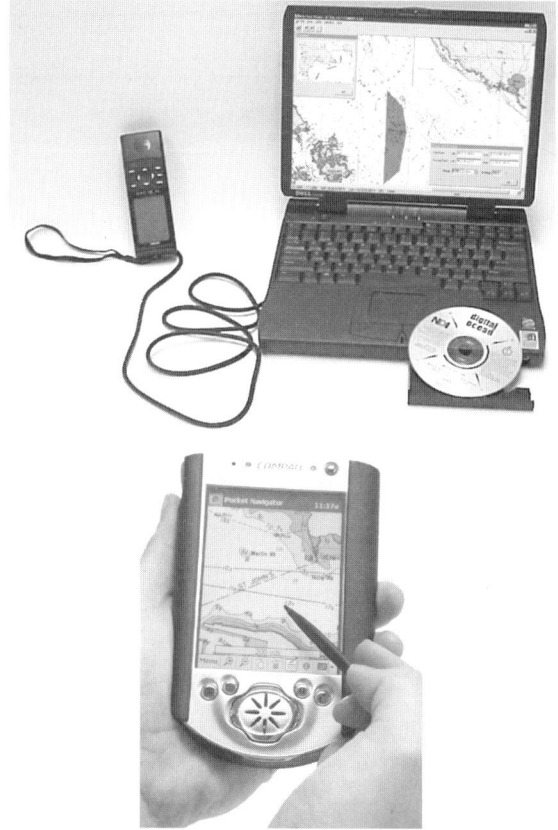

Figure 47. Detail of an electronic chart showing the ship's course, direction and speed. Note the larger chart from which the detail is derived in the upper left-hand window. Though most ships equipped with ECDIS would have a built-in monitor and processor, navigators can also use portable devices like the two shown here to link into the ship's navigational systems.

(© 2006 Canadian Hydrographic Service/Nautical Data International, www.digitalocean.ca)

Electrification and Automation: Coastal Aids to Navigation

The purpose of coastal aids to navigation, like that of shipboard navigational tools, has remained largely unchanged since ancient times — to identify hazards and lead mariners into safe, navigable channels. Twentieth-century authorities, like their predecessors, continued to search for ways to make seamarks more visible and easier to distinguish from one another and to develop uniform systems of marking that could be understood by all mariners. At the same time, faced with the steady growth in the number of navigational aids, they also had to find ways to contain the costs of building, operating, and maintaining these varied and far-flung devices. To address these problems they devised new and more efficient forms of illumination and extended the use of light from stations and ships to buoys and beacons. They developed enhanced sounding systems for use in fog and applied advances in radio and radar to seamarking. Authorities adopted electricity as a power source wherever possible, and this allowed them to simplify power plants and use more powerful and versatile forms of lights. This reduced the number of staff needed and paved the way for gradual automation of many seamarks.

Technological Advances in Aids to Navigation

The twentieth century witnessed dramatic changes in aids to navigation largely brought about by two interrelated trends — electrification and automation — and by the emergence of ever more precise electronic navigational systems. Thus, while the first half of the century witnessed a fairly steady expansion in the number and variety of aids established worldwide, the decades since 1970 have seen a gradual decline in the number and importance of major aids such as light stations and a redeployment of many minor ones to meet those navigational requirements that are not addressed by more sophisticated aids such as vessel traffic control and satellite positioning systems.

Despite their recent decline, lighthouses played a pivotal role in the aids-to-navigation system through most of the twentieth century. From 1900 on, the international network of lights grew steadily to meet the increasing demands of sea-going and coastal trade and commerce. Engineers and builders focused much of their attention on enhancing illumination while at the same time reducing the complexity of the lights and their power requirements and developing more durable and efficient structures to house the lights. All of these advances were aimed at reducing the cost of building and maintaining lights while ensuring that coastlines were marked more thoroughly and effectively.

Improvements in illumination began early in the century with the concurrent introduction of oil vapour and acetylene lights. First used by the French lighthouse service in 1898, the oil vapour light trebled "the power of all former wick lamps" by using an incandescent mantle instead of a flat wick for burning the fuel. Authorities in Europe, the United States, and Britain adopted this form of light and began to produce improved versions of it for use in their lighthouses. In 1920 David Hood, engineer-in-chief of Britain's Trinity House, made one of the most important innovations in the design of oil vapour lights when he introduced an improved viscous silk mantle that doubled the brilliance of existing mantle lamps.[208] These types of lights became and remained among the most common in many lighthouse services until the introduction of electric lamps.

Figure 48. *Fourth-order light from Victoria Island, Ontario, equipped with a gas mantle lamp. This technology represented an enormous improvement in illumination over the wick-style lamps.*

(Library and Archives Canada, neg. PA 135446)

Acetylene is colourless gas produced by immersing calcium carbide in water. Canadian Thomas L. Willson discovered a commercially viable process for producing calcium carbide in 1892, and within ten years, engineers had adapted a variety of lamps to burn this new fuel. Tests showed that it burned more brightly and cleanly than kerosene, thus increasing the visibility of lights and eliminating some of the lightkeeper's daily maintenance work. Though acetylene was used in some lighthouses, its most important and widespread application was as an illuminant for buoys and other unattended lights, where it proved to be a relatively safe, reliable, and efficient form of fuel.[209]

The next major improvement in illumination came with the introduction of electrical light sources. British lighthouse authorities had attempted to use arc lamps as early as the 1850s but found that the cost and difficulty of supplying the fuel and water needed to run the generators and the maintenance requirements of the arc lamps themselves made this form of illumination impractical. By the early twentieth century, however, reliable supplies of electricity were more readily accessible, for engineers had developed both large-scale generation and delivery systems and more efficient small generators. Concurrently, electrical companies had introduced a variety of smaller, more powerful and durable lights. The first of these was the tungsten filament bulb, introduced about 1907 and used widely across Europe and North America.

In the decades after the Second World War, lighthouse authorities also began to install mercury vapour and xenon lamps. The former not only produced light of a higher intensity than incandescent filament bulbs but also lasted much longer and were smaller. The xenon lamp is also small and durable. Because it produces a light of "unprecedented intensity" and a beam that is very concentrated, its use is limited to situations where thick fog demands the strongest possible light and where "a bright light by day and sharply defined beam are required."[210] By the 1970s, authorities also adopted lighting systems and techniques developed elsewhere, including sealed beam units identical to those used for railway locomotive headlights and halogen lights similar to the type found in slide projectors.[211]

Electrification and the development of brighter, smaller, and more efficient lamps paved the way for other improvements in lighthouses and lightships. Electric motors could now be adapted to rotate the lights, replacing mechanical clockwork mechanisms that had to be wound and adjusted constantly. Moreover, authorities soon discovered that with more intense light sources, the large, expensive, and high-maintenance Fresnel lenses could be dispensed with in favour of much simpler and lighter moulded glass or plastic optics. These significantly smaller assemblies powered by electric motors made it easier and cheaper to vary light characteristics such as colour and flash sequence. Widespread adoption of electric lights also made possible the use of automatic lamp changers and light sensors, which further reduced the need for constant attendance to the light.

The shift toward automated lights was a gradual but steady one. Initially, automation simply freed lightkeepers from the onerous daily chores of cleaning the lanterns and lenses, replenishing the fuel and grooming the wicks, and the nightly tasks of lighting and minding the lamps. In most cases, they remained on station and focused their attention on other duties, including taking care of the electrical generators, overseeing other navigational aids including fog alarms,

Figure 49. Canadian marine authorities began to install electric lights in their navigational aids around the time of the First World War. This particular lamp probably dates from after the Second World War, and included a sun valve that automatically turned the light on when the sky got dark.

(Library and Archives Canada, neg. e003719350)

Figure 50. Adoption of high-power electrical lights made it possible to replace many of the large, expensive, and high-maintenance Fresnel lenses. This image shows a staff member working on the third-order Fresnel apparatus from the Point Ferolle light.
(Library and Archives Canada, neg. e003719347)

meteorological equipment, and radio systems, and carrying out long-term maintenance on the installation.

By the 1970s, however, more and more navigational aids had been or were being completely automated. The cost of staffing light stations had grown dramatically due to a number of factors, including demands by keepers that their terms of service be improved — fewer hours, healthier working environments, shorter periods on duty especially at isolated sites, and so on. This coincided with technological developments that made it possible to reduce the number of staffed lighthouses. By the 1970s, marine authorities worldwide were setting up new and more precise positioning systems that made some seamarks obsolete. Concurrently, engineers began to introduce computerized control systems that allowed staff at remote locations to monitor and control lights. Where these systems were put in place, lighthouses were "de-staffed" and visited only periodically by supply and maintenance personnel based at centralized lighthouse depots.[212]

Advances in lighthouse tower construction also helped authorities reduce costs. Steel and reinforced concrete became the materials of choice for new light towers. These materials were more durable and versatile than masonry, stone, or wood and required less maintenance than these or cast iron. There were also new design requirements for twentieth-century light stations, including new buildings to house generators, radio systems, fog alarms, and a variety of sensors for automatic equipment. After 1950, helicopter landing pads became common especially at isolated, wave-swept stations, where they had to be built at the top of the tower above the lantern. These aluminum lattice-work decks did not improve the aesthetic appearance of the towers, but they certainly made the keepers' lives safer and more tolerable.[213]

Lightships underwent a similar transformation to that of lighthouses. Engineers were able to apply many of the advances made in lighthouse design to lightships. Improvements in illumination were especially important, since lightships carried their lanterns on masts that could seldom hold the weight of a heavy Fresnel lens and thus were dependent on reflection for concentrating the beam and extending its visibility. Maritime authorities thus gradually changed lightships' lanterns from oil lamps to more powerful alternatives, eventually converting all to electricity, using generators to produce the necessary power. This change allowed engineers and designers to incorporate smaller and more versatile lights in the vessels, helping to make them more visible and to distinguish them from other floating and stationary illuminated aids.

Ship construction also benefited from technological advances. Steel hulls and superstructure gradually replaced wood and iron, permitting more flexibility in design of the vessels while providing necessary strength. Although no amount of technological improvement could alleviate the discomfort of living in a vessel moored in shallow, often choppy waters, crew living quarters were gradually expanded and enhanced to make the best of a bad situation. Where possible, lightships, like lighthouses, were completely automated and, in some countries including Canada, entirely replaced with stationary pillar lights.[214]

So little has been written about minor aids such as buoys and beacons in the twentieth century that it is difficult to trace their technological evolution in any detail. Engineers seem to have pursued trends established in previous decades to make floating and coastal marks more visible, more durable, and more "readable." Marine authorities worldwide expanded their use of illumination for important buoys. In addition to the Pintsch gas buoy, they began to use acetylene buoys. During the early years of the century, at least two basic types of acetylene buoy were available — one using

Figure 51. Fog alarm building at Cape Croker, Ontario. The horn is conspicuous in the second-floor window. Equally conspicuous are the fuel tanks below. Steam-powered alarms consumed a lot of fuel, which increased the resupply requirements of many light stations.
(Library and Archives Canada, neg. e003719336)

pressurized gas and the other using calcium carbide powder as a fuel source.

Acetylene gas, though an efficient and reliable fuel, posed significant dangers in its pressurized form. Gustav Dalén, a notable Swedish inventor of lighting systems for seamarks, was blinded by an explosion while experimenting with acetylene, and in 1906, four employees of the Canadian Department of Marine and Fisheries died in a blast caused by a pressurized buoy. One solution to this problem was the self-generating water to carbide buoy developed by Thomas Willson around 1904. This device contained calcium carbide to which water was periodically added to generate a steady supply of acetylene gas. Pressure never exceeded more than a few pounds per square inch, and the device could carry sufficient calcium carbide to produce four times as much acetylene fuel as the standard pressurized buoy. Thus Willson buoys not only required less servicing but could also be serviced by smaller vessels, since they did not have to carry compression equipment to refuel the tanks. This meant that the use of lighted buoys could be extended even to very remote waterways.[215]

Scientists eventually found a way "to stabilize acetylene gas by dissolving it in acetone retained in a porous mass containing charcoal," allowing the further use and development of the pressurized buoy. Among the many improvements to these devices, one

Figure 52. The first illuminated buoys were powered either by gas or, later, pressurized acetylene, both of which required regular refuelling or charging. Note the buoy at the right, tethered to the ship, and the large pressurized vessel on deck.
(Library and Archives Canada, neg. e003719354)

of the most notable was Gustav Dalén's control system that made a flashing sequence possible. In his Nobel Prize–winning invention, a pilot light burned constantly and ignited the acetylene gas as it was released in timed puffs through a diaphragm valve. The flash sequence was controlled by adjusting the diaphragm. Dalén also introduced the first workable sun-valve, a photometric device that automatically switched the light on or off by controlling the flow of gas with a rod. When heated by the sun the rod expanded and closed off the fuel supply. In low light conditions, it contracted to allow gas to flow to the lantern again. By the 1980s, engineers had devised a way to use gas pressure "to rotate a lightweight optic around the light source," a capability that was especially useful for larger floating buoys and for fixed beacon lights.[216]

After the 1960s, engineers also began to look for ways to apply advances in electrical illumination to smaller lights. This meant that they had to develop reliable and efficient devices for generating and storing electricity that were small enough to fit onto a buoy and robust enough to withstand the rigours of wind, water, and wave motion. Maritime authorities experimented with several different generation techniques, including basic dry cell batteries and batteries charged by solar, wind, or wave power. In their initial stages, all of these approaches posed problems. Electrical connections with the lamps were subject to corrosion from exposure to sea water. Solar panels of the type required were too expensive to compete with acetylene. Wind recharging systems required prohibitively expensive maintenance work, and wave-powered turbines could only use air flowing in one direction. In the past decade, however, many of these obstacles have been overcome, allowing marine authorities to convert many of their minor lights to electrical operation, to light many more buoys and beacons, and to add special light characteristics that help mariners distinguish one marker from another.[217]

In addition to improved lighting technology, engineers also applied advances in materials and design to the production of navigational aids, especially buoys. Steel gradually replaced iron and wood as the construction material of choice. Buoys made of steel were lighter than iron ones and more durable than those constructed of wood. They still required regular painting to reduce corrosion, however, and when punctured in a collision with a vessel could sink. Also the largest buoys were heavy — up to 5 400 kilograms for a lighted buoy — and this made the task of removing them for maintenance and then redeploying them all the more demanding.

As a result of these disadvantages, marine authorities began experimenting with plastic buoys in the 1970s. Compared to steel, plastic is light, does not corrode, and does not require painting, since the colour is dispersed throughout the material. As with any new technology, there were some problems with the first generation of synthetic buoys. For example, Irish authorities found that the glass-reinforced plastic model they used developed cracks during deployment, exposing the foam interior to water absorption over time. By the mid-1980s, though, engineers and manufacturers had produced a number of successful designs, which European governments began adopting for use in their jurisdictions.

U.S. marine authorities were slower to adopt plastic buoys. According to one analyst, the U.S. "Coast Guard looked at plastic in the mid-1970s but saw too many problems." They did not reconsider this decision until the 1990s. By this time, materials and construction techniques had improved significantly and the cost of maintaining steel buoys had risen significantly due to a number of factors, including new environmental regulations that limited the use of quick-drying vinyl paints. As a consequence of this, the Americans began market study and test programs with a view to finding a replacement for the largest lighted buoys then in service. They identified three different types of plastic buoy and eventually selected a buoy made by Gilman, which consisted of "an inner steel structure surrounded by ionomer foam with densified skin." Although the new plastic buoys cost more than their steel equivalents, US$18,000 to $20,000 each, officials expected the lifetime costs to be significantly lower because they would not have to be painted. Moreover, once the USCG had adjusted its buoy-laying equipment and practices to handle the less robust plastic devices, they would be easier to deploy and take up because of their relatively light weight (6,000 to 7,000 pounds [2 700 to 3 200 kg] compared to 12,000 pounds [5 400 kg] for a comparable steel buoy).[218] If the tests proved successful, the USCG planned to replace steel buoys gradually over many years.

Over the course of the twentieth century, engineers also found ways to make lighthouses, lightships, buoys, and beacons more conspicuous to mariners. They continued to incorporate sounding devices wherever possible — bells and whistles on buoys and beacons

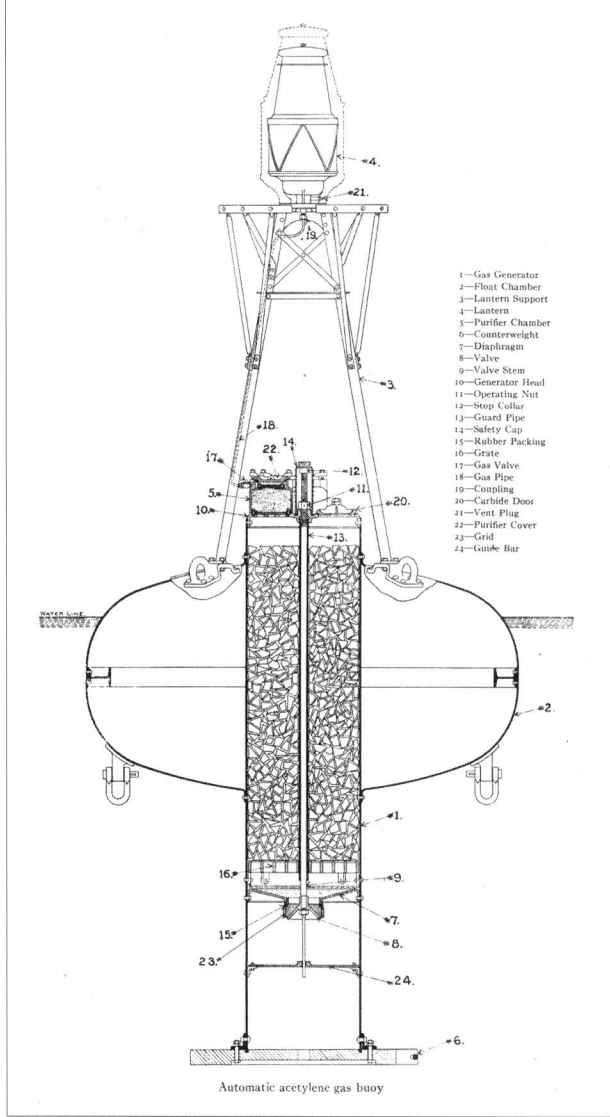

Figure 53. *Diagram showing Thomas Willson's automatic acetylene gas buoy. It eliminated the need for compression equipment, since it was charged with dry calcium carbide granules to which water was periodically added to create acetylene gas.*
(Canada: Her Natural Resources, Navigation, Principal Steamer Lines and Trans-Continental Railways [Ottawa: Department of Marine and Fisheries, 1912], 136)

and more elaborate fog alarms at light stations. For the latter, they experimented with and developed a variety of compressed air–fuelled devices that emitted stronger and more penetrating signals. The Canadian-invented diaphone was one such fog alarm that gained widespread popularity around the turn of the century, despite its large operating plant. It produced signals "by the reciprocal action of a hollow pierced piston within a cylinder with similarly pierced sides." As authorities gradually converted many installations to electrical power, they were able to take advantage of advances in electronic engineering that made much smaller electrical diaphragm emitters viable. Also, while some earlier fog alarms could be set to come on automatically under certain conditions, the adoption of electronic systems made full remote monitoring and control possible.[219]

In addition to audible signals, engineers have also used radio as a way of making buoys more conspicuous. As more and more shipping companies began equipping their vessels with radar sets after the Second World War, it became clear that some buoys could be picked up on receivers, allowing navigators to "see" them even in the fog. Based on this experience, technicians began to design fixtures that would enhance radar pickup of certain important buoys. The first devices, deployed in the late 1940s, were simple reflectors that gave the buoys a more "visible" radar profile, allowing navigators to detect them on their receivers at much greater range. At first, these reflectors were just added to the existing buoys. By the mid-1950s, though, their utility was proven, and marine services not only stepped up production and deployment but also began to look at ways of incorporating them into the buoy superstructure, making them stronger and more reliable.[220]

More recently, technicians have developed the radar beacon, or racon. This device is attached to a buoy, beacon, or light station and is activated by radar signals from an approaching ship. Once activated, it sends back a strong signal "which appears on the ship's screen as a bright blip." Each racon can be set to send out an identifying letter signal that distinguishes it from other transponders in the same general area.[221]

Canadian Aids to Navigation

Though Canadian marine officials had made great progress in the marking of our coastal and inland waters in the nineteenth century, much remained to be done. Navigational infrastructure had to be built to service new ports such as Churchill, Manitoba, and existing facilities had to be upgraded to meet the demands of increasing traffic and larger and faster vessels. To fulfill these costly requirements, Canadian

Figure 54. Marine authorities in Canada also applied new lighting technologies to smaller shore-based aids like this pole light on Hudson Bay in 1914.
(Library and Archives Canada, neg. e003719342)

marine officials, like their nineteenth-century predecessors, had to balance their desire to utilize the latest technologies with the realities of a limited budget, long coastlines, and an extremely harsh climate. This meant that they were eager to obtain, develop, and test new devices and systems, especially those that promised to improve navigation without increasing (and perhaps even reducing) the costs of constructing, operating, and maintaining the network. At the same time, however, they often adopted these new technologies gradually, leaving old but reliable devices in place at some minor sites long after they had become obsolete.

Apart from these particular concerns, officials at the departments of Marine and Fisheries and Transport were influenced by the same factors and trends that propelled navigational aid developments in the wider world. Foremost among these were electrification and automation, which shaped the evolution of lighthouses, buoys and beacons, and fog alarms throughout the century and which were especially important in a country where there were so many aids to navigation in isolated places. Canadian marine authorities were also preoccupied with the same practical objectives that motivated their colleagues in other countries — making aids more visible, more durable, and more "readable."

Canadian officials were quick to adopt the new lighting technologies that became available to improve the performance of their lighthouses. In 1902, the Department of Marine and Fisheries installed its first acetylene light, in the station at Father Point on the St Lawrence. It doubled the range of visibility, and the following year, the department decided to convert all of the kerosene lights on the upper St Lawrence to acetylene. In the same year, officials began to replace certain other kerosene lights with incandescent petroleum vapour lights. While this conversion was under way, technicians at the Dominion Lighthouse Depot continued to experiment with these and other types of lights in order to determine which were best suited for use in various locations and applications. Eventually, the department decided that petroleum vapour lights were the most appropriate choice for lighthouses, while acetylene was used mainly to illuminate buoys. Bush noted that there was at least one Canadian supplier of petroleum vapour lights, Diamond Heating and Light Co. of Montréal, though he does not say how many, if any, lights the government bought from them.[222]

Although they were quick to embrace these new illuminants, Canadian marine officials could not afford to abandon older technologies given that, by the 1940s, they had some two thousand lights to maintain. Though departmental annual reports for the first half of the twentieth century do not specify the type of illuminant used in Canadian lighthouses, the Department of Transport report for 1966 noted that there were still ninety-five oil wick lights in service in Canada. In this context, it seems reasonable to assume that, in keeping with previous practice, marine officials began by converting the most important lights to petroleum vapour and only gradually replaced this obsolescent technology at secondary stations. Some minor stations, such as those mentioned in the 1966 report, were probably never converted to petroleum vapour lights but went directly from oil wick to electric lights.[223]

The conversion to electric lights was similarly gradual. Once again, Canadian officials were immediately interested in the great potential of both electric lighting and electrical power to enhance the effectiveness of their network. They installed the first electric light at Reed Point, New Brunswick, in 1895. In 1902, the Cape Croker lighthouse on Georgian Bay became the first electrically operated light and fog alarm, using a generating plant supplied by A. Trudeau of Ottawa. By 1915, there were 23 electrically equipped lights — including 8 in Nova Scotia, 6 in British Columbia, and 5 in Ontario — and by 1928, 96 of the department's 1,771 lights were electric. Increasingly electricity was being used to supply both the lights and the rotary power needed to turn the lamps.[224]

Electrification progressed rapidly after the Second World War. Electrical utility companies gradually extended their networks into more and more small communities, including many coastal ones. At the same time, taking advantage of war-related research and development, engineers developed increasingly reliable and efficient diesel generators. Marine officials tested these at a number of sites and found that they were appropriate both as primary power sources at remote lighthouses and as backup for those already connected to the electrical grid. Thus, even the most isolated lighthouses, such as those in the Arctic, could be electrified.[225]

The gradual conversion to electricity also involved the development and deployment of new electric light sources. The first electric light bulbs — presumably the tungsten filament bulbs used by other lighthouse services in the first half of the twentieth century — were used in combination with the existing dioptric lens apparatus that concentrated and focused the light beam. By the 1960s, though, Canadian authorities had begun adopting mercury vapour and xenon lamps. The xenon light installed at Prince Shoal in 1964 was so powerful that it was only used in dense fog.[226]

The introduction of these enormously powerful lights allowed Canadian lighthouse authorities to implement additional cost- and work-saving devices. They were able gradually to replace the large, heavy, expensive, and demanding Fresnel lenses with simpler moulded glass and plastic lenses that were lighter, cheaper, and easier to clean. This in turn made it possible for authorities to use lighter lanterns for mounting the lenses. During the 1950s DOT engineers developed a new aluminum alloy lantern that was both light and non-corrosive, a significant improvement over the heavy cast-iron type it replaced. Over the fiscal year 1955–56, staff installed this type of lantern in fifteen stations.[227]

As in other countries, these developments paved the way for the gradual automation of light stations. The first stage of automation in Canada involved the introduction of equipment that brought standby devices such as light bulbs and generators into service when needed. By the late 1950s, though, departmental engineers and National Research Council of Canada (NRC) researchers were already exploring the application of electronic circuits and transistors to navigational lights. In 1956 they began working on an electronic flasher and the following year had a device that featured "constant speed operation and provision for all flashing and coded light characteristics." By 1959, the "new transistor-type flasher" was a proven success and had been deployed in the field. The department continued to expand its use of electronic systems and components through the 1960s and 1970s, by which time engineers had begun to develop and install computerized remote control systems that allowed staff to monitor and operate stations from a central location.[228]

The development of automatic systems combined with the introduction of new sources of power such as batteries and solar cells made it possible to remove onsite staff completely from many sites and to reduce the level of maintenance required to keep lights operating reliably. Diesel generators not only needed regular refuelling and maintenance, but also large and elaborate buildings to house them and their fuel supplies safely and securely, especially at exposed sites. Department officials hoped that, once perfected, other power sources would last longer, take up less space, and require less attention from technicians. With this goal in mind, the Department of Transport began exploring the possibility of using solar power in aids to navigation as early as 1956. In that year, DOT officials began working with scientists at the NRC on what they called a "solar-battery sun-switch." It was designed to extinguish battery-operated lights during daylight hours to save precious battery power. By 1958–59, officials of the department were reporting that their newly developed "sun valve" had "proven very satisfactory" and was "being used extensively in the field."[229]

As successful as these early experiments were, it took many more years before engineers developed solar power systems that were reliable enough to meet the needs of a lighthouse for a full year. In the 1980s, Goudge Island, B.C., became the first light in Canada to be solarized and last a full year. After this, larger lights were also solarized, and the solar cells proved so reliable that the generators that provided backup power were eventually removed.[230]

The Department of Transport began the process of "de-staffing" its lighthouses in 1970, at which time there were 264 staffed installations. By 1991, there were just 70 staffed lighthouses remaining, and by 2000, the number had dropped to 60. Opposition from the lightkeepers' union, local communities, and user groups, however, forced the government to slow down implementation of its new policy. Opposition was particularly effective in British Columbia and Newfoundland, where local mariners, recreational boaters, and others pointed out the essential services lightkeepers provided,

especially in emergencies. This opposition eventually led Coast Guard officials to reconsider their policy of full automation and to explore other roles for staff that will help to justify the cost of having keepers for some lights. As of 2004, 51 staffed lights employing 128 lightkeepers remained in operation.[231]

Despite this reprieve, it is clear that the traditional role of the lighthouse has been transformed and that, since the introduction and widespread adoption of GPS and other sophisticated navigational systems, some of them have even become superfluous as aids to navigation. This, combined with the fact that they are expensive to build, maintain, and operate, makes their long-term future uncertain at best.[232]

Canadian marine officials also took advantage of improvements in construction techniques and materials to increase the strength and durability of lighthouses. Engineers began to introduce reinforced concrete as a building material early in the twentieth century.

Figure 55. This light tower at Belle Isle, Newfoundland, is a good example of early reinforced-concrete construction. Uncertain of the strength of this new material, builders added buttresses for extra support.
(Library and Archives Canada, neg. PA 172437)

Initially, they were reluctant to design towers that relied entirely on this new and relatively unknown substance for strength. Instead, they used it in combination with other supporting structures. For example, the cast-iron tower at Cape Bauld on the Strait of Belle Isle (1906) was coated with reinforced concrete a few years after it was erected. Supporting buttresses were also added to enhance its stability and durability. The first towers built entirely out of reinforced concrete — Estevan Point, Caribou Island, and Father Point — also had support buttresses. Eventually, experience proved that reinforced concrete was strong enough to provide sufficient stability without the need for additional support structures. By 1917, departmental engineers had constructed a number of reinforced-concrete towers. The use of skeleton steel for tower construction followed a similar chronology.[233]

Though the adoption of new designs and construction materials made lighthouses more durable and the advent of automated equipment made the task of building the towers easier, these advances did not solve all the problems associated with lighthouse construction. Some structures still fell prey to the ravages of the ocean environment. In 1917 the existing wooden lighthouse on Sable Island was replaced by a skeleton steel structure with specially constructed foundations designed to cope with the shifting sands of the island. Apparently this design worked well, but the first tower had to be replaced after only nine years due to serious corrosion caused by the salt air. Despite this problem and despite a recommendation to replace the steel structure with a concrete tower, departmental officials decided in 1935 to rebuild the light using "open-work steel construction." As late as the mid-1970s, this remained the preferred building form for Sable Island.[234]

In addition to the challenges of corrosion on Sable Island, DOT officials also had to deal with the problems posed by the erosion of the island. The light tower was repeatedly put at risk by the loss of land at the west end of the island. In 1951, it "was again moved back to higher ground" where it was, as DOT officials put it, "safe for the time being."[235]

On the west coast, engineers and contractors were confronted with an equally daunting challenge in building a lighthouse on Triple Island, near Prince Rupert, in 1919. This wind- and wave-swept rocky island was inundated whenever "a strong westerly wind coincided with spring and fall flood tides," damaging buildings and washing away supplies and anything else "of a temporary nature." The first contractor withdrew from the project, believing that it was not practical. The second contractor and his workers were plagued by "savage weather" but managed to finish the reinforced-concrete tower and building in about seventeen months.[236]

Canadian lightships also underwent significant change and improvement in the twentieth century. To begin with, marine officials began ordering purpose-built vessels from Canadian shipbuilders instead of buying foreign-built craft or refitting existing vessels to serve as lightships. In 1903 the government ordered two new lightships to mark Lurcher Shoal and Anticosti Island. They "were 112 feet [34 m] long, were built of steel, and had two masts and no bowsprit." Unlike many earlier lightships they had their own propelling machinery and so did not have to be towed onto and off station. Most importantly, they had a strong mooring system consisting of "oversize mushroom anchors and Lloyd's tested stud link cable fitted to generous

Figure 56. This unusual open steel tower built on special foundations was chosen for Sable Island to help cope with the problem of shifting sands. Despite this design, the tower still had to be moved due to erosion at the west end of the island.
(Library and Archives Canada, neg. e003719344)

Figure 57. Of all the construction challenges faced by contractors, Triple Island near Prince Rupert, B.C., was perhaps the greatest. The first builder quit, calling the project impractical, and the second lost money on the project.
(Library and Archives Canada, neg. e003719358)

Figure 58. Lighthouses were often a challenge to supply and maintain, as can be seen in this image of the Bird Rocks station in the Gulf of St Lawrence. Note the long, steep stairs and supply ramp.
(Library and Archives Canada, neg. e003719339)

hawse-pipe merging into the stem." They each had seventh-order electric lights on each mast, which were visible 13 miles (21 km) away. They also had diaphone fog signals as well as a backup steam whistle and a bell.[237]

By the 1950s, lightships had reached the height of their technological development in Canada, as the series of vessels commissioned at the turn of the century were gradually replaced with new vessels. Constructed of welded steel to ensure that they would be able to stay on station in all conditions, these ships were 128 feet (39 m) long and powered entirely by electricity provided by diesel generators. In addition to powerful lights and fog signals, they were also equipped with all the latest navigational and communication systems — radio beacons, radiotelegraph, radiotelephone, and radio direction finding. The builders also paid careful attention to the quality of life aboard the ship, providing individual cabins, messes for the officers and crew, and television and radio for entertainment.[238]

Though these advances and improvements in design and construction made modern lightships superior in many respects to the older models, serving on lightships remained a difficult and dangerous duty. Stationed in exposed locations, they had few defences against other vessels or against the weather. In 1914, a modern British-built lightship, *Halifax No. 19*, was lost in a gale "after stranding on a rocky shore at Liscombe [sic], N.S. in course of delivery." All crew were lost in this mishap. In windy weather, the lack of forward movement of the moored ships made them less steady than moving vessels. This, combined with the general hardship

Figure 59. *Placed on station near the entrance to Halifax Harbour in 1956, the Sambro Island lightship was one of the last generation of lightships and represented the apex of this technology. By 1968, all lightships had been replaced either by pillar lights or large offshore buoys.*
(Library and Archives Canada, neg. e003719356)

all sailors face of living and working on board a cramped, isolated, and constantly moving ship for six-month stretches, made work on board lightships especially demanding, even for the independent and hardy souls who tended to be attracted to the lightkeeping profession.

Because of these hazards and hardships, the Canadian government began exploring ways to replace its lightships even before this last group of lightships was launched. By the 1950s, the experience gained from earlier lighthouse construction challenges and the progress made by engineers in working with steel and concrete made it possible for lighthouse designers to develop new specialized structures that could withstand even the harshest weather, ice, and wave conditions. These structures, which became known as pillar lights, differed in design and construction to suit the particular conditions of the sea, lake, or riverbed and the climate. All were offshore towers, though, and were built of steel, concrete, or some combination of the two.

The Department of Transport built its first pillar light in 1953 at Gros Cap Reef on Lake Superior. It consisted of a prow-shaped foundation of steel-reinforced concrete specially designed to "withstand ice pressure." This structure was built in drydock and then towed to the site, secured in place, and then the light tower was constructed on top of it. Though not much larger than the converted naval trawler it replaced, this light station could be operated and maintained by a much smaller crew.[239]

The light towers that replaced the lightships at White Island Shoal and Prince Shoal were a slightly different design. Their foundations were conical steel piers upon which rested inverted cones that provided a base for the lighthouse and other buildings as well as a landing pad for helicopters. These stations were an enormously successful design for Canadian conditions and were used extensively, especially in the St Lawrence River and Gulf region. The last Canadian lightship, *Lurcher No. 4*, was retired in October 1969 and replaced by a large gas and bell buoy.[240]

Yet while the pillar lights may have been a triumph of engineering and a definite improvement over lightships, they, like the vessels they replaced, were lonely and inhospitable places for human beings. On most pillars, as on some insular lights, there was, quite simply, no place to go. A walk around the turret provided little exercise and even less enjoyable distraction from duty; in stormy conditions, even this small pleasure was denied light station staff. Keepers had to pass their spare time indoors pursuing mainly sedentary hobbies. At White Island, because of the harsh conditions, families were not allowed to accompany the keepers, and until 1970, there were no relief crews from September through to Christmas due to the bad weather. After 1970, new staff came in by helicopter every two weeks.[241]

The hardships associated with life on the pillars and other isolated and insular light stations contributed to the government's decision to automate many of its lights after 1970. It began a pilot project in the Laurentian region, which included among its twenty-nine manned lighthouses a number of isolated lights. By the early 1970s, nine of these stations had been successfully automated, and the government decided to implement a policy that would have seen all Canadian

Figure 60. *The White Island pillar light with the tower almost complete, 26 November 1955. The caisson was built in a shipyard and towed out to its station, where it was secured in place. Construction then began on the tower. The lightships of the St Lawrence were among the first to be replaced by this unique Canadian design, which successfully withstands both wave motion and severe ice conditions.*
(Library and Archives Canada, neg. e003719361)

lighthouses automated and "de-staffed" through the 1980s. As mentioned earlier, by 2004 the policy of full automation was under review, but by this time, both the Laurentian and Central and Arctic regions (the latter region covering Ontario, the prairie provinces, and all of the Arctic except the western Yukon) were already fully automated.[242]

In the area of smaller aids to navigation — buoys, beacons, and fog alarms — the twentieth century was an era of enormous expansion. Canada experienced not only a steady growth in marine traffic along its established trade and transportation routes, but also a significant extension of its navigable waterways, with, for example, the opening of the port of Churchill (1931) and of the Great Lakes to sea-going ships (1959).

The government responded to the challenges posed by the steady increase in demands on its marine infrastructure in two ways. First it added more aids. In 1905, the Department of Marine and Fisheries reported 4,200 buoys of all kinds; by 1935 that number had grown to include more than 5,600 unlighted buoys in addition to 606 gas and signal buoys and over 3,000 other markers. In 1965 there were some 10,000 buoys, of which about 1,500 were major markers with light or sound or both. There were also "nearly 5000 minor, unlighted shore-based beacons, dolphins, stakes and other markers." Unlike other areas of navigational aids such as lighthouses, this expansion continued into the late 1990s. In 1998 the government reported 13,000 floating and 6,000 land-based fixed aids to navigation.[243]

The second strategy adopted by the government was to introduce new technologies that would improve the effectiveness, durability, and longevity of aids. The latter two objectives were particularly important in the Canadian context, where icy conditions and twice-yearly removal and repositioning took a particularly high toll on the many hundreds of seasonal floating aids stationed across the country. In the search for new and better technologies, the government relied increasingly on the research staff at the Dominion Lighthouse Depot. These engineers, technicians, and designers not only tested all the latest materials and equipment produced by outside organizations and manufacturers, they also developed their own devices, often in co-operation with National Research Council staff after the Second World War.

In the area of buoys, Canadian authorities were quick to recognize and incorporate the major improvements made around the world. They were early adopters of the Willson acetylene buoy, which was manufactured by the International Marine Signalling Co. of Ottawa. By 1912 they had already placed 62 of these markers in Canadian waters and had found that the largest models held enough fuel to maintain the light for nine months. Just over twenty years later, the Department of Transport had 584 gas and audible signal buoys (bell or whistle) in operation.[244] Though not all of these were acetylene, many of them were.

Figures 61 and 62. *Two early-twentieth-century beacons, one wave-swept (Burnaby Shoal, B.C., 1913) and the other on shore (Black Rock, Georgian Bay, circa 1913). The former has a bell to provide an audible warning of danger.* (Library and Archives Canada, negs. e003719341 and e003719340)

In the years after the Second World War, Department of Transport officials, with the assistance of the NRC, also began to explore new methods of lighting buoys and new sources of power to maintain the lights. As early as 1950, staff at the Dominion Lighthouse Depot were looking for alternatives to acetylene, testing both propane, which was "coming into wide use in European countries," and battery-operated units. The tests were intended "to determine the relative cost and efficiency under Canadian conditions" of the two systems.[245] By the late 1950s, as noted earlier in this section, depot and NRC researchers had developed an electronic sun-valve to turn lights on and off as needed. This particular device was used widely in Canada and, according to one source, also adopted by the Americans.[246]

Following the lead of the international maritime community, DOT officials also took advantage of the development of radar to make their buoys more "visible." In 1948–49, they fitted several buoys along the east coast with experimental radar reflectors. Within a year they had declared the experiment complete and had begun installing the devices "on buoys where long range radar reflection is required." They also noted that work was continuing on the development of "special lightweight reflectors for small buoys." The growing use of radar reflectors prompted officials to establish a production "set-up" at the Prescott depot in 1954–55. The following year, technicians designed and began building a reflector that formed "part of the buoy superstructure," thereby "giving greater strength and reliability."[247] DOT technicians also added radar transponders to some buoys and beacons sometime after 1969.[248]

Canadian marine officials also followed developments in the construction materials for buoys. They began testing plastic buoys as early as 1961–62 and were

Figure 63. Buoy-tending was a difficult and demanding task, especially with large light buoys like the Cove Island fairway buoy pictured here. Even in fair weather this work required superior ship-handling and expert teamwork by an experienced crew.
(Library and Archives Canada, neg. e003719349)

Figure 64. After 1945, Canadian marine authorities began to incorporate radar into their aids to navigation. This lightweight electric lantern has a radar reflector attached to it, allowing radar-equipped vessels to "see" the seamark to which it was attached even in foggy conditions.
(Library and Archives Canada, neg. e003719351)

sufficiently encouraged by the results to continue their work in the area. That year, they sent a number of fibreglass and plastic buoys to St John's "for experimental use in sea water" and were planning to send some to the west coast as well. As promising as these tests seemed at the time, little seems to have come of them during this early period, probably for some of the same reasons noted by U.S. officials in their experiments of the 1970s. In the mid-1990s Canadian marine authorities, like their American counterparts, began another round of extensive tests with the new generation of plastic buoys, some made by the same group of manufacturers used by the Americans.[249]

Government technicians were also actively engaged in the design of new buoys to suit Canadian requirements. As early as 1950, DOT officials had developed a buoy that could "withstand the ice pressure and movement." They used these to mark the navigable channels of the St Lawrence River for icebreakers and shipping early in the season, when ice conditions sometimes made it impossible to lay the regular buoys. In the early 1960s, staff were actively developing new designs for buoys to be used in the Northwest Territories and also designed a small, foam-filled steel buoy for use in "minor waters."[250]

Fog signals also received some attention from marine officials. At the turn of the twentieth century, the diaphone, another Canadian invention, was quickly becoming the fog alarm of choice. Developed in 1902 by Toronto manufacturer J. P. Northey, the diaphone was a modification of the widely used Scotch siren. It operated "on the principle of a high-velocity pulsating piston rather than a rotating drum" and "produced a blast of more constant pitch for about one-eighth the power expended by the Scotch siren."[251] Unlike the older compressed air horns it replaced, which in their late-nineteenth-century incarnation were found to be unreliable in stormy weather, the diaphone was thoroughly tested and found to penetrate well in all conditions, up to a distance of 45 miles (72 km). By 1912 the department had installed 82 and had plans to add 8 more in the near future.[252]

The diaphone, along with other less sophisticated fog alarms — hand foghorns and bells and a Swedish-manufactured compressed-air fog signal called the Tyfon — continued in service for many decades.[253] Beginning in the mid-1960s, however, engineers and manufacturers began to develop new and more efficient types of fog signals. In 1965–56, the department began replacing its smaller diaphones with an improved version of the air horn. One of these was the Canadian-developed Airchine, a small air horn that produced "a signal of almost comparable range" to the diaphone but which was far more economical to operate. Its air compressors were driven by small electrical motors.

The department also adopted various other small foghorns "for ranges up to two miles [3.2 km]." By 1968, many of the larger stations had also been converted to compressed-air signals, though much larger and more powerful.[254]

In the mid-1960s, departmental technicians were also looking into the possibility of operating fog signals by remote control. By that time, they already had several remote control systems in operation and were actively seeking "more effective, maintenance-free systems" to examine. As well, they were testing two types of automatic fog detectors, a crucial component of any remote control set-up. The successful automation of fog signals, which was accomplished by the 1970s, was one of many prerequisites to full automation and ultimate de-staffing of Canada's many lighthouses.[255]

Traffic Management Systems

The dramatic increase in the size, number, and speed of ships travelling on the world's waterways since 1945 has put great pressure on navigational infrastructure, especially in confined areas such as harbours, channels, and straits. In these congested areas there was a high risk of collisions, groundings, and other mishaps. For example, before 1969, authorities recorded an average thirty collisions a year in the Dover Strait between England and France. This risk, combined with the growth in oil tanker and other potentially hazardous traffic, prompted marine authorities to increase monitoring, direction, and control of marine traffic.[256]

Historically, ships and their officers were never subject to the kind of strict control imposed on aircraft pilots. Nevertheless, there were long-standing precedents for managing marine traffic, especially in busy, congested, or treacherous waterways. For example, many countries established compulsory pilotage zones within their national waters beginning in the nineteenth century. In these zones, vessels had to take on board a pilot who knew the local waters and could guide the vessels safely into port or through a hazard.

In the first half of the twentieth century, both national and international marine authorities established a series of "passive" controls whereby ships abide by "regulations or agreements which do not require any pragmatic involvement of persons not on the ships concerned." These included what are known as "rules of the road," that is, rules governing how ships should proceed when meeting, passing, or crossing the tracks of other vessels. At the international level, these rules were eventually formalized and became the IMO's collision regulations. National governments also implemented their own rules restricting access, for example, to certain waters for security or military reasons. As well, large passenger liner companies established a voluntary traffic separation scheme known as the North Atlantic Track Agreement to help ensure safe and efficient travel on this busy route.[257]

Recognizing that these systems were increasingly inadequate, marine authorities began to introduce new and more active forms of direction and control. In 1948, the port of Liverpool began operating the world's first Vessel Traffic System, or VTS. This system relied on radio and radar to monitor vessels entering the area and to ensure that they were progressing at a safe speed and on a safe course in relation to their destination and the other ships in the area. If a problem arose, the VTS officer could contact the ship and recommend that they alter speed and/or course. This system proved so useful that by the mid-1960s four other port authorities had adopted it.

Canadian transport officials with the support of the NRC had begun experimenting with harbour radar in the mid-1940s, setting up systems at Camperdown near Halifax in 1946–47 and at the Lions Gate Bridge in Vancouver in 1948–49. Though used to monitor harbour traffic, these do not seem to have been part of a larger control system. Canada's first VTS was installed in Montréal Harbour in 1968 to deal with "increasing traffic volumes, particularly of oil and oil products." The St Lawrence had long been a compulsory pilotage zone and was covered by a network of radio stations and other aids to navigation. Officials believed, however, that more active intervention was needed in order to prevent collisions and maintain safe and efficient traffic movement.

The radars for the Montréal VTS were designed and built in Canada by Decca Radar Canada of Toronto. DOT asked that, as much as possible, the company use "standard marine equipment to keep initial costs low, to ensure reliability, and to guarantee reparability." The radio equipment was also off-the-shelf, purchased and installed by DOT staff.[258] When completed in 1968, the Montréal centre was staffed by three marine traffic regulators and a supervisor and operated twenty-four hours a day. The radars had a range of about six nautical miles and were set to cover different areas of the harbour. The whole system cost just $186,000 and yet "operated completely satisfactorily for 22 years until it was replaced in 1990." By 1992, there were eleven VTS centres in Canada.[259]

VTS, like most marine technologies, has evolved with changes in radio, radar, and position-finding technology. In 1993, marine authorities in the United States set up a pilot program that combined radar with Differential GPS, Digital Selective Calling, and electronic charts to create "an integrated tracking system that presumably will provide Coast Guard watchstanders ashore with more information for guiding ships in crowded harbors." The site chosen for the project was Prince William Sound, where the *Exxon Valdez* had run aground so disastrously in March 1989. This was one of eight operational VTS systems run by the USCG at the time.[260]

Although VTS was an effective control mechanism in and around ports or confined waterways such as the Houston ship channel in Houston, Texas, other techniques were needed for busy open sea routes and approaches to harbours. In the 1960s and 1970s, regulators began to implement what are called traffic separation schemes, in which ships travelling in one direction are separated from ships moving in the opposite direction. The routes are depicted on the charts for the area, and there is no active intervention from the control centres that monitor the traffic.

The first traffic separation scheme was introduced in 1967 in the Dover Strait, the world's busiest international waterway and, as noted above, an area plagued by collisions. In this early period, the directions

Figure 65. *Canadian officials began experimenting with harbour radar in the late 1940s, setting up systems at Camperdown, Nova Scotia, in 1946–47 and the following year on the Lions Gate Bridge in Vancouver, shown here. These systems were a precursor to the more elaborate vessel traffic systems established in the late 1960s.*
(Library and Archives Canada, neg. e003719353)

were not compulsory but only "recommended." These schemes, though, gradually came to be seen as an indispensable tool in the struggle to prevent collisions and other mishaps. By 1972 the IMO, working with national regulators, had devised a series of rules governing the conduct of vessels in these zones. These are now part of the International Regulations for Preventing Collisions at Sea.[261]

As noted in the overview section of this chapter, Canadian officials implemented Canada's first traffic separation scheme in the aftermath of the *Arrow* accident in Chedabucto Bay, N.S., in February 1970. By the mid-1990s there were two additional IMO-sanctioned schemes operating, one in the Bay of Fundy and its approaches and one in the Strait of Juan de Fuca and its approaches. The Coast Guard also "recommends routing measures in the Johnstone and Broughton Straits (between Vancouver Island and the mainland), in the St. Lawrence at Les Escoumins, in the Gulf and River St. Lawrence, in Halifax Harbour and its approaches, and throughout the Great Lakes."[262]

Notes

1. Donald Kerr and Deryck W. Holdsworth, eds., *The Historical Atlas of Canada*, vol. 3, *Addressing the Twentieth Century, 1891–1961* (Toronto: University of Toronto Press, 1990), Plate 3, "Economic Growth."
2. Robert J. McCalla, *Water Transport in Canada* (Halifax: Formac Publishing, 1994), xii.
3. Ibid., xi, 8–9.
4. Ambrose Greenway, introduction to *The Golden Age of Shipping: The Classic Merchant Ship, 1900–1960*, ed. Ambrose Greenway (London: Conway Maritime Press, 1994), 7, and Charles E. Mathieu, "Modern Merchant Ship Propulsion," in *The Shipping Revolution: The Modern Merchant Ship*, ed. Alastair Couper (London: Conway Maritime Press, 1992), 184–7. See also Graeme Maclennan, "Marine Propulsion," in Greenway, ed., *Golden Age*, 152–63.
5. See J. Strange, "Oil Tankers, Chemical Carriers and Gas Carriers," in Couper, ed., *Shipping Revolution*, 65–7, for a discussion of economies of scale in shipping and the relationship between size and efficiency.
6. P. B. Watson, "Bulk Cargo Carriers," in Greenway, ed., *Golden Age*, 61–79; Laurence Dunn, "Cargo Ships," in Greenway, ed., *Golden Age*, 38–58; also Greenway, *Golden Age*, 7–13; D. K. Fleming, "Modern Tramp Ships, Bulk Carriers and Combination Carriers," in Couper, ed., *Shipping Revolution*, 12–31; Jacques Marcadon, "Conventional General Cargo Liners and Refrigerated Ships," in Couper, ed., *Shipping Revolution*, 32–40; and Alastair Couper, introduction to *Shipping Revolution*, 7–11.
7. McCalla, *Water Transport*, xiv; P. B. Watson, 75–9; and D. K. Fleming, 21–3.
8. Greenway, *Golden Age*, 10, upper photo caption.
9. Ambrose Greenway, "Passenger Vessels," in Greenway, ed., *Golden Age*, 33–5, and Captain Steven Cross and Bruce E. Marti, "Passenger Ships: Ferries and Cruise Ships," in Couper, ed., *Shipping Revolution*, 84–100.
10. McCalla, *Water Transport*, xiv.
11. Peter Hunter, *The Magic Box: A History of Containerization* (ICHCA Canada, 1993), 7–9; Cy Martin, *Gold Rush Narrow Gauge: The Story of the White Pass and Yukon Route* (Los Angeles: Trans-Anglo Books, 1969), 63–8; and Sidney Gilman, "Container Shipping," in Couper, ed., *Shipping Revolution*, 42–5.
12. Gilman, "Container Shipping," 42–61.
13. David McGee, "Marine Engineering in Canada: An Historical Assessment," National Museum of Science and Technology, 1997, 198–200.
14. Gilman, "Container Shipping," 42–4.
15. Strange, "Oil Tankers," 66.
16. As early as 1967, one observer noted that while over the previous twelve years Britain's merchant fleet had grown by 3 million gross tons (2.7 million tonnes) (though made up of 1,300 ships), it was being operated by 25,000 fewer personnel. George Bonwick, ed., *Automation on Shipboard*, Proceedings of a conference held at Geneva by the International Institute of Labour Studies (London: Macmillan & Co., 1967), 6.
17. A. G. Corbet, "Modern Merchant Ship Navigation," in Couper, ed., *Shipping Revolution*, 180–2.
18. Corbet's example is the *Ditlev Lauritzen*, a 14,406 g.r.t. cargo ship that can be operated by a crew of just six individuals. See 180–2, including photo captions.
19. McCalla, *Water Transport*, 68 (and footnote); Shannon Bentley, "Ship Registers and the Use of Flags," in Couper, ed., *Shipping Revolution*, 193–6.
20. Strange, "Oil Tankers," 74.
21. Ibid., 64–75; "A Decade of Achievement: The Activities of IMCO 1960–1970," *Shipping World and Shipbuilder* 164, no. 3853 (January 1971): 81, and "The Shrinking American Tanker Fleet," *Professional Mariner* 14 (August/September 1995): 27–30.
22. See Canada Shipping Act, Chap. 44, 24–25 Geo. V. 1934, 269–450.
23. "A Decade of Achievement," 81–5.
24. Most of the information on international maritime organizations came from Kamil A. Bekiashev and Bitali V. Serebriakov, *International Marine Organizations: Essays on Structure and Activities* (The Hague: Marinus Nijhoff Publishers, 1981). See the various chapter headings for specific groups discussed.
25. This information was gleaned from a review of recent issues of trade journals such as *Professional Mariner* and *Shipping World and Shipbuilder*, which contain numerous articles that deal with or touch upon the issue of regulation and its application.
26. Kerr and Holdsworth, eds., *Historical Atlas*, Plate 3, "Economic Growth."
27. *World Almanac and Book of Facts* (Mahwah, N.J.: World Almanac Books, 1998), 112.
28. Canada, Department of Marine and Fisheries, *Annual Report 1927–28* (Ottawa: King's Printer, 1928), 18, and Canada, Department of Marine and Fisheries, *Annual Report 1935–36* (Ottawa: King's Printer, 1936), 102.
29. McCalla, *Water Transport*, 69–70.
30. Ibid., 1–10, and Statistics Canada, Transportation Division, Multimodal Transport Section, *Shipping in Canada, 1995*, Catalogue no. 54-205-XPB (Ottawa: Statistics Canada, 1997), 39.
31. McCalla, *Water Transport*, 78, and McGee, "Marine Engineering," 199–200. See also various articles and advertisements in *Canadian Shipping and Marine Engineering News* throughout the 1960s. One ad (no page number) in the September 1965 issue (vol. 36, no. 12) announced the launching of the SS *Tarantau* and claimed that "her fast-moving automatic system of hoppers,

conveyer belts and bucket elevators" enabled her to "transfer 6000 tons [5 450 tonnes] from ship to shore in a single hour."
32. John Edward Belliveau, Silver Donald Cameron, and Michael Harrington, *Iceboats to Superferries: An Illustrated History of Marine Atlantic* (St John's: Breakwater, 1992), 10–2, and McCalla, *Water Transport*, 81–6.
33. Gary and Patricia Bannerman, *The Ships of British Columbia: An Illustrated History of the British Columbia Ferry Corporation* (Surrey, B.C.: Hancock House Publishers, 1985), 11, 14, 17–8, 31; "B.C. Ferries Business Is Almost Too Good," *Canadian Shipping and Marine Engineering News* 36, no. 9 (June 1965): 83; telephone interview with BC Ferries Corporation communications officer, Oct. 1998; and McCalla, *Water Transport*, 82–7.
34. Canadian Coast Guard, "Service Profile 96 — Ferry Services," on website at www.ccg-gcc.gc.ca.
35. McCalla, *Water Transport*, 108, 137; "Containerization Reduces Costs," *Canadian Shipping and Marine Engineering News* 36, no.8 (May 1965): 28–9; "Canada Probably *Can* Support Six Container Ports," *Canadian Transportation and Distribution Management* 75, no. 6 (June 1972), 14; and "The 100,000th Container through Halifax," *Canadian Transportation and Distribution Management* 75, no. 6 (June 1972): 46.
36. McCalla, *Water Transport*, 131–9.
37. *The Canadian Encyclopaedia*, 2nd ed. (Edmonton: Hurtig Publishers, 1988), s.v. "Thunder Bay"; G. P. deT. Glazebrook, *A History of Transportation in Canada*, vol. 2 (Toronto: McClelland & Stewart, 1964), 226–34, and Robert Nicholls, "Mobility Canada: An Historical Perspective, 1825–1975," unpublished report (Montréal, 1978), 91–2. For a description of harbour developments including the construction of grain elevators, see Department of Marine and Fisheries, *Annual Report 1927–28*, 105–35.
38. McCalla, *Water Transport*, 81–2.
39. Strange, "Oil Tankers," 66–7.
40. Canada, Statistics Canada, *Shipping in Canada, 1995*, 25.
41. McCalla, *Water Transport*, 158–80; Nicholls, "Mobility Canada," 121–3; and Glazebrook, *History of Transportation*, 234–40. Glazebrook's work only covers the period up to 1936 but gives some idea of how long the idea had been around and just how much estimates of the ultimate value of the project differed.
42. McCalla, *Water Transport*, 108.
43. "Seaway: Long-Range Plans Depend on Traffic Developments," *Canadian Transportation and Distribution Management* 75, no.8 (August 1972): 28.
44. Overfishing had, by this time, already led to a serious decline in the Great Lakes commercial fleet and had forced the federal government to negotiate a series of conservation treaties with the Americans on the west coast. The economic problems in the Atlantic fishery were so profound that, in 1927, the government appointed a royal commission to investigate and to suggest solutions. *Canadian Encyclopaedia*, 2nd ed., s.v. "Fisheries History."
45. Ibid., and J. M. Bumsted, *The Peoples of Canada: A Post-Confederation History* (Toronto: Oxford University Press, 1992), 295–6. Though there seems to be general agreement that the fisheries on both coasts grew substantially after 1945, the statistics make it difficult to establish exactly how this growth was reflected over time in the number and relative size of vessels engaged in the fishery. What does seem apparent is that there was a marked increase in the number of large vessels involved in the fishery.
46. See McCalla, *Water Transport*, 6–10, and Canada, *Shipping in Canada, 1995*, 7.
47. Canadian Coast Guard, "Service Profile 96 — Commercial Fishing Industry," on CCG website, www.ccg-gcc.gc.ca, and Canada, Department of Transport, *List of Ships*, vol. 2, *Fishing Vessels on Register in Canada 1997* (Ottawa: Department of Transport, 1998), no page nos.
48. See Department of Transport, *Annual Reports* for years 1945 to 1966, "Nautical Services" and "Marine Services" sections. See also Canadian Coast Guard, "Service Profile 96 — Recreational Boating," on CCG website, www.ccg-gcc.gc.ca.
49. Since Confederation, marine matters have been overseen by Marine and Fisheries (1867–1884 and 1892–1930), Marine (1884–1892 and 1930–1936), Transport (1936 to present), and Fisheries and Oceans (1995 to present). In 1995 the Canadian Coast Guard and the aids to navigation program were moved to Fisheries and Oceans while shipping regulation remained with Transport.
50. Edward W. Bush, *The Canadian Lighthouse*, Canadian Historic Sites 9 (Ottawa: Indian and Northern Affairs, 1975), 31.
51. Captain Ernest J. Chambers, *The Canadian Marine: A History of the Department of Marine and Fisheries* (Toronto: Canadian Marine and Fisheries History, 1905), 51, 55, and Bush, *Canadian Lighthouse*, 31.
52. *Canadian Encyclopaedia*, s.v. "Canadian Coast Guard."
53. See, for example, Thomas E. Appleton, *Usque ad Mare: A History of the Canadian Coast Guard and Marine Services* (Ottawa: Department of Transport, 1968), 275–300 for a list of marine service/Canadian Coast Guard ships up to 1968. *Canadian Encyclopaedia*, s.v. "Canadian Coast Guard."
54. Chambers, *Canadian Marine*, 33; Canada, Department of Transport, *Annual Report 1951–52* (Ottawa: Queen's Printer, 1953), 17–18; and Canada, Department of Transport, *Annual Report 1965–66* (Ottawa: Queen's Printer, 1967), 53.
55. *Canadian Encyclopaedia*, s.v. "Canadian Coast Guard."
56. According to Ben Hutchin of the Canadian Coast Guard (interviewed 9 June 2004), there are still some 51 staffed lighthouses in Canada. The original plan to automate all of these by the year 2000 is under review as part of the Marine Aids Modernization Project according to Mike Clements, also of CCG (interviewed same date). See also Lynn Tanod and Chris Jaksa, "Keepers of the Light," *Explore* 81 (October/November 1996): 26–32, and Ross Howard, "Why He's Still a Keeper of the Flame," *Toronto Globe and Mail*, 20 April 1998. For the recommendations relating to harbours and pilotage, see the Coast Guard College website at www.cgc.ns.ca/~jim/stndcomm/stndcomm.htm. The Department of Transport website, www.tc.gc.ca, also contains information on pilotage and pilotage statistics, which, for one district, include a category called "entrepreneur pilots."
57. See the Coast Guard's website at www.ccg-gcc.gc.ca/archives/profile/marineaids.htm.
58. Eric W. Sager, *Seafaring Labour: The Merchant Marine of Atlantic Canada, 1820–1914* (Kingston: McGill-Queen's University Press, 1989), 93–101.
59. Appleton, *Usque ad Mare*, 194–5.
60. Canada Shipping Act, 269–450.
61. McCalla, *Water Transport*, 60–8.
62. Canada, Department of Marine and Fisheries, *Annual Report 1904* (Ottawa: King's Printer, 1905), 111. See 112 for a point form description of the course content and a summary of the attendance at the schools.

63. "Examinations for Certificates of Sea-Going Masters and Mates," *Canadian Railway and Marine World*, September 1936, 441.
64. Appleton, *Usque ad Mare*, 268.
65. Canada, Department of Transport, *Annual Report 1941-42* (Ottawa: King's Printer, 1942), 9-12; Canada, Department of Transport, *Annual Report 1942-43* (Ottawa: King's Printer, 1943), 10; and Director of Merchant Seaman, *Training for the Merchant Navy* (Ottawa: King's Printer, 1942), no page nos.
66. Canada, Department of Transport, *Annual Report 1944-45* (Ottawa: King's Printer, 1945), 11.
67. Ibid., 10.
68. Canada, Department of Transport, *Annual Report 1948-49* (Ottawa: King's Printer, 1949), 52-3.
69. Appleton, *Usque ad Mare*, 268-9.
70. The federal government continued to operate some seasonal or specialized schools and to provide direct financial support to others. See various departmental reports for the 1950s and 1960s.
71. In 1952-53 the government took three important actions related to certification requirements. It installed radio direction finding equipment in several centres to test candidates' (masters and mates') abilities to obtain radio bearings. It also established an optional examination for Extra Master's Certificate as "an inducement to higher studies." Finally, it set up Able Seamen's schools to comply with a recently passed ILO convention. Canada, Department of Transport, *Annual Report 1952-53* (Ottawa: Queen's Printer, 1953), 74-5.
72. Ibid., 67-8.
73. "Radar Navigation Course Offered in Nova Scotia," *Canadian Shipping and Marine Engineering News* (October 1964): 74.
74. "Ontario to Provide Marine School," *Canadian Shipping and Marine Engineering News* 36, no. 4 (January 1965): 18-9.
75. Appleton, *Usque ad Mare*, 269.
76. Ibid., 271.
77. This is not a comprehensive description of the programs currently available in Canada, but rather a sample of typical programs. The information comes from the websites of the various institutions and from electronic and telephone interviews with staff at the Nautical Institute of the Nova Scotia Community College. My contacts there are Peter Dunford, Director of Marine Training, and Mike Kruger, Marine Navigation Instructor. The websites consulted were British Columbia Institute of Technology, www.transportation.bcit.ca/marine/index.html; Camosun College, www.camosum.bc.ca/schools/tradesntech/nautical/index.htm; Nautical Institute at Nova Scotia Community College, www.nscc.ns.ca/marine/Nautical/index.html; Memorial University of Newfoundland, www.mi.mun.ca; and L'Institut maritime du Québec, www.imq.qc.ca/eng/careers/naviga_a.htm.
78. At one time the responsibility for operating at least some of these systems was assigned to the specially trained radio officer. With the increased automation and integration of radio into bridge operations generally, though, the industry decided that the radio officer was no longer necessary.
79. See websites for course outlines.
80. See websites for information on simulator-based courses. Of the schools included here, only MUN mentions the use of a full mission ship's bridge simulator. According to Peter Dunford, MUN is also working with the Department of Transport on the development of an ice navigation simulator.
81. These observations are based on exchanges and commentaries I have followed on the Marine List (listserv), where many experienced mariners — masters, mates, pilots, and others — frequently discuss the problems with seafaring today.
82. Paul H. Savet, ed., *Gyroscopes: Theory and Design with Application to Instrumentation, Guidance, and Control* (New York: McGraw-Hill Book Company, 1961), 78.
83. Peter Kemp, ed., *The Oxford Companion to Ships and the Sea* (London: Oxford University Press, 1979), 191.
84. P. V. H. Weems, *Marine Navigation* (New York: D. Van Nostrand Company, 1943), 63.
85. Savet, ed., *Gyroscopes*, 78, 81-4; J. E. D. Williams, *From Sails to Satellites: The Origin and Development of Navigational Science* (Oxford: Oxford University Press, 1994), 155-9; Kemp, ed., *Oxford Companion*, 191; Weems, *Marine Navigation*, 63-74; Bernard Dixon, Dougal Dixon, Linda Gamlin, Iain Nicolson, and Candida Hunt, eds., *The Encyclopedic Dictionary of Science* (New York: Facts on File Publications, 1988), s.v. "Gyroscope."
86. Weems, *Marine Navigation*, 63; Savet, ed., *Gyroscopes*, 78-81; Williams, *Sails to Satellites*, 158-60; and Kemp, ed., *Oxford Companion*, 191.
87. Williams, *Sails to Satellites*, 160-1; Savet, ed., *Gyroscopes*, 122-9. In these devices, containers of mercury act like slow-moving pendulous weights working to keep the gyrocompass stable. The motion of the mercury from one container to the other is slow in comparison to the motion of the rolling ship, and so the containers do not react as an ordinary pendulum would to every erratic movement of the vessel. Because of this, the mercury control exerts a damping effect on the motion of the gyrocompass. Weems, *Marine Navigation*, 69-71.
88. Savet, ed., *Gyroscopes*, 78-9.
89. Ibid., 79; Kemp, ed., *Oxford Companion*, 191; and Richard Woodman, "Navigation 1900-1960," in Greenway, ed., *Golden Age*, 176.
90. Woodman, "Navigation 1900-1960," 176.
91. Weems, *Marine Navigation*, 83; Kemp, ed., *Oxford Companion*, 191.
92. Williams, *Sails to Satellites*, 162; Woodman, "Navigation 1900-1960," 176; Savet, ed., *Gyroscopes*, 79; and Kemp, ed., *Oxford Companion*, 48, 191.
93. Corbet, "Modern Merchant Ship Navigation," in Couper, ed., *Shipping Revolution*, 178; Weems, *Marine Navigation*, 103-4; and Kemp, ed., *Oxford Companion*, 282, 816.
94. Kemp, ed., *Oxford Companion*, 42-3.
95. Weems, *Marine Navigation*, 103-4; Kemp, ed., *Oxford Companion*, 42-3, 282, 816.
96. Woodman, "Navigation 1900-1960," 179, photo caption.
97. The Doppler effect, first predicted in 1842 by physicist Christian Doppler, is the apparent change in the frequency of light or sound waves caused by the relative motion of the source and receiver. The magnitude of that change, known as the Doppler shift, can be used to measure the direction and speed of movement in coastal waters. Kemp, ed., *Oxford Companion*, 816, and Williams, *Sails to Satellites*, 234-8.
98. Woodman, "Navigation 1900-1960," 176-7.
99. Weems, *Marine Navigation*, 99-100; Benjamin Dutton, *Navigation and Nautical Astronomy* (Annapolis, Md.: United States Naval Institute, 1942), 29-30; Woodman, "Navigation 1900-1960," 177; and Harvey B. Loomis, ed., *Navigation* (New York: Time-Life Books, 1975), 93.
100. Woodman, "Navigation 1900-1960," 177; Kemp, ed., *Oxford Companion*, 493; Weems, *Marine Navigation*, 99-100; and Dutton, *Navigation and Nautical Astronomy*, 27-31.
101. Kemp, ed., *Oxford Companion*, 493-4.

102. Woodman, "Navigation 1900–1960," 176–7.
103. Corbet, "Modern Merchant Ship Navigation," 178.
104. Ibid. Corbet maintains that Doppler sonar "is not very commonly carried by merchant ships," while Williams, *Sails to Satellites*, 237–8, states that "doppler logs are now widely fitted to ships." In one of their newsletter/bulletins, Offshore Resources also suggests that Doppler logs are a common fixture on vessels. Captain L. J. Swann and Barry Ridgewell, "Study to Set Standards Suggested," *Offshore Resources* 4/5 (September/October 1984): 14.
105. Corbet, "Modern Merchant Ship Navigation," 178, and Williams, *Sails to Satellites*, 237–8.
106. Williams, *Sails to Satellites*, 237–8.
107. Woodman, "Navigation 1900–1960," 178.
108. Sharon A. Babaian, *Radio Communication in Canada: An Historical and Technological Survey*, Transformation Series 1 (Ottawa: National Museum of Science and Technology, 1992), 23.
109. Canada, Department of Marine and Fisheries, *Annual Report 1906–07* (Ottawa: King's Printer, 1907), 11.
110. Babaian, *Radio Communication*, 88, and Woodman, "Navigation 1900–1960," 178.
111. Babaian, *Radio Communication*, 34–6.
112. See Department of Marine and Fisheries and Department of Transport annual reports beginning in the 1920s.
113. Department of Transport, *Annual Report 1948–49*, 232, and Stephan Dubreuil, *Come Quick, Danger: A History of Marine Radio in Canada* (Ottawa: Minister of Public Works and Government Services Canada, 1998), 72–3.
114. Dubreuil, *Come Quick*, 75.
115. Canada, Department of Transport, *Annual Report 1961–62* (Ottawa: Queen's Printer, 1962), 17. See also DOT *Annual Report 1968–69* (Ottawa: Queen's Printer, 1970), where plans to establish a VHF network to improve radio coverage of the Great Lakes are mentioned on page 11.
116. Edward M. Noll, *Radio Transmitter Principles and Projects* (Indianapolis: Howard M. Sams & Company, 1973), 127.
117. Department of Transport, *Annual Report 1961–62*, 17–8; Canada, Department of Transport, *Annual Report 1964–65* (Ottawa: Queen's Printer, 1965), 16; Dubreuil, *Come Quick*, 76; Charles Maginley, *History of the Canadian Coast Guard since 1968* (St Catharines, Ont.: Vanwell Publishing, 2003), 7. For information on VHF radio, see also Canadian Coast Guard (CCG), Laurentian Region, "History of Telecommunication and Electronics" (unpublished report, 1982), 21, 22, 26, 31, 36.
118. CCG, Laurentian Region, "History of Telecommunication and Electronics," 38.
119. Canada, Fisheries and Oceans Canada, *Global Marine Distress and Safety System (GMDSS)* (Ottawa: Minister of Public Works and Government Services Canada, 1997), no page nos.
120. CCG, Laurentian Region, "History of Telecommunication and Electronics," 27; Maginley, *Canadian Coast Guard*, 113–4; and Garth Wilson, "Acquisition Proposal: First Canadian Vessel Traffic Services Centre," CMST curatorial files. For more information on the uses of bridge-to-bridge radio communication in this period, see also R. Bier, "Efficient Communications at Sea," *Shipping World and Shipbuilder* 164, no. 3859 (July 1971): 789, and "Bridge-to-Bridge Radiotelephones — New USA Legislation," *Shipping World and Shipbuilder* 165, no. 3868 (April 1972): 525.
121. CCG, Laurentian Region, "History of Telecommunication and Electronics," 27; Maginley, *Canadian Coast Guard*, 113–4.
122. David F. Tver, *The Norton Encyclopedic Dictionary of Navigation* (New York: W. W. Norton & Company, 1987), 173.
123. Canada, Fisheries and Oceans Canada, GMDSS, no page nos.; "Product Report, New on the Market," *Professional Mariner* 24 (April/May 1997): 80. See references to channel 70 in *Professional Mariner* 1 (June/July 1993): 14–5. For current information on GMDSS, consult the Canadian Coast Guard's website at www.ccg.gcc.gc.ca.
124. Glyn Smith, "Manufacturers Await IMO Performance Standards," *Shipping World and Shipbuilder* 179, no. 4002 (December 1983): 661.
125. INMARSAT is an international communications organization founded in 1979 with the purpose of developing satellite systems using UHF transponders to provide communications service to ships at sea via small, low-cost shipboard terminals. See Doris Jelly, *Canada: 25 Years in Space* (Montréal: Polyscience Publications, 1988), 58–9.
126. See "Product Report, New on the Market."
127. Canada, Fisheries and Oceans Canada, GMDSS pamphlet; Tver, *Norton Encyclopedic Dictionary*, 172–3.
128. Tim Queeney, "Satcom Options Increase," *Professional Mariner* 29 (December/January 1998): 61–2.
129. Kemp, ed., *Oxford Companion*, 686.
130. Ibid.
131. Williams, *Sails to Satellites*, 181.
132. Dutton, *Navigation and Nautical Astronomy*, 150 (emphasis in original).
133. Williams, *Sails to Satellites*, 184. In keeping with the 1929 International Convention for the Safety of Life at Sea, the Canada Shipping Act of 1934 gave owners of vessels 5,000 gross tons (4 545 tonnes) and over two years from the ratification of the convention to install "approved direction-finding apparatus." See pages 801 and 828.
134. Dutton, *Navigation and Nautical Astronomy*, 151; Weems, *Marine Navigation*, 170–2; "Canadian Government Radio Direction Finding Stations," *Canadian Railway and Marine World (CRMW)*, August 1923, 408; and "Radio Aids to Navigation," *Canadian Railway and Marine World*, August 1936, 394.
135. Weems, *Marine Navigation*, 172; Dutton, *Navigation and Nautical Astronomy*, 151; and "Canadian Government Radio Direction Finding Stations," 408.
136. Canada, Department of Marine and Fisheries, *Annual Report 1922–23* (Ottawa: King's Printer, 1923), 140.
137. Canada, Department of Marine and Fisheries, *Annual Report 1928–29* (Ottawa: King's Printer, 1929), 163.
138. Canada, Department of Transport, *Annual Report 1949–50* (Ottawa: King's Printer, 1951), 163, and Department of Transport, *Annual Report 1964–65*, 18.
139. Telephone interview with DOT, CCG officials, 1998.
140. Corbet, "Modern Merchant Ship Navigation," 178.
141. British patent quoted in Williams, *Sails to Satellites*, 202.
142. Ibid., 202–16.
143. Ibid., 216.
144. Woodman, "Navigation 1900–1960," 179.
145. Williams, *Sails to Satellites*, 216.
146. Kemp, ed., *Oxford Companion*, 685; Woodman, "Navigation 1900–1960," 179–80; and Williams, *Sails to Satellites*, 216–7.
147. Excerpt from Nicholas J. Healy and Joseph C. Sweeney, *The Law of Marine Collision* (Centreville, Md.: Cornell Maritime Press, 1988), which appeared in *Professional Mariner* 35 (October/November 1998): 64–9.
148. Excerpt from Healy and Sweeney, *Law of Marine Collision*, 67.

149. Williams, *Sails to Satellites*, 217.
150. Commander J. B. Hewson, *A History of the Practice of Navigation* (Glasgow: Brown, Son & Ferguson, 1983), 226–7, and Tver, *Norton Encyclopedic Dictionary*, 162–3 and 168. See also W. Burger, *Radar Observer's Handbook for Merchant Navy Officers*, 5th ed. (Glasgow: Brown, Son & Ferguson, 1975).
151. Hewson, *Practice of Navigation*, 268, and B. C. Piercy, "Radar Collision Avoidance Equipment," *Shipping World and Shipbuilder* 165, no. 3865 (January 1972): 67. This is one of several articles in this journal in the early 1970s about collision avoidance navigation systems. See, for example, March 1972, 349; March 1973, 303; and August 1973, 876.
152. Excerpt from Healy and Sweeney, *Law of Marine Collision*, 68.
153. Corbet, "Modern Merchant Ship Navigation," 178. For a discussion of the limitations of collision avoidance systems including ARPA and the problems posed by IMCO's decision to make these systems compulsory, see Captain A. N. Cockcroft et al., "The Compulsory Fitting of Seaborne Radar Collision Avoidance Systems, A Discussion," *Journal of Navigation* 33, no. 3 (1980): 389–97. The discussants were members of the Technical Committee of IMCO charged with looking into the implications of the new measures.
154. Williams, *Sails to Satellites*, 217.
155. Canada, Department of Transport, *Annual Report 1951–52* (Ottawa: Queen's Printer, 1953), 155.
156. "Navigation News," *Shipping World and Shipbuilder* 178, no. 3997 (June 1983): 333.
157. Kemp, ed., *Oxford Companion*, 584.
158. Williams, *Sails to Satellites*, 223–4; Kemp, ed., *Oxford Companion*, 384; and Corbet, "Modern Merchant Ship Navigation," 179.
159. Kemp, ed., *Oxford Companion*, 197; Williams, *Sails to Satellites*, 226; and John S. Hall, ed., *Radar Aids to Navigation* (New York: McGraw-Hill Book Company, 1947), 47–50.
160. Williams, *Sails to Satellites*, 226; Corbet, "Modern Merchant Ship Navigation," 179.
161. Kemp, ed., *Oxford Companion*, 236; Williams, *Sails to Satellites*, 226–7; Corbet, 179; and Hall, *Radar Aids to Navigation*, 76–7. See also E. W. Anderson, *The Principles of Navigation* (London: Hollis & Carter, 1966), 531–4 and 543.
162. Williams, *Sails to Satellites*, 226–8; Corbet, 177 and 179; and telephone interviews with Val Smith, Standards Officer, Long Range Aids to Navigation, Canadian Coast Guard, 9 March 1999, and Charles Maginley, Canadian Coast Guard, 9 March 1999. According to Mr. Maginley there may still be some active Decca sites along the coasts of Britain and Europe.
163. Williams, *Sails to Satellites*, 228–9.
164. Ibid., 228–9; Corbet, "Modern Merchant Ship Navigation," 179; Kemp, ed., *Oxford Companion*, 580; Anderson, *Principles of Navigation*, 537 and 542–3.
165. Anderson, *Principles of Navigation*, 506–8; Williams, *Sails to Satellites*, 230–2; and E. W. Anderson, "Navigational Equipment," in *A History of Technology*, vol. 7, *The Twentieth Century c. 1900 to c. 1950, Part II*, ed. Trevor I. Williams (Oxford: Oxford University Press, 1978), 847.
166. Williams, *Sails to Satellites*, 232; Anderson, *Principles of Navigation*, 526–9 and 543; Kemp, ed., *Oxford Companion*, 498; and Corbet, "Modern Merchant Ship Navigation," 179.
167. Kemp, ed., *Oxford Companion*, 498; Williams, *Sails to Satellites*, 232–3; and interview with Val Smith, 9 March 1999.
168. Williams, *Sails to Satellites*, 232–4; Anderson, *Principles of Navigation*, 529–30; Corbet, "Modern Merchant Ship Navigation," 179; and interview with Val Smith, 9 March 1999. Mr. Smith stated that the American government, despite a recommendation from the department responsible for Loran C to extend service into 2008, has refused to provide the funding necessary to continue operation of the U.S. stations. See also recent issues (1996–1999) of *Professional Mariner* for discussions of the latest developments in the story and the various points of view on abandoning Loran C.
169. Department of Transport, *Annual Report 1948–49*, 233; Canada, Department of Transport, *Annual Report 1957–58* (Ottawa: Queen's Printer, 1959), 11; Canada, Department of Transport, *Annual Report 1958–59* (Ottawa: Queen's Printer, 1960), 11; Canada, Department of Transport, *Annual Report 1959–60* (Ottawa: Queen's Printer, 1961), 13; Canada, Department of Transport, *Annual Report 1960–61* (Ottawa: Queen's Printer, 1962), 16; and Maginley, *Canadian Coast Guard*, 4.
170. Maginley, *Canadian Coast Guard*, 4–5.
171. Department of Transport, *Annual Report 1968–69*, 10–11; and Maginley, *Canadian Coast Guard*, 5.
172. Williams, *Sails to Satellites*, 238–41; Corbet, "Modern Merchant Ship Navigation," 179; Anderson, *Principles of Navigation*, 574–6; and Bradford W. Parkinson, "History and Operation of NAVSTAR, the Global Positioning system," *IEEE Transactions on Aerospace and Electronic Systems* 30, no. 1 (January 1994): 1145–61.
173. Williams, *Sails to Satellites*, 238, and Parkinson, "History and Operation of NAVSTAR," 1146.
174. Anderson, *Principles of Navigation*, 575, and Corbet, "Modern Merchant Ship Navigation," 179. See also "Navigation by Satellite," *Shipping World and Shipbuilder* 64, no. 3855 (March 1971): 351, for a contemporary description of the system as well as some of the contradictory findings about its performance.
175. According to Anderson, *Principles of Navigation*, 575, the process of reducing the copious data to a position would have taken about an hour even for a skilled navigator using a mechanical calculator.
176. Williams, *Sails to Satellites*, 238–9; Corbet, "Modern Merchant Ship Navigation," 179; and interview with Val Smith, 9 March 1999.
177. Williams, *Sails to Satellites*, 240; Parkinson, "History and Operation of NAVSTAR," 1149; and Corbet, "Modern Merchant Ship Navigation," 179.
178. Corbet, "Modern Merchant Ship Navigation," 179–80; Parkinson, "History and Operation of NAVSTAR," 1149–50; Canadian Coast Guard, "Differential Global Positioning System," on website at www.ccg-gcc.gc.ca; "Navigation," *Shipping World and Shipbuilder* 198, no. 4136 (September 1997): 10; Jon Copley, "Pinpoint Precision," *New Scientist* 159, no. 2151 (12 September 1998): 22; and Williams, *Sails to Satellites*, 240–1.
179. Tim Queeney, "Marine Technology," *Professional Mariner* 37 (December/January 1999): 69; "Differential Global Positioning System" and "Marine DGPS Update," CCGS website; and *McGraw-Hill Yearbook of Science and Technology 1994* (New York: McGraw-Hill, 1993), s.v. "Satellite Navigation Systems."
180. Maginley, *Canadian Coast Guard*, 5. The U.S. Department of Defense has since stopped downgrading the GPS signals for civilian use but can at any time resume this practice or take the system entirely offline if deemed necessary for security reasons. In this context, it is not clear whether the DGPS stations will continue to operate or not.
181. Stanley Fillmore and R. W. Sandilands, *The Chartmakers: A History of Nautical Surveying in Canada* (Toronto:

NC Press, 1983), 2, 58, and 67–9. For a detailed description of the work of the CHS from 1883 to 1945, see O. M. Meehan, *The Canadian Hydrographic Service from the Time of Its Inception in 1883 to the End of the Second World War*, ed. William Glover with David Gray in *The Northern Mariner* 14, no. 1 (January 2004): 1–158.

182. Canadian inventor Reginald Fessenden is often given credit for developing the first such device, which he called the fathometer, as a means of detecting underwater objects such as icebergs. See Peter Whitfield, "Portolan Reflections," *Mercator's World*, November/December 1998, 60–1.
183. Whitfield, "Portolan Reflections," 61.
184. Fillmore and Sandilands, *Chartmakers*, 74–5 and 92–5; Whitfield, "Portolan Reflections," 60–1.
185. Fillmore and Sandilands, 74–5 and 92–6; see also Whitfield, "Portolan Reflections," 61.
186. Whitfield, "Portolan Reflections," 62.
187. See Canadian Hydrographic Service (CHS) website at www.chs-shc.dfo-mpo.gc.ca.
188. Fillmore and Sandilands, *Chartmakers*, 128.
189. Ibid., 133.
190. See CHS website: www.chs-shc.dfo-mpo.gc.ca/chs/en/educational/developing.htm.
191. Fillmore and Sandilands, *Chartmakers*, 138–9; CHS website.
192. *The Concise Oxford English Dictionary* defines a vector as: "a quantity having direction as well as magnitude, especially as determining the position of one point in space relative to another." Tenth ed., revised, ed. Judy Pearsall (Oxford: Oxford University Press, 2002).
193. Tim Queeney, "Issues Facing Raster Charts," *Professional Mariner* 25 (June/July 1997): 54–5; CHS website: www.chs-shc.dfo-mpo.gc.ca/chs/en/products/raster.htm.
194. Robert G. Lyall and David G. Michelson, "Automatic Radar Positioning Systems: A New Era in Radar Navigation," paper in files (subject: PINS) of Curator of Transportation, no page nos.
195. See Curator's Acquisition File for PINS 9000.
196. Technically speaking, the U.S. government owns and controls the GPS system and has the right to limit access as it sees fit. In the past, for example, the U.S. military introduced errors into the signals so that civilian and foreign military users could not benefit from the same level of accuracy as the U.S. military. This practice, which has since been ended, led to the development of differential GPS (DGPS), which corrected the errors.
197. Christian Hempstead, "ECDIS Is a Powerful Navigation Tool But Requires Solid Training," *Professional Mariner* 66 (September 2002): 24. See also CHS website, "ECDIS."
198. Hempstead, "Powerful Navigation Tool," 22 (photograph and caption). See also advertisement facing p. 24 in the same article.
199. See CHS website, "IEC Test Standards/Procedures for ECDIS," *Contour*, Fall 1996, 1of 3. See also "Government Response to Report Recommendations" (report refers to "The Marine Electronic Highway — An ECDIS Vision for Canada," by John Pace) on the Transport Canada website at www.tc.gc.ca/cmac/documents/ecdisvisione.htm, especially p. 2.
200. Julian Goodyear, Scott Strong, and Captain Andrew Rae, "Confined Waterways — A Challenge," *Contour*, Fall 1996, 3 (available on CHS website), and M. J. Casey, "Hey! Why Is My Ship Showing Up on the Dock?" *Contour*, Fall 1996, 3–6.
201. "Government Response to Report Recommendations," 2.
202. Brian Terry and Stephen MacPhee, "Public/Private Sector Partnership in Electronic Charting," *Contour*, Fall 1996, 1–4, and Brian Terry, "NDI's New Products," *Contour*, Fall 1996, 1–3.
203. Goodyear, Strong, and Rae, "Confined Waterways — A Challenge," 1–2.
204. Olaf Gundersrud, "DNV Nautical Safety Class," *Contour*, Fall 1996, 1–4.
205. Hempstead, "Powerful Navigation Tool," 24.
206. Marine Safety Directorate, Simulated Electronic Navigation Courses (TP 4958E), 2000, 48–61. See Transport Canada website at www.tc.gc.ca/marinesafety/tp/tp4958/tp4958e.htm.
207. Hempstead, "Powerful Navigation Tool," 22–6.
208. Bush, *Canadian Lighthouse*, 18; Douglas B. Hague and Rosemary Christie, *Lighthouses: Their Architecture, History and Archaeology* (Llandysul Dyfed, U.K.: Gomer Press, 1985), 156–7.
209. Bush, *Canadian Lighthouse*, 18–19; Jennifer Paton, in *Dictionary of Canadian Biography*, vol. 14, *1911 to 1920*, ed. Ramsay Cook (Toronto: University of Toronto Press, 1998), s.v. "Willson, Thomas Leopold." According to Hague and Christie, *Lighthouses*, 160–1, acetylene was also used as a backup light source in electrified stations beginning in the 1930s.
210. Bush, *Canadian Lighthouse*, 20–3; John Naish, *Seamarks: Their History and Development* (London: Stanford Maritime, 1985), 158–9; Hague and Christie, *Lighthouses*, 172–3.
211. Naish, *Seamarks*, 138–9; Hague and Christie, *Lighthouses*, 172–4; Maginley, *Canadian Coast Guard*, 105–7.
212. Naish, *Seamarks*, 158–67; Hague and Christie, *Lighthouses*, 172–5; Maginley, *Canadian Coast Guard*, 105–7.
213. Bush, *Canadian Lighthouse*, 14; Naish, *Seamarks*, 156–63.
214. Hague and Christie, *Lighthouses*, 203–4; Naish, *Seamarks*, 110–5; Bush, *Canadian Lighthouse*, 14.
215. Naish, *Seamarks*, 65–6; Bush, *Canadian Lighthouse*, 21–2; Department of Marine and Fisheries, *Annual Report 1904*, 61–2; Appleton, Usque ad Mare, 110–2; Thomas Carpenter, *Inventors: Profiles in Canadian Genius* (Camden East, Ont.: Camden House Publishing, 1990), 92–4.
216. Naish, *Seamarks*, 65–6; Bush, *Canadian Lighthouse*, 21–2; Hague and Christie, *Lighthouses*, 159.
217. Naish, *Seamarks*, 66–7, 162–4; Maginley, *Canadian Coast Guard*, 105–7.
218. Jennifer Worster, "More Synthetic Buoys Urged for U.S. Coastline," *Professional Mariner* 10 (December/January 1995): 68–9.
219. Hague and Christie, *Lighthouses*, 191–2; Maginley, *Canadian Coast Guard*, 105–7; Naish, *Seamarks*, 161. See Hague and Christie, 192, and Naish, 162, for descriptions of modern systems.
220. Canada, Department of Transport, *Annual Report 1948–49* (Ottawa: King's Printer, 1950), 234; Canada, Department of Transport, *Annual Report 1954–55* (Ottawa: King's Printer, 1956), 67; and Canada, Department of Transport, *Annual Report 1955–56* (Ottawa: King's Printer, 1957), 66.
221. Naish, *Seamarks*, 164–5; Maginley, *Canadian Coast Guard*, 105–7; Hague and Christie, *Lighthouses*, 192.
222. Department of Marine and Fisheries, *Annual Report 1904*, 58–9, and Bush, *Canadian Lighthouse*, 18–9.
223. Canada, Department of Transport, *Annual Report 1965–66* (Ottawa: Queen's Printer, 1967), 33. Out of a total of 3,536 lights, there were 40 oil vapour, 95 oil wick, 1084 commercial electric, 142 station-generated electric, 2009 battery electric, and 166 acetylene lights.
224. Bush, *Canadian Lighthouse*, 20–1, and Department of Marine and Fisheries, *Annual Report 1927–28*, 24.
225. Bush, *Canadian Lighthouse*, 21–3.

226. Ibid., 23, and Canada, Department of Transport, *Annual Report 1962–63* (Ottawa: Queen's Printer, 1964), 27.
227. Department of Transport, *Annual Report 1955–56*, 66, and Bush, *Canadian Lighthouse*, 23.
228. Normand Lafrenière, *Lightkeeping on the St. Lawrence* (Toronto: Dundurn Press, 1996), 31–4 including photographs.
229. Canada, Department of Transport, *Annual Report 1956–57* (Ottawa: Queen's Printer, 1958), 15; Department of Transport, *Annual Report 1958–59*, 18.
230. Maginley, *Canadian Coast Guard*, 105–7.
231. Ibid., and interviews with CCG officials Ben Hutchin and Mike Clements, 9 June 2004.
232. Maginley, *Canadian Coast Guard*, 105–7, and CCG website at www.ccg-gcc.gc.ca/iala-aism/chapter1.htm.
233. Canadian Coast Guard website at www.ccg-gcc.gc.ca/iala-aism/chapter1.htm, and Bush, *Canadian Lighthouse*, 14.
234. Bush, *Canadian Lighthouse*, 14.
235. Canada, Department of Transport, *Annual Report 1950–51* (Ottawa: King's Printer, 1951), 55.
236. Bush, *Canadian Lighthouse*, 80–1.
237. Appleton, Usque ad Mare, 120–1.
238. Ibid., 121; Department of Transport, draft press releases, 20 October and 8 December 1956; and P. F. Boisvert, "The Life of a Lightship," unpublished manuscript, CCGC, 7 January 1978, in files provided by Charles Maginley.
239. Appleton, Usque ad Mare, 122, and Bush, *Canadian Lighthouse*, 14.
240. Boisvert, "Life of a Lightship," 4; Bush, *Canadian Lighthouse*, 14; Department of Transport, *Annual Report 1961–62*, 26 (and photo after p. 23); Department of Transport, *Annual Report 1958–59*, 17; and Appleton, Usque ad Mare, 122–4 and photo p. 125.
241. Lafrenière, *Lightkeeping*, 72–83, including photographs.
242. Ibid., 85–8, and interviews with CCG officials Ben Hutchin and Mike Clements.
243. Chambers, *Canadian Marine*, 55; Department of Transport, *Annual Report 1935–36*, 79; Department of Transport, *Annual Report 1964–65*, 27; and Canada, Department of Transport, *Transportation in Canada Annual Report* (Ottawa: Public Works and Government Services Canada, 1999), 191.
244. J. G. Macphail, "The Lighthouse Service of Canada," *The Engineering Journal*, August 1931, 446.
245. Department of Transport, *Annual Report 1950–51*, 57.
246. W. J. Manning, "How Marine Works Branch Functions," *Canadian Shipping and Marine Engineering News* 35, no. 11 (August 1964): 64; and Department of Transport, *Annual Report 1954–55*, 67.
247. Department of Transport, *Annual Report 1948–49*, 234; Department of Transport, *Annual Report 1949–50*, 65; Canada, Department of Transport, *Annual Report 1951–52* (Ottawa: Queen's Printer, 1952), 155; Department of Transport, *Annual Report 1954–55*, 67; and Department of Transport, *Annual Report 1955–56*, 66.
248. Maginley, *Canadian Coast Guard*, 107. He mentions the use of this technology in the period after 1968 but gives no date for its adoption.
249. Department of Transport, *Annual Report 1961–62*, 27, and Worster, 70.
250. Department of Transport, *Annual Report 1950–51*, 56; and Department of Transport, *Annual Report 1961–62*, 27.
251. Bush, *Canadian Lighthouse*, 24.
252. Canada, Department of Marine and Fisheries, *Canada: Her Natural Resources, Navigation, Principal Steamer Lines and Transcontinental Railways*, 12th Congress of the Permanent International Association of Navigational Congresses (Ottawa: Government Printing Bureau, 1912), 131–3, and Macphail, "Lighthouse Service," 440.
253. According to Bush, *Canadian Lighthouse*, 24, the diaphone was still in use in the mid-1970s.
254. Department of Transport, *Annual Report 1965–66*, 32; Maginley, *Canadian Coast Guard*, 3; and Bush, *Canadian Lighthouse*, 24. For information on the department's fog alarms, see the tables in any DOT annual report for the 1940s or 1950s.
255. Department of Transport, *Annual Report 1965–66*, 32, and Maginley, *Canadian Coast Guard*, 109.
256. Corbet, "Modern Merchant Ship Navigation," 183, photo caption, and McCalla, *Water Transport*, 65. See also L. Barker to G. Wilson, 15 May 1992, Montreal Harbour Radar Equipment, p. 1, letter in acquisition file held by Curator.
257. Corbet, "Modern Merchant Ship Navigation," 182.
258. Canada, Department of Transport, *Annual Report 1946–47* (Ottawa: King's Printer, 1947), 195; Canada, Department of Transport, *Annual Report 1947–48* (Ottawa: King's Printer, 1947), 201; Department of Transport, *Annual Report 1948–49*, 234; and L. Barker to G. Wilson, 15 May 1992, 1–3.
259. L. Barker to G. Wilson, 15 May 1992, 1–3, and Tony K. S. Quon, "Risk Analysis of Vessel Traffic Systems," *Maritime Policy Management* 19, no. 4 (1992): 319.
260. Tim Queeney, "Using Differential GPS to Upgrade VTS Systems," *Professional Mariner* 1 (June/July 1993): 12; and Robert McKenna, "VTS Takes On a Life of Its Own," *Professional Mariner* 3 (October/November 1993): 50.
261. Corbet, "Modern Merchant Ship Navigation," 182–3, and McCalla, *Water Transport*, 66–7.
262. McCalla, *Water Transport*, 66–7.

Conclusion

For centuries, Canada, like much of the rest of the world, has depended on marine transportation to facilitate trade and sustain its economic prosperity. Today, over "90 per cent of world trade by weight moves by sea transport," including most of the primary resources that Canada produces.[1] Yet the ships that carry our exports and imports are only one part of the complex transportation system that allows billions of tonnes of goods to move safely and efficiently across the world's oceans. Equally important are the navigational systems that mariners use to find and maintain their routes and to avoid the many hazards that confront them on their voyages.

Historical Context

Marine navigational instruments and aids are as old as water-borne travel itself, but it was the advent of transoceanic exploration in the late fifteenth century that provided the major impetus for the systematic development and refinement of these devices. Locked in competition for the riches of the Far East and the New World, the European powers needed to establish safe and reliable trade routes for the vessels travelling back and forth across the oceans. These same routes were essential to sustain the colonies the Europeans set up to secure and exploit their "discoveries." These requirements gave great impetus to governments, navies, scientists, inventors, and mariners to develop better ways to navigate.

The era of exploration laid the foundation for the creation of an increasingly international economy in the eighteenth and nineteenth centuries. As imperial powers such as Spain, England, and France conquered and integrated many formerly isolated regions into their trading spheres, the scope and level of trade increased, as did the frequency of commercial and military conflict. The Industrial Revolution not only created enormous new productive capacity, including larger, faster steam-propelled ships, it also created a demand for raw materials from distant colonies and countries. It produced a growing mass of landless workers who were dependent on trade and commerce to supply the basic necessities of life, and it contributed to large-scale migrations within Europe and from Europe to North and South America. This meant that there were more ships, carrying more people and goods, than ever before on the world's waterways. Increased shipping activity, in turn, highlighted certain chronic safety problems that attracted public attention and debate. All of these factors placed constant pressure on maritime authorities, both naval and mercantile, to improve the safety and efficiency of marine transportation around the world. Enhancing navigational tools, skills, and infrastructure was an essential component of this long-term goal.

These pressures continued to grow over the course of the twentieth century as economic and population growth and almost constant war or fear of war gave rise to rapid technological change in the transportation industry. Most of the major advances in navigational technology originated in military research but were readily embraced by mercantile interests as a means of coping with the increasingly competitive reality of international shipping. Shipping companies commissioned larger, faster ships that could carry more goods and sail on tighter timetables. This allowed them to keep pace with other forms of transportation, especially trucking and aviation, and to cater to the needs of an increasingly interconnected world economy. In this context, accurate and expeditious navigation became more critical than ever. Also, technological change in industry brought a greater dependence on oil, liquid natural gas, and various dangerous chemicals, all of which had to be transported to distant sites. The potential danger posed by ships carrying these hazardous substances placed additional demands on mariners and marine infrastructure.

The Technology of Marine Navigation

The tools and systems of marine navigation are designed to address two critical needs: the need to establish a vessel's position and course accurately, particularly on the featureless open ocean, and the need to identify, monitor, and avoid hazards, especially in coastal waters. These imperatives have not changed since the turn of the fifteenth century. What has changed is the technology mariners use to address them.

Over the past five hundred years, mariners, scientists, instrument makers, and engineers have produced many notable advances in the technology of marine navigation. A great many of their most important accomplishments are clustered into three very active periods of scientific and technological innovation, inspired, in part, by intense commercial and military rivalries among the European powers. From the mid-eighteenth to the early nineteenth centuries mariners benefited from the introduction of the octant, the sextant, the chronometer, and the first mechanical logs and sounders. They also gained access to work of astronomers who had carefully recorded the movements of celestial bodies and of hydrographic services that were producing and compiling better and more up-to-date charts. All of these advances greatly enhanced the ability of mariners to establish their position by celestial navigation and to plot and follow a safe course from one destination to another.

Navigation was also made safer and more expeditious in this period by improvements in coastal aids. Marine authorities set up the first lightships, adopted the Argand lamp and parabolic reflectors, and introduced the first revolving lights before the end of the eighteenth century. In the 1820s, they began to use the recently developed Fresnel lens. Along with many general improvements in the design of floating aids including, for example, the use of iron, these innovations made aids more reliable, more visible, and more durable.

Many of these early innovations remained central to marine navigation well into the late nineteenth and early twentieth century, when they were augmented by another group of important inventions. The field of coastal aids to navigation benefited from the introduction of acetylene and electric lights and concrete and steel as building materials for light towers. Marine officials also began to develop and use electrical power sources for lights and fog signals. Spurred on by imperial rivalries and international conflict, inventors also produced radio, radio direction finding, and sonar, all of which ultimately made an important contribution to coastal communication and navigation.

These and the many other incremental improvements made by scientists, mariners, and engineers between 1500 and 1945 added significantly to the accuracy, effectiveness, and reach of the instruments and infrastructure of navigation. As far-reaching as these changes were, though, they did not fundamentally alter the basic methods of marine navigation; they simply gave mariners and marine authorities some new and better tools with which to work. Mariners still relied on the sextant and the compass for oceanic navigation but could use the additional information provided by RDF to confirm or clarify their position whenever they were within range of a station. Governments still built and staffed lighthouses but by using electric lights and power increased their visibility and decreased staff time devoted to maintenance work.

After the Second World War, the incremental pace of change in marine navigation gradually gave way to a wholesale transformation. In the years leading up to the war, during the war, and in the years immediately following it, scientists and engineers made several critical breakthroughs in the field of electronics that laid the groundwork for a new approach to navigation. Among the most important advances were the development of radar, the creation and deployment of the first hyperbolic radio navigation systems, and the invention of semiconductors. Other important innovations that contributed to the transformation were the refinement and widespread adoption of the gyrocompass and the steady improvement in the capabilities of radio communication systems.

Some of these new technologies had obvious applications to merchant shipping and were readily embraced in the decades following the war. Others had a much less immediate but more profound impact. Throughout the 1960s, 1970s, and 1980s, scientists and engineers were busy developing and perfecting the integrated circuit, microprocessors, and supercomputers needed to design, build, and control the sophisticated military vehicles and weapons systems and spacecraft the U.S. government wanted to fight the Cold War. One pivotal result of this work was the development of satellite navigation systems, most notably GPS. Another important offshoot was the rapid evolution and dissemination of computing technology after 1980. With smaller, more powerful, and less costly microprocessors available to them, equipment designers began to produce increasingly automated and integrated systems for shipboard use and for coastal aids to navigation.

These technological changes coincided with an equally profound transformation of government in the West. Plagued by high budget deficits and large accumulated debts, many governments fell under the sway of a new right-wing political agenda that called for major spending cuts and a new business-friendly approach to governance. Corporations lobbied for deregulation of markets and utilities and sales of profitable public assets, all based on the argument that increased competition would create more jobs and would be good for the consumer and the economy as a whole.

This new ethos translated into substantial and ongoing program, service, and staff reductions in most western governments. In those areas where programs had to be maintained to meet international commitments — aids to navigation was one such area — governments looked to technology to help them provide essential services while at the same time reducing labour and other costs. In the shipping industry, already one of the most competitive in the world, a constant search for greater efficiency and less regulation led many companies to flag their ships offshore and to reduce crew levels to unprecedented lows. The latter was facilitated to a great extent by substituting technology for people.

The results of these developments have been dramatic. Whereas in the 1980s, governments were using computerized control systems to automate and de-staff lighthouses, by the 1990s, they were talking about abandoning some of what were once the most important lights. The pervasive adoption of GPS systems, even by the owners and operators of small craft, has, according to government and industry officials, made certain lights redundant. It has also made some in the industry question the need to learn basic celestial navigation or to carry sextants and chronometers at all. They are, after all, not as accurate as GPS and much more time-consuming and complicated to use.

During the same period, the development of reliable long-distance voice radio systems made it possible for the shipping industry and marine authorities to phase out the use of Morse code, to reduce the number of coastal radio stations, and to eliminate the position of radio officer on board ships. Though radio communication is as important as ever — more important, perhaps, when you consider the number of vessel traffic systems and controlled waterways around the world — it has become just one of many functions for which the officer of the watch is now responsible.

Similarly, electronic charts have recently begun to displace paper charts as the method of choice for setting and following a safe and expeditious course. ECDIS relieves bridge officers of the laborious task of manually plotting the ship's course and speed and can provide more accurate fixes. Because it now requires much less time and attention, it too can be part of general duties assigned a bridge officer.

There can be no doubt that these innovations have improved the accuracy and reliability of marine navigation, in many cases significantly, or that most mariners welcome these improvements. At the same time, new technologies have created new problems and challenges that cannot be ignored. Although improved navigational tools provide much more accurate and plentiful course, position, and other information, this constant stream of data can be overwhelming and even contradictory. The officer of the watch needs to sort and evaluate it in the context of other information and therefore must balance attention to the monitors with attention to the radio, radars, and the "manual" watch. Thus, while there may be no requirement for sextant readings and hand plotting, the workload and related risks are still significant.

As in many fields, however, sophisticated technology has been used as a convenient excuse for cutting staff. Within the shipping industry the prevailing notion seems to be that the art of navigation is now so integrated, automated, accurate, and dependable that only a tiny complement of skilled officers is needed to manage a ship. In some cases this can mean just one officer in charge of a ship and responsible for processing and acting upon all the information supplied by an integrated bridge system that deals not just with navigation but also with many of the other systems and functions of a modern vessel.

Another problem posed by the new navigational technology arises from the tendency to rely too heavily on it. Most people who live in developed societies believe very strongly in the efficacy and reliability of technology. We now rely on microprocessors and other sophisticated devices to carry out tasks that once had to be done by hand. Cashiers, for example, no longer have to know how to calculate the correct change because the cash register does it for them. When the computers "go down" or the power goes off, we are suddenly confronted with our inability to do simple but essential tasks. This may be a humbling experience but it generally would not pose a danger to us or to society. The same cannot be said for a ship that loses its computerized navigational systems when out at sea or entering a busy channel or harbour. Will there be someone on board who knows how to use a sextant or plot a course on a paper chart? Will there even be a paper chart on the vessel?

Even when navigational systems are functioning, they are not infallible. Technology, especially sophisticated integrated systems, is only as accurate and reliable as the inputs it receives. Many factors can cause distorted position and other readings, from a badly sited antenna to temporary signal loss or pre-GPS chart data. The system takes and uses whatever data it is fed; it cannot judge whether that data is good or bad. Only humans can do this, and they can only do it by comparing what they are seeing on the monitors with what is actually happening in the water. As one experienced mariner recently put it: "Technology is great, but you still have to look out the window."[2]

Notes

1. Robert J. McCalla, *Water Transport in Canada* (Halifax: Formac Publishing, 1994), 8 (table 1.1) and 3.
2. Joel N. Kouyoumjian, "Correspondence," *Professional Mariner* 75 (October/November 2003): 62. This is the title of Mr. Kouyoumjian's article. In it he elaborates on the idea by stating: "There isn't a piece of equipment on the bridge that deserves more of your attention than what is visible outside the window. I've always maintained that if I need to know where I am within 10 feet, I'm not going to be inside looking at the computer. I'm going to be outside looking at the reason."

Bibliography

Monographs

Andrews, Kenneth. *Trade, Plunder and Settlement: Maritime Enterprise and the Genesis of the British Empire, 1480–1630.* Cambridge: Cambridge University Press, 1984.

Appleton, Thomas E. Usque ad Mare: *A History of the Canadian Coast Guard and Marine Services.* Ottawa: Department of Transport, 1968. Available on the Canadian Coast Guard website, www.ccg-gcc.gc.ca/usque-ad-mare/main_e.htm

Babaian, Sharon A. *Radio Communication in Canada: An Historical and Technological Survey.* Transformation Series 1. Ottawa: National Museum of Science and Technology, 1992.

Bannerman, Gary and Patricia. *The Ships of British Columbia: An Illustrated History of the British Columbia Ferry Corporation.* Surrey, B.C.: Hancock House Publishers, 1985.

Beaglehole, J. C. *The Life of Captain James Cook.* London: Hakluyt Society, 1974.

Bekiashev, Kamil A., and Bitali V. Serebriakov. *International Marine Organizations: Essays on Structure and Activities.* The Hague: Marinus Nijhoff Publishers, 1981.

Belliveau, John Edward, Silver Donald Cameron, and Michael Harrington. *Iceboats to Superferries: An Illustrated History of Marine Atlantic.* St John's: Breakwater, 1992.

Bennett, J. A. *The Divided Circle: A History of Instruments for Astronomy, Navigation and Surveying.* Oxford: Phaidon-Christie's, 1987.

Blake, John. *The Sea Chart: The Illustrated History of Nautical Maps and Navigational Charts.* London: Conway Maritime Press, 2004.

Bliss, Michael. *Northern Enterprise: Five Centuries of Canadian Business.* Toronto: McClelland & Stewart, 1987.

Boxer, C. R. *The Dutch Seaborne Empire, 1600–1800.* London: Hutchinson & Company, 1965.

Braudel, Fernand. *Civilization and Capitalism: 15th–18th Century,* vol. 1, *The Structures of Everyday Life: The Limits of the Possible.* Translation from the French, revised by Sian Reynolds. New York: Harper & Row, 1981.

Bumsted, J. M. *The Peoples of Canada: A Post-Confederation History.* Toronto: Oxford University Press, 1992.

———. *The Peoples of Canada: A Pre-Confederation History.* Toronto: Oxford University Press, 1992.

Burstyn, Harold L. *At the Sign of the Quadrant: An Account of the Contributions to American Hydrography Made by Edward March Blunt and his Sons.* Mystic, Conn.: Marine Historical Association, 1957.

Bush, Edward W. *The Canadian Lighthouse.* Canadian Historic Sites 9. Ottawa: Indian and Northern Affairs, 1975.

Cameron, Ian. *Lodestone and Evening Star.* New York: E. P. Dutton & Company, 1966.

Carpenter, Thomas. *Inventors: Profiles in Canadian Genius.* Camden East, Ont.: Camden House Publishing, 1990.

Cotter, Charles. H. *A History of the Navigator's Sextant.* Glasgow: Brown, Son & Ferguson, 1983.

Crone, G. R. *Maps and Their Makers: An Introduction to the History of Cartography,* 5th ed. Chatham, U.K.: W. & J. Mackay, 1978.

Dubreuil, Stephan. *Come Quick, Danger: A History of Marine Radio in Canada.* Ottawa: Minister of Public Works and Government Services Canada, 1998.

Evans, G. N. D. *Uncommon Obdurate: The Several Public Careers of J. F. W. DesBarres.* Salem, Mass.: Peabody Museum, 1969.

Fillmore, Stanley, and R. W. Sandilands. *The Chartmakers: A History of Nautical Surveying in Canada.* Toronto: NC Press, 1983.

Firstbrook, Peter. *The Voyage of the* Matthew: *John Cabot and the Discovery of America.* Toronto: McClelland & Stewart, 1997.

Fisher, Robin. *Vancouver's Voyage: Charting the Northwest Coast, 1791–1795.* Vancouver: Douglas & McIntyre, 1992.

Forbes, Eric G. *The Birth of Scientific Navigation: The Solving in the 18th century of the Problem of Finding Longitude at Sea.* Maritime Monographs and Reports Series 10. Greenwich: National Maritime Museum, 1974.

Glazebrook, G. P. deT. *A History of Transportation in Canada*, vol. 2. Toronto: McClelland & Stewart, 1964.

Gould, R. T. *The Marine Chronometer: Its History and Development*. Woodbridge, U.K.: Antique Collectors Club, 1989. Originally published in London, 1923.

Gurney, Alan. *Compass: A Story of Exploration and Innovation*. New York: W. W. Norton & Company, 2004.

Gutsche, Andre, Barbara Chisholm, and Russel Floren. *Alone in the Night: Lighthouses of Georgian Bay, Manitoulin Island and the North Channel*. Toronto: Lynx Images, 1996.

Hague, Douglas B., and Rosemary Christie. *Lighthouses: Their Architecture, History and Archaeology*. Llandysul Dyfed, U.K.: Gomer Press, 1985.

Holland, Francis Ross Jr. *America's Lighthouses: Their Illustrated History since 1716*. Brattleboro, Vt.: Stephen Greene Press, 1972.

Howse, Derek. *Greenwich Time and the Discovery of the Longitude*. Oxford: Oxford University Press, 1980.

———. *Greenwich Time and the Longitude*. London: Philip Wilson Publishers, 1997.

Howse, Derek, and Michael Sanderson. *The Sea Chart: An Historical Survey based on the Collections in the National Maritime Museum*. Newton Abbot, U.K.: David & Charles, 1973.

Hunter, Peter. *The Magic Box: A History of Containerization*. n.p.: ICHCA Canada, 1993.

Ifland, Peter. *Taking the Stars: Celestial Navigation from Argonauts to Astronauts*. Malabar, Fla.: Krieger Publishing Company, 1998.

Inglis, Robin. *The Lost Voyage of Lapérouse*. Vancouver: Vancouver Maritime Museum, 1986.

Innis, Harold. *The Cod Fisheries: The History of an International Economy*. Toronto: University of Toronto Press, 1954.

Jelly, Doris. *Canada: 25 Years in Space*. Montréal: Polyscience Publications, 1988.

Kendrick, John, and Robin Inglis. *Enlightened Voyages: Malaspina and Galiano on the Northwest Coast, 1791–1792*. Vancouver: Vancouver Maritime Museum, 1991.

Lafrenière, Normand. *Lightkeeping on the St. Lawrence*. Toronto: Dundurn Press, 1996.

Levere, Trevor H. *Science and the Canadian Arctic: A Century of Exploration, 1818–1918*. Cambridge: Cambridge University Press, 1993.

Litalien, Raymonde. *Les explorateurs de l'Amérique du Nord, 1492–1795*. Sillery, Que.: Les editions du Septentrion, 1993.

Maginley, Charles. *History of the Canadian Coast Guard since 1968*. St Catharines, Ont.: Vanwell Publishing, 2003.

Martin, Cy. *Gold Rush Narrow Gauge: The Story of the White Pass and Yukon Route*. Los Angeles: Trans-Anglo Books, 1969.

May, Commander W. E. *A History of Marine Navigation*. New York: W. W. Norton & Company, 1973.

McCalla, Robert J. *Water Transport in Canada*. Halifax: Formac Publishing, 1994.

McGhee, Robert. *Canada Rediscovered*. Ottawa: Canadian Museum of Civilization, 1991.

McKenzie, Ruth. *Admiral Bayfield: Pioneer Nautical Surveyor*. Ottawa: Environment Canada, Fisheries and Marine Service, 1976.

Molloy, David J. *The First Landfall: Historic Lighthouses of Newfoundland and Labrador*. St John's: Breakwater, 1994.

Morison, Samuel Eliot. *The European Discovery of America: The Northern Voyages, A.D. 500–1600*. New York: Oxford University Press, 1971.

———. *The European Discovery of America: The Southern Voyages, A.D. 1492–1616*. New York: Oxford University Press, 1974.

Morton, Desmond. *A Short History of Canada*. Edmonton: Hurtig Publishers, 1983.

Mörzer Bruyns, W. F. J. *The Cross-Staff: History and Development of a Navigational Instrument*. Zutphen, Netherlands: Vereeniging Nederlandsch Historisch Scheepvaart Museum, 1994.

Naish, John. *Seamarks: Their History and Development*. London: Stanford Maritime, 1985.

Nebenzahl, Kenneth. *Maps from the Age of Discovery: Columbus to Mercator*. London: Time Books, 1990.

O'Dea, Fabian. *The 17th Century Cartography of Newfoundland*. Cartographica. Monograph 1, 1971.

Parry, J. H. *The Discovery of the Sea*. Berkeley: University of California Press, 1981.

———. *The Establishment of the European Hegemony, 1415–1715*. New York: Harper & Row, 1966.

Pope, Peter E. *The Many Landfalls of John Cabot*. Toronto: University of Toronto Press, 1997.

Proulx, Gilles. *Between France and New France: Life Aboard the Tall Sailing Ships*. Toronto: Dundurn Press, 1984.

Proulx, Jean-Pierre. *Basque Whaling in Labrador in the 16th Century*. Ottawa: Environment Canada, 1992.

Pullen, Hugh F. *The Sea Road to Halifax: Being an Account of the Lights and Buoys of Halifax Harbour*. Occasional Paper No. 1. Halifax: Maritime Museum of the Atlantic, 1980.

Quinn, David B. *England and the Discovery of America, 1481–1620*. New York: Alfred A. Knopf, 1974.

Randier, Jean. *Marine Navigational Instruments*. Translated from the French by John E. Powell. London: John Murray, 1980.

Ritchie, G. S. *The Admiralty Chart: British Naval Hydrography in the Nineteenth Century*. New York: American Elsevier Publishing Company, 1967.

Sager, Eric W. *Seafaring Labour: The Merchant Marine of Atlantic Canada, 1820–1914*. Kingston: McGill-Queen's University Press, 1989.

Sager, Eric W., and Gerald E. Panting. *Maritime Capital: The Shipping Industry in Atlantic Canada, 1820–1914*. Montréal and Kingston: McGill-Queen's University Press, 1990.

Sobel, Dava. *Longitude: The True Story of a Lone Genius Who Solved the Greatest Scientific Problem of His Time*. New York: Walker & Company, 1995.

Stimson, Alan. *The Mariner's Astrolabe: A Survey of Known, Surviving Sea Astrolabes*. Utrecht: HES Publishers, 1988.

Taylor, E. G. R. *The Haven-Finding Art: A History of Navigation from Odysseus to Captain Cook*. New York: Abelard-Schuman, 1957.

Thomson, Don W. *Men and Meridians: The History of Surveying and Mapping in Canada*, vol. 1, *Prior to 1867*. Ottawa: Queen's Printer, 1966.

Up North: The Discovery and Mapping of the Canadian Arctic. Toronto: Royal Ontario Museum, 1958. An exhibition catalogue.

Vickers, Daniel. *Farmers and Fishermen: Two Centuries of Work in Essex County, Massachusetts, 1630–1850*. Chapel Hill, N.C.: University of North Carolina Press, 1994.

Wagner, Henry R. *Cartography of the Northwest Coast of America to the Year 1800*. Amsterdam: N. Israel, 1968.

Wallace, Frederick William. *Wooden Ships and Iron Men*. Belleville, Ont.: Mika Publishing Company, 1976.

Wallace, Hugh N. *The Navy, the Company, and Richard King: British Exploration in the Canadian Arctic, 1829–1860*. Montréal: McGill-Queen's University Press, 1980.

Waters, David W. *The Art of Navigation in England in Elizabethan and Early Stuart Times*. London: Hollis & Carter, 1958.

Webb, R. K. *Modern England from the 18th Century to the Present*. New York: Dodd, Mead & Company, 1975.

Whitfield, Peter. *The Charting of the Oceans: Ten Centuries of Maritime Maps*. London: British Library, 1996.

Williams, Alan F. *John Cabot and Newfoundland*. St John's: Newfoundland Historical Society, 1996.

Williams, J. E. D. *From Sails to Satellites: The Origin and Development of Navigational Science*. Oxford: Oxford University Press, 1994.

Williamson, James A. *The Cabot Voyages and Bristol Discovery under Henry VII*. Hakluyt Society, 2nd Series, No. 120. Cambridge: Cambridge University Press, 1962.

Wilson, Garth. *A History of Shipbuilding and Naval Architecture in Canada*. Transformation Series 4. Ottawa: National Museum of Science and Technology, 1994.

Zaslow, Morris. *The Opening of the Canadian North, 1870–1914*. Toronto: McClelland & Stewart, 1971.

Edited Volumes and Collected Works

Anderson, E. W. "Navigational Equipment." In *A History of Technology*, vol. 7, *The Twentieth Century, c. 1900 to c. 1950, Part II*, edited by Trevor I. Williams, 837–56. Oxford: Oxford University Press, 1978.

Andrew, David, ed. *The Charts and Coastal Views of Captain Cook's Voyages: The Voyages of the Endeavour, 1768–1771*. London: Hakluyt Society, 1988.

———. "Vancouver's Survey Methods and Surveys." In *From Maps to Metaphors: The Pacific World of George Vancouver*, edited by Robin Fisher and Hugh Johnston, 51–69. Vancouver: University of British Columbia Press, 1993.

Andrewes, W. H., ed. *The Quest for Longitude*. Cambridge, Mass.: Collection of Historical Scientific Instruments, 1996.

Baugh, Daniel A. " Seapower and Science: The Motives for Pacific Exploration." In *Scientific Aspects of European Exploration*, edited by William K. Storey, 85–139. Expanding World Series, vol. 6. Aldershot, U.K.: Variorum, 1996.

Bentley, Shannon, "Ship Registers and the Use of Flags." In *The Shipping Revolution: The Modern Merchant Ship*, edited by Alastair Couper, 192–6. Conway's History of the Ship, ed. Robert Gardiner. London: Conway Maritime Press, 1992.

Bogaard, Paul A., ed. *Profiles of Science and Society in the Maritimes prior to 1914*. Sackville, N.B.: Acadiensis Press and Centre for Canadian Studies, Mount Allison University, 1990.

Bonwick, George, ed. *Automation on Shipboard*. Proceedings of a conference held at Geneva by the International Institute of Labour Studies. London: Macmillan & Company, 1967.

Brooks, Randall C. "Time, Longitude Determination and Public Reliance upon Early Observatories." In *Profiles of Science and Society in the Maritimes prior to 1914*, edited by Paul A. Bogaard, 162–92. Sackville, N.B.: Acadiensis Press and Centre for Canadian Studies, Mount Allison University, 1990.

Cell, Gillian T. "The Cupids Cove Settlement: A Case Study of the Problems of Colonisation." In *Early European Settlement and Exploration in Atlantic Canada*, edited by G. M. Story, 97–114. St John's: Memorial University of Newfoundland, 1982.

Corbet, A. G. "Modern Merchant Ship Navigation." In *The Shipping Revolution: The Modern Merchant Ship*, edited by Alastair Couper, 177–83. Conway's History of the Ship, ed. Robert Gardiner. London: Conway Maritime Press, 1992.

Couper, Alastair. Introduction to *The Shipping Revolution: The Modern Merchant Ship*, edited by Alastair Couper, 7–11. Conway's History of the Ship, ed. Robert Gardiner. London: Conway Maritime Press, 1992.

———, ed. *The Shipping Revolution: The Modern Merchant Ship*, Conway's History of the Ship, ed. Robert Gardiner. London: Conway Maritime Press, 1992.

Cross, Captain Steven, and Bruce E. Marti. "Passenger Ships: Ferries and Cruise Ships." In *The Shipping Revolution: The Modern Merchant Ship*, edited by Alastair Couper, 84–102. Conway's History of the Ship, ed. Robert Gardiner. London: Conway Maritime Press, 1992.

De Vorsey, Louis. "Amerindian Contributions to the Mapping of North America: A Preliminary View." In *Scientific Aspects of European Exploration*, edited by William K. Storey, 211–8. Expanding World Series, vol. 6. Aldershot, U.K.: Variorum, 1996.

Dunn, Laurence. "Cargo Ships." In *The Golden Age of Shipping: The Classic Merchant Ship*, edited by Ambrose Greenway, 38–58. Conway's History of the Ship, ed. Robert Gardiner. London: Conway Maritime Press, 1994.

Easterbrook, W. T., and M. H. Watkins, eds. *Approaches to Canadian Economic History*. Toronto: Macmillan Company of Canada, 1978.

Fernandez-Armesto, Felipe, ed. *The European Opportunity*. Expanding World Series, vol. 2. Aldershot, U.K.: Variorum, 1995.

Fisher, Robin, and Hugh Johnston, eds. *From Maps to Metaphors: The Pacific World of George Vancouver*. Vancouver: University of British Columbia Press, 1993.

Fleming, D. K. "Modern Tramp Ships, Bulk Carriers and Combination Carriers." In *The Shipping Revolution: The Modern Merchant Ship*, edited by Alastair Couper, 12–31. Conway's History of the Ship, ed. Robert Gardiner. London: Conway Maritime Press, 1992.

Frost, Alan. "Science for Political Purposes: European Exploration of the Pacific Ocean, 1764–1806." In *Scientific Aspects of European Exploration*, edited by William K. Storey, 67–84. Expanding World Series, vol. 6. Aldershot, U.K.: Variorum, 1996.

Fuson, Robert. "The John Cabot Mystique." In *Essays on the History of North American Discovery and Exploration*, edited by Stanley H. Palmer and Dennis Reinhartz, 35–51. College Station, Tex.: Texas A&M University Press, 1988.

Gilchrist, John. "Exploration and Enterprise: The Newfoundland Fishery, c. 1497–1677." In David S. Macmillan, ed., *Canadian Business History Selected Studies, 1497–1971*, 7–26. Toronto: McClelland & Stewart, 1972.

Gilman, Sidney. "Container Shipping." In *The Shipping Revolution: The Modern Merchant Ship*, edited by Alastair Couper, 42–62. Conway's History of the Ship, ed. Robert Gardiner. London: Conway Maritime Press, 1992.

Greenway, Ambrose, ed. *The Golden Age of Shipping: The Classic Merchant Ship, 1900–1960*. Conway's History of the Ship, ed. Robert Gardiner. London: Conway Maritime Press, 1994.

———. Introduction to *The Golden Age of Shipping: The Classic Merchant Ship*, edited by Ambrose Greenway, 7–13. Conway's History of the Ship, ed. Robert Gardiner. London: Conway Maritime Press, 1994.

———. "Passenger Vessels." In *The Golden Age of Shipping: The Classic Merchant Ship*, edited by Ambrose Greenway, 14–37. Conway's History of the Ship, ed. Robert Gardiner. London: Conway Maritime Press, 1994.

Harley, J. B. "Silences and Secrets: The Hidden Agenda of Cartography in Early Modern Europe." In *Scientific Aspects of European Exploration*, edited by William K. Storey, 161–80. Expanding World Series, vol. 6. Aldershot, U.K.: Variorum, 1996.

Howse, Derek, ed. *Five Hundred Years of Nautical Science, 1400–1900*. Proceedings of the Third International Reunion for the History of Nautical Science and Hydrography. London: National Maritime Museum, 1981.

———. "The Lunar Distance Method of Measuring Longitude." In *The Quest for Longitude*, edited by W. H. Andrewes, 149–62. Cambridge, Mass.: Collection of Historical Scientific Instruments, 1996.

Kemp, Peter, ed. *The Oxford Companion to Ships and the Sea*. London: Oxford University Press, 1979.

Lahey, Raymond J. "Avalon: Lord Baltimore's Colony in Newfoundland." In *Early European Settlement and Exploration in Atlantic Canada*, edited by G. M. Story, 115–38. St John's: Memorial University of Newfoundland, 1982.

Lewis, G. Malcolm. "Indicators of Unacknowledged Assimilations from Amerindian Maps on Euro-American Maps of North America: Some General Principles Arising from the Study of La Verendrye's Composite Map, 1728–29." In *Scientific Aspects of European Exploration*, edited by William K. Storey, 219–46. Expanding World Series, vol. 6. Aldershot, U.K.: Variorum, 1996.

Mackintosh, W.A. "Economic Factors in Canadian History." In *Approaches to Canadian Economic History*, edited by W. T. Easterbrook and M. H. Watkins, 1–15. Toronto: Macmillan Company of Canada, 1978.

Maclennan, Graeme. "Marine Propulsion." In *The Golden Age of Shipping: The Classic Merchant Ship*, edited by Ambrose Greenway, 152–63. Conway's History of the Ship, ed. Robert Gardiner. London: Conway Maritime Press, 1994.

Macmillan, David S., ed. *Canadian Business History Selected Studies, 1497–1971*. Toronto: McClelland & Stewart, 1972.

Marcadon, Jacques. "Conventional General Cargo Liners and Refrigerated Ships." In *The Shipping Revolution: The Modern Merchant Ship*, edited by Alastair Couper, 32–41. Conway's History of the Ship, ed. Robert Gardiner. London: Conway Maritime Press, 1992.

Martijn, Charles A., ed. *Les Micmacs et la mer*. Montréal: Recherches amérindiennes au Québec, 1986.

Mathieu, Charles E. "Modern Merchant Ship Propulsion." In *The Shipping Revolution: The Modern Merchant Ship*, edited by Alastair Couper, 184–7. Conway's History of the Ship, ed. Robert Gardiner. London: Conway Maritime Press, 1992.

Mollat, Michel, ed. *Histoire de pêches maritimes en France*. Toulouse: Editions Privat, 1987.

Moskowitz, Saul. "The Method of Lunar Distances and Technological Advance." In *Three Studies in the History of Celestial Navigation*, 101–21. Marblehead, Mass.: History of Technology Press, 1974.

Palmer, Stanley H., and Dennis Reinhartz, eds. *Essays on the History of North American Discovery and Exploration*. College Station, Tex.: Texas A&M University Press, 1988.

Pope, Peter. "Early Estimates: Assessment of Catches in the Newfoundland Cod Fishery, 1660–1690." In Daniel Vickers, ed., *Marine Resources and Human Societies in the North Atlantic since 1500*, 7–40. ISER Conference Paper Number 5. St John's: Memorial University of Newfoundland, Institute of Social and Economic Research, 1995.

Pritchard, James S. "French Charting of the East Coast of Canada" In *Five Hundred Years of Nautical Science, 1400–1900*, edited by Derek Howse, 119–29. Proceedings of the Third International Reunion for the History of Nautical Science and Hydrography. London: National Maritime Museum, 1981.

Quinn, David B. *New American World: A Documentary History of North America to 1612*, vol. 4, *Newfoundland from Fishery to Colony: Northwest Passage Searches*. New York: Arno Press, 1979.

———. "Newfoundland in the Consciousness of Europe in the Sixteenth and Early Seventeenth Centuries." In *Early European Settlement and Exploration in Atlantic Canada*, edited by G. M. Story, 9–30. St John's: Memorial University of Newfoundland, 1982.

———. ed. *North American Discovery circa 1000–1612*. Columbia, S.C.: University of South Carolina Press, 1971.

———. *The Voyages and Colonising Enterprises of Sir Humphrey Gilbert*. Nendeln/Liechtenstein: Kraus Reprint, 1967. Originally published by the Hakluyt Society, 1940.

Storey, William K., ed. *Scientific Aspects of European Exploration*. Expanding World series, vol. 6. Aldershot, U.K: Variorum, 1996.

Story, G. M., ed. *Early European Settlement and Exploration in Atlantic Canada*. St John's: Memorial University of Newfoundland, 1982.

Strange, J. "Oil Tankers, Chemical Carriers and Gas Carriers." In *The Shipping Revolution: The Modern Merchant Ship*, edited by Alastair Couper, 63–83. Conway's History of the Ship, ed. Robert Gardiner. London: Conway Maritime Press, 1992.

Turgeon, Laurier. "Le temps des pêches lointaines. Permanences et transformations (vers 1500–vers 1850)." In *Histoire de pêches maritimes en France*, edited by Michel Mollat, 133–81. Toulouse: Editions Privat, 1987.

Vancouver, George. *A Voyage of Discovery to the North Pacific Ocean and Round the World, 1791–1795*, vol. 1. Edited by W. Kaye Lamb. London: Hakluyt Society, 1984.

Vickers, Daniel, ed. *Marine Resources and Human Societies in the North Atlantic since 1500*. ISER Conference Paper 5. St John's: Memorial University of Newfoundland, Institute of Social and Economic Research, 1995.

Wallace, Brigitta L. "The L'Anse aux Meadows Site." In *The Norse Atlantic Saga*, edited by G. Jones, 285–304. Oxford: Oxford University Press, 1986.

Waters, D. W. "Science and the Techniques of Navigation in the Renaissance." In *Art, Science, and History in the Renaissance*, edited by Charles S. Singleton, 189–237. Baltimore: Johns Hopkins Press, 1967.

Watson, P. B. "Bulk Cargo Carriers." In *The Golden Age of Shipping: The Classic Merchant Ship*, edited by Ambrose Greenway, 61–80. Conway's History of the Ship, ed. Robert Gardiner. London: Conway Maritime Press, 1994.

Williams, Trevor I., ed. *A History of Technology*, vol. 7, *The Twentieth Century, c. 1900 to c. 1950, Part 2*. Oxford: Oxford University Press, 1978.

Woodman, Richard "Navigation 1900–1960." In *The Golden Age of Shipping: The Classic Merchant Ship*, edited by Ambrose Greenway, 175–80. Conway's History of the Ship, ed. Robert Gardiner. London: Conway Maritime Press, 1994.

Journal Articles

General

Bennett, J. A. "Science Lost and Longitude Found: The Tercentenary of John Harrison." *Journal of the History of Astronomy* 24, no. 77 (November 1993): 281–7.

Brooks, Randall C. "Nautical Instrument-Makers in Atlantic Canada." *Nova Scotia Historical Review* 6, no. 2 (1986): 36–54.

Casey, M. J. "The *Asia* Tragedy." *Lighthouse*. No volume, no number, no date, no page numbers. Published in Burlington, Ont., by the Canadian Hydrographers' Association.

Copley, Jon. "Pinpoint Precision." *New Scientist* 159, no. 2151 (12 September 1998): 22.

Farrell, David. " Keeping the Local Economy Afloat: Canadian Pacific Navigation and Shipowning in Victoria, 1883–1901." *The Northern Mariner* 6, no. 1 (January 1996): 31, 40–1.

Glover, William. "The Challenge of Navigation to Hydrography on the British Columbia Coast, 1850–1930." *The Northern Mariner* 6, no. 4 (October 1996): 1–16

Jackson, Ian. "A Bearing on Good Fortune." *Geographical* (November 1993): 10–12.

Kelley, James E. Jr. "The Distortions of Sixteenth-Century Maps of America." *Cartographica* 32, no. 4 (Winter 1995): 1–13.

Maddison, Francis. "On the Origin of the Mariner's Astrolabe." *Sphæra*, Occasional Papers 2. Oxford: Museum of the History of Science, 1997.

Meehan, O. M. *The Canadian Hydrographic Service from the Time of Its Inception in 1883 to the End of the Second World War*. Edited by William Glover with David Gray in *The Northern Mariner* 14, no. 1 (January 2004): 1–158.

Mercer, F. A., and Kevin Haydon. "Finding the Longitude: The Trials and Rewards of John Harrison, the Inventor of the Marine Chronometer." *Sea History* 66 (Summer 1993): 22–3.

Moskowitz, Saul. "The World's First Sextants." *Navigation* 34, no. 1 (Spring 1987): 22–42.

Sandilands, R. W. "Charting the Beaufort Sea." *Lighthouse*, no. 24 (November 1981): 10.

———. "The History of Hydrographic Surveying in British Columbia." *The Canadian Cartographer* 7, no. 2 (December 1970): 105–15.

———. "Hydrographic Surveying in the Great Lakes during the Nineteenth Century." *The Canadian Surveyor* 36, no. 2 (June 1982): 139–63.

Smith, Julian A. "Charles Potter, Optician and Instrument Maker." *Journal of the Royal Astronomical Society of Canada* 87, no. 1 [640] (February 1993): 14–33.

Sorrenson, Richard. "The Ship as a Scientific Instrument in the Eighteenth Century." *OSIRIS* 2nd series, 11 (1996): 221–36.

Tanod, Lynn, and Chris Jaksa. "Keepers of the Light." *Explore* 81 (October/November 1996): 26–32.

Topham, W. R. "A Re-discovered Chronometer Maker: Richard U. Marsters." *NAWCC Bulletin* (August 1987): 269–75.

Turgeon, Laurier. "Pour redécouvrir notre 16e siècle: les pêches à Terre-Neuve d'apres les archives notariales de Bordeaux." *Revue d'Histoire de l'Amerique Française* 39 (1986): 523–49.

Whiteley, William. "James Cook and British Policy in the Newfoundland Fisheries, 1763–7." *Canadian Historical Review* 54, no. 3 (September 1973): 245–72.

Whitfield, Peter. "Portolan Reflections." *Mercator's World*, November/December 1998, 17–63.

Maritime Industry Journals

"B.C. Ferries Business Is Almost Too Good." *Canadian Shipping and Marine Engineering News* 36, no. 9 (June 1965): 83.

Bier, R. "Efficient Communications at Sea." *Shipping World and Shipbuilder* 164, no. 3859 (July 1971): 789.

"Bridge-to-Bridge Radiotelephones — New USA legislation." *Shipping World and Shipbuilder* 165, no. 3868 (April 1972): 525.

Brogdon, Bill. "A History of Range Lights." *Professional Mariner* 3 (October/November, 1993): 60–3.

"Canada Probably *Can* Support Six Container Ports." *Canadian Transportation and Distribution Management* 75, no. 6 (June 1972): 14, 17–8.

"Canadian Government Radio Direction Finding Stations." *Canadian Railway and Marine World*, August 1923, 407–8.

Cockcroft, Captain A. N., et al. "The Compulsory Fitting of Seaborne Radar Collision Avoidance Systems, A Discussion." *Journal of Navigation* 33, no. 3 (1980): 389–97.

"Containerization Reduces Costs." *Canadian Shipping and Marine Engineering News* 36, no. 8 (May 1965): 28–9.

"A Decade of Achievement: The Activities of IMCO 1960–1970." *Shipping World and Shipbuilder* 164, no. 3853 (January 1971): 81–5.

"Examinations for Certificates of Sea-Going Masters and Mates." *Canadian Railway and Marine World*, September 1936, 441.

Healy, Nicholas J., and Joseph C. Sweeney. *The Law of Marine Collision.* Centreville, Md.: Cornell Maritime Press, 1988. Excerpt that appeared in *Professional Mariner* 35 (October/November 1998): 64–9.

Hempstead, Christian. "ECDIS Is a Powerful Navigation Tool But Requires Solid Training." *Professional Mariner* 66 (September 2002): 24.

Kouyoumjian, Joel N. "Correspondence." *Professional Mariner* 75 (October/November 2003): 62.

Macphail, J. G. "The Lighthouse Service of Canada." *Engineering Journal*, August 1931, 446–51.

Manning, W. J. "How Marine Works Branch Functions." *Canadian Shipping and Marine Engineering News* 35, no. 11 (August 1964): 64.

McKenna, Robert. "VTS Takes On a Life of Its Own." *Professional Mariner* 3 (October/November 1993): 46–50.

"Navigation." *Shipping World and Shipbuilder* 198, no. 4136 (September 1997): 10.

"Navigation by Satellite." *Shipping World and Shipbuilder* 64, no. 3855 (March 1971): 351.

"Navigation News." *Shipping World and Shipbuilder* 178, no. 3997 (June 1983): 333.

"The 100,000th Container through Halifax." *Canadian Transportation and Distribution Management* 75, no. 6 (June 1972): 46.

"Ontario to Provide Marine School." *Canadian Shipping and Marine Engineering News* 36, no. 4 (January 1965): 18–9.

Parkinson, Bradford W. "History and Operation of NAVSTAR, the Global Positioning System." *IEEE Transactions on Aerospace and Electronic Systems* 30, no. 1 (January 1994): 1145–61.

Piercy, B. C. "Radar Collision Avoidance Equipment." *Shipping World and Shipbuilder* 165, no. 3865 (January 1972): 67–70.

"Product Report, New on the Market." *Professional Mariner* 24 (April/May 1997): 80.

Queeney, Tim. "Issues Facing Raster Charts." *Professional Mariner* 25 (June/July 1997): 54–5.

———. "Marine Technology." *Professional Mariner* 37 (December/January, 1999): 69–71.

———. "Satcom Options Increase." *Professional Mariner* 29 (December/January 1998): 61–2.

———. "Solar Power." *Professional Mariner* 8 (August/September 1994): 56–9.

———. "Using Differential GPS to Upgrade VTS Systems." *Professional Mariner* 1 (June/July 1993): 12–5.

Quon, Tony K. S. "Risk Analysis of Vessel Traffic Systems." *Maritime Policy Management* 19, no. 4 (1992): 319–36.

"Radar Navigation Course Offered in Nova Scotia." *Canadian Shipping and Marine Engineering News* 36, no. 1 (October 1964): 74.

"Radio Aids to Navigation." *Canadian Railway and Marine World*, August 1936, 394.

"Seaway: Long-Range Plans Depend on Traffic Developments." *Canadian Transportation and Distribution Management* 75, no. 8 (August 1972): 24, 28.

"The Shrinking American Tanker Fleet." *Professional Mariner* 14 (August/September 1995): 27–30.

Smith, Glyn. "Manufacturers Await IMO Performance Standards." *Shipping World and Shipbuilder* 179, no. 4002 (December 1983): 659–63.

Swann, Captain L. J., and Barry Ridgewell. "Study to Set Standards Suggested." *Offshore Resources* 4/5 (September/October 1984): 14.

Wash, Greg. "Tracking Traffic in New York." *Professional Mariner* 1 (June/July 1993): 51–7.

Worster, Jennifer. "More Synthetic Buoys Urged for U.S. Coastline." *Professional Mariner* 10 (December/January 1995): 68–70.

Other

Howard, Ross. "Why He's Still a Keeper of the Flame." *Toronto Globe and Mail*, 20 April 1998.

Dictionaries, Encyclopedias, and Atlases

Burghardt, Andrew F. "Emergence of a Transportation System, 1837–1852." Plate 25 in *Historical Atlas of Canada*. Vol. 2, *The Land Transformed, 1800–1891*, edited by R. Louis Gentilcore. Toronto: University of Toronto Press, 1993.

The Canadian Encyclopaedia, 2nd ed. Edmonton: Hurtig Publishers, 1988. s.v. "Canadian Coast Guard," "Fisheries History," "Thunder Bay."

Cornell, Paul G. "Owen, William Fitzwilliam." In *Dictionary of Canadian Biography*, vol. 8, edited by Francess G. Halpenny. Toronto: University of Toronto Press, 1985.

Dixon, Bernard, Dougal Dixon, Linda Gamlin, Iain Nicolson, and Candida Hunt, eds. *The Encyclopedic Dictionary of Science*. New York: Facts on File Publications, 1988. s.v. "Gyroscope."

Galois, R. M., and R. Cole Harris. "The Gold Rushes in British Columbia, 1858–1881." Plate 36 in *Historical Atlas of Canada*. Vol. 2, *The Land Transformed, 1800–1891*, edited by R. Louis Gentilcore. Toronto: University of Toronto Press, 1993.

Gentilcore, R Louis, ed. *Historical Atlas of Canada*. Vol. 2, *The Land Transformed, 1800–1891*. Toronto: University of Toronto Press, 1993.

Head, C. Grant "Economies in Transition." In *Historical Atlas of Canada*. Vol. 2, *The Land Transformed, 1800–1891*, edited by R. Louis Gentilcore, 95–7. Toronto: University of Toronto Press, 1993.

Head, C. Grant, Rosemary E. Ommer, and Patricia A. Thornton. "Canadian Fisheries, 1850–1900." Plate 37 in *Historical Atlas of Canada*. Vol. 2, *The Land Transformed, 1800–1891*, edited by R. Louis Gentilcore. Toronto: University of Toronto Press, 1993.

Kerr, Donald, and Deryck W. Holdsworth, eds. *The Historical Atlas of Canada*. Vol. 3, *Addressing the Twentieth Century, 1891–1961*. Toronto: University of Toronto Press, 1990.

McGraw-Hill Yearbook of Science and Technology 1994. New York: McGraw-Hill, 1993. s.v. "Satellite Navigation Systems."

McInnis, Marvin. "Economic Growth." Plate 3 in *The Historical Atlas of Canada*. Vol. 3, *Addressing the Twentieth Century, 1891–1961*, edited by Donald Kerr and Deryck W. Holdsworth. Toronto: University of Toronto Press, 1990.

McKenzie, Ruth. "Bayfield, Henry Wolsey." In *Dictionary of Canadian Biography*, vol. 11, *1881 to 1890*, edited by Francess G. Halpenny. Toronto: University of Toronto Press, 1982.

Ommer, Rosemary E. "Ships and Shipping, 1863–1914." Plate 39 in *Historical Atlas of Canada*. Vol. 2, *The Land Transformed, 1800–1891*, edited by R. Louis Gentilcore. Toronto: University of Toronto Press, 1993.

Osborne, Brian S. "Expanding Economies." In *Historical Atlas of Canada*. Vol. 2, *The Land Transformed, 1800–1891*, edited by R. Louis Gentilcore, 33–5. Toronto: University of Toronto Press, 1993.

Osborne, Brian S., Jean-Claude Robert, and David A. Sutherland. "Population in the Canadas and the Maritimes to 1851." Plate 10 in *Historical Atlas of Canada*. Vol. 2, *The Land Transformed, 1800–1891*, edited by R. Louis Gentilcore. Toronto: University of Toronto Press, 1993.

Paton, Jennifer. "Willson, Thomas Leopold." In *Dictionary of Canadian Biography*, vol. 14, *1911 to 1920*, edited by Ramsay Cook. Toronto: University of Toronto Press, 1998.

Richtik, James A., and Don Measner. "Homesteading and Agriculture in the West, 1872–1891." Plate 42 in *Historical Atlas of Canada*. Vol. 2, *The Land Transformed, 1800–1891*, edited by R. Louis Gentilcore. Toronto: University of Toronto Press, 1993.

Robert, Jean-Claude, Normand Séguin, and Serge Courville (seigneurial land rents). "An Established Agriculture: Lower Canada to 1851." Plate 13 in *Historical Atlas of Canada*. Vol. 2, *The Land Transformed, 1800–1891*, edited by R. Louis Gentilcore. Toronto: University of Toronto Press, 1993.

Sutherland, David A. "International Trade to 1891." Plate 43 in *Historical Atlas of Canada*. Vol. 2, *The Land Transformed, 1800–1891*, edited by R. Louis Gentilcore. Toronto: University of Toronto Press, 1993.

———. "Trade to Mid-century." Plate 15 in *Historical Atlas of Canada*. Vol. 2, *The Land Transformed, 1800–1891*, edited by R. Louis Gentilcore. Toronto: University of Toronto Press, 1993.

Tver, David F. *The Norton Encyclopedic Dictionary of Navigation*. New York: W. W. Norton & Company, 1987.

Walder, Ronald H., and David A. Sutherland (Maritime shipbuilding). "By Hand and By Water: Manufacturing to 1851." Plate 16 in *Historical Atlas of Canada*. Vol. 2, *The Land Transformed, 1800–1891*, edited by R. Louis Gentilcore. Toronto: University of Toronto Press, 1993.

Wood, David J., Peter Ennals (Hamilton Township), and Thomas E. McIlwraith (cleared land, 1842). "A New Agriculture: Upper Canada to 1851." Plate 14 in *Historical Atlas of Canada*. Vol. 2, *The Land Transformed, 1800–1891*, edited by R. Louis Gentilcore. Toronto: University of Toronto Press, 1993.

World Almanac and Book of Facts. Mahwah, N.J.: World Almanac Books, 1998.

Wynn, Graeme. "Timber Production and Trade to 1850." Plate 11 in *Historical Atlas of Canada*. Vol. 2, *The Land Transformed, 1800–1891*, edited by R. Louis Gentilcore. Toronto: University of Toronto Press, 1993.

Guides, Handbooks, Textbooks, and Bibliographies

Anderson, E. W. *The Principles of Navigation*. London: Hollis & Carter, 1966.

Burger, W. *Radar Observer's Handbook for Merchant Navy Officers*, 5th ed. Glasgow: Brown, Son & Ferguson, 1975.

Campbell, John F. *History and Bibliography of* The New American Practical Navigator *and* The American Coast Pilot. Salem, Mass.: Peabody Museum, 1964.

Dutton, Benjamin. *Navigation and Nautical Astronomy*. Annapolis, Md.: United States Naval Institute, 1942.

Findlay, Alexander. *A Description and List of the Lighthouses of the World, 1861*. London: Richard Holmes Laurie, 1861.

Fisher, William, and John Thornton. *The English Pilot: The Fourth Book*. Reprint published by Theatrum Orbis Terrarum, 1967. Originally published in London, 1689.

Hall, John S., ed. *Radar Aids to Navigation*. New York: McGraw-Hill Book Company, 1947.

Hewson, Commander J. B. *A History of the Practice of Navigation*. Glasgow: Brown, Son & Ferguson, 1983.

Loomis, Harvey B., ed. *Navigation*. New York: Time-Life Books, 1975.

McNally, John St Vincent. *Seamanship Examiner and Instructor of Masters and Mates for the Marine Board Examination in Canada*. Saint John, N.B.: Barnes & Company, 1873.

Nicholls, A. E. *Nicholls's Seamanship and Viva Voce Guide*. Glasgow: James Brown & Son, 1913.

Nicholson, N. L., and L. M. Sebert. *The Maps of Canada: A Guide to Official Canadian Maps, Charts, Atlases and Gazetteers*. Folkestone, U.K.: Wm. Dawson & Sons, 1981.

Noll, Edward M. *Radio Transmitter Principles and Projects*. Indianapolis: Howard M. Sams & Company, 1973.

Savet, Paul H., ed. *Gyroscopes: Theory and Design with Application to Instrumentation, Guidance, and Control*. New York: McGraw-Hill Book Company, 1961.

Skelton, R. A., and R. V. Tooley. *The Marine Surveys of James Cook in North America, 1758–1768, Particularly the Survey of Newfoundland: A Bibliography of Printed Charts and Sailing Directions*. London: Map Collectors' Circle, 1967.

Wallis, Helen M., and Arthur H. Robinson, eds. *Cartographical Innovations: An International Handbook of Mapping Terms to 1900.* Tring, U.K.: Map Collectors Publication, 1982.

Weems, P. V. H. *Marine Navigation.* New York: D. Van Nostrand Company, 1943.

Wharton, Rear Admiral Sir William. *Hydrographical Surveying: A Description of the Means and Methods Employed in Constructing Marine Charts*, 2nd rev. ed. London: John Murray, 1898.

Theses, Unpublished Papers, and Reports

Baugh, Daniel A. "The Sea-Trial of John Harrison's Chronometer, 1736." Source unknown.

Bosher, J. F. "What Was 'Mercantilism' in the Age of New France?" Paper originally read at a conference at the University of Ottawa, 3 November 1989.

Brooks, Randall. "Report on Selected Marine Navigational Instruments." Prepared for National Museum of Science and Technology (now the CSTM), July 1990.

Haslam, Rear Admiral D. W. "The British Contribution to the Hydrography of Canada." Unpublished and unpaginated paper provided by Ed Dahl, formerly of the National Archives of Canada.

McGee, David. "Marine Engineering in Canada: An Historical Assessment." Report written for the National Museum of Science and Technology, now Canada Science and Technology Museum (CSTM), 1997. Available in CSTM Library.

Meehan, O. M. *The Canadian Hydrographic Service: A Chronology of Its Early History between the Years 1883 and 1947.* Unpublished manuscript, quoted in Stanley Fillmore and R. W. Sandilands, *The Chartmakers: A History of Nautical Surveying in Canada.* Toronto: NC Press, 1983.

Nicholls, Robert. "Mobility Canada: An Historical Perspective, 1825–1975." Unpublished report dated Montréal, 1978. Available in CSTM Library.

Pope, Peter E. "The South Avalon Planters, 1630 to 1700: Residence, Labour, Demand and Exchange in Seventeenth Century Newfoundland." DPhil thesis, Memorial University of Newfoundland, 1992.

Pritchard, James S. "Ships, Men and Commerce: A Study of Maritime Activity in New France." Unpublished PhD thesis, University of Toronto, 1971.

Ritchie, G. S. "500 Years of Graphical and Symbolic Representation on Marine Charts." Paper presented to the International Hydrographic Organization Sixth International Conference on the History of Cartography, 1975.

Schilder, Gunther. "Development and Achievements of Dutch Northern and Arctic Cartography in the 16th and 17th Centuries." Unpublished paper/presentation, 1981.

Walker, David. "A Survey of Major Technological Developments in Canadian Marine Transportation from the Earliest Times to the Present." Unpublished research report for Curator of Transportation, Canada Science and Technology Museum, circa 1990.

Government Publications

Annual Reports

The most important sources of information on marine matters in Canada from Confederation to the present day are the annual reports of the federal departments responsible. These include Marine and Fisheries (1867 to 1884 and 1892 to 1930), Marine (1884 to 1892 and 1930 to 1936), Transport (1936 to the present), and Fisheries and Oceans (1995 to the present). In 1995, the Canadian Coast Guard and the aids to navigation program were moved to Fisheries and Oceans while shipping regulation remained with Transport. Responsibility for radio communication and navigation also resided in different departments over time, including the Naval Service, Transport, and Communications.

I consulted most of the twentieth-century reports up to the late 1960s and two nineteenth-century reports — for 1872 and 1884. Those that I used extensively or from which I quoted directly are cited in the endnotes.

Journals and Statutes

Canada. Canada Shipping Act, Chap. 44, 24–25 Geo. V. 1934, pp. 269–450.

———. *Journals of the House of Assembly of the Province of Canada, 1858*, App. 38, Return to an Address from the Legislative Assembly of the 19th April, 1858.

———. *Journals of the Legislative Assembly of the Province of Canada 1857*, App. 19, General Report of the Commissioners of Public Works.

Lower Canada. *Report of the Special Committee of the House of Assembly of Lower-Canada on the Petition of the Merchants, Ship-owners, Masters of Vessels and Pilots, with an instruction to enquire in the expediency of erecting Lighthouses on the St. Lawrence.* Quebec: House of Assembly, 1829.

———. *Statutes*, 45 Geo. III, cap. 12.

Other

Canada. Department of Marine and Fisheries. *Canada: Her Natural Resources, Navigation, Principal Steamer Lines and Transcontinental Railways.* 12th Congress of the Permanent International Association of Navigational Congresses. Compiled, arranged, and edited by William W. Stumbles. Ottawa: Government Printing Bureau, 1912.

Canada. Department of Transport. *List of Ships.* Vol. 2, *Fishing Vessels on Register in Canada 1997.* Ottawa: Department of Transport, 1998.

———. *Transportation in Canada Annual Report.* Ottawa: Public Works and Government Services Canada, 1999.

Canada. Director of Merchant Seamen. *Training for the Merchant Navy.* Ottawa: King's Printer, 1942.

Canada. Fisheries and Oceans Canada. *Global Marine Distress and Safety System.* Ottawa: Minister of Public Works and Government Services Canada, 1997.

Canada. Statistics Canada. Transportation Division, Multimodal Transport Section. *Shipping in Canada, 1995.* Ottawa: Statistics Canada, 1997.

Canadian Coast Guard, Laurentian Region. "History of Telecommunication and Electronics." Unpublished report, 1982.

Chambers, Captain Ernest J. *The Canadian Marine: A History of the Department of Marine and Fisheries.* Toronto: Canadian Marine and Fisheries History, 1905.

CSTM **Documents and Files**

Canada Science and Technology Museum. "Collection Development Strategy." November 2000.

Curator's Files, Transportation Subject Area

Files relating to the acquisition of the first Canadian Vessel Traffic Services Centre. These include the acquisition proposal as well as correspondence relating to the acquisition between L. Barker to G. Wilson, 1992.

Files relating to the acquisition of the Precise Integrated Navigational System (PINS) for Offshore Systems Ltd., including the acquisition proposal and background articles such as Robert G. Lyall and David G. Michelson, "Automatic Radar Positioning Systems: A New Era in Radar Navigation."

Files supplied by Charles Maginley, including copies of pamphlets on GPS and GMDSS, Department of Transport, draft press releases, 20 October and 8 December 1956, and an unpublished Canadian Coast Guard report written by P. F. Boisvert, "The Life of a Lightship," 7 January 1978.

Interviews

Over the course of my research on the recent history of marine navigation in Canada I contacted a number of people who supplied me with information on two main subjects: the recent history of aids to navigation in Canada and current government policy regarding navigational instruction, education, and certification in Canada.

Aids to Navigation

I spoke to a number of officials at the Canadian Coast Guard, Fisheries and Oceans, and Transport Canada in 1998–99 and again in 2004 when completing revisions to the manuscript. These included:

Mike Clements, Canadian Coast Guard, 9 June 2004.

Ben Hutchin, Canadian Coast Guard, 9 June 2004.

Charles Maginley, Canadian Coast Guard, 9 March 1999.

Val Smith, Standards Officer, Long Range Aids to Navigation, Canadian Coast Guard, 9 March 1999.

Education and Certification

I spoke to and interviewed electronically staff at the Nautical Institute of the Nova Scotia Community College. My contacts there were Peter Dunford, Director of Marine Training, and Mike Kruger, Marine Navigation Instructor.

Other

I also spoke to a communications officer with BC Ferries regarding the current status of their fleet and its growth in recent years.

Websites

I consulted a large number of websites both national and international in my search for reliable and current information on marine navigation. Because these consultations took place over the course of several years, I cannot be certain that electronic addresses have not changed or that articles once posted have since been removed or significantly revised. Some of my electronic sources, most notably the Canadian Hydrographic Service's newsletter *Contour*, are probably available in printed form through interlibrary loan services.

During the course of this project I also subscribed to a marine listserv operated by the Canadian Coast Guard, where I followed the wide-ranging discussions of experienced mariners — masters, mates, pilots, and others. They debated everything from the latest technology to changes to certification and international maritime policy and regulations.

Canadian Coast Guard

Coast Guard College website,
www.cgc.ns.ca/~jim/stndcomm/stndcomm.htm

"Differential Global Positioning System," www.ccg-gcc.gc.ca

"Service Profile 96 — Commercial Fishing Industry, Ferry Services, Recreational Boating," www.ccg-gcc.gc.ca

Canadian Hydrographic Service

CHS website. www.chs-shc.dfo-mpo.gc.ca

Contour Articles

Casey, M. J. "Hey! Why Is My Ship Showing Up On the Dock?" *Contour*, Fall 1996.

Goodyear, Julian, Scott Strong, and Captain Andrew Rae. "Confined Waterways — A Challenge." *Contour*, Fall 1996.

Gundersrud, Olaf. "DNV Nautical Safety Class." *Contour*, Fall 1996.

"IEC Test Standards/Procedures for ECDIS." *Contour*, Fall 1996.

Terry, Brian. "NDI's New Products." *Contour*, Fall 1996.

Terry, Brian, and Stephen MacPhee. "Public/Private Sector Partnership in Electronic Charting." *Contour*, Fall 1996.

Transport Canada

Transport Canada website, www.tc.gc.ca/cmac/documents/ecdisvisione.htm

Marine Safety Directorate, Simulated Electronic Navigation Courses (TP 4958E), 2000, www.tc.gc.ca/marinesafety/tp/tp4958/tp4958e.htm

Nautical Schools

British Columbia Institute of Technology, www.transportation.bcit.ca/marine/index.html

Camosun College, www.camosum.bc.ca/schools/tradesntech/nautical/index.htm

L'Institut maritime du Québec, www.imq.qc.ca/eng/careers/naviga_a.htm

Memorial University of Newfoundland, www.mi.mun.ca

Nautical Institute at Nova Scotia Community College, www.nscc.ns.ca/marine/Nautical/index.html

Other

In researching navigational instrument makers in Canada in the nineteenth century, I consulted a number of directories for port cities including Halifax, Saint John, St John's, Québec, Montréal, Kingston, Toronto, and Victoria. I began with the 1850s and worked forward to the 1890s, selecting one or two volumes for each decade as available. The directories I used included *McAlpine's*, *Hutchinson's*, and *Lovell's*.

Index

An italic page number indicates that the item appears only in a figure. The letter "n" following a page number indicates that the item is in a note: e.g., 34n65 indicates that the item is in note 65 on page 34.

Acadia, HMS, *110*
accidents
    See also safety, marine
    impact on education and training, 46
    loss statistics (1836), 42
    risk of, 83–84
Admiralty. *See* Royal Navy
agriculture, 12, 41–42, 44, 45
aids to navigation
    See also beacons; buoys; leading marks; lighthouses; lightships; seamarks
    Canadian, 30–32, 66–73, 123–32
    early, 2, 7, 28–32
    land-based, 28–32, 60–63, 66, 67–73, 117–34, 142
    responsibility for in Canada, 30–32, 40, 42–43, 45–46, 60, 66–67, 87–89, 123–24
    technological advances, 30–32, 60–66, 117–23, 141–42
    two-way, 96–109. *See also* Electronic Chart Display Information System (ECDIS); hyperbolic navigation; integrated navigational systems; radar; radio; satellite navigation systems
air horns, compressed, 132
    See also fog signals
Airy, G. B., 50
Allied Submarine Detection Investigation Committee (Asdic), 94–95
    See also depth measurement; sonar
Amadi, Giovanni, 66
Amoco Cadiz, 84
Anschütz-Kaempfer, Hermann, 93
Arctic, exploration and charting
    eighteenth century, 11, 13, 14, 23
    nineteenth century, 54, 57–58
Arctic Waters Pollution Prevention Act, 89
Argand, Ami, 31
Arnold, John, 49
Arrow, 84
Asia, 59
astrolabe, 14–15
astronomical navigation. *See* celestial navigation
astronomy, marine navigation and, 14–21, 48
Atlantic Neptune (DesBarres), 24
atlases, 22, 24
automatic radar plotting aids (ARPAs), 105
automation
    aids to navigation, 117, 120–24
    cargo-handling, 82–83, 85
    hydrographic surveys, 110–11, 113
    lighthouses, 89, 118–19, 124–25, 129–30, 143
    Loran C, 107
    radar plotting, 105

Back, George, 57
back-staff, 16–17
    See also Davis, John

Baffin, William, 11
Balboa, Vasco Núñez, 8
Bayfield, Henry Wolsey, 24, 40, 42, 54–57
BC Ferries, 85–86
beacons
    Canadian use of, 71, 72, 130
    construction of, 64–65
    directional, 101
    early, 28
    lighting of, 121–22
    radar, 123, 131
    radio, 102, 103
bearing. *See* direction finding
Beechey, Frederick, 57
Bering, Vitus, 13
Berthoud, Louis, 49
binnacle, 50
    See also compass
Bird, John, 17
Blaeu, W. J., 23
Blunt, Edward March, 54
Bordier-Marcet, J. A., 61
bottom log, 95–96. *See also* log
Boulton, John George, 59–60, 109
boundary disputes, 40, 53, 54–55, 58–59
Breguet, Abraham-Louis, 49
British Columbia
    aids to navigation, 67, 68, 69, *70*, 71, 133
    exploration and economic development, 13–14, 44–45, 85–86
    hydrographic surveys, 24–27, 58–59, 60, *110*
    lighthouses, *70*, 71, 125, 126, *127*
    radar, 133
British Columbia Institute of Technology (BCIT), 92
British Empire Loyalists, 39, 40
British North America Act of 1867, 89
Brown, S. G., 94
Brulé, Etienne, 12–13
Bullock, Frederick, 54
buoy tenders, 87–88, *121*, *131*
buoys
    acetylene, 118, 119–21, *122*, 130
    audible or sound, 64, 122–23
    Canadian, 30, 64, *65*, 71–72, 130–32
    design and construction of, 28–29, 64, 77n150, *122*, 131–32
    early, 28–29, 30
    identification of, 65–66, 71–72
    illumination of, *65*, 118, 119–22, 130
    spar, 77n150
    wreck markers, 71
Button, Thomas, 11
Bylot, Robert, 11

Cabot, John (Zuan Caboto), 8, 15, 21, 22, 28
Cabot, Sebastian, 8, 10
Cabot Strait, 42, 66
cairns, 28, 29
Camosun College, 92
Campbell, John, 17, 19, 34n65
Canada Shipping Act (1906), 89–90
Canadian Coast Guard, 86–87, 88, 99, 109

157

Canadian Coast Guard College, 91–92
Canadian Ferry Operators' Association, 86
Canadian Hydrographic Service, 59, 109, 110, 111, 115
Canadian Merchant Navy, 90, 91
Canadian Pacific Railway, 45, 105
canals and channels, 42, 43, 45, 86
Cape Breton Island, 24, 56
cargo ships (twentieth-century), 87–88
cargo-handling, 82–83, 85, 86
Caribou, MV, 113
Cartier, Jacques, 9, *10*, 21, 22, 30
cartography, 22–25, 35n85, 66, 35n93
    See also charts and charting; hydrography
Cassini de Thury, Jacques-Dominique, 19
celestial navigation, 1, 10, 14–20, 24, 25, 34n51, 46–48, 54, 92, 143
certification, mariner, 46–48, 90, 92, 93
    See also education and training, mariner
Champlain, Samuel de, 11, 12, 23
charts and charting, 1, 2, 7, 14, 21–27, 52–60, *97*, *98*, 109–16, 143
    See also cartography; hydrography; surveys, hydrographic
Chernikeeff, Captain, 95
children, employment at sea, 84, 89
chip log, 21–22
    See also log; speed, measurement of
chronometer
    Canadian maker, 52
    invention and refinement, 19–20, 35n72–74, 48, 49, 75n65
    use in hydrographical surveys, 25, 57, 109
Churchill, Manitoba, *85*
Civil War, United States, and demand for ships, 45
Coast Guard Watchkeeping Certificate, 92
coastal navigation, definition, 1
cod fishery. *See* fishery, Newfoundland
Cold War, impact on navigational technology, 108
collision avoidance systems, 104–5
    See also radar
collisions
    radar-assisted and resulting regulations, 104–6
    traffic management systems resulting from, 132–34
colonization, European, 9, 11–12, 13, 21, 23, 30, 33n33, 39–44
Columbus, Christopher, 7–8, 15
communication, radio, 39, 83, 96–101
compass, 14, 21, 23, 25, 48, 50–51, 93–94, 110
compensation balance (in chronometer), 49
computers
    charts and charting, 111–16
    navigational systems, 105, 108–9
    risks of complexity, dependence on, 143
Confederation, impact on trade and development, 44, 45–46, 67
containerization, 82, 86
Cook, James, 13, 24–25, 26, 30
Cosa, Juan de la, 22
court cases and the use of radar, 104
crews, 83, 92. *See also* staffing
Crimean War, and the demand for ships, 45
cross-staff, 15, 16

d'Alembert, Jean, 19
Dalén, Gustav, 120
Dalrymple, Alexander, 27
Davis, John, 11, 16, 21–22, 23
Davis quadrant. *See* back-staff
dead reckoning, 1, 14, 15, 49
Decca Navigator, 106, 111
    See also hyperbolic navigation

Decca Radar Canada, 133
Department of Marine and Fisheries. *See* aids to navigation; education and training; legislation and regulation; lighthouses; marine infrastructure
Department of Transport (DOT). *See* aids to navigation; education and training; legislation and regulation; lighthouses; marine infrastructure
depth measurement, 14, 49, 50, 75n74, 94
DesBarres, J. F. W., 24, 55
Desceliers, Pierre, 22
Deshayes, Jean, 23, 24
Det Norske Veritas, 116
Diamond Heating and Lighting Company, 124
diaphone, 123, 132
d'Iberville, Pierre Lemoyne, 24
Differential GPS (DGPS), 108–9, 114
digital selective calling (DSC), 100
direction finding
    in education and training, 46, 48
    importance for explorers, 14–15
    longitude, 18
    magnetic variation, 21
    radio, 101–3, 142
Discovery, HMS, 26
distance measurement, 1, 14, 20–21, 25, 35n74, 49–50, 56
distress signals, 100
Dominion Lighthouse Depot, 87, 124, 130, 131
Drake, Francis, 10
Dutch chart-making, 22–24

Earnshaw, Thomas, 49
echo-sounders, 93, 94–95, 110
education and training, mariner, 10, 23, 46–48, 60, 90–92, 105, 115, 116
    See also certification, mariner; schools, navigation
Electronic Chart Display Information System (ECDIS), 113–16, 143
electronic navigation charts (ENCS), 109, 115, 143
Enhanced Group Call-Safety-NET (EGC), 100
Ericsson, John, 50
exploration, Canadian waters, 7–14, 21–27, 53, 57–58, 76n113

ferries, 82, 85–86
fire, seamarks using, 28, 29–30
    See also lighthouses
First World War, 101, 110
fishery, 30, 41, 44, 45, 53, 87
fishery, Newfoundland, 8, 9, 11, 12, 13, 23, 24, 32n8
"flag of convenience," 83, 84
Fletcher, John, 49
Flinders, Matthew, 50
Flinders Bar, 50
    See also binnacle; compass
fog signals, 46, 61, 66, 72–73, *120*, 122–23, 132, 142
Foulis, Robert, 66, 72
Fox, Luke, 11
Franklin, John, 57–58
Fraser, Peter, 40
Fraser River, 44, 45, 59, 71
Fresnel, Augustin, 61
Frobisher, Martin, 11, 23
Fundy, Bay of, 23, 56, 66, 67, 73
fur trade, 11, 12–13, 14, 44

Galiano, Dionisio Alcala, 14, 25
Gaspé Bay, 24
Gellibrand, Henry, 18
Georgian Bay
    exploration and settlement, 23, 45
    fog signal, 73

hydrographic surveys, 59–60
lighthouses, 67, 69, *70*, 73
Royal Navy base, 40
Gesner, Abraham, 62
Gilbert, Humphrey, 11
Global Marine Distress and Safety System (GMDSS), 100
Global Positioning System (GPS), 108–9, 142, 143
globes, 23
gnomic projection, 54
Godfray, Hugh, 54
Godfrey, Thomas, 17
gold rushes, B.C., 44, 45, 59
Great Lakes
    aids to navigation, 42–43, 67, 69, 71, 99, 103, 107, 117, *130, 131*
    exploration and development, 23, 40–42, 43, 44, 85, 86–87
    fog signals, 73, *120*
    hydrographic surveys, 42, 54–57, 59–60
    lighthouses, 70, 129
Great Lakes Survey, 60
Greenwich meridian, 1, 18
Groseilliers, Médard Chouart des, 13
guides, to navigation, 53–54
Gundersrud, Olaf, 116
gyrocompass, 93–94, 110

Hadley, John, 17
Halifax, Nova Scotia
    aids to navigation, 30–31, 71, 72
    hydrographic surveys, 24, 56
    instrument trade, 52
    lighthouses, 31–32
    port development, 39, 86
    traffic separation scheme, 133
Halley, Edmond, 19
Hanseatic League, 28
harbours. *See* ports
harpoon log, 49, 50. *See also* log
Harrison, John, 19–20, 35n71, 49
hazards, marking. *See* aids to navigation; seamarking
Hearne, Samuel, 13
Hertz, Heinrich, 103
Holland, Samuel, 24, 55
Hood, David, 117
Hudson, Henry, 11, 23
Hudson Bay, 23
Hudson's Bay Company, 13, 23, 45, 58, 59
Hülsmeyer, Christian, 103
Huron, Lake
    See also Georgian Bay; Great Lakes
    aids to navigation, *130*
    exploration and development, 12–13, 43, 44, 45, 85, 86, 87
    hydrographic surveys, 40, 55, *56*
    lighthouses, 67, *70*
Hutchinson, William, 31
Hydrographic Survey of Canada, 109
    See also Canadian Hydrographic Service
hydrography, 22–27, 40, 53–60, 66, 109–11, 113, 142
    See also cartography; charts and charting; surveys, hydrographic
hyperbolic navigation systems, 101, 105–7, 142
    See also Decca; Loran; Omega; Sonne/Consol

icebreakers, *82*, 86–88
identification friend or foe (IFF), 103
    See also radar
immigration, 40–41, 45
Imray, James, 54
indigenous peoples, 7, 9, 23, 26, 36n105

infrastructure, marine, 1–2, 28, 39–40, 45–46, 53, 60, 66–73
    See also aids to navigation; legislation and regulation; ports; seamarking; shipping industry
instrument development, 16–18, 19–20, 48–51, 93–96
instrument trade, Canada, 51–53
integrated navigational systems, 113–16.
    See also Electronic Chart Display and Information System (ECDIS); Precise Integrated Navigational System (PINS)
International Association of Lighthouse Authorities (IALA), 84
International Convention for the Safety of Life at Sea (SOLAS), 84, 89
International Convention on Standards of Training, Certification and Watchkeeping for Seafarers (STCW-95), 93
International Conventions for the Prevention of Pollution of the Sea by Oil, 89
International Hydrographic Organization (IHO), 84, 115
International Load Line Convention, 84
International Marine Organization, 93
International Maritime Conference, 66
International Maritime Organization (IMO), 84, 100, 132–33, 134
International Maritime Satellite Organization (INMARSAT), 84, 100–101
International Regulations for Preventing Collisions at Sea (COLREGS), 104, 132–34
International Telecommunications Union, 99

James, Thomas, 11, 18
James Bay, 23
John A. Macdonald, CCGS, 99
journals, navigational, 15, 23, 24, 25
Juan de Fuca, Strait of, 58

Kellett, Henry, 58
Kerr, James, 54
Kingston, George, 46–47
Kingston, Ontario, 40, *41*
knots, as a measure of speed, 21
Krupp Atlas-Elektronik, 105

La Salle, René-Robert Cavelier, Sieur de, 9, 13
Labrador, 30, 54, 55
lamps and lanterns
    See also lighthouses; lights
    Canadian applications, 31–32, 69–70, 124–25, 128, 130–31
    early, 30–32
    electric, 63, 118, 124, *131*
    flashing apparatus, *62*, 63, 118, 124–25
    oil vapour, gas mantle, and acetylene, 62–63, 117, 119–22, *123*
    reflective apparatus and lenses, 31, 61–62, 118, *119*
land claims. *See* exploration, Canadian waters
Lane, Michael, 24
Lapérouse, Jean-François de, 13–14, 25
latitude, determining, 14, 15–17, 21, 23, 25, 48, 57, 108, 109
Le Roy, Pierre, 20, 49
lead and line, 1, 14, 48, 50, 57, 109, *110*
leading marks, 29, 71, 72
legislation and regulation
    collision, 132–33
    conferences, navigation, 66
    destruction of seamarks, 30
    mariner certification, 46, 47, 90
    merchant shipping, 46, 89
    navigation, 40, 45–46, 83–84, 87–90

legislation and regulation *(cont'd)*
    radar, 104–5
    radio, 98, 100
    standards: aids to navigation, 61, 66, 71, 72; charts including ECDIS, 53, 54, 114–15
Lemonnier, Pierre-Charles, 19
lenses and reflective apparatus, 31, 61, 62, 70, *117*, *118*, *119*, 124
    See also lamps and lanterns; lighthouses
light stations. *See* lighthouses
lighthouses
    automation of, 89, 119, 124–25, 129–30, 143
    Belle Isle, *125*
    Bird Rocks, 127, *127*
    Cape North, *69*
    Cove Island, *70*
    design, building, and maintenance, 31–32, 40, 66–70, 124–26
    Fisgard, 69, *70*
    fog alarms at, 72–73, 132
    Green Island, *67*
    identification of, 63, 70, 125. S*ee also* lamps and lanterns: flashing apparatus
    illumination of, 30–32, 62–63, 69–71, 117–19, 124–25, 142. *See also* lamps and lanterns
    Louisbourg, 31, *31*, 73, 99
    Race Rocks, 69
    Red Islet, *68*
    Sable Island, 126, *126*
    Sambro Island, 31, *31*
    Triple Island, 126, *127*
    White Island, *129*
lighting, seamark, 28, 30–32, 61–65, 69–70, 71, 119–22, 130–31
lightkeepers, 88, 128–29
lightships, 63–64, 71, 118, 119, 126, 128–29
Lockwood, Anthony, 54
log, 20–22, 49–50, 95–96, 142
    See also speed, measurement of
log-line. *See* log
logs, ships', 23, 25
log-ship. *See* log
longitude
    in education and training, 57
    in hydrographic surveying, 25, 57, 75n102
    solution of, 18–21
Loran, 106–7, 113–14
    See also hyperbolic navigation systems

Mackenzie, Alexander, 14
Mackenzie River, 58
Magellan, Ferdinand, 8
magnetic deviation, 50
magnetic variation
    as a way to find longitude, 18
    identification of and solutions to, 21, 23, 30, 34n68, 94
magneto-striction transducer recording sounders, 110
Malaspina, Alejandro, 14, 25, 34n47
manuals, navigating, 22
map-makers. *See* hydrography
map-making, 22, 23, 35n85, 54
    See also charts and charting; hydrography; surveys, hydrographic
maps. *See* charts and charting
Marconi, Guglielmo, 96, 97
Marett, J. L., 42
marine charts. *See* charts and charting
Marine Engineering Instructional School, 90–91
Marine Navi-Sailor, 114
markers. *See* seamarking
Marsters, Richard Upham, 52

Martinez, Esteban José, 14
Maskelyne, Nevil, 19
Mason, John, 23
Massey, Edward, 49, 50
Mauritania, RMS, 101
Maxwell, William F., 54, 59
Mayer, Tobias, 17
McLean, Alexander "Sandy," *102*
M'Clure, Robert, 58
mechanical log, 95, 142. *See also* log
Memorial University of Newfoundland (MUN), 92
Mercantile Marine Act (1850), 46
Mercator, Gerardus, 22, 23
Mercator projection, 22, 23
merchant shipping, 42, 46, 47, 89, 90, 91, 142
Merchant Shipping Act (1854), 89
Merchant Shipping (Colonial) Act (1869), 89
meridians, convergence of, 22
    See also gnomic projection; Mercator projection
meteorology, 46
metric system, 54
Mini-M, 100–101
Montréal, exploration and development, 9, 39, 42, 86, *88*
mooring, of buoys and lightships, 28–29, 61, 64, 128

Napoleonic Wars, 40, 53
National Research Council (NRC), 125, 130, 131
Nautical Almanac (Maskelyne), 19
nautical cartography. *See* charts and charting; surveys, hydrographic
Nautical Data International, 115
Nautical Institute of Nova Scotia Community College, 92
navigation
    See also celestial navigation; dead reckoning, radio: direction finding (RDF)
    definition, 1
    position-finding devices, 14–18, 20–21, 48–51, 93–95, 101–9, 113–14
    positioning systems: hyperbolic, 105–7; integrated, 113–15; radio, 101–5; satellite, 107–9
navigational aids. *See* aids to navigation
navigational instruments. *See* astrolabe; back-staff; chronometer; compass; cross-staff; lead and line; log; nocturnal; octant; quadrant; sandglass; sextant; traverse board
Navstar. *See* Global Positioning System (GPS); satellite positioning systems
NAVTEX, 100
New Brunswick
    fog signals, 72
    hydrographic surveys, 54, 55, 56
    lighthouses, 32, 42, 66, 68, 124
    lightships, 71
New France
    aids to navigation, 30, 31
    exploration and development, 12–13
    hydrographic surveys, 23–24
Newfoundland
    exploration and development, 9, 12, 24
    fishery, 8, 11, 13, 23, 32n8, 41, 44
    fog alarm, 73
    hydrographic surveys, 22, 24, 25, 35n89, 54, 55
    lighthouses, 42, 45, 66, 67, 68, 69, 70, *125*
    radio, 97
Newton, Henry, 32
Niagara River, 55
nocturnal, 16
Nootka Sound, 14
Norberg, Jonas, 63
Nories, John, 54
North Atlantic Track Agreement, 133

north magnetic pole, 57
North West Company, 14
Northey, J. P., 132
Northwest Passage, exploration of
	before nineteenth century, 7, 8, 9, 10-11, 13, 14, 21, 22, 27
	nineteenth century, 57-58
Nova Scotia
	fog signals, 73
	hydrographic surveys, 24, 54, 56
	lighthouses, 31-32, 42, 67, 68, *126*
	lightships, 71, *128*
Nova Scotia Marine Navigation School, 91

observatories, astronomical, 18-19
oceanic navigation. *See* navigation
octant, 17, 19, 48, 142
Offshore Systems Ltd., 114
	See also Precise Integrated Navigational System (PINS)
oil tankers, 84, 86
	See also ultra large crude carriers (ULCCs); very large crude carriers (VLCCs)
Omega, 106, 107
	See also hyperbolic navigation systems
Ontario, Lake, 43, 66, 69, 71
Ontario Department of Education, Technological and Trades Training Branch, 91
Orlebar, John, 54
Ortelius, Abraham, 22
Owen, Francis, 54
Owen, William Fitzwilliam, 54-55

Pacific coast, exploration and charting
	eighteenth century, 13-14, 24-27
	nineteenth century, 58-59, 60
Parry, Edward, 57
Perez, Juan, 13
Permanent International Association of Navigation Conferences, 66
Pierce, J. A., 106
pillar lights, 119, 128-30
pilotage zones, 132
piloting, 21, 53, 54, 56
	See also sailing directions
pitometer. *See* bottom log
Pitot, Henry, 95
pleasure boats, 87
plotting course, 15, 22, 25, 30, 105
pole light, *123*
pollution, 83-84, 89
ports, 23, 30, 39-40, 43, 45, 54, 61, 83, 85, 86
position-finding devices. *See under* navigation
positioning systems. *See under* navigation
Precise Integrated Navigation System 9000 (PINS 9000), *113*, 114
Prince Edward Island
	hydrographic survey, 56
	lighthouse, 70
projections, map, 22, 23, 54
	See also gnomic projection; Mercator projection
Pullen, William, 57

Quadra, CGS, 110
quadrant, Davis, 16-17
quadrant, seaman's, 14, 15
Québec
	aids to navigation, 30-31, 71
	exploration and development, 9-10, 12-13, 22-23, 39, 41-45, 85, 86, *88*
	hydrographic surveys, 23-24, 55
	lighthouses, 39-40, 66-68, *127*, 129-30
Queen Charlotte Islands, 59

racon, 123
radar, 103-5, 123, 131, 133
radio
	communication, 96-101, 133
	direction finding (RDF), 101-3, 142
radiotelegraph, 99
Radiotelegraph Act, 89
radiotelephone. *See* radio communication
Radisson, Pierre Esprit, 13
railways, 43, 45
Raleigh, Walter, 10
range marks. *See* leading marks
regulations. *See* legislation and regulation
regulatory bodies, 84
research, war-related, 94-95, 99, 102, 103, 105, 106-7, 108, 110
resources, natural, 7, 11-12, 23, 30, 39, 44, 45, 81, 84, 85, 86, 87
rhumb line, 21
Ribero, Diego, 22
Rimouski, HMCS, *94*
roads, 43
Roberval, Jean-François de La Rocque, 9
Ross, James Clark, 57
Ross, John, 57
Rosselli, Francesco, 22
Rotz, Jean, 22
Royal Navy, 24, 27, 39, 40, 42, 53-60, 66, 70, 71
Rupert's Land, 45

Sable Island, 56
	See also under lighthouses
safety, marine, 42, 46, 48, 54, 55, 84, 100
Saguenay River, 9, 22, 30, 40
sailing directions, 21, 23, 28, 42, 53-54, 55, 56, 60
St John, New Brunswick, 32, 39, 72
St John's, Newfoundland, 39, 54, 66
St Lawrence, Gulf of
	exploration and development, 22, 30
	hydrographic surveys, 23, 24, 54, 55
	lighthouses, 67, 68-69, 126, *127*, 129-30
	lightships, 126
	sailing directions for, 56
St Lawrence River
	aids to navigation, 30, 40, 42, *65*
	exploration and development, 9, 43
	fog signals, 72-73
	hydrographic surveys, 23, 24, 54-55
	lighthouses, 66, 67, *68*, 70, 124, *127*, 129-30
	lightships, 71, 128-30
	sailing directions for, 56
St Lawrence Seaway, 86
St Margaret's Sea Training School, 90-91
Sambro Island, 31-32, 128
sampling, seabed, 14
	See also lead and line
sandglass, 14, 15, 20-21, 49
	See also speed, measurement of
satellite communication systems, 84, 99, 100-101
	See also radio
satellite navigation systems, 107-9, 142
scale reader, 48
schools, navigation, 46-48, 74n56, 90-92
Schulze, Gustav, 52
Scotch siren, 132
	See also fog signals

161

Sea Beam, 110
sea lanes, 66
seamarking, 1, 3n2, 28-32, 40, 42-43, 46, 54, 60-73, 77n189, 117-32
    See also beacons; buoys; fog signals; lamps and lanterns; lighthouses; lightships
seamen, rights of, 84, 89
Second World War
    navigational aids resulting from, 99, 103, 105, 106-7, 124, 131, 142
    post-war commercial growth, 83, 84-85, 87
settlement, post Confederation, 44-45
sextant, 17-18, 19, 20, 25, 48, 49, 57, 142, 143
shipbuilding, 41, 42, 43, 44, 45, 53, 81-82, 87-88
shipping industry
    containerization, 82, 83, 86
    fishery and, 8, 41, 87
    growth in, 42, 43, 45, 53, 81, 83, 85
    instrument trade and, 51-53
    marine infrastructure and, 1, 42-43, 45-46, 83, 85-86
    regulation of, 46, 89-90
    technological improvements, 42, 43, 81, 82-83
signal poles, 28
Simpson, Thomas, 57
simulators
    integrated navigational systems, 92-93
    radar, 105
single-sideband (SSB), 99
    See also radio communication
solar power, 118, 121, 125
    See also sun valve
sonar, 93, 94, 96, 110, 142
    See also depth measurement; echo-sounders
Sonne/Consol, 106
    See also hyperbolic navigation systems
sound devices
    on buoys, 61, 64, 122-23, 130
    fog signals, 66, 72-73, 132
speed, measurement of, 14, 15, 20-21, 49-50, 95-96
Sperry, Elmer, 94
staffing
    general marine services, 45-46, 88
    lighthouses, 119, 125, 129-30
    on ships, 115, 142, 143
steam
    fog signals, 72-73
    propulsion, impact on navigation and charting, 54, 55, 59-60
steamships, 43, 45, 46, 54, 55, 57
Stevenson, Robert, 64
Stewart, William, 60, 112
streaming the log, 20
    See also measurement of speed
sun-valve, 118, 125, 131
Superior, Lake, 45, 55
Supreme Court of Canada, 104
survey methods
    Bayfield, 57
    Cook, 24
    twentieth-century, 109-11
    Vancouver, 25-27
surveys, hydrographic, 14, 21-27, 40, 42, 53-60, 109-11
symbols, chart, 54, 115
system electronic navigation charts (SENCs), 115

tables, navigational, 14, 17, 18, 19, 54
tachometers, 95
Talon, Jean, 30
telegraphic code
    in radio, 98, 99, 102
    on sound buoys, 66
tellurometer, 111
terminal facilities. See ports
theodolite, 57, 109-10
Thompson River, 44, 45
Thomson, William, 50, 51
Thornton, John, 23
tides, 23, 48, 54
timber trade, 39, 40, 41-42, 44-45
time, measurement of, 14, 16, 18, 19-20, 108
    See also chronometer; Global Positioning System (GPS)
Titanic, RMS, 97, 98
tolls and tariffs, to finance aids to navigation, 28, 31, 32
Tooker, William, 54
trade
    colonial, 10, 11, 12-13, 32, 33n33, 42-45
    international, 1, 8-9, 14, 21, 22, 28, 81, 83, 84-85, 86-87
    marine infrastructure and, 39-40, 42-43
traffail log. See harpoon log
traffic management systems, 89-90, 132-34
Transas Marine, 114
transit, 60
Transit, satellite navigation system, 108
traverse board, 14, 15, 21
traverse table, 21-22
Treaty of Paris, 24
triangulation
    in charting, 24, 57, 111
    in GPS, 108-9
    in radio direction finding, 101
Trinity Houses, 40, 42, 45, 46, 69
"true motion" plan position indicator (PPI), 104
    See also radar
Tyfon, fog signal, 132

ultra large crude carriers (ULCCs), 83
United States Navy, 106, 108
Upper Canada, 40, 41, 42

Vancouver, George, 14, 24, 25-27, 36n119, n124
Vancouver Island, 27, 60, 68
Verazzano, Giovanni, 21, 22
very large crude carriers (VLCCs), 83, 86
Vessel Traffic System (VTS), 100, 133
vessels, specialized, 45, 82, 83, 86, 87-88
Victoria, British Columbia, 58
von Wellbach, Carl Auer, 62
voyages of discovery. See exploration, Canadian waters

Wagenaer, Lucas Janszoon, 22
Waldseemüller, Martin, 22
Walker, Thomas Ferdinand, 49, 50
War of 1812
    impact on maritime activity, 40
    need for charts, 53
War of Independence, 13, 24
Watchkeeping Mate Unrestricted Certificate of Competency, 92
waterways, inland, 45-46
weather observation, 25
Werner, Johannes, 18, 19
Wigham, John, 62
Willson, Thomas L., 118, 120
Winnipeg, Lake, 67, 69-70, 112
wireless telegraph network, 97, 98
    See also radio communication
Wright, Edward, 22